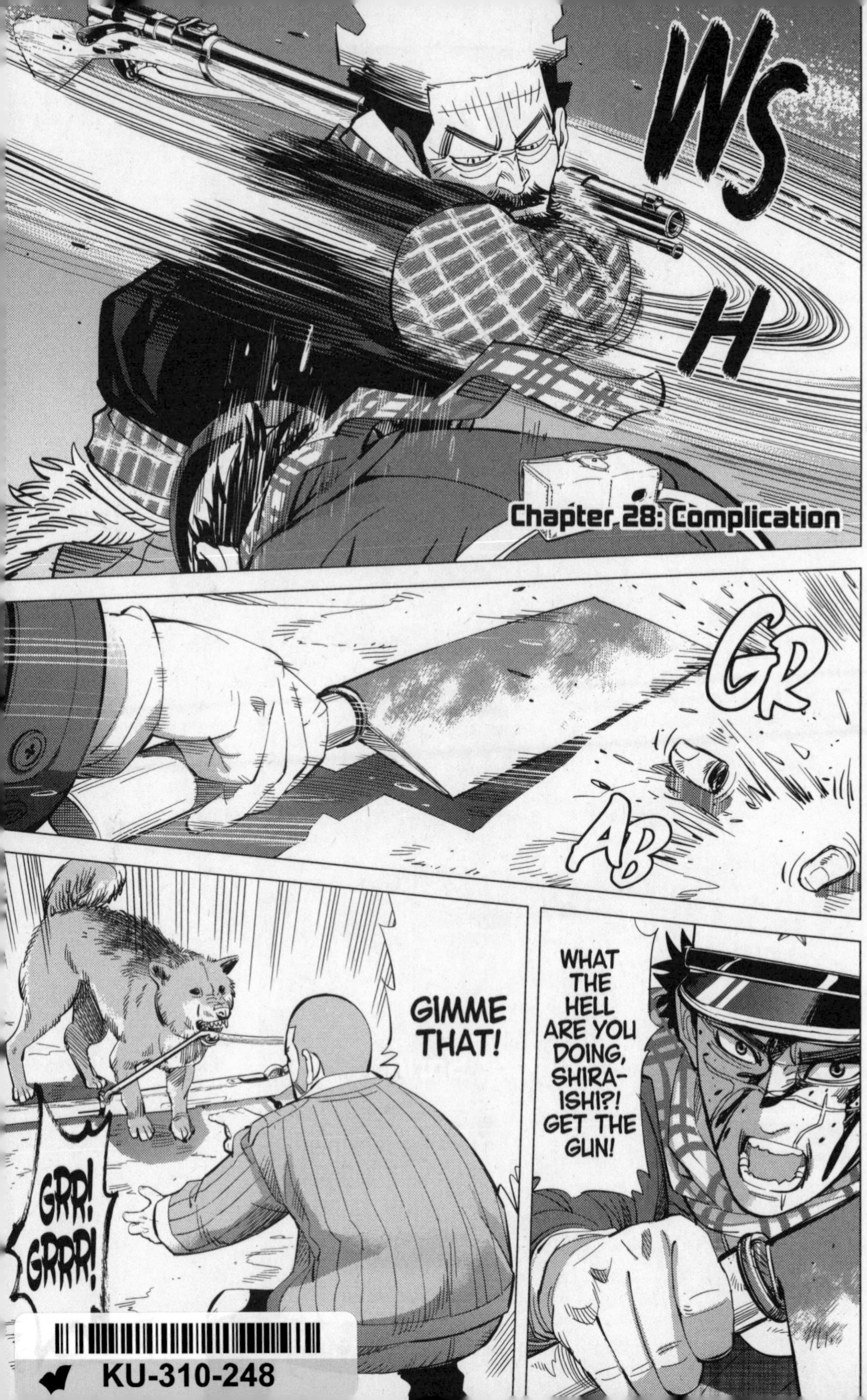
WSH
Chapter 28: Complication
GR
AB
WHAT THE HELL ARE YOU DOING, SHIRA-ISHI?! GET THE GUN!
GIMME THAT!
GRR! GRRR!

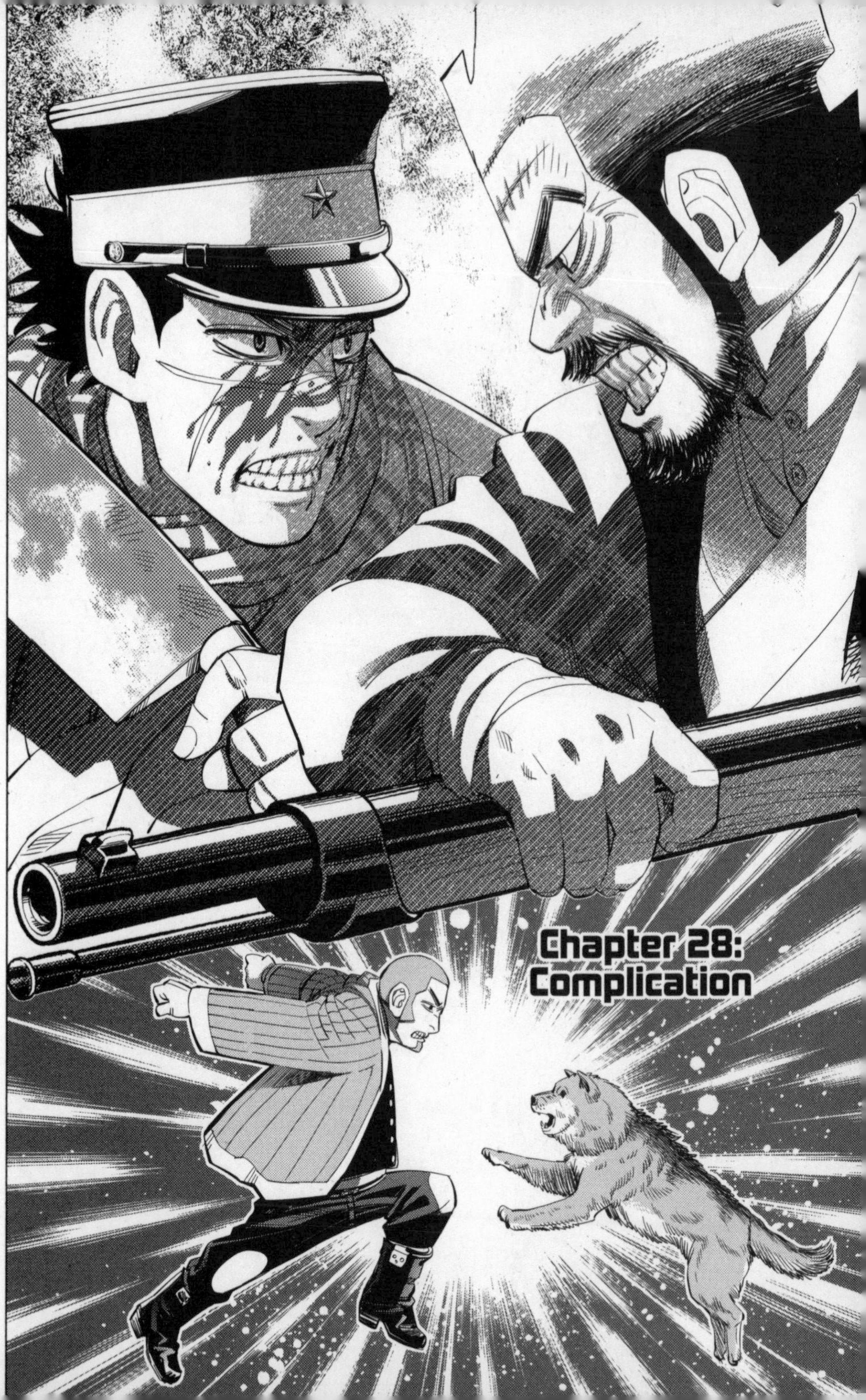
Chapter 28:
Complication

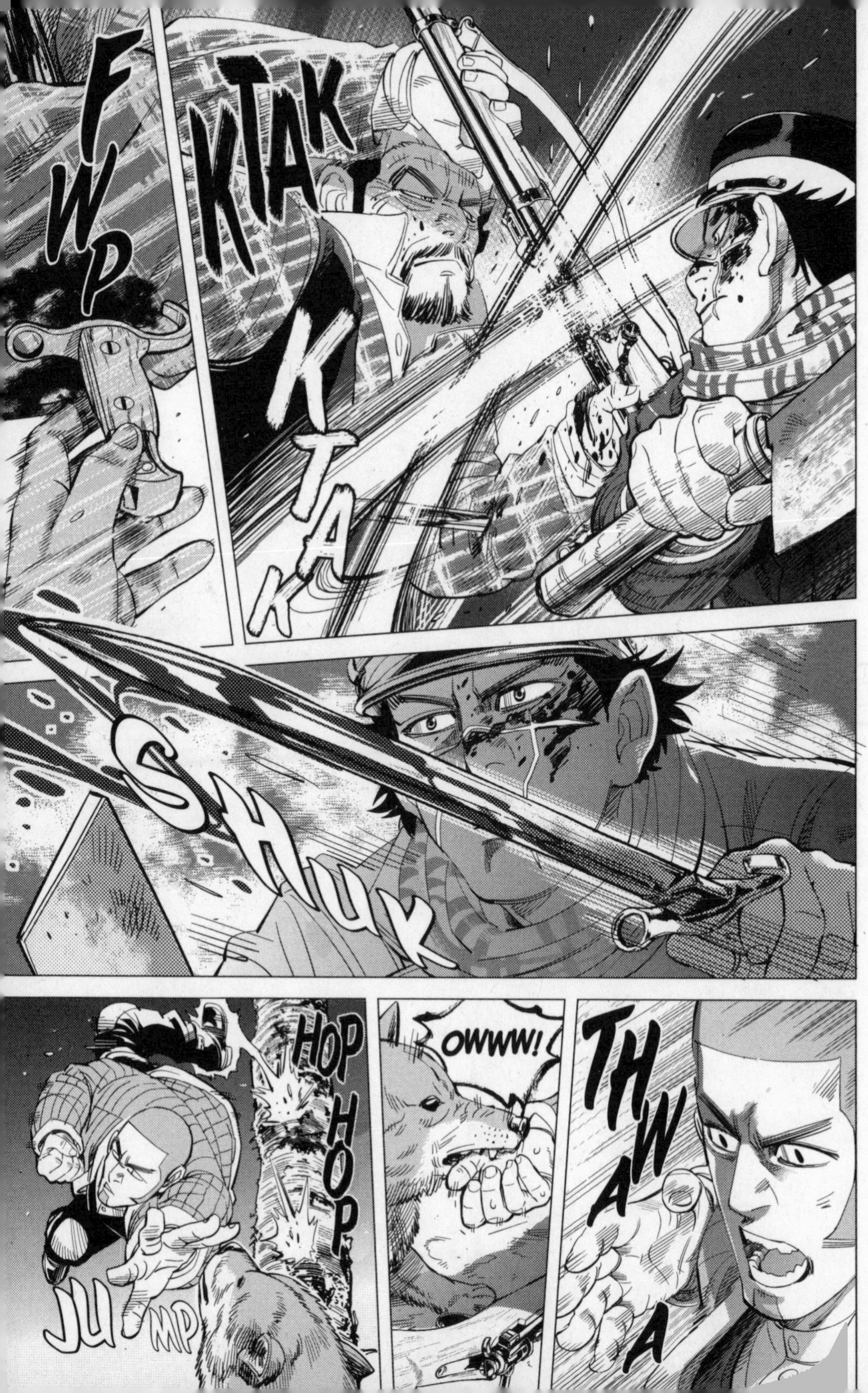
KTAK
KTAK
FWP
SHUUK
THWAA
OWWW!
HOP HOP HOP
JUMP

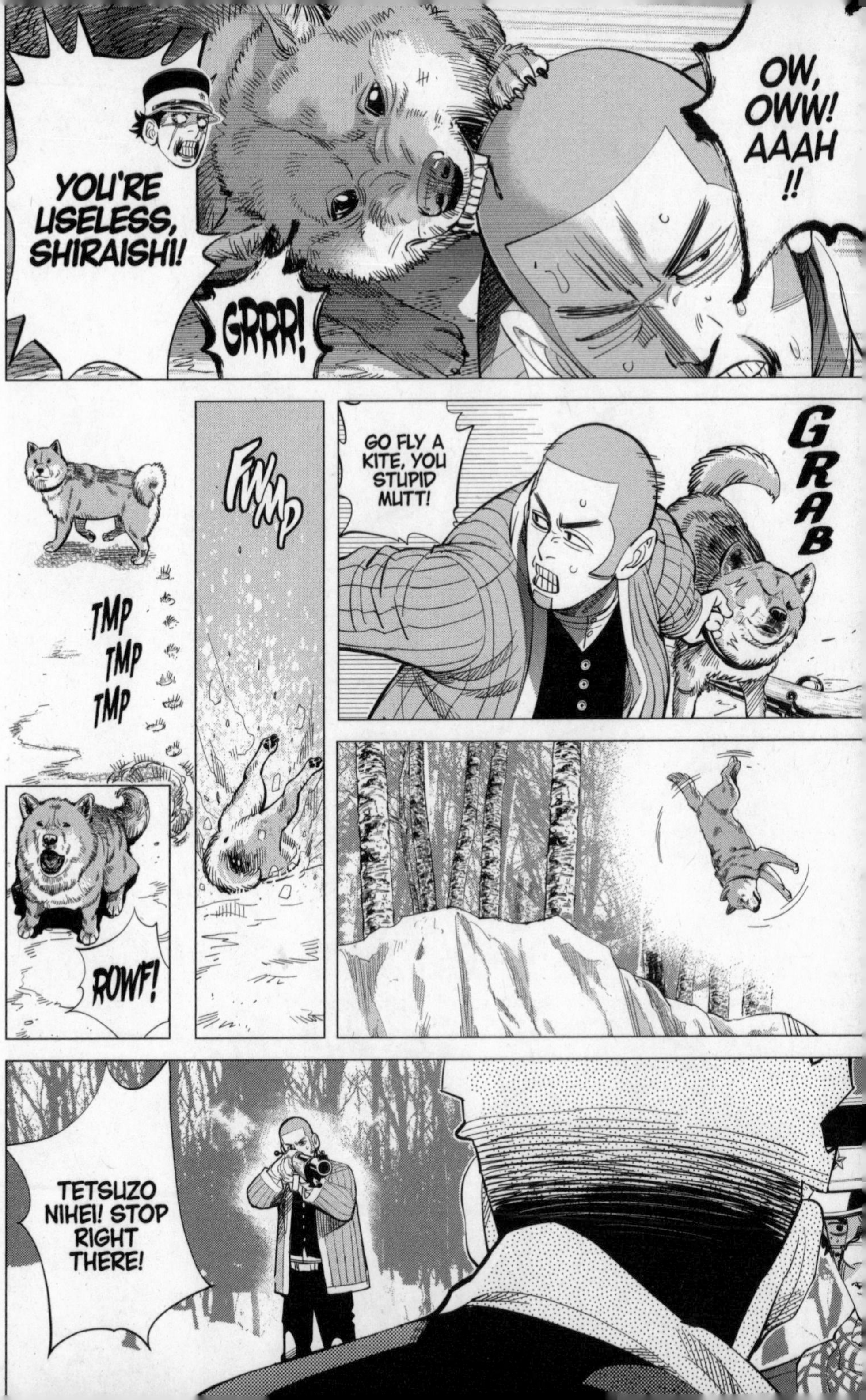
OW, OWW! AAAH!!
GRRR!
YOU'RE USELESS, SHIRAISHI!
GRAB
GO FLY A KITE, YOU STUPID MUTT!
FWMP
TMP TMP TMP
ROWF!
TETSUZO NIHEI! STOP RIGHT THERE!

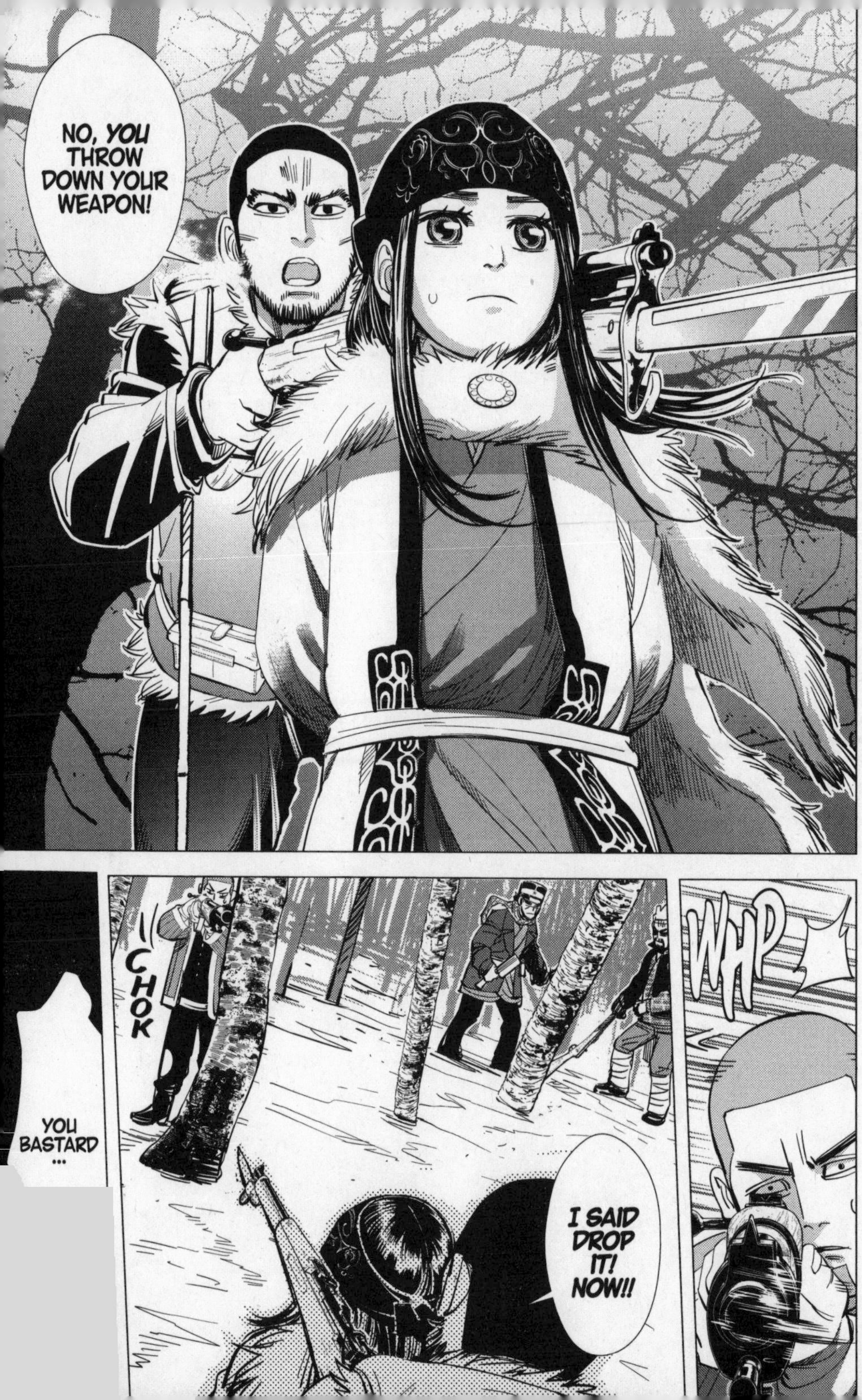
NO, YOU THROW DOWN YOUR WEAPON!
WHP
I SAID DROP IT! NOW!!
CHOK
YOU BASTARD...

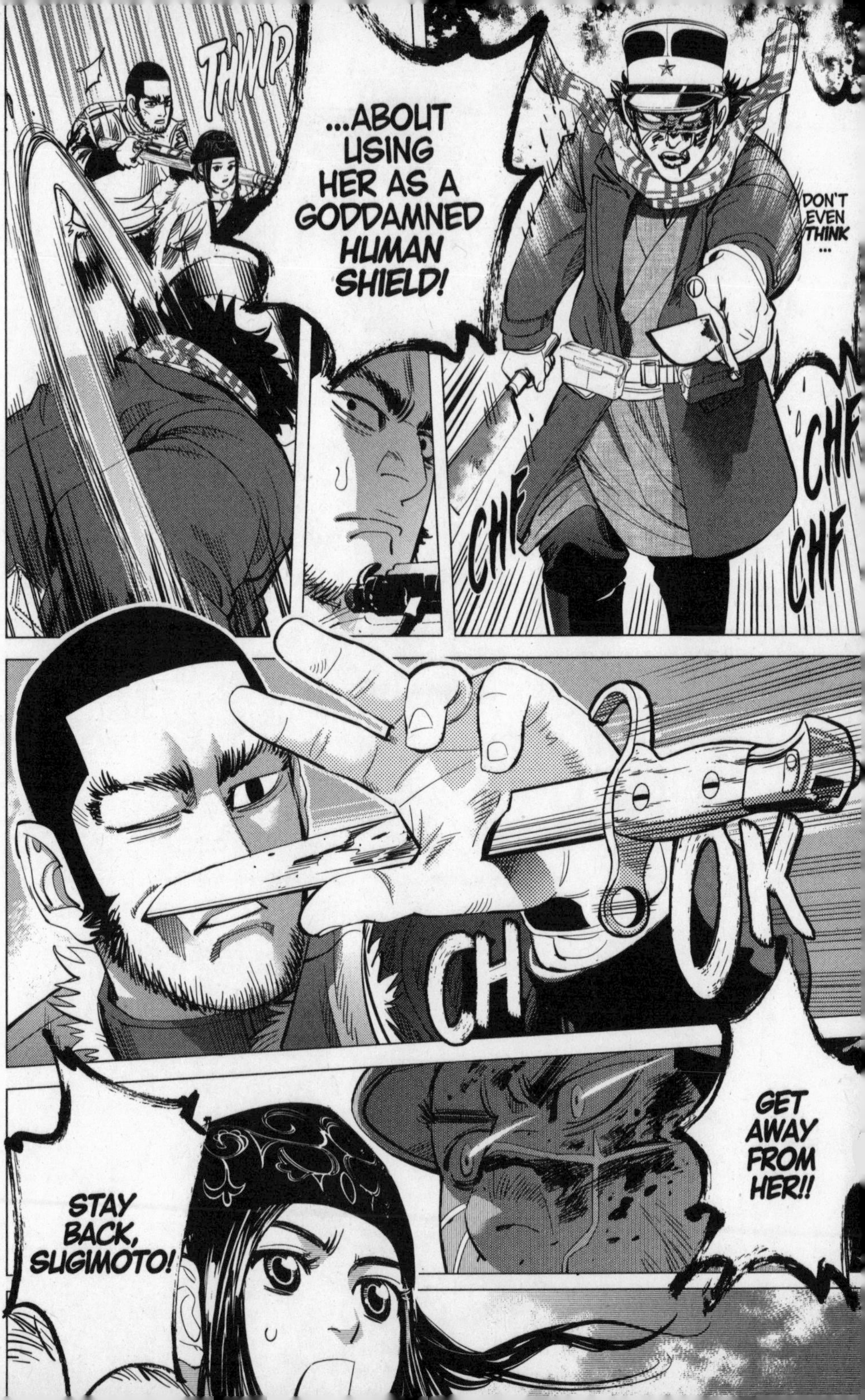
DON'T EVEN THINK ...
CHF CHF
CHF
...ABOUT USING HER AS A GODDAMNED HUMAN SHIELD!
THWIP
CHOK
GET AWAY FROM HER!!
STAY BACK, SUGIMOTO!

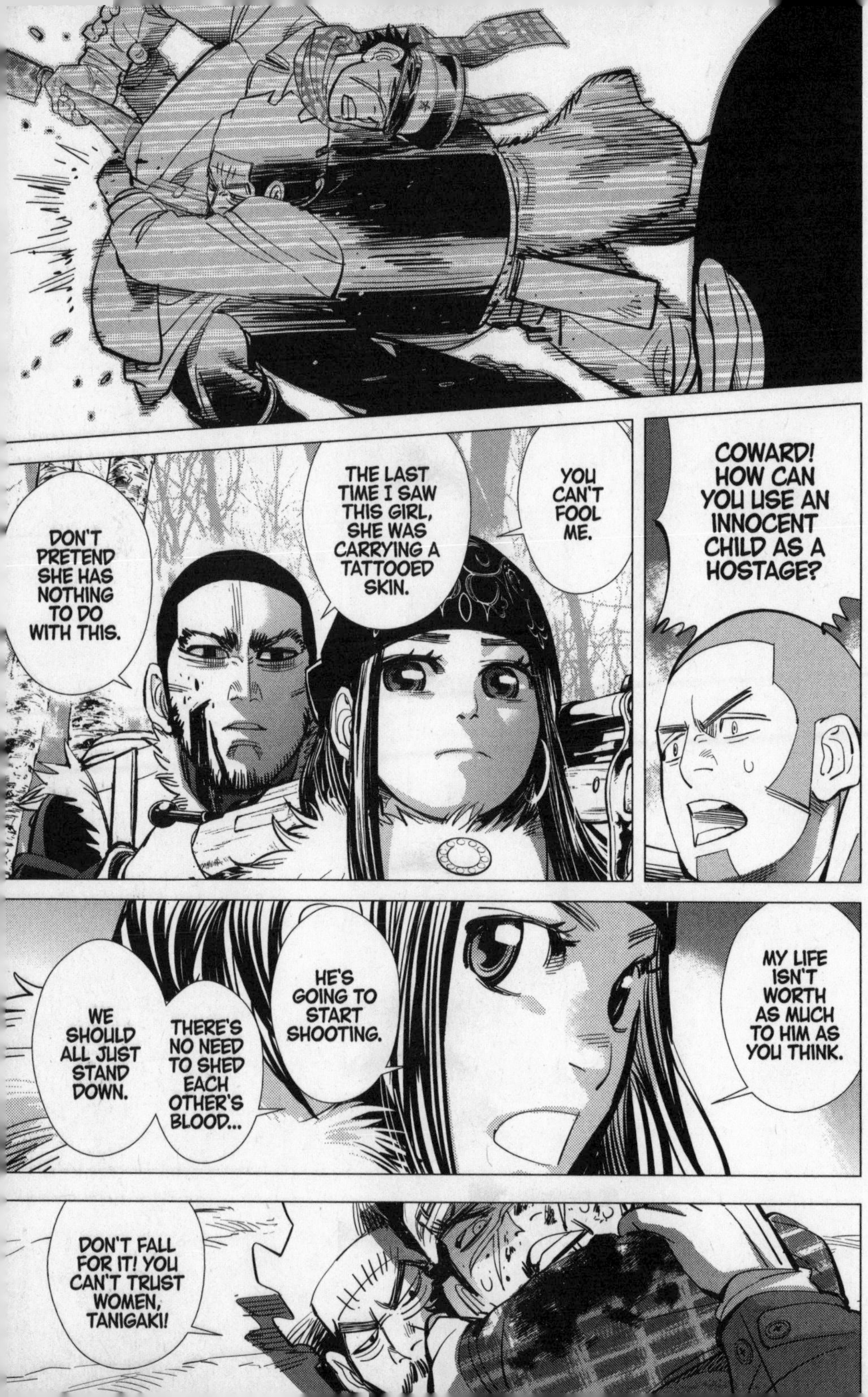
COWARD! HOW CAN YOU USE AN INNOCENT CHILD AS A HOSTAGE?
YOU CAN'T FOOL ME.
THE LAST TIME I SAW THIS GIRL, SHE WAS CARRYING A TATTOOED SKIN.
DON'T PRETEND SHE HAS NOTHING TO DO WITH THIS.
MY LIFE ISN'T WORTH AS MUCH TO HIM AS YOU THINK.
HE'S GOING TO START SHOOTING.
THERE'S NO NEED TO SHED EACH OTHER'S BLOOD...
WE SHOULD ALL JUST STAND DOWN.
DON'T FALL FOR IT! YOU CAN'T TRUST WOMEN, TANIGAKI!

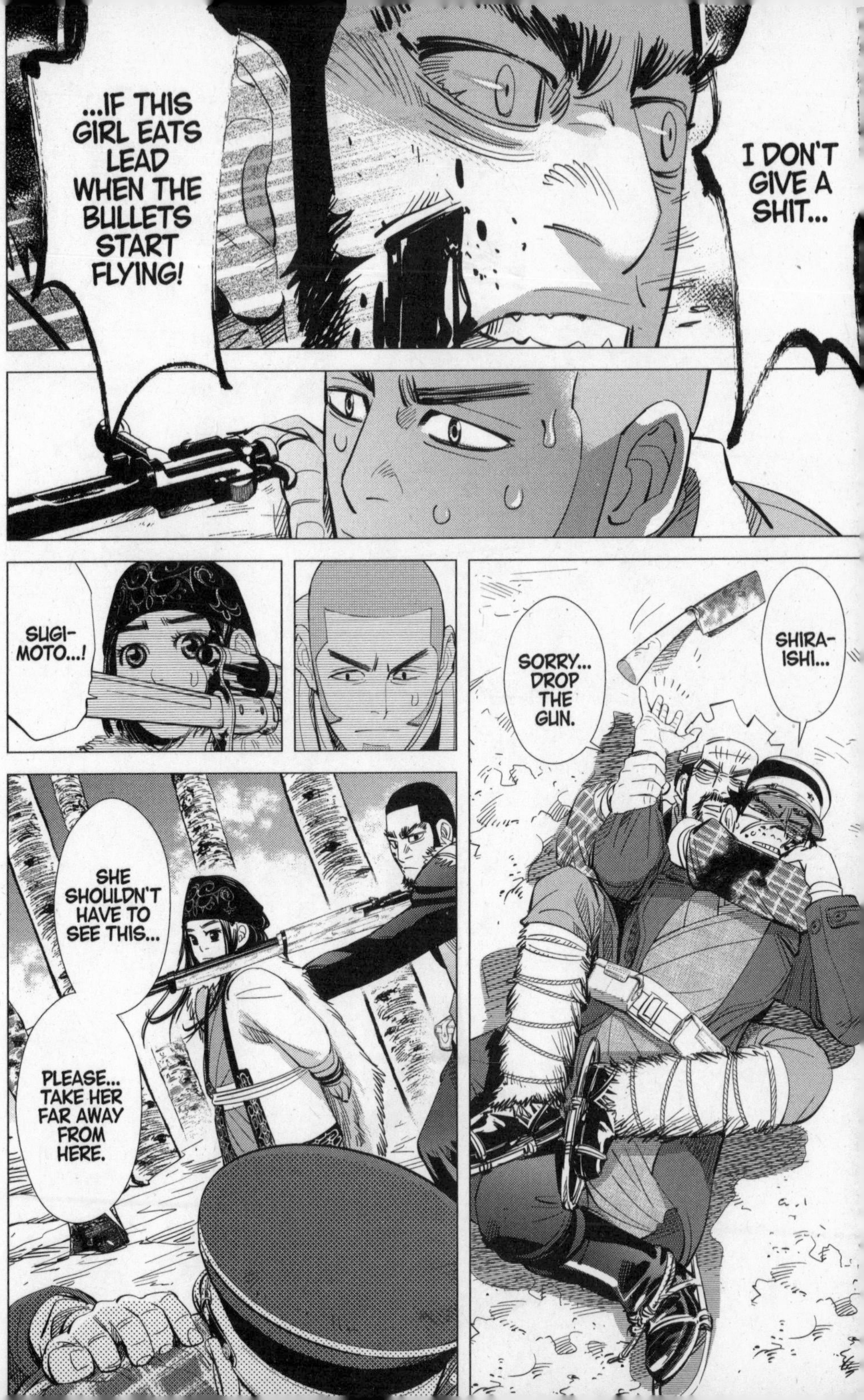
I DON'T GIVE A SHIT...
...IF THIS GIRL EATS LEAD WHEN THE BULLETS START FLYING!
SHIRA-ISHI...
SORRY... DROP THE GUN.
SUGI-MOTO...!
SHE SHOULDN'T HAVE TO SEE THIS...
PLEASE... TAKE HER FAR AWAY FROM HERE.

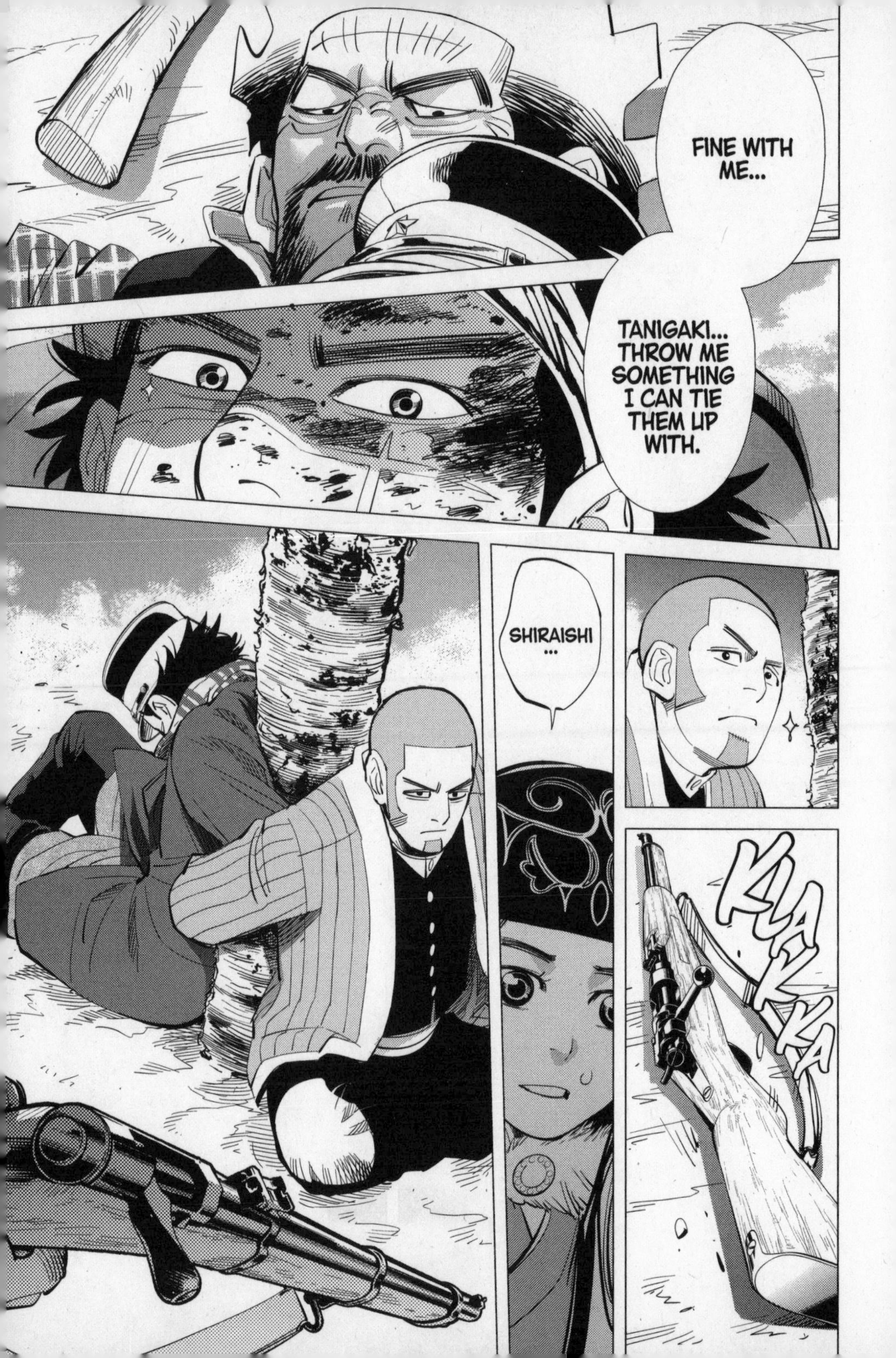
FINE WITH ME...
TANIGAKI... THROW ME SOMETHING I CAN TIE THEM UP WITH.
SHIRAISHI ...
KLAKKA

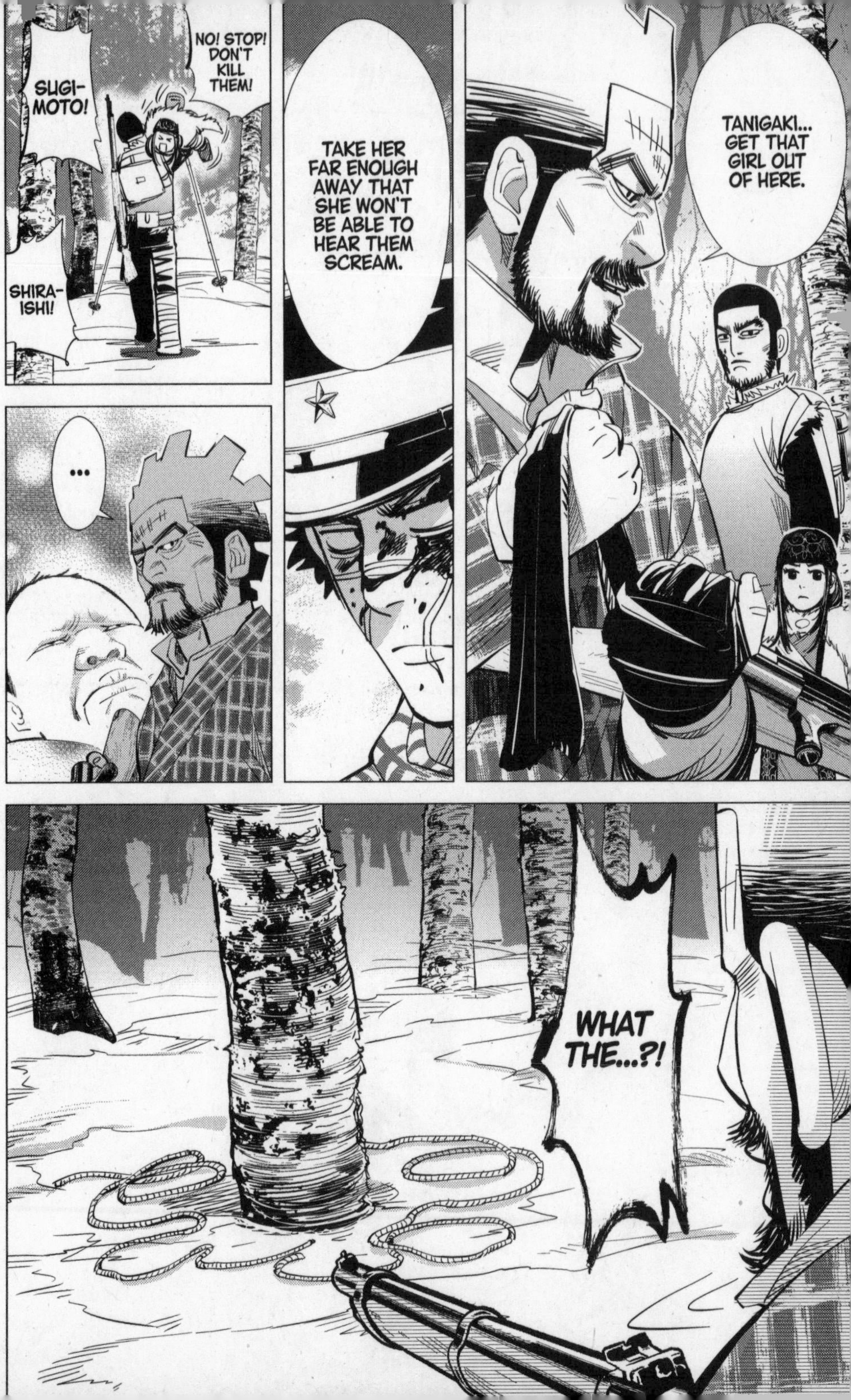
TANIGAKI... GET THAT GIRL OUT OF HERE.
TAKE HER FAR ENOUGH AWAY THAT SHE WON'T BE ABLE TO HEAR THEM SCREAM.
NO! STOP! DON'T KILL THEM!
SUGI-MOTO!
SHIRA-ISHI!
...
WHAT THE...?!

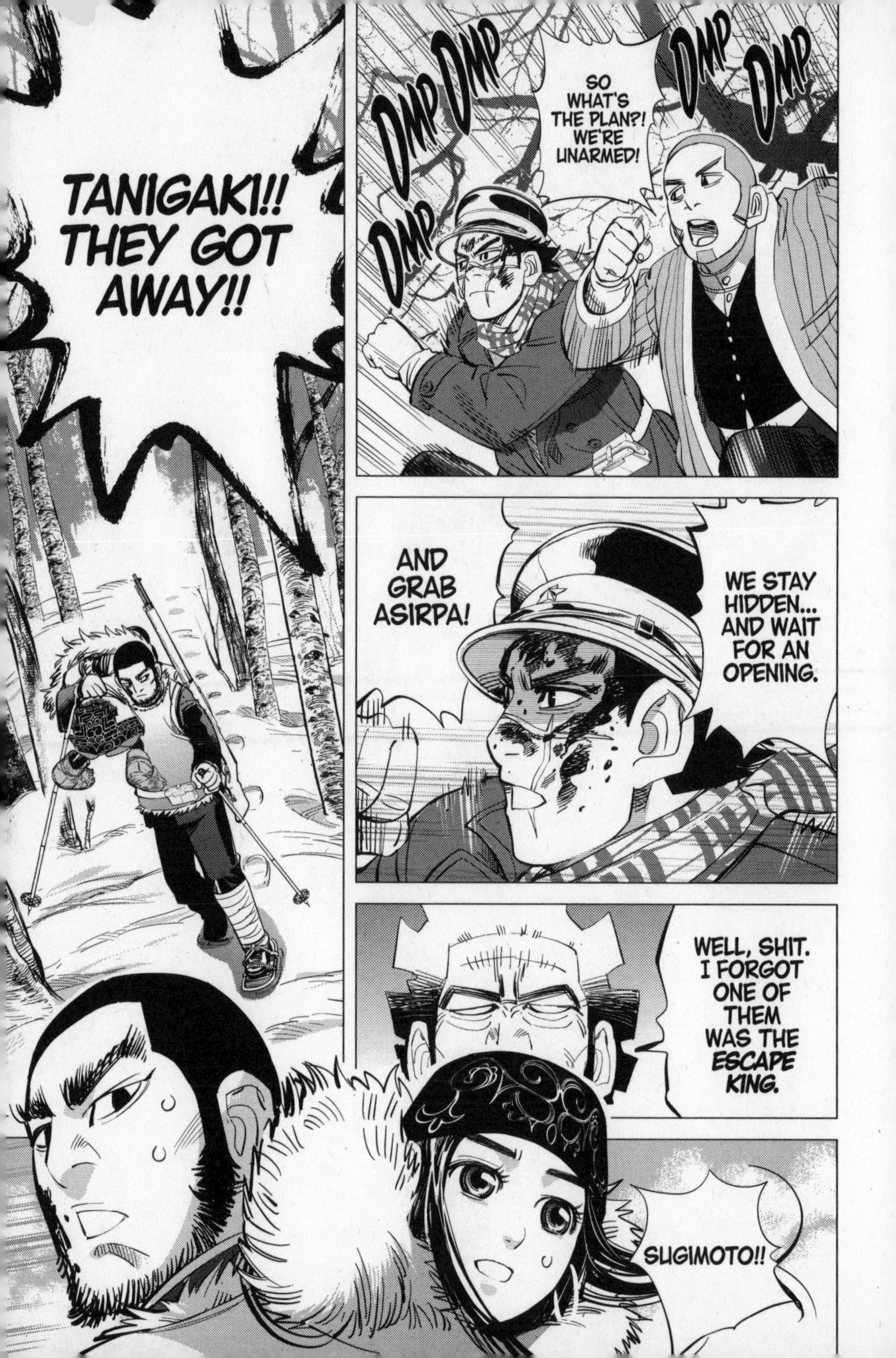
DMP DMP
DMP
SO WHAT'S THE PLAN?! WE'RE UNARMED!
DMP DMP
WE STAY HIDDEN... AND WAIT FOR AN OPENING.
AND GRAB ASIRPA!
WELL, SHIT. I FORGOT ONE OF THEM WAS THE ESCAPE KING.
TANIGAKI!! THEY GOT AWAY!!
SUGIMOTO!!

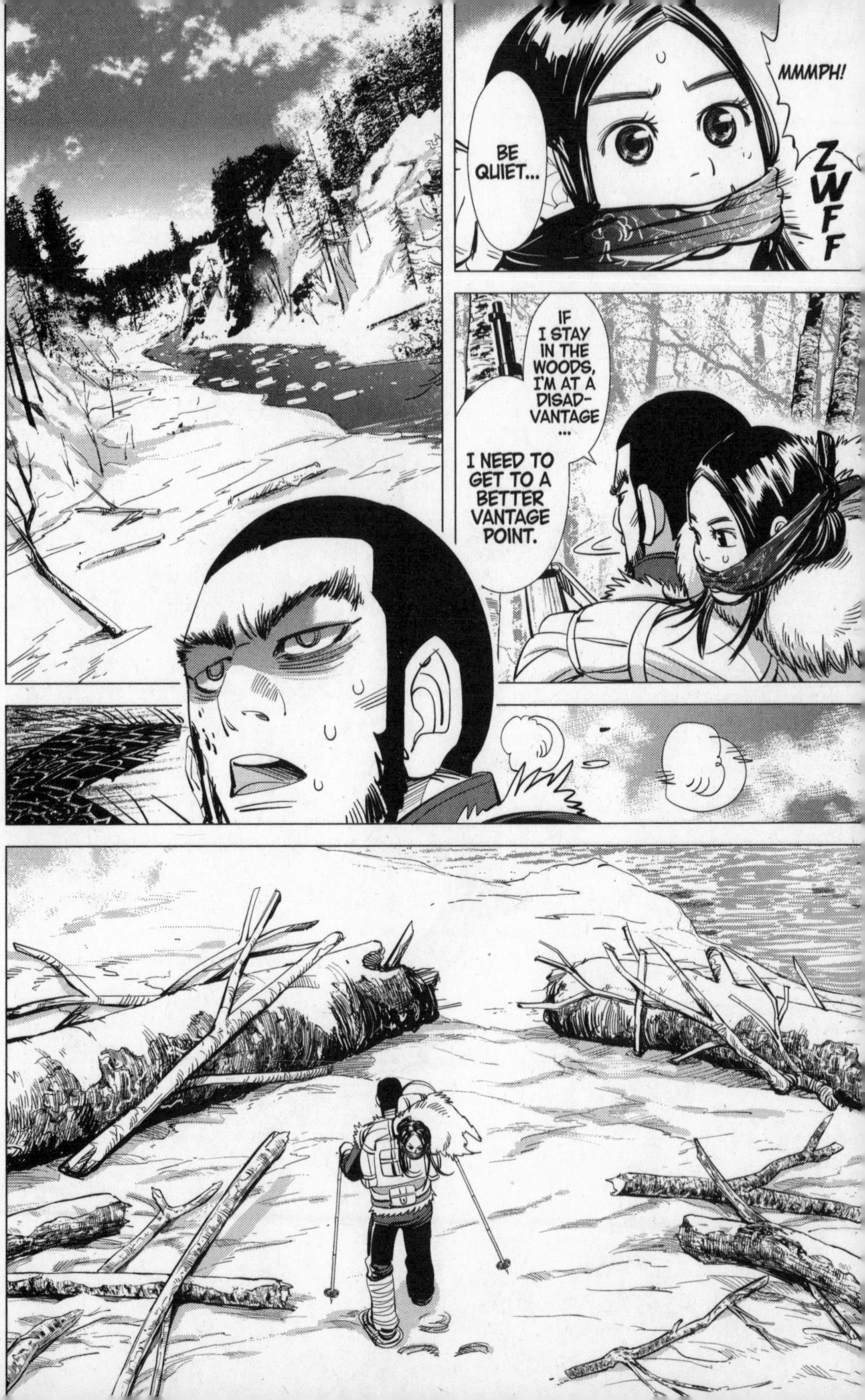
MMMPH!
ZWFF
BE QUIET...
IF I STAY IN THE WOODS, I'M AT A DISADVANTAGE...
I NEED TO GET TO A BETTER VANTAGE POINT.

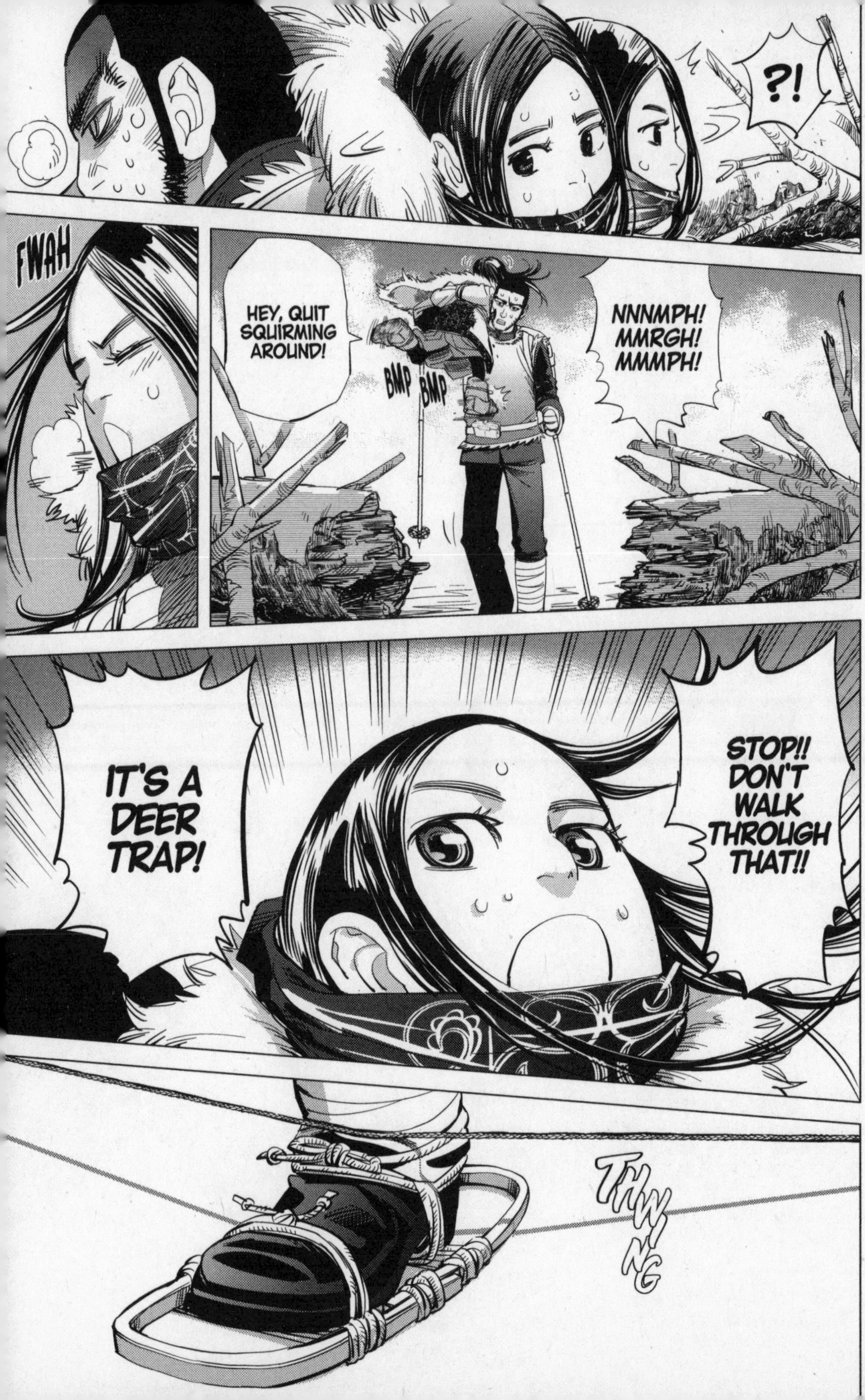
?!
NNNMPH! MMRGH! MMMPH!
HEY, QUIT SQUIRMING AROUND!
BMP BMP
FWAH
STOP!! DON'T WALK THROUGH THAT!!
IT'S A DEER TRAP!
THWING

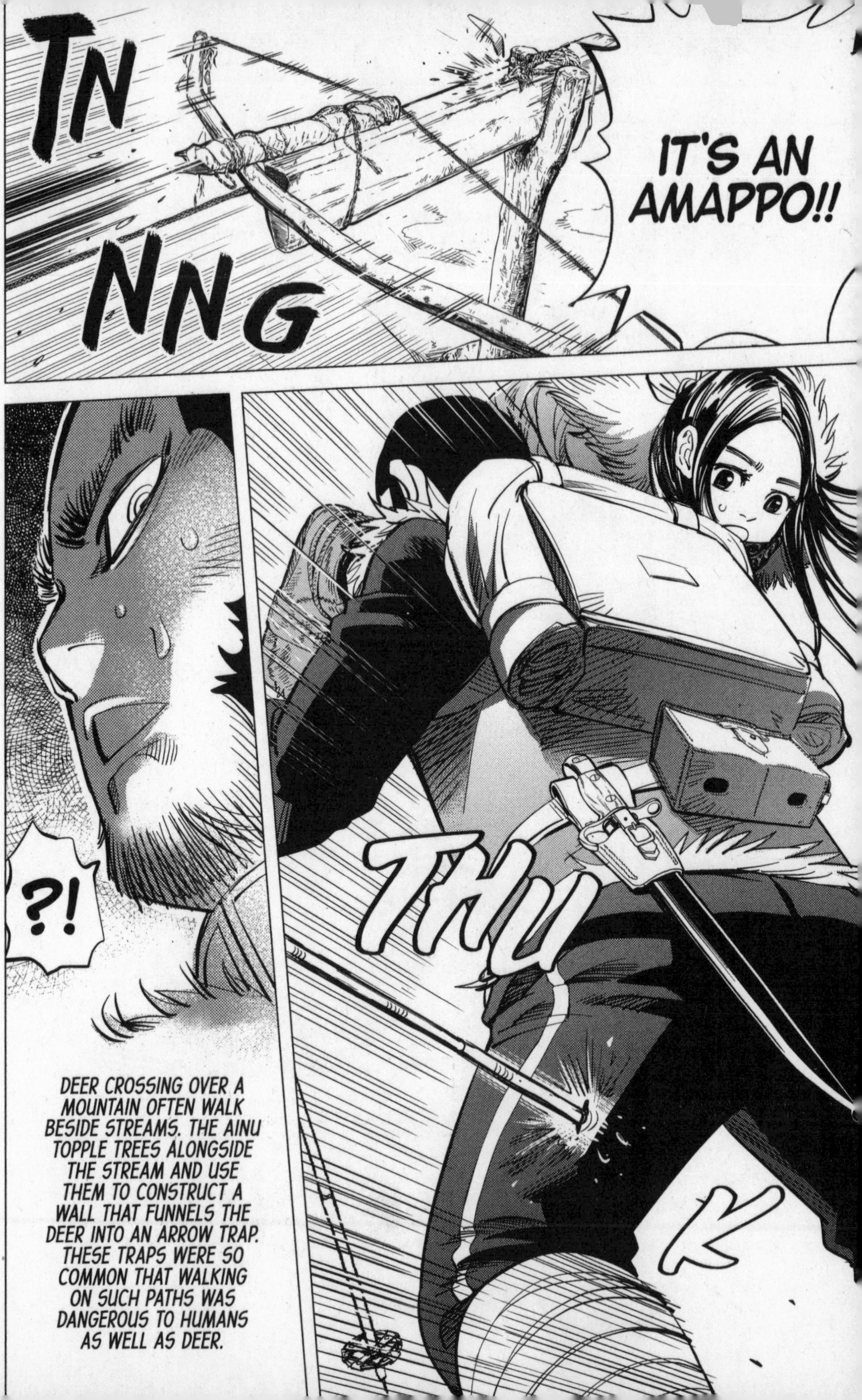
IT'S AN AMAPPO!!
TN NNG
THU
K
?!
DEER CROSSING OVER A MOUNTAIN OFTEN WALK BESIDE STREAMS. THE AINU TOPPLE TREES ALONGSIDE THE STREAM AND USE THEM TO CONSTRUCT A WALL THAT FUNNELS THE DEER INTO AN ARROW TRAP. THESE TRAPS WERE SO COMMON THAT WALKING ON SUCH PATHS WAS DANGEROUS TO HUMANS AS WELL AS DEER.

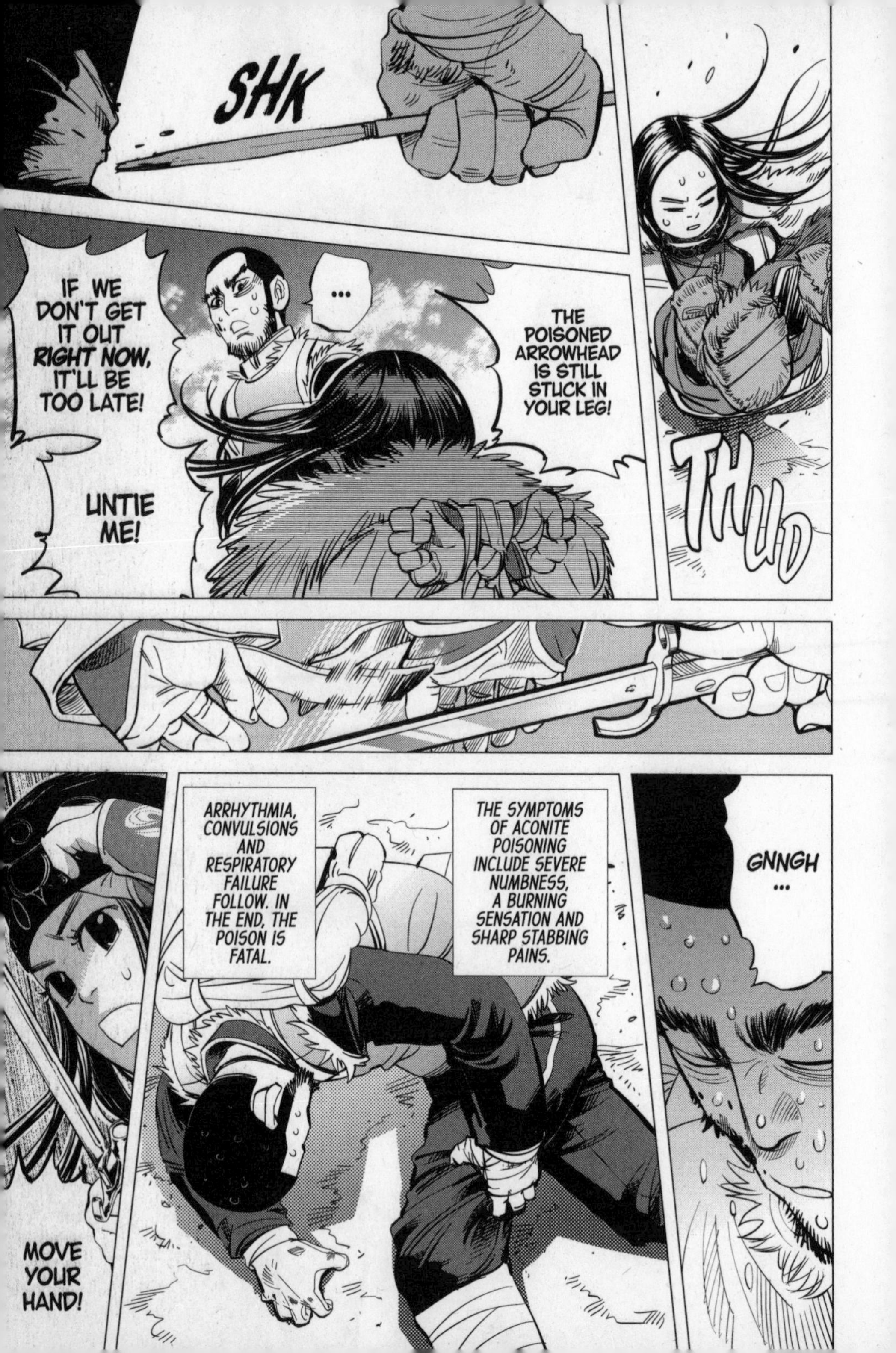
THUD
SHK
THE POISONED ARROWHEAD IS STILL STUCK IN YOUR LEG!
...
IF WE DON'T GET IT OUT RIGHT NOW, IT'LL BE TOO LATE!
UNTIE ME!
GNNGH ...
THE SYMPTOMS OF ACONITE POISONING INCLUDE SEVERE NUMBNESS, A BURNING SENSATION AND SHARP STABBING PAINS.
ARRHYTHMIA, CONVULSIONS AND RESPIRATORY FAILURE FOLLOW. IN THE END, THE POISON IS FATAL.
MOVE YOUR HAND!

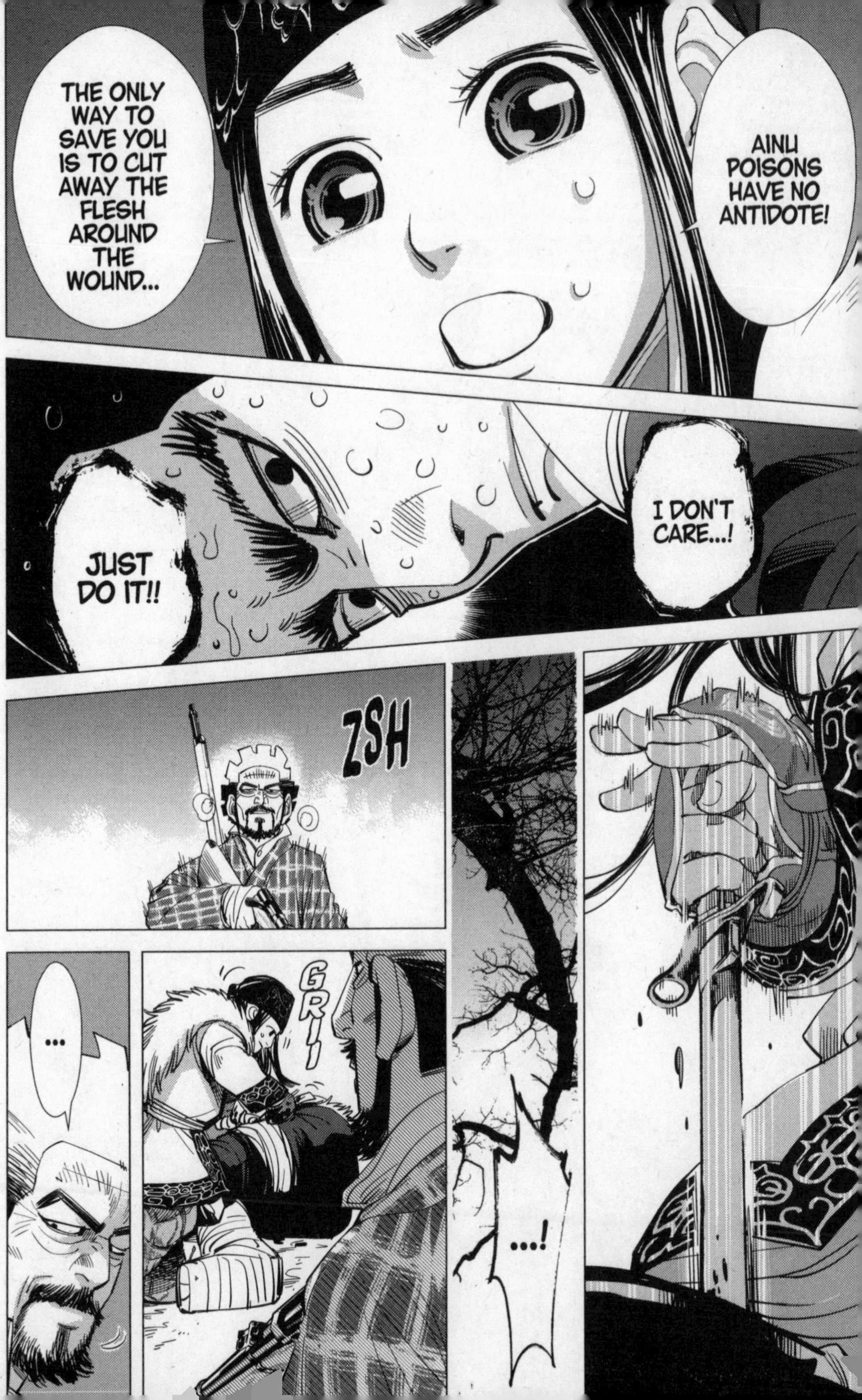
AINU POISONS HAVE NO ANTIDOTE!
THE ONLY WAY TO SAVE YOU IS TO CUT AWAY THE FLESH AROUND THE WOUND...
I DON'T CARE...!
JUST DO IT!!
...!
ZSH
GRII
...

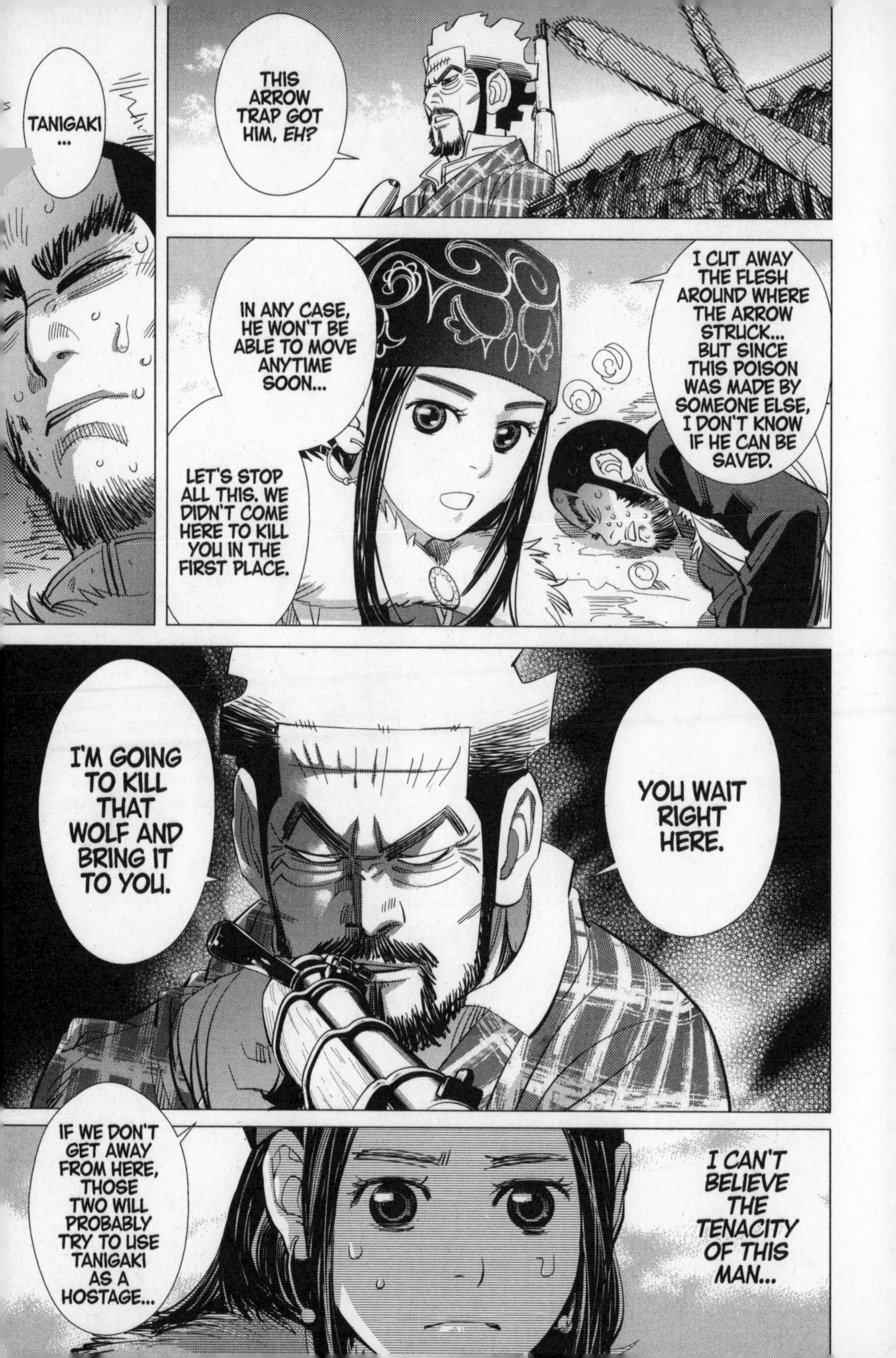
THIS ARROW TRAP GOT HIM, EH?
I CUT AWAY THE FLESH AROUND WHERE THE ARROW STRUCK... BUT SINCE THIS POISON WAS MADE BY SOMEONE ELSE, I DON'T KNOW IF HE CAN BE SAVED.
IN ANY CASE, HE WON'T BE ABLE TO MOVE ANYTIME SOON...
LET'S STOP ALL THIS. WE DIDN'T COME HERE TO KILL YOU IN THE FIRST PLACE.
TANIGAKI ...
YOU WAIT RIGHT HERE.
I'M GOING TO KILL THAT WOLF AND BRING IT TO YOU.
I CAN'T BELIEVE THE TENACITY OF THIS MAN...
IF WE DON'T GET AWAY FROM HERE, THOSE TWO WILL PROBABLY TRY TO USE TANIGAKI AS A HOSTAGE...

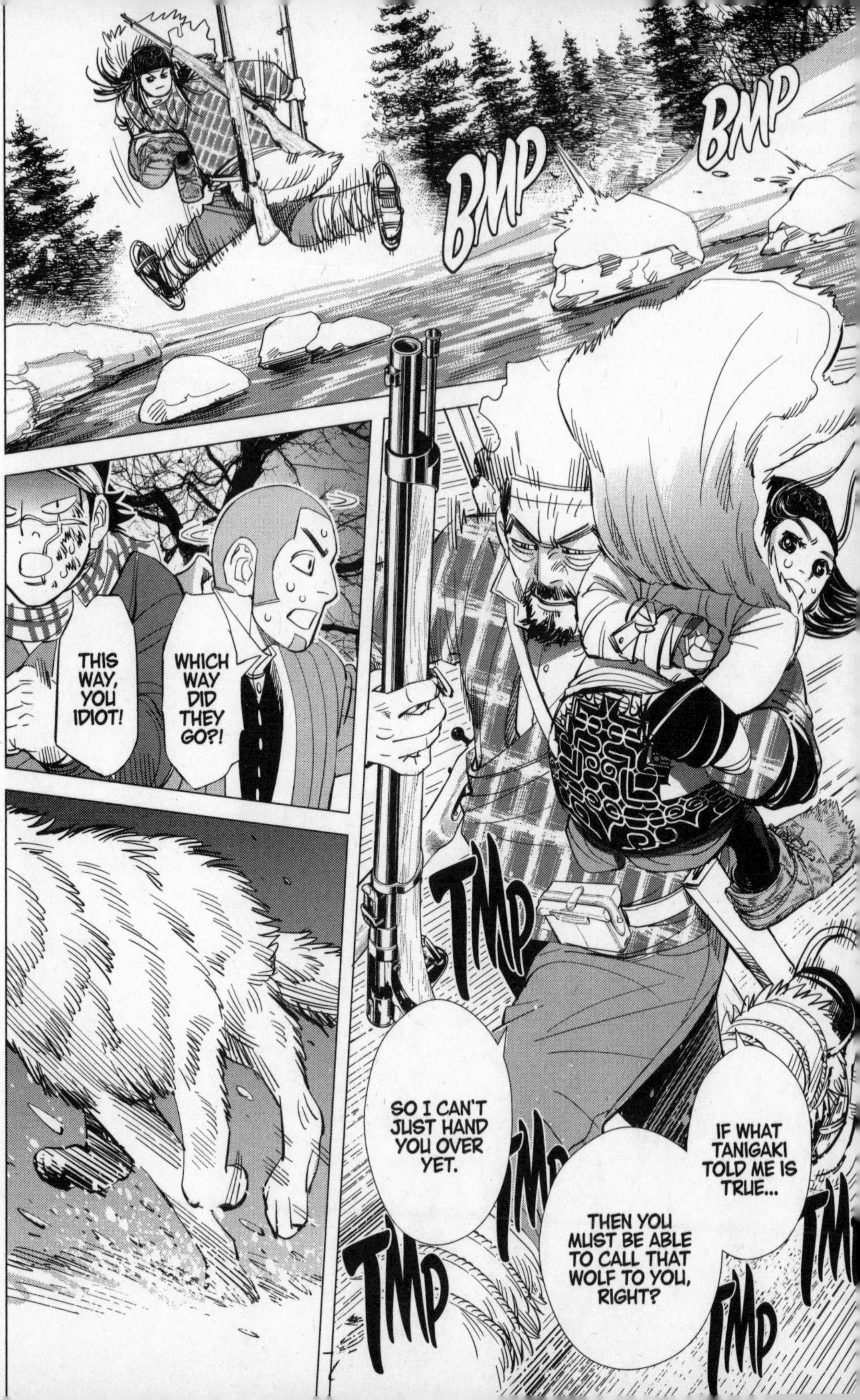
BMP
BMP
TMP
IF WHAT TANIGAKI TOLD ME IS TRUE...
THEN YOU MUST BE ABLE TO CALL THAT WOLF TO YOU, RIGHT?
SO I CAN'T JUST HAND YOU OVER YET.
TMP
TMP
TMP
TMP
WHICH WAY DID THEY GO?!
THIS WAY, YOU IDIOT!

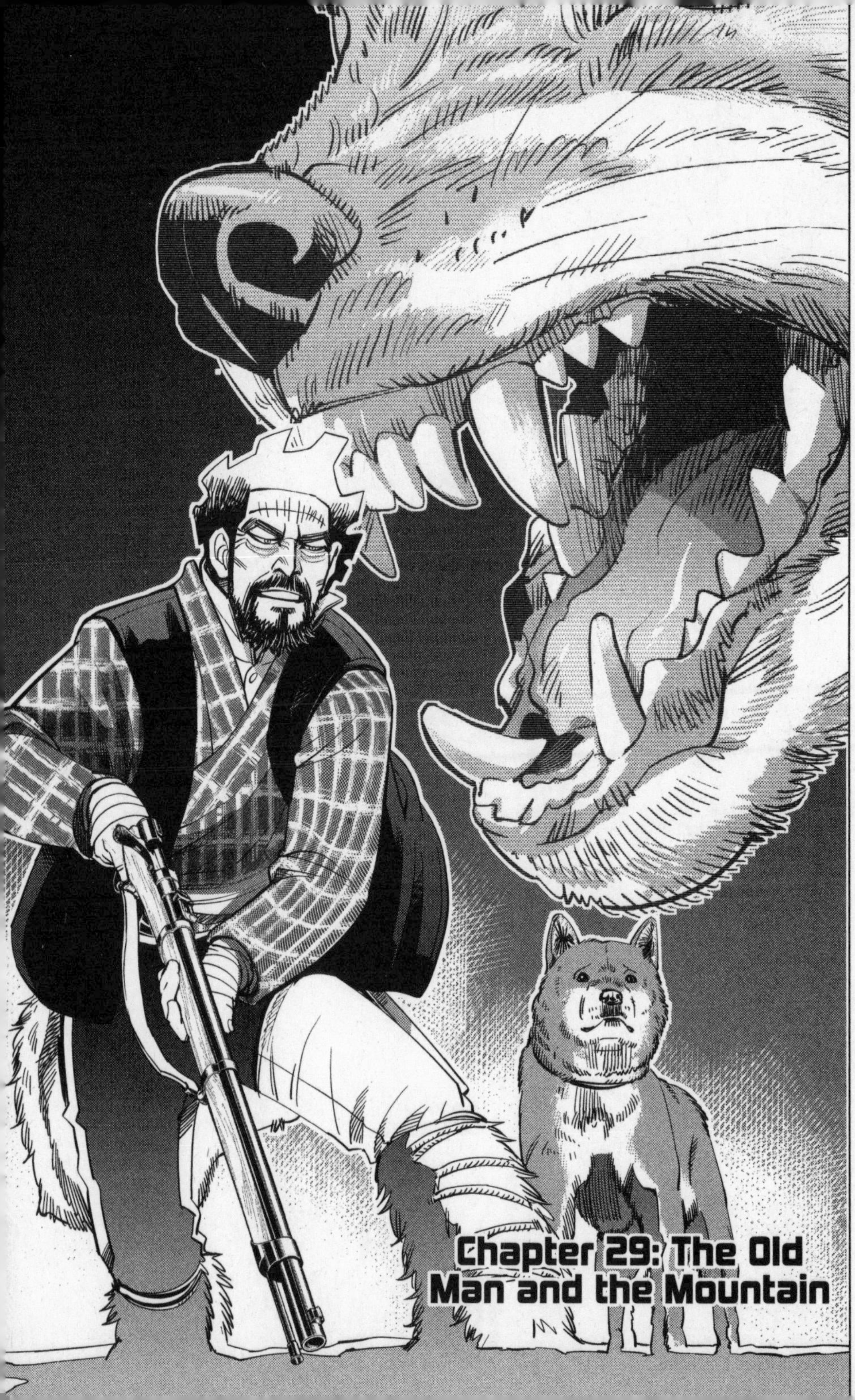
Chapter 29: The Old
Man and the Mountain

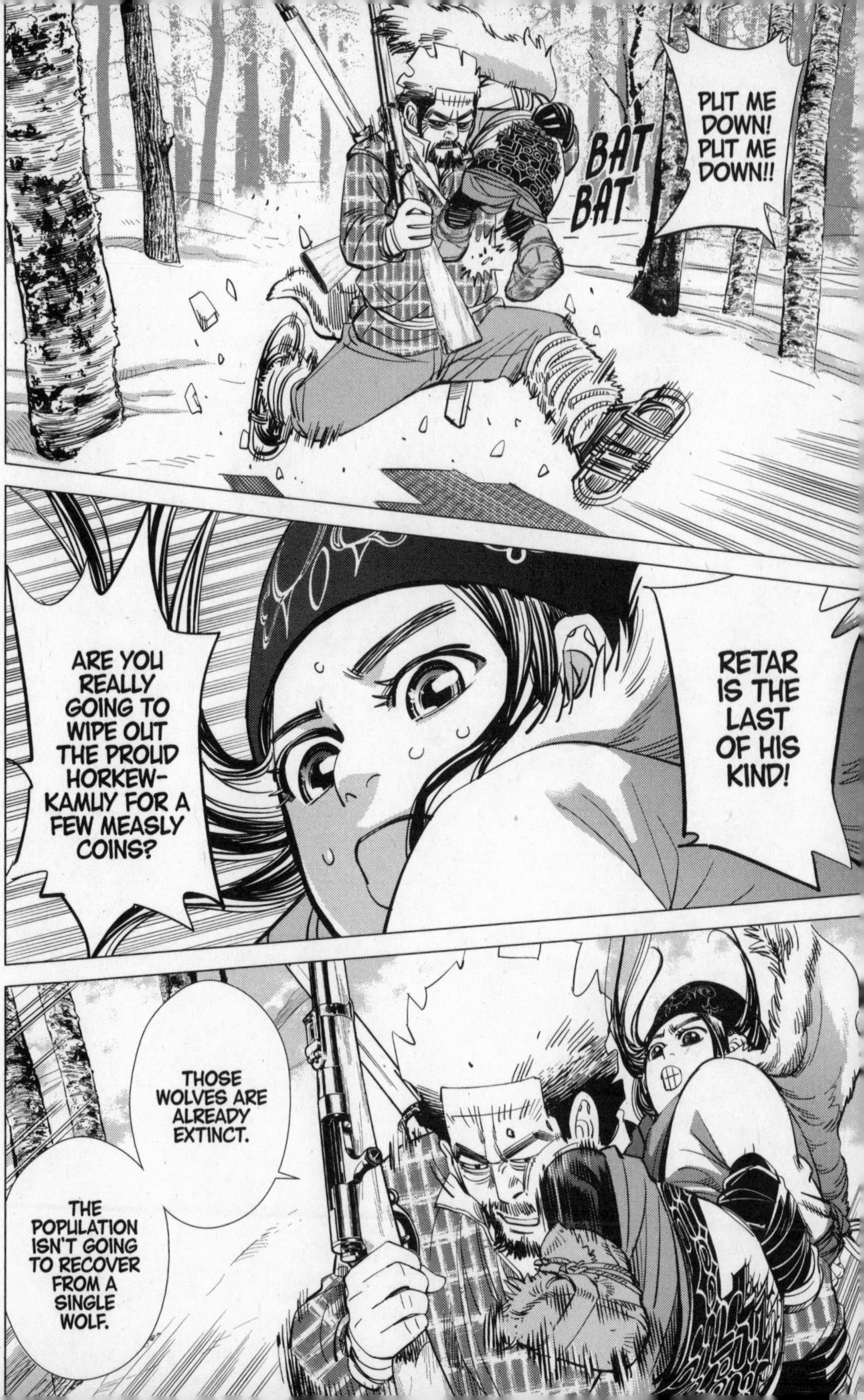
PUT ME DOWN! PUT ME DOWN!!
BAT BAT
RETAR IS THE LAST OF HIS KIND!
ARE YOU REALLY GOING TO WIPE OUT THE PROUD HORKEW-KAMUY FOR A FEW MEASLY COINS?
THOSE WOLVES ARE ALREADY EXTINCT.
THE POPULATION ISN'T GOING TO RECOVER FROM A SINGLE WOLF.

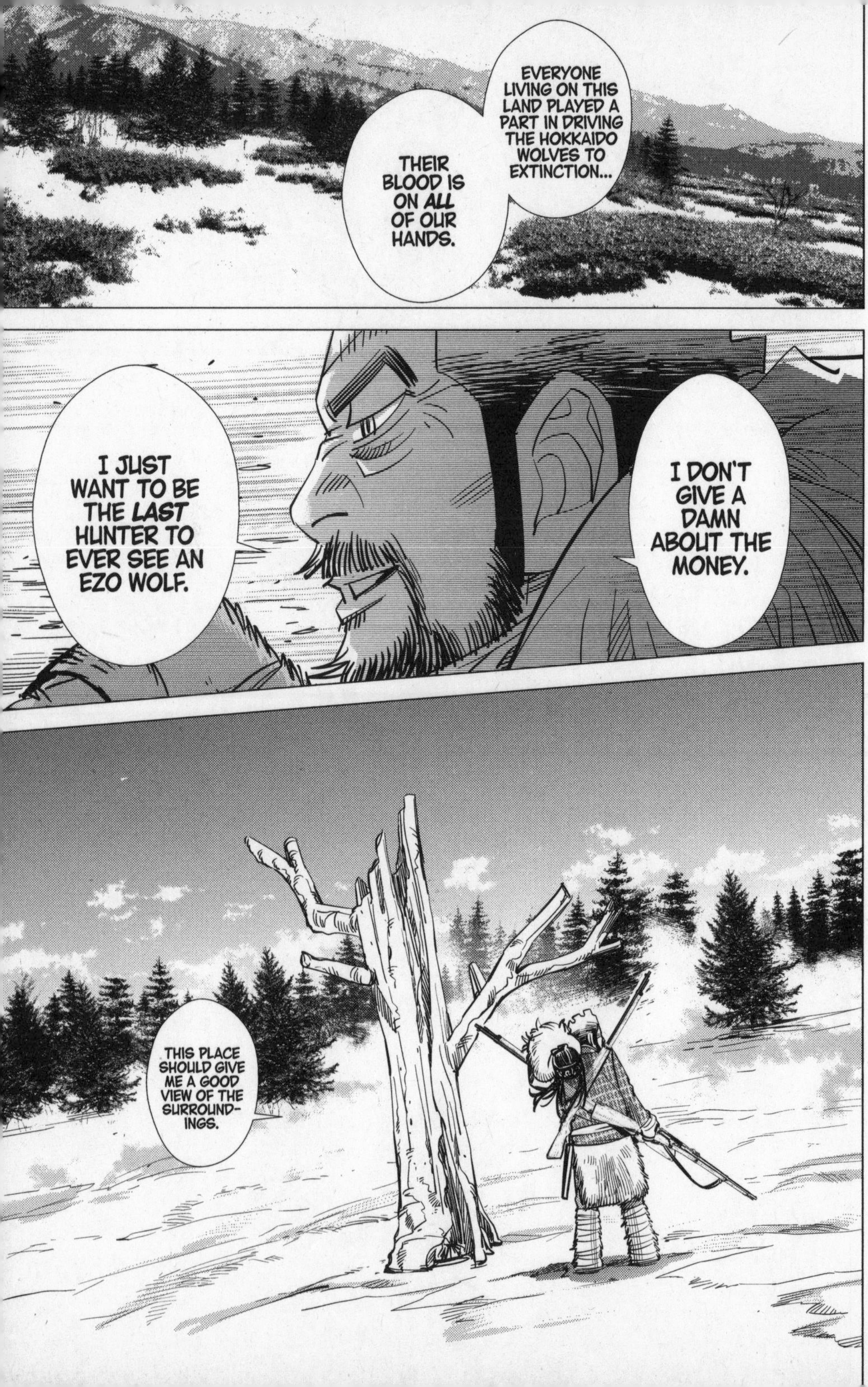
EVERYONE LIVING ON THIS LAND PLAYED A PART IN DRIVING THE HOKKAIDO WOLVES TO EXTINCTION...
THEIR BLOOD IS ON *ALL* OF OUR HANDS.
I DON'T GIVE A DAMN ABOUT THE MONEY.
I JUST WANT TO BE THE *LAST* HUNTER TO EVER SEE AN EZO WOLF.
THIS PLACE SHOULD GIVE ME A GOOD VIEW OF THE SURROUND-INGS.

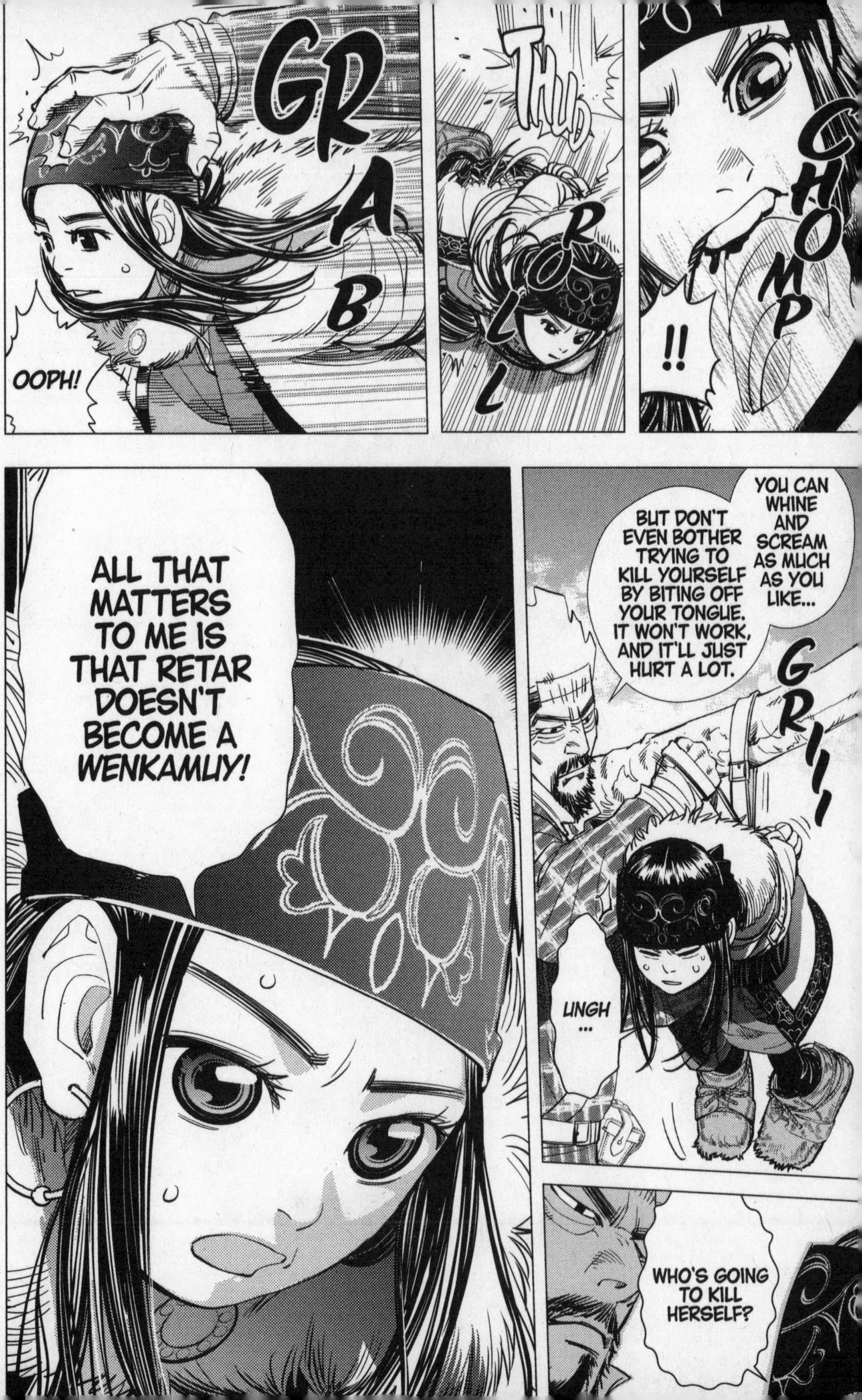
CHOMP
!!
THUD
ROLL
GRAB
OOPH!
YOU CAN WHINE AND SCREAM AS MUCH AS YOU LIKE...
BUT DON'T EVEN BOTHER TRYING TO KILL YOURSELF BY BITING OFF YOUR TONGUE. IT WON'T WORK, AND IT'LL JUST HURT A LOT.
GRI
UNGH...
WHO'S GOING TO KILL HERSELF?
ALL THAT MATTERS TO ME IS THAT RETAR DOESN'T BECOME A WENKAMUY!

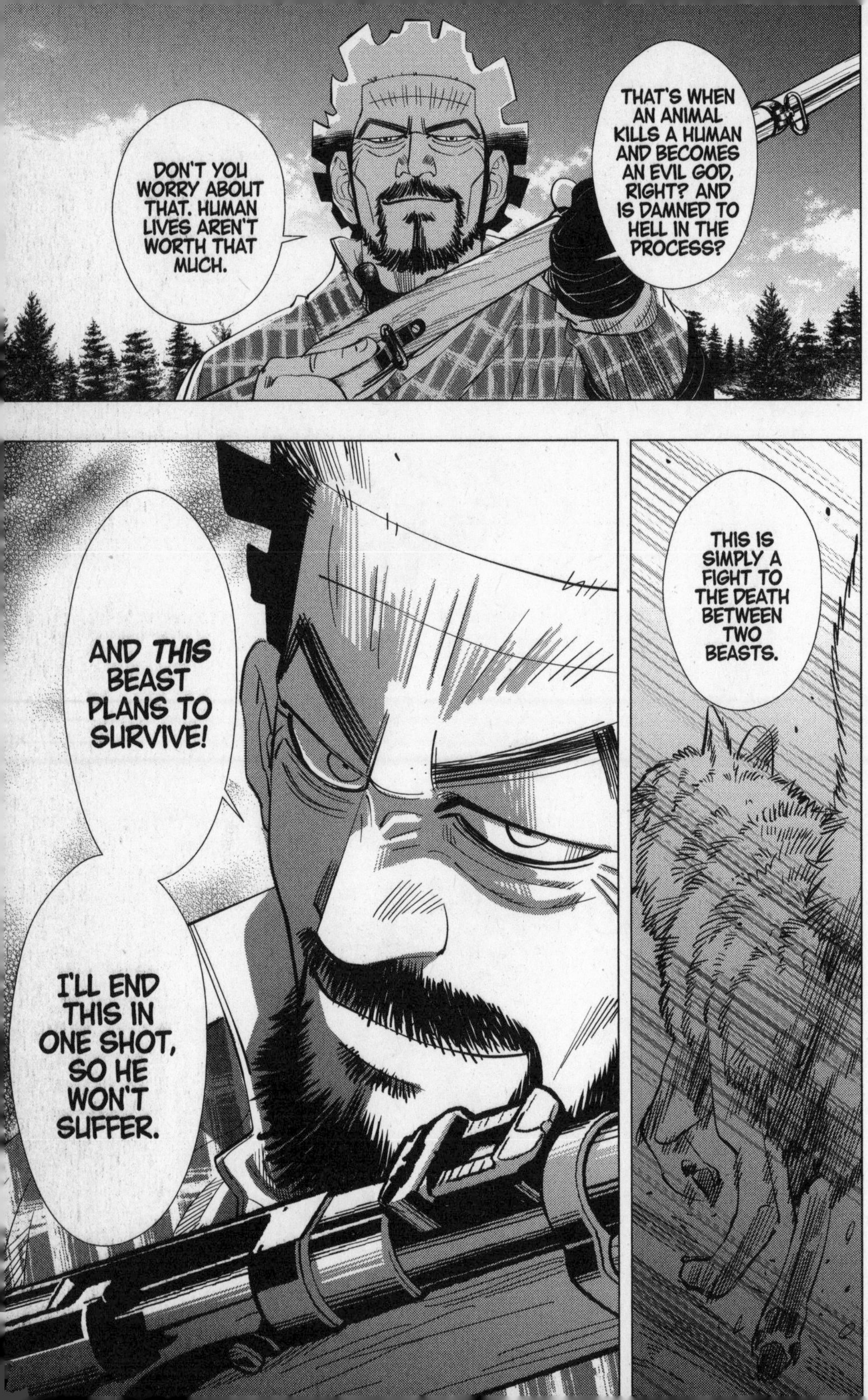
THAT'S WHEN AN ANIMAL KILLS A HUMAN AND BECOMES AN EVIL GOD, RIGHT? AND IS DAMNED TO HELL IN THE PROCESS?
DON'T YOU WORRY ABOUT THAT. HUMAN LIVES AREN'T WORTH THAT MUCH.
THIS IS SIMPLY A FIGHT TO THE DEATH BETWEEN TWO BEASTS.
AND THIS BEAST PLANS TO SURVIVE!
I'LL END THIS IN ONE SHOT, SO HE WON'T SUFFER.

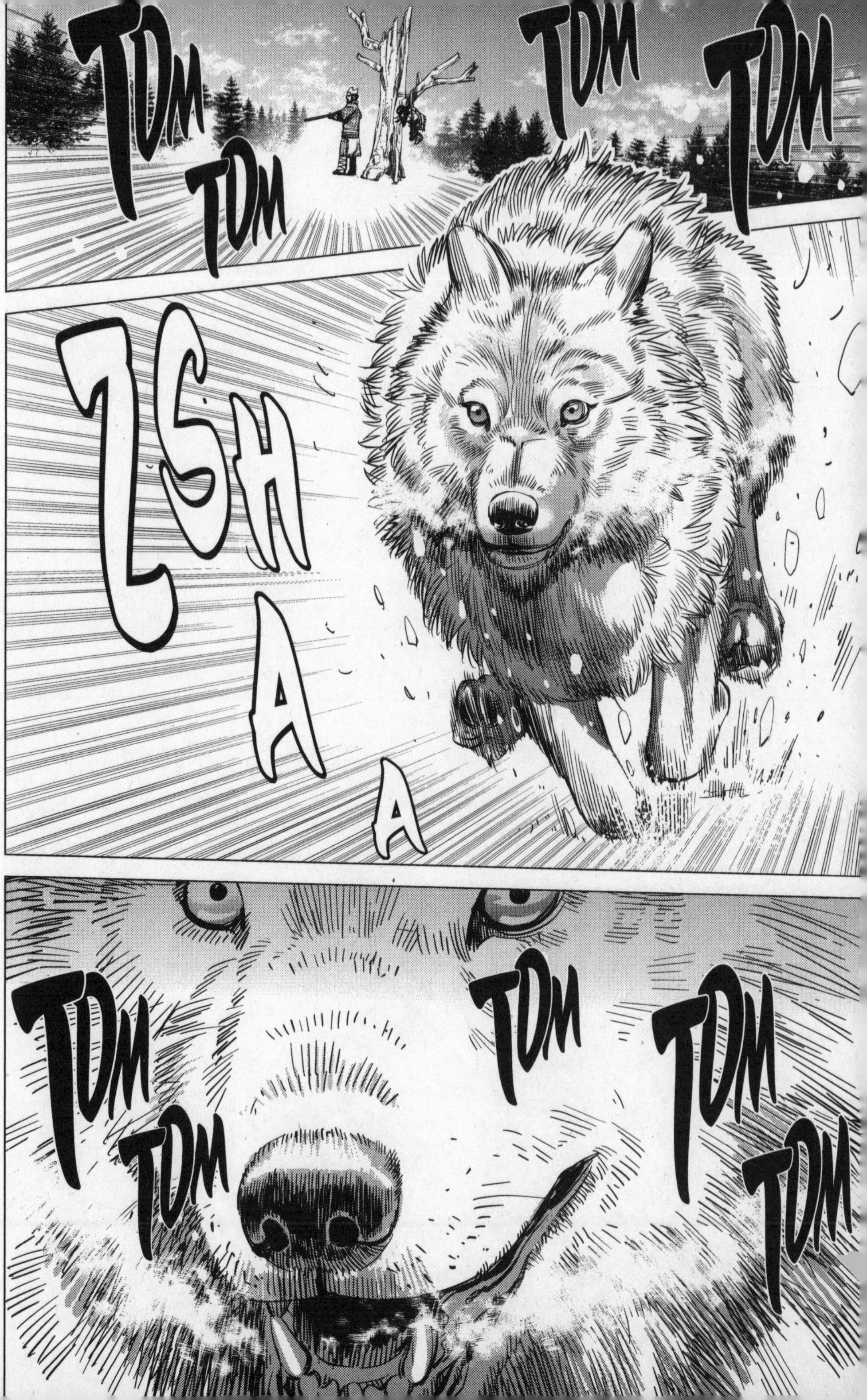
TOM TOM
TOM TOM
TOM TOM
ZSHAA
TOM TOM TOM
TOM TOM
TOM TOM

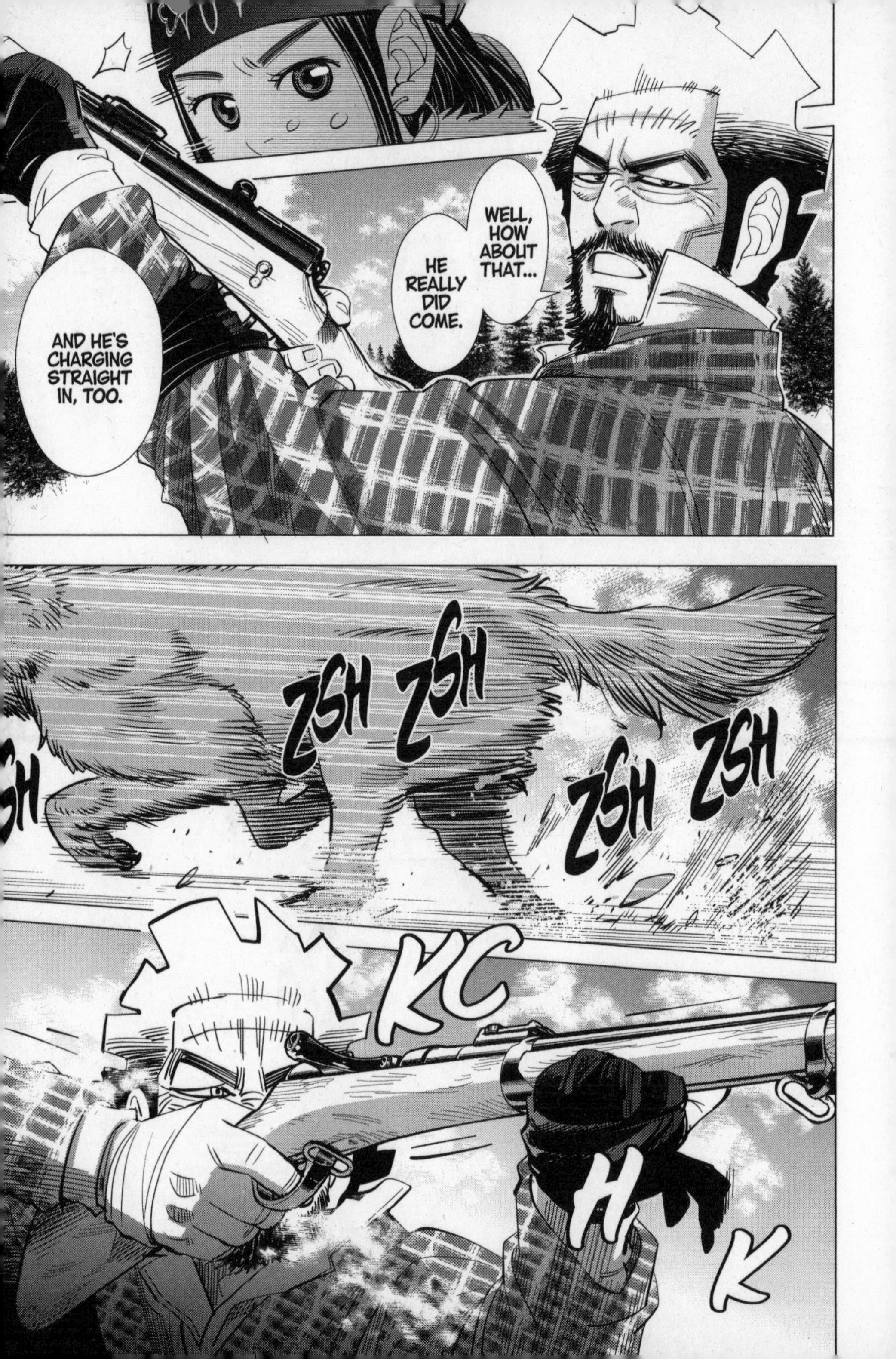
WELL, HOW ABOUT THAT...
HE REALLY DID COME.
AND HE'S CHARGING STRAIGHT IN, TOO.
ZSH ZSH
ZSH ZSH
KC
H
K

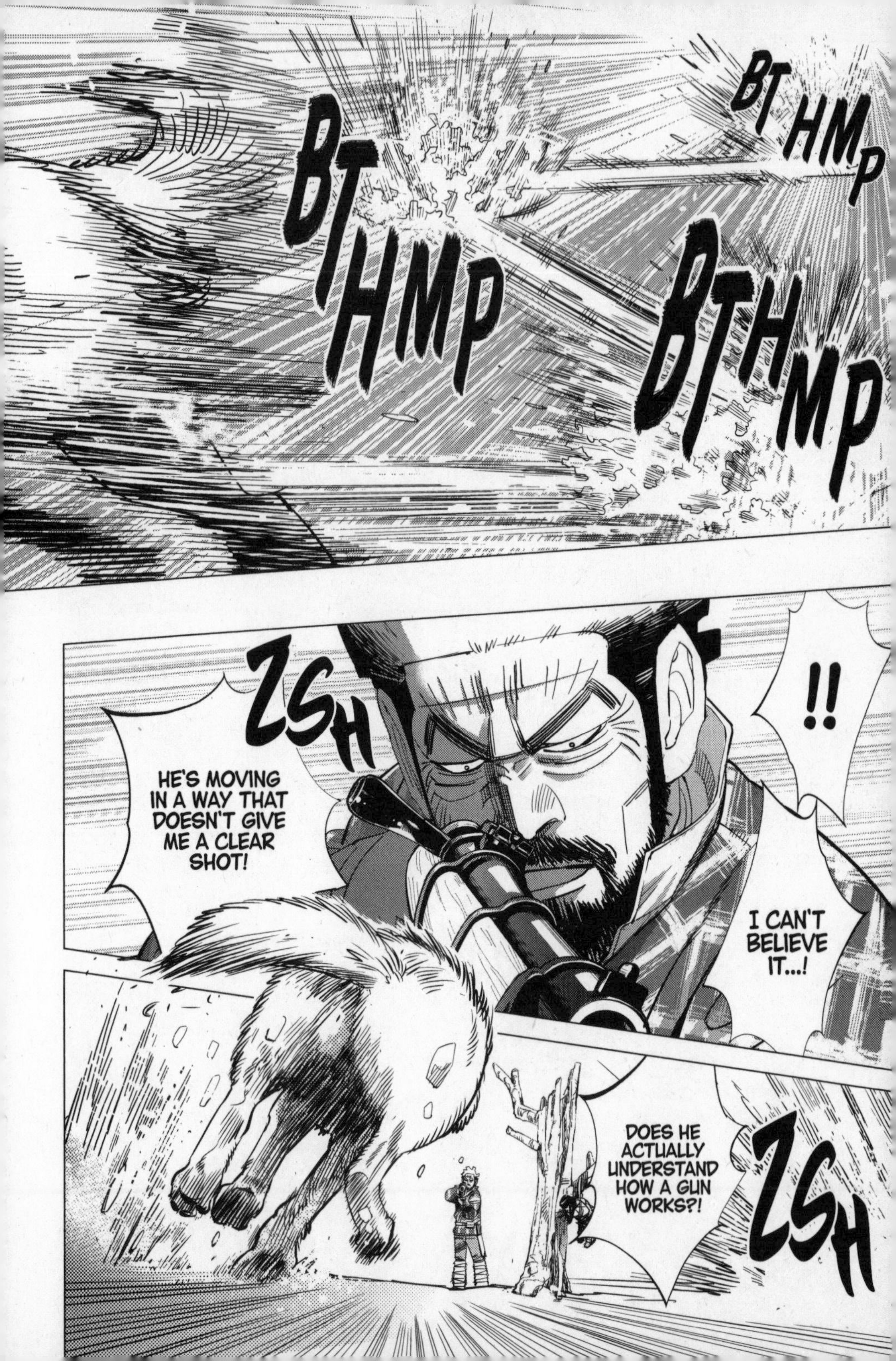
BTHMP
BTHMP
BTHMP
!!
ZSH
HE'S MOVING IN A WAY THAT DOESN'T GIVE ME A CLEAR SHOT!
I CAN'T BELIEVE IT...!
ZSH
DOES HE ACTUALLY UNDERSTAND HOW A GUN WORKS?!

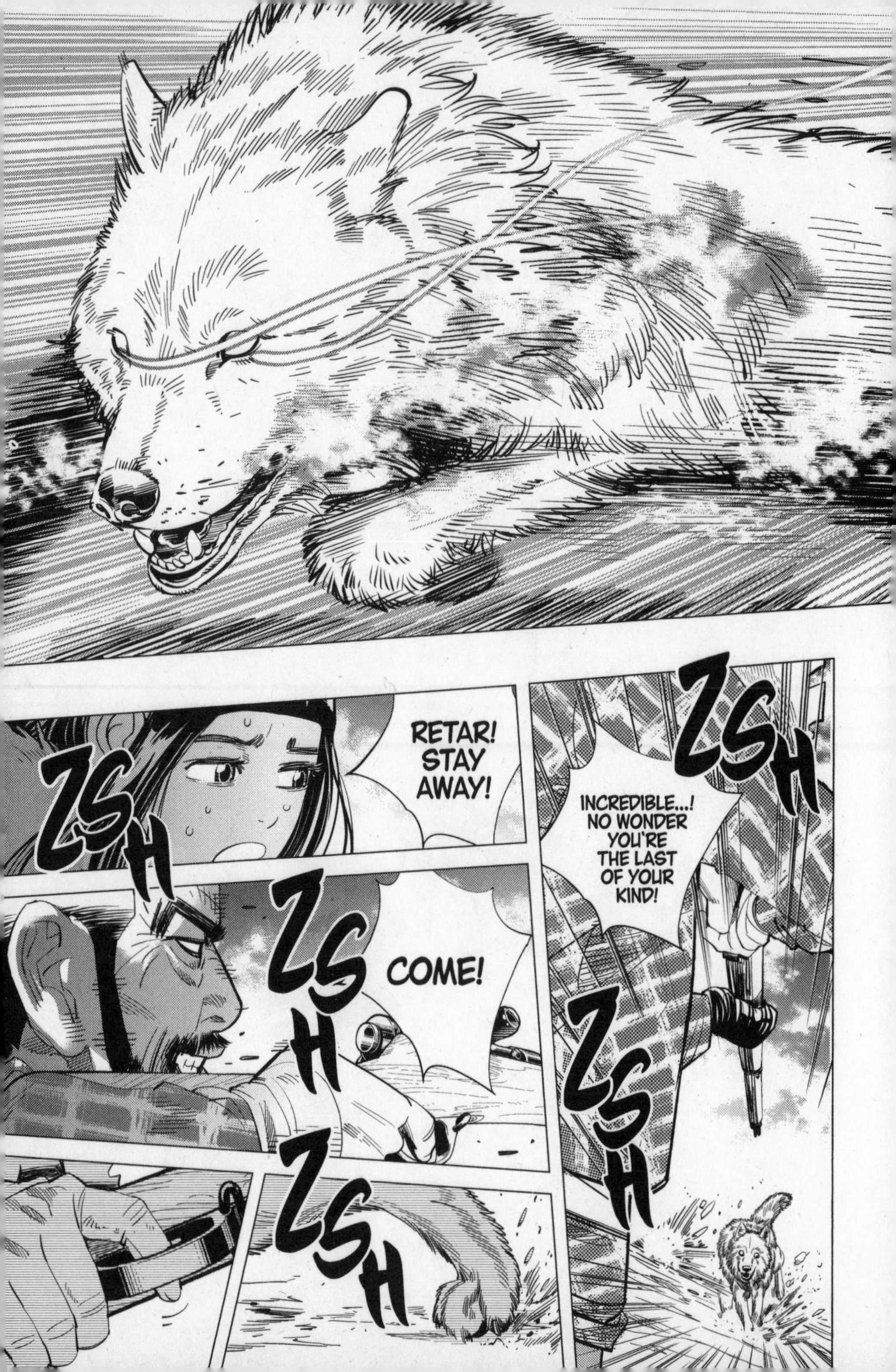
ZSH
INCREDIBLE...! NO WONDER YOU'RE THE LAST OF YOUR KIND!
ZSH
RETAR! STAY AWAY!
ZSH
ZSH
COME!
ZSH

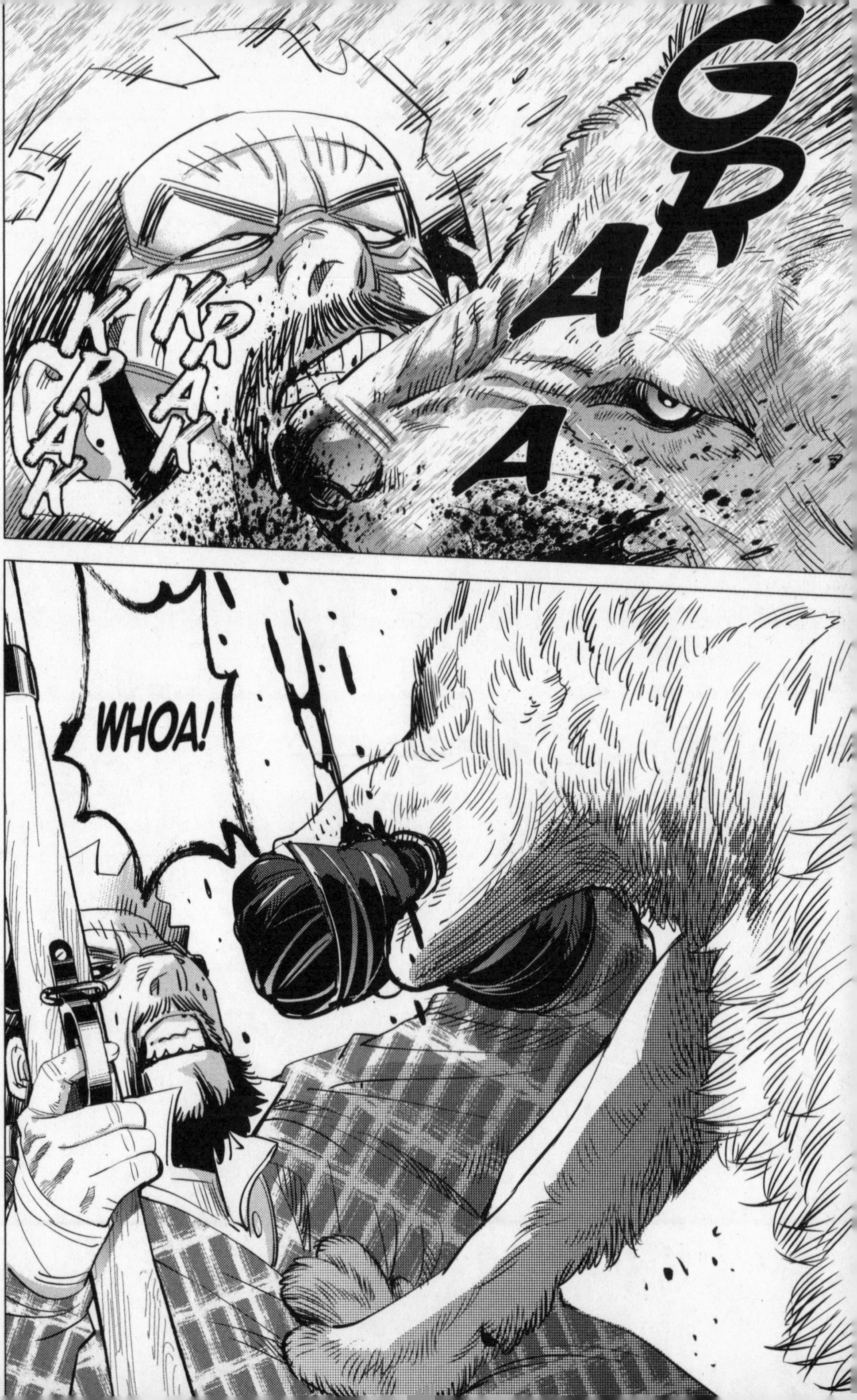
GRAAA
KRAK
KRAK
WHOA!

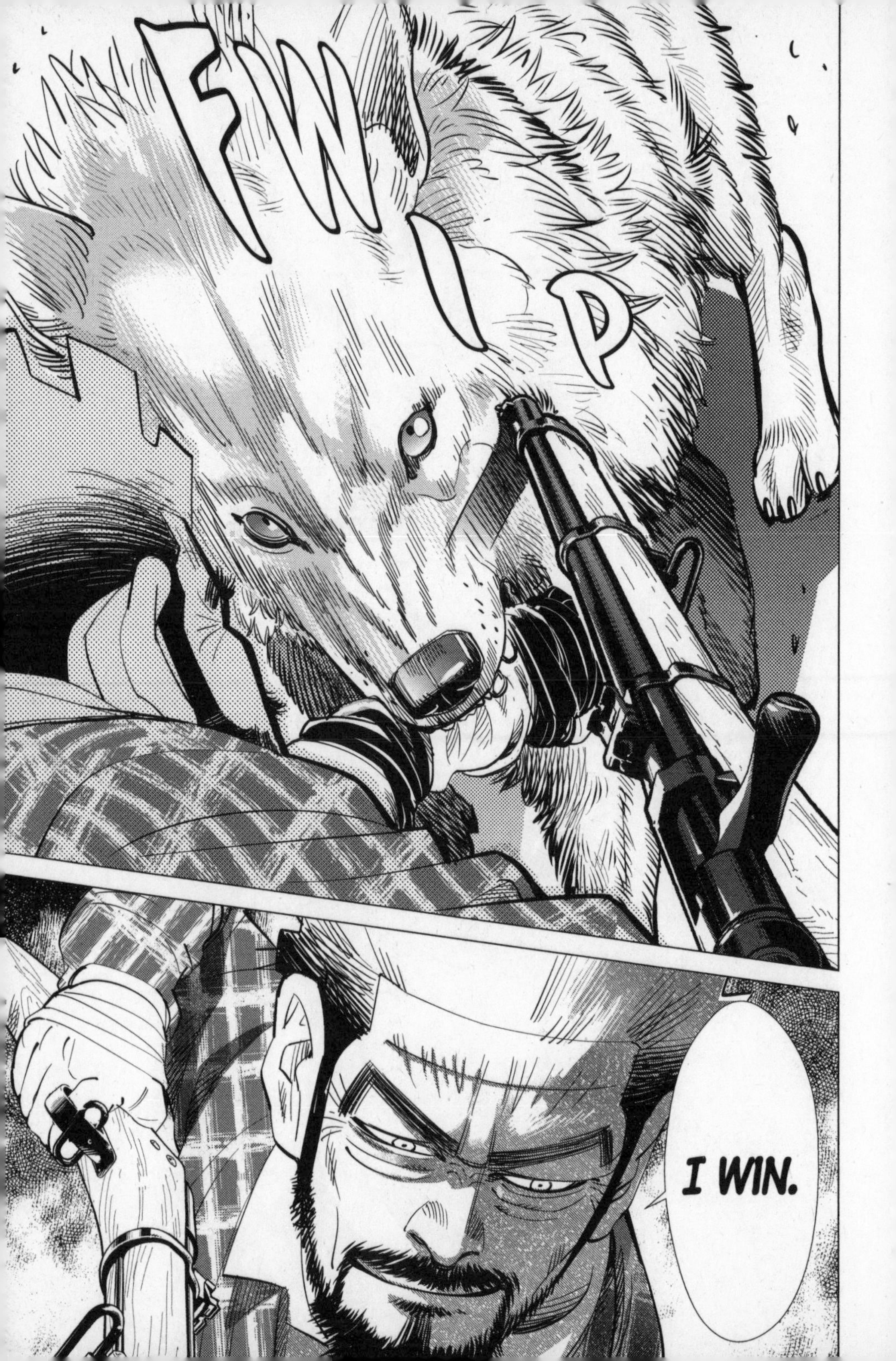
FWIP
I WIN.

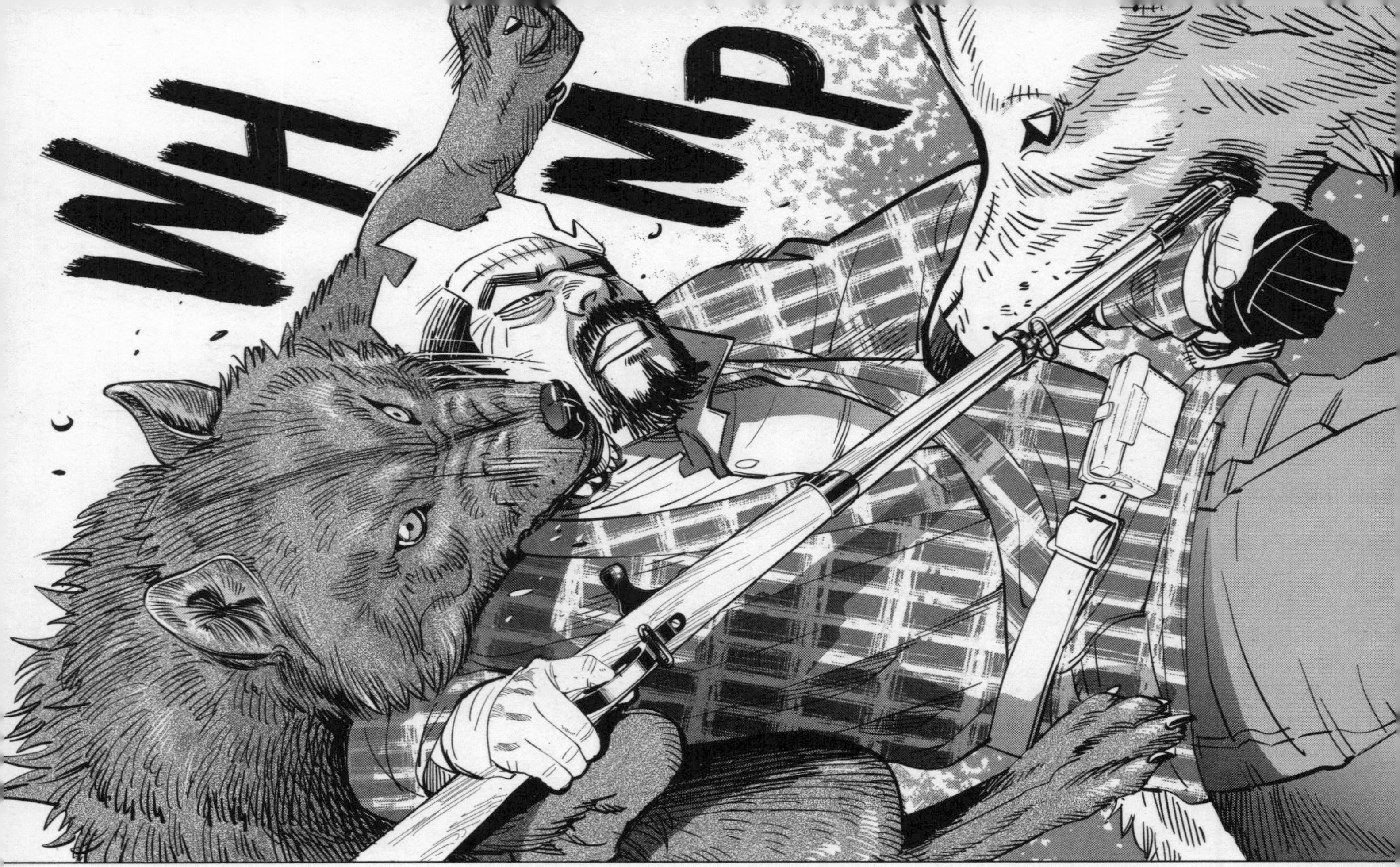
WHUMP

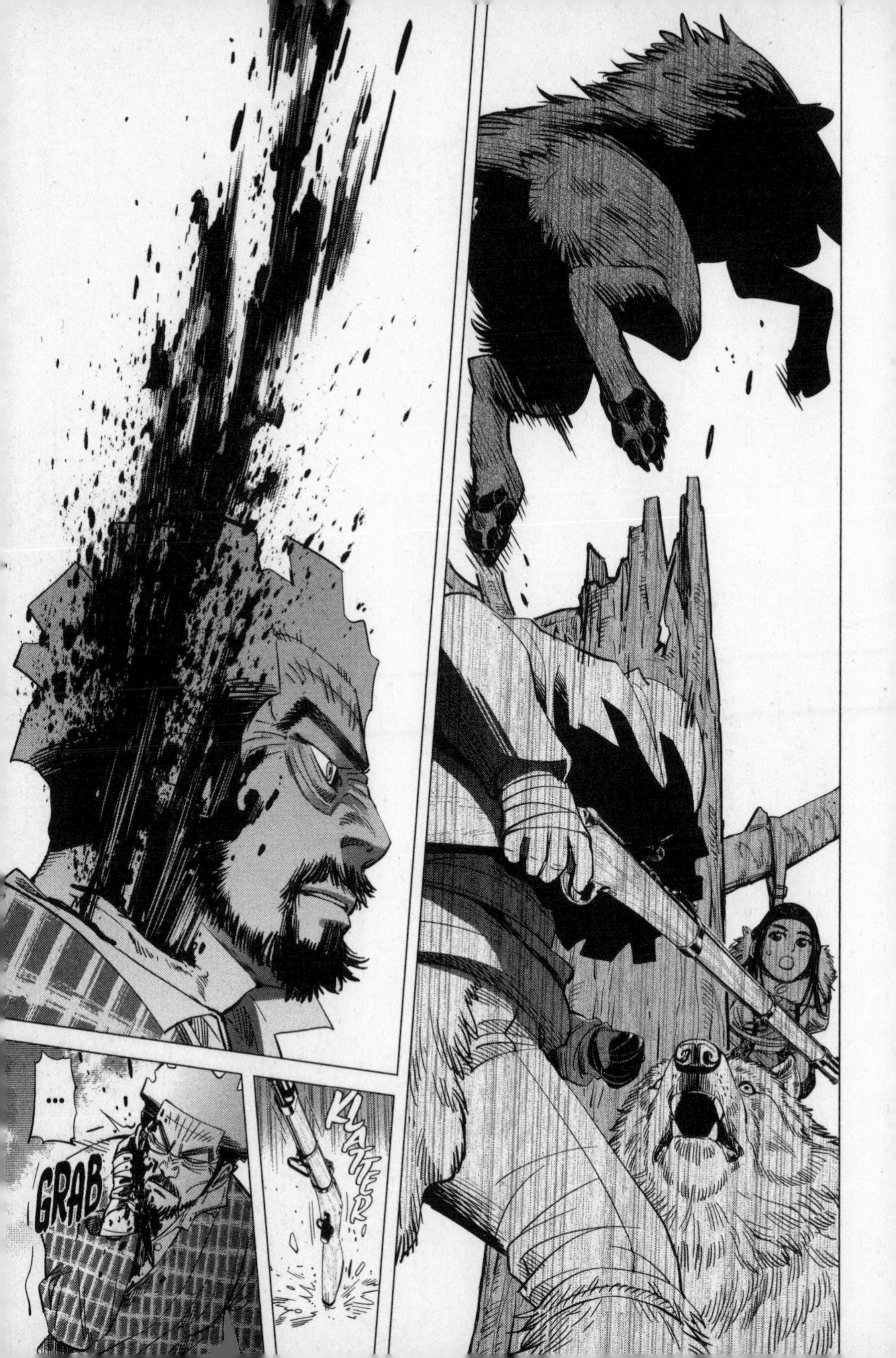
KLATTER!
GRAB
...

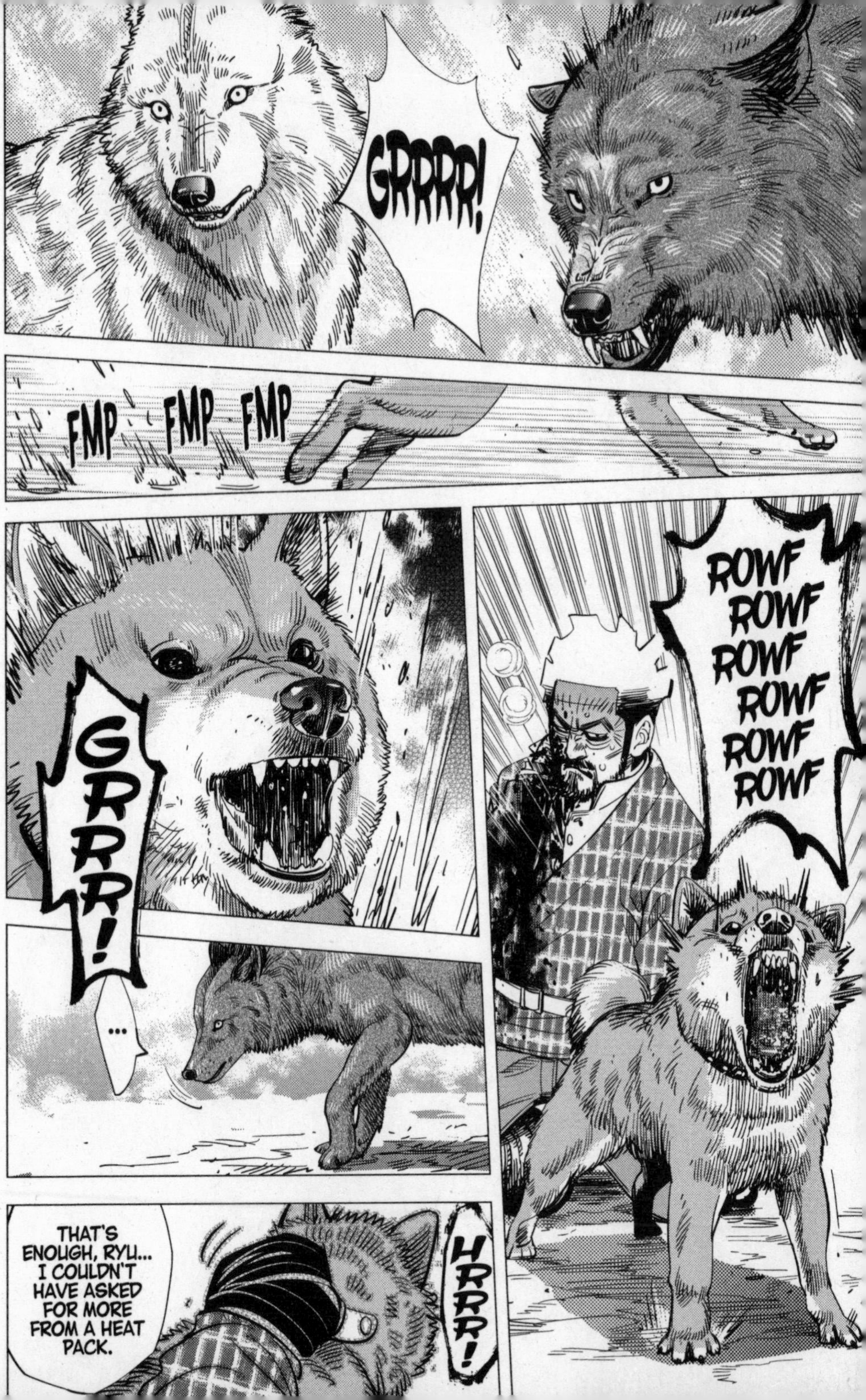
GRRRR!
FMP FMP FMP
ROWF ROWF ROWF ROWF ROWF ROWF ROWF
GRRR!
...
HRRR!
THAT'S ENOUGH, RYU... I COULDN'T HAVE ASKED FOR MORE FROM A HEAT PACK.

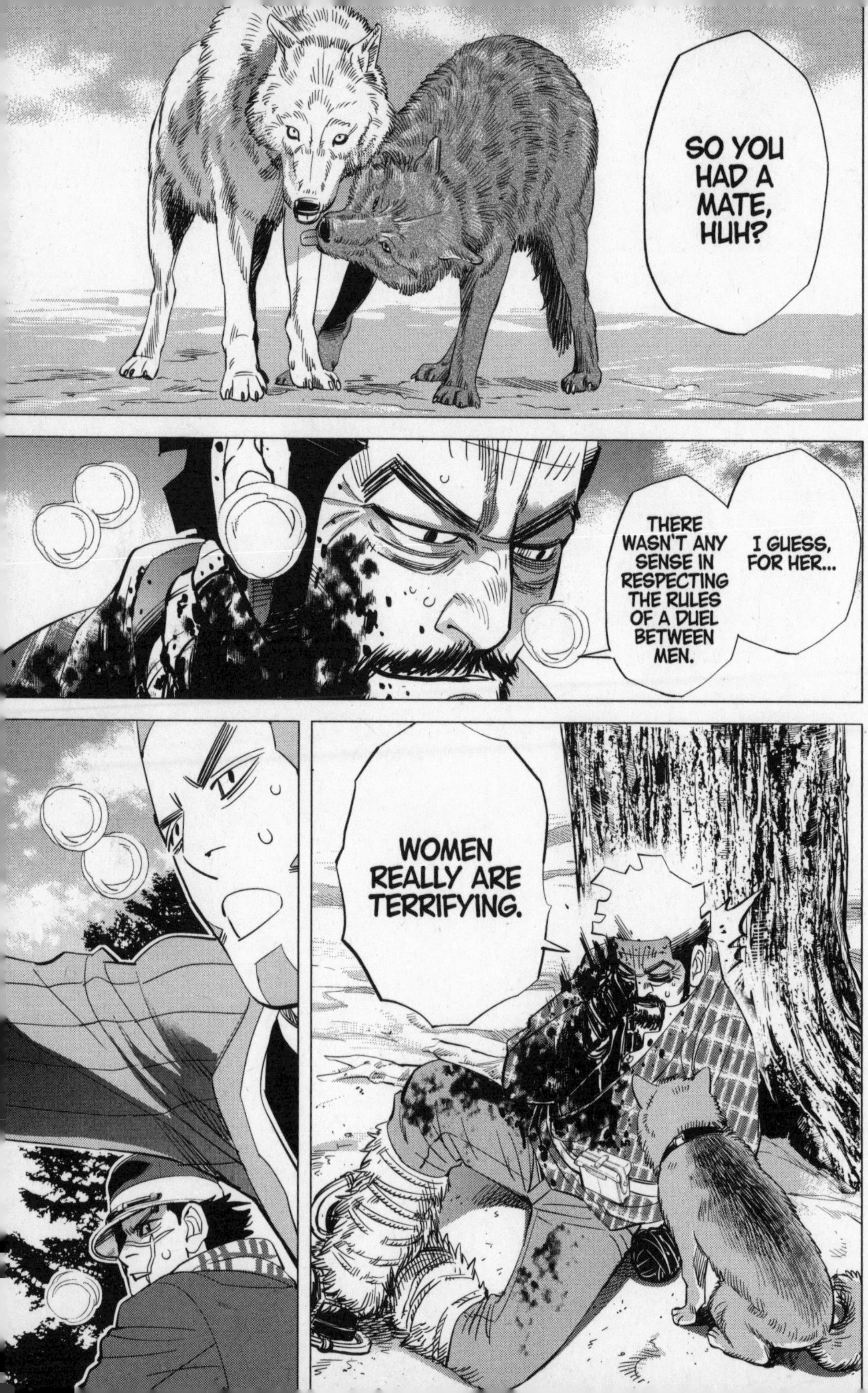
SO YOU HAD A MATE, HUH?
I GUESS, FOR HER...
THERE WASN'T ANY SENSE IN RESPECTING THE RULES OF A DUEL BETWEEN MEN.
WOMEN REALLY ARE TERRIFYING.

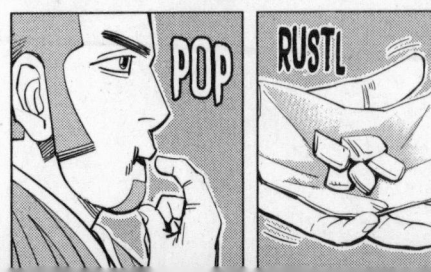

WHINE

POP

RUSTL

BUT... I AM SATISFIED.

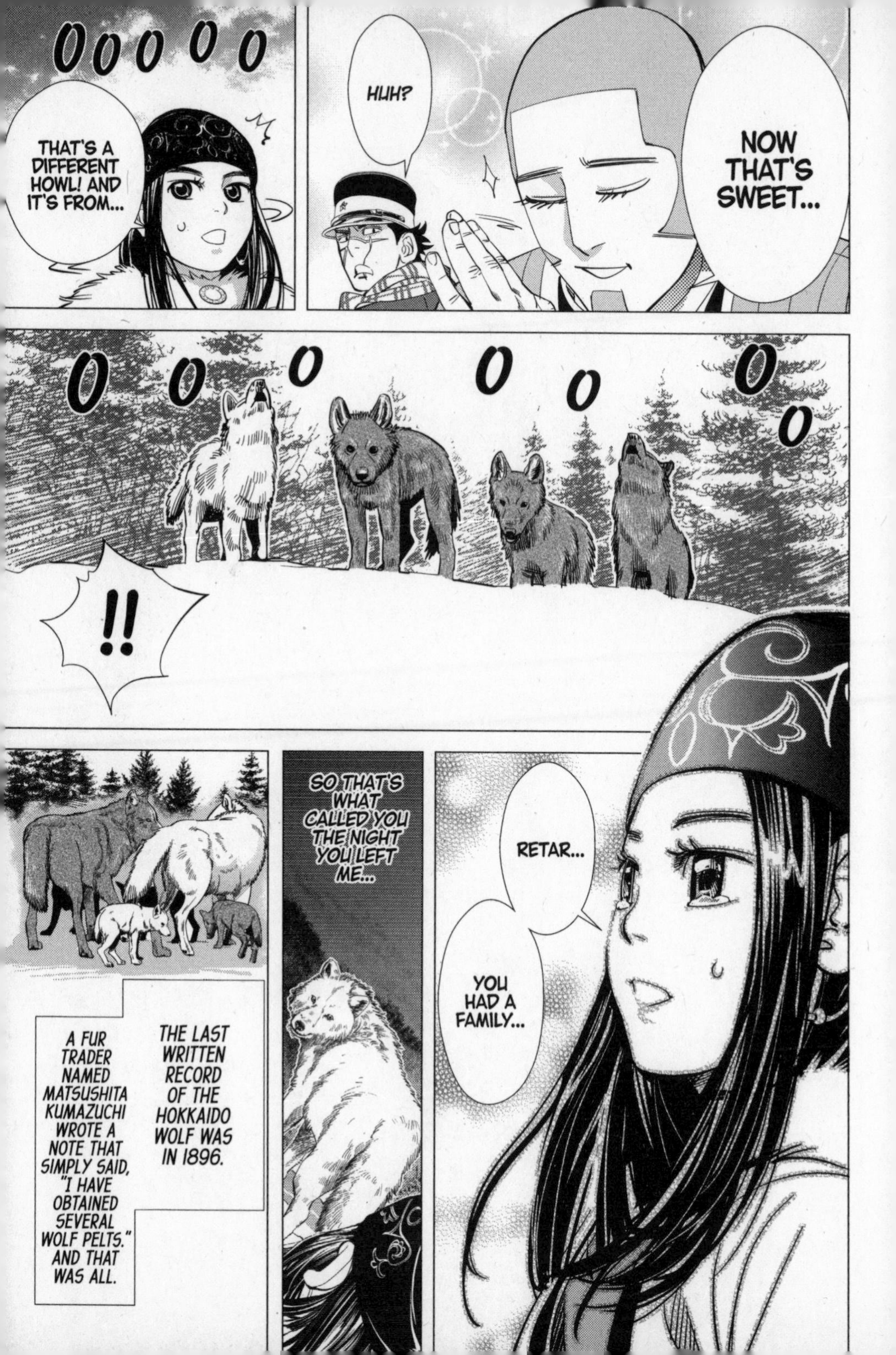
NOW THAT'S SWEET...
HUH?
OOOOO
THAT'S A DIFFERENT HOWL! AND IT'S FROM...
OO
O
O
O
O
O
!!
RETAR...
YOU HAD A FAMILY...
SO THAT'S WHAT CALLED YOU THE NIGHT YOU LEFT ME...
THE LAST WRITTEN RECORD OF THE HOKKAIDO WOLF WAS IN 1896.
A FUR TRADER NAMED MATSUSHITA KUMAZUCHI WROTE A NOTE THAT SIMPLY SAID, "I HAVE OBTAINED SEVERAL WOLF PELTS." AND THAT WAS ALL.

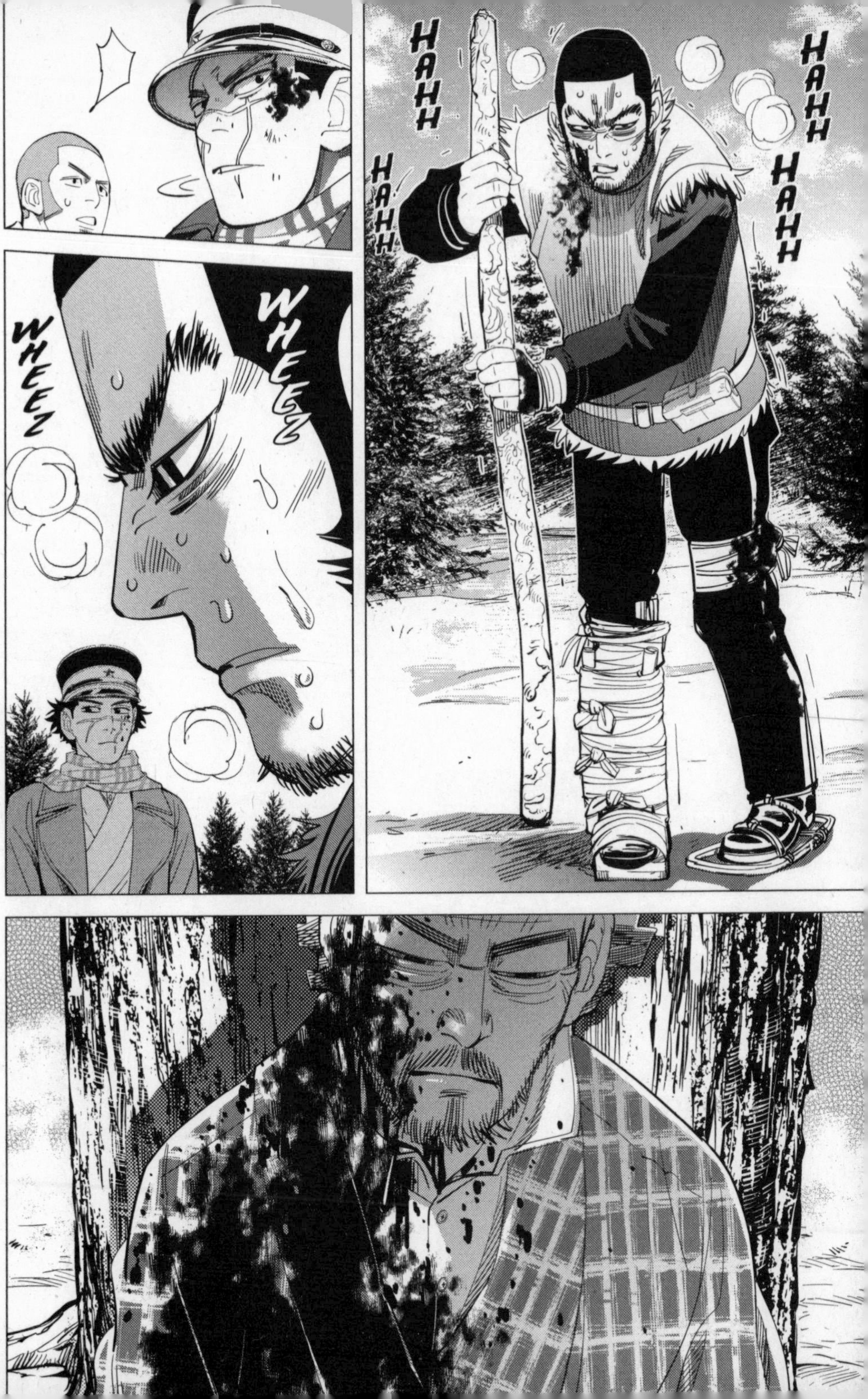
HAHH
HAHH
HAHH
HAHH
WHEEZ
WHEEZ

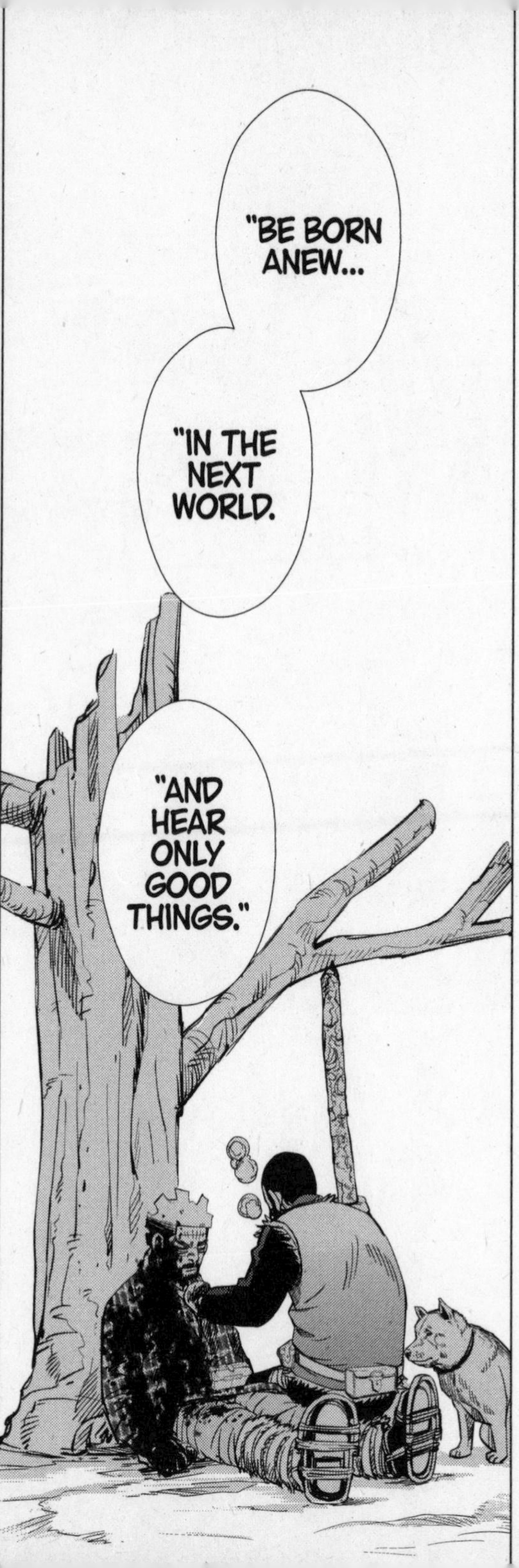
"BE BORN ANEW...
"IN THE NEXT WORLD.
"AND HEAR ONLY GOOD THINGS."
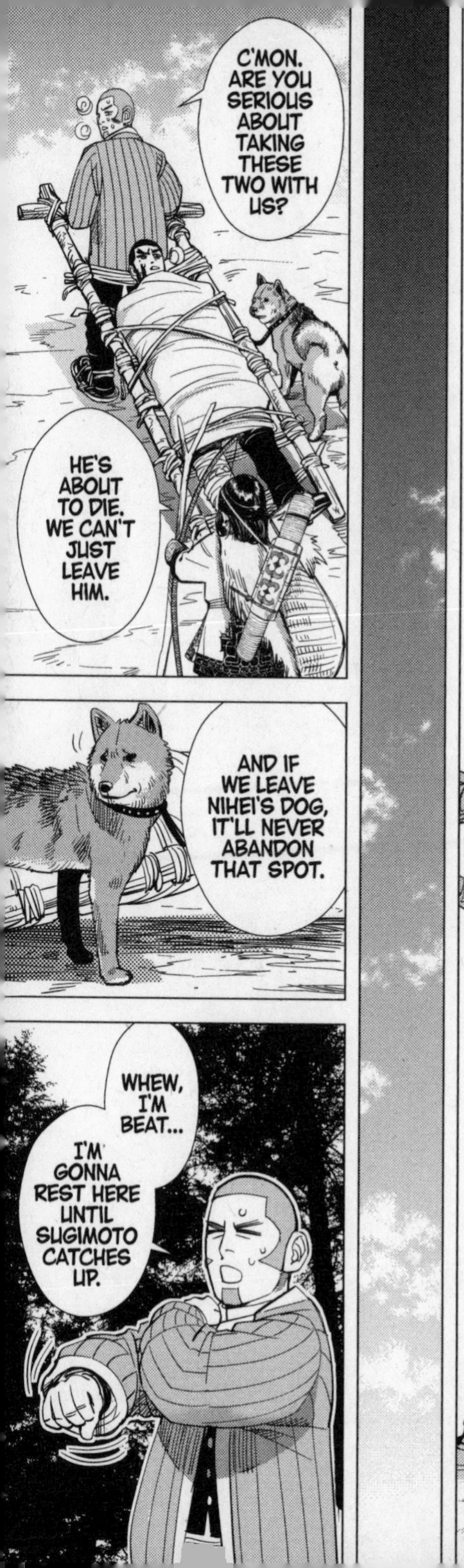
C'MON. ARE YOU SERIOUS ABOUT TAKING THESE TWO WITH US?
HE'S ABOUT TO DIE. WE CAN'T JUST LEAVE HIM.
AND IF WE LEAVE NIHEI'S DOG, IT'LL NEVER ABANDON THAT SPOT.
WHEW, I'M BEAT...
I'M GONNA REST HERE UNTIL SUGIMOTO CATCHES UP.

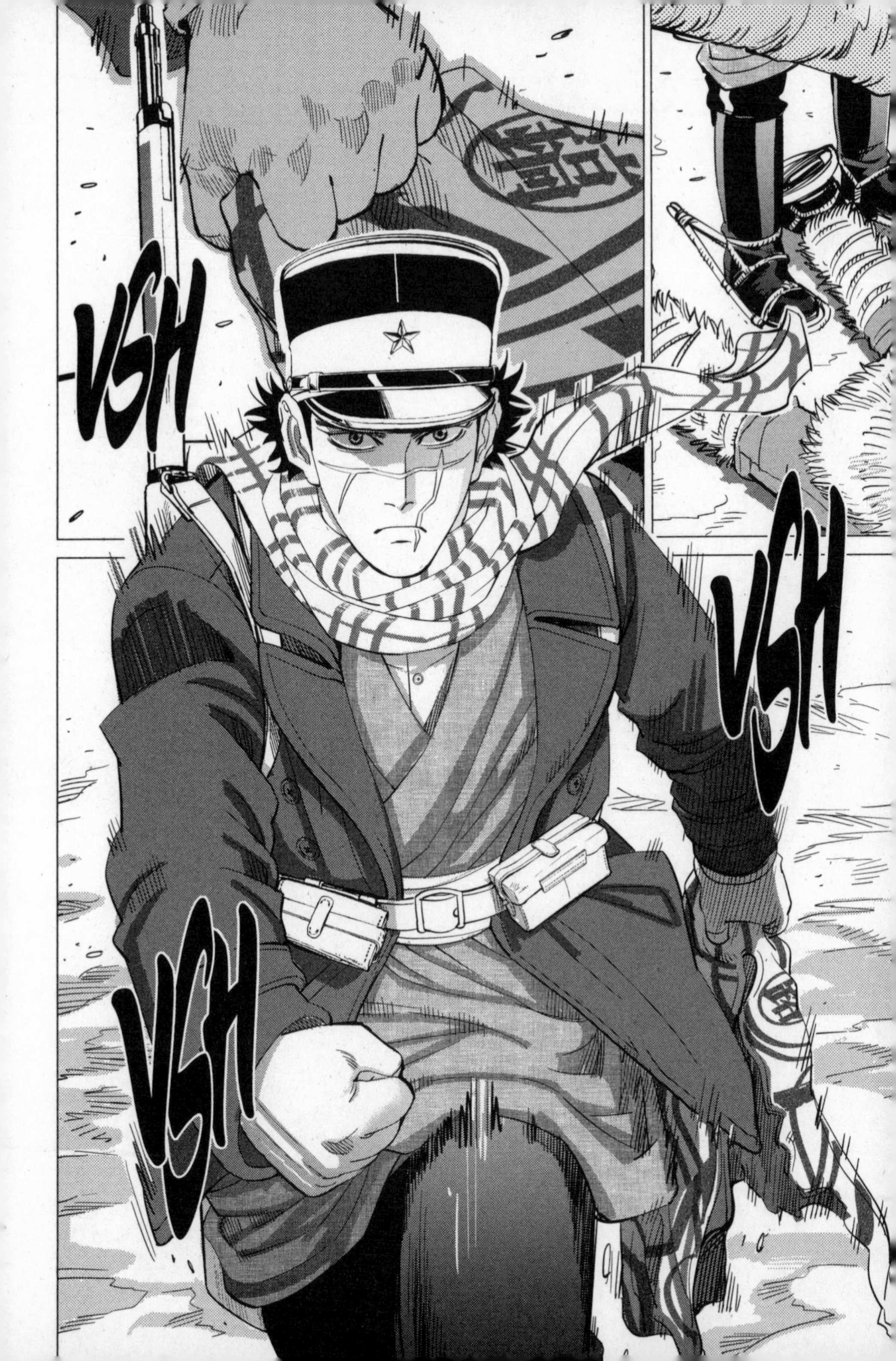
VSH
VSH
VSH

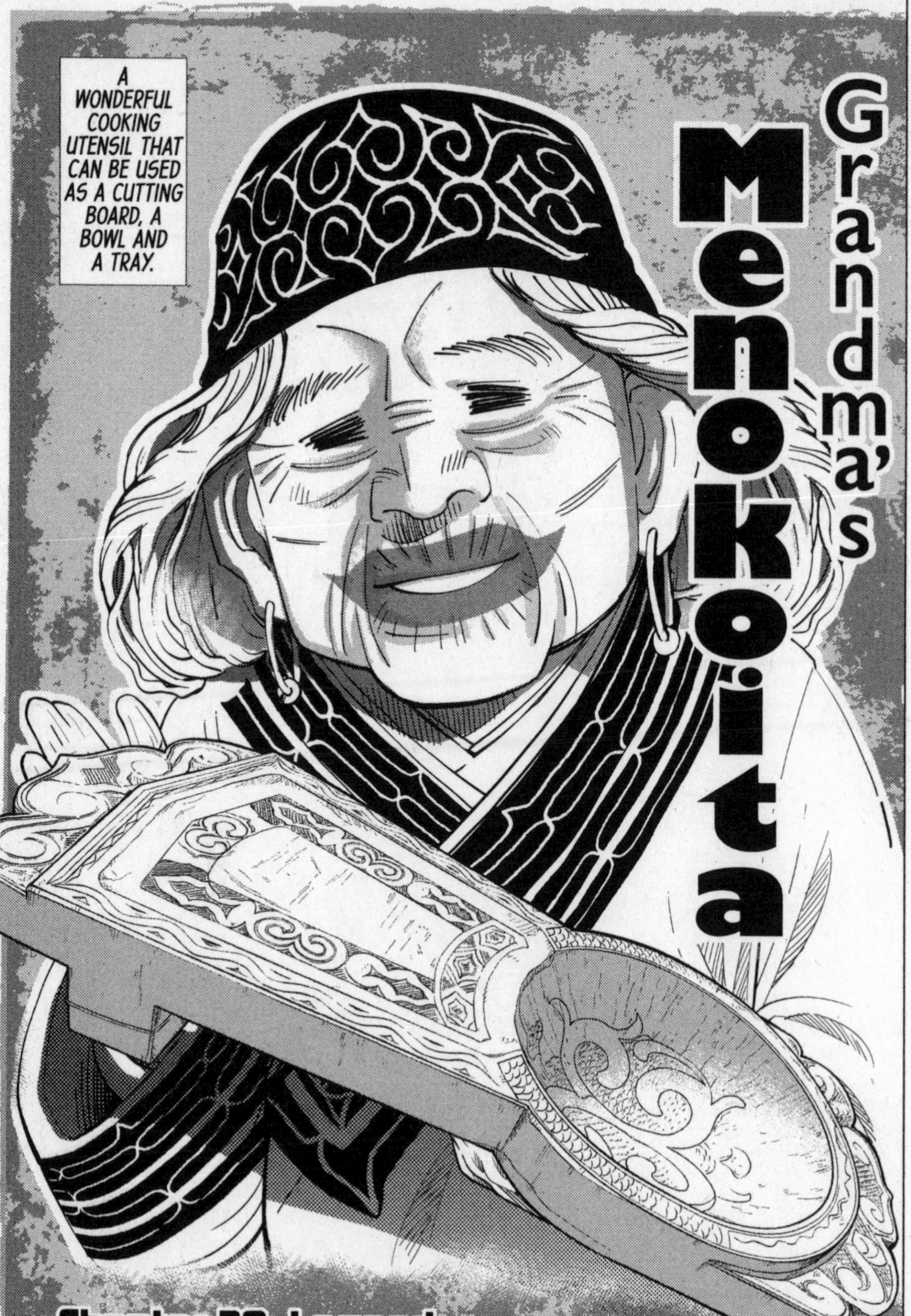
Grandma's Menoko Ita
A WONDERFUL COOKING UTENSIL THAT CAN BE USED AS A CUTTING BOARD, A BOWL AND A TRAY.
Chapter 30: Legend

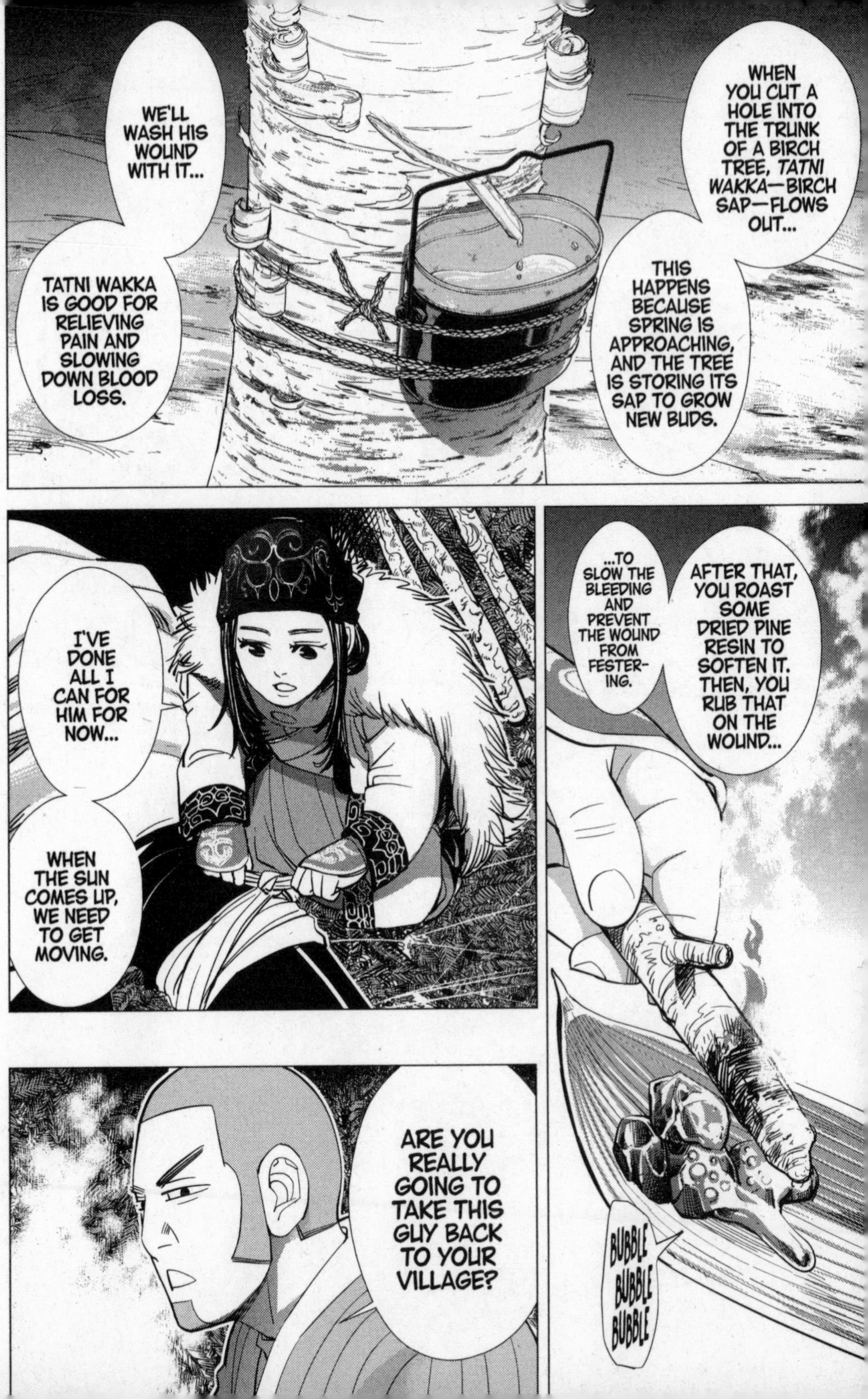
WHEN YOU CUT A HOLE INTO THE TRUNK OF A BIRCH TREE, *TATNI WAKKA*—BIRCH SAP—FLOWS OUT...
THIS HAPPENS BECAUSE SPRING IS APPROACHING, AND THE TREE IS STORING ITS SAP TO GROW NEW BUDS.
WE'LL WASH HIS WOUND WITH IT...
TATNI WAKKA IS GOOD FOR RELIEVING PAIN AND SLOWING DOWN BLOOD LOSS.
AFTER THAT, YOU ROAST SOME DRIED PINE RESIN TO SOFTEN IT. THEN, YOU RUB THAT ON THE WOUND...
...TO SLOW THE BLEEDING AND PREVENT THE WOUND FROM FESTER-ING.
BUBBLE BUBBLE BUBBLE
I'VE DONE ALL I CAN FOR HIM FOR NOW...
WHEN THE SUN COMES UP, WE NEED TO GET MOVING.
ARE YOU REALLY GOING TO TAKE THIS GUY BACK TO YOUR VILLAGE?

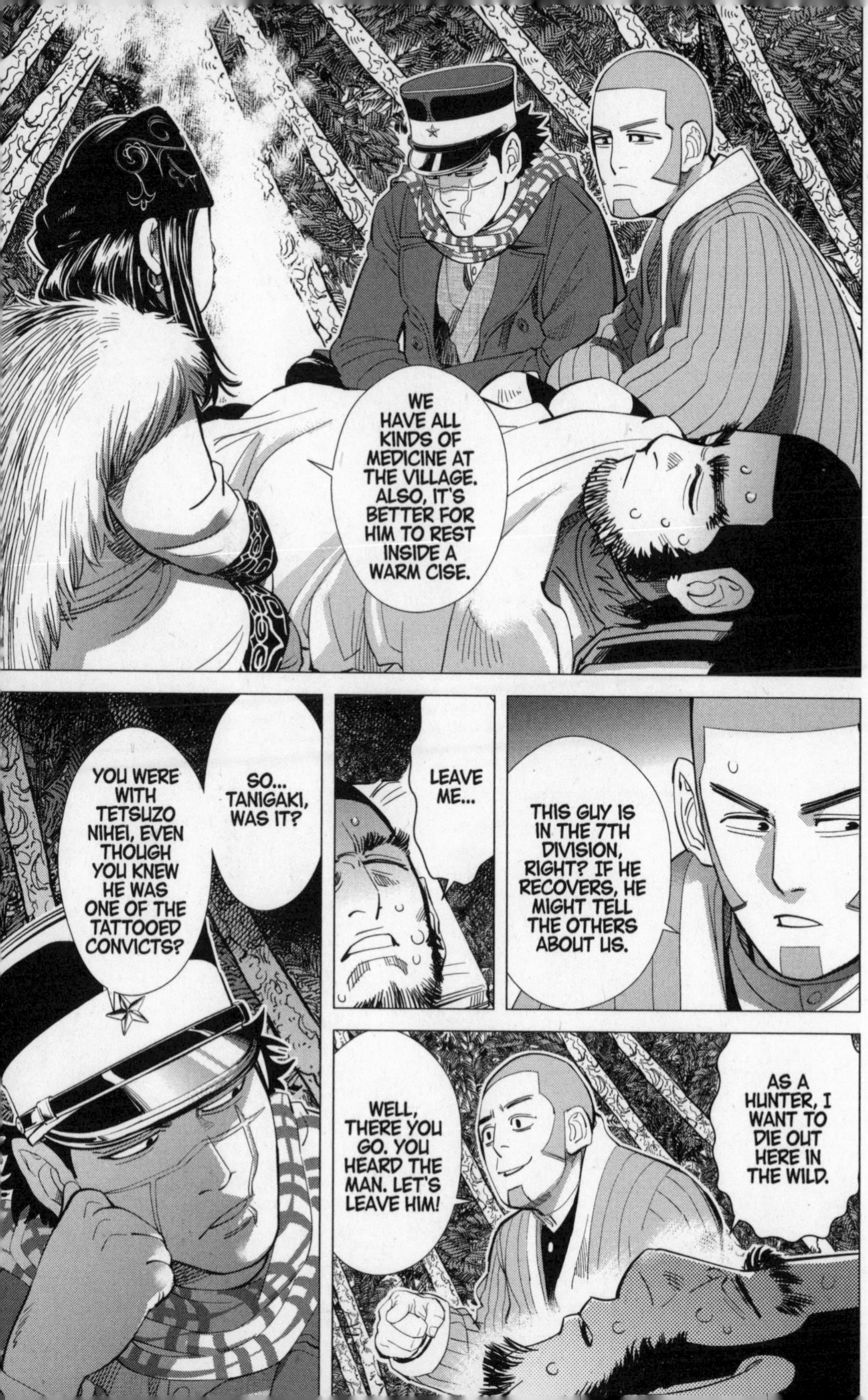
WE HAVE ALL KINDS OF MEDICINE AT THE VILLAGE. ALSO, IT'S BETTER FOR HIM TO REST INSIDE A WARM CISE.
THIS GUY IS IN THE 7TH DIVISION, RIGHT? IF HE RECOVERS, HE MIGHT TELL THE OTHERS ABOUT US.
LEAVE ME...
AS A HUNTER, I WANT TO DIE OUT HERE IN THE WILD.
WELL, THERE YOU GO. YOU HEARD THE MAN. LET'S LEAVE HIM!
SO... TANIGAKI, WAS IT?
YOU WERE WITH TETSUZO NIHEI, EVEN THOUGH YOU KNEW HE WAS ONE OF THE TATTOOED CONVICTS?

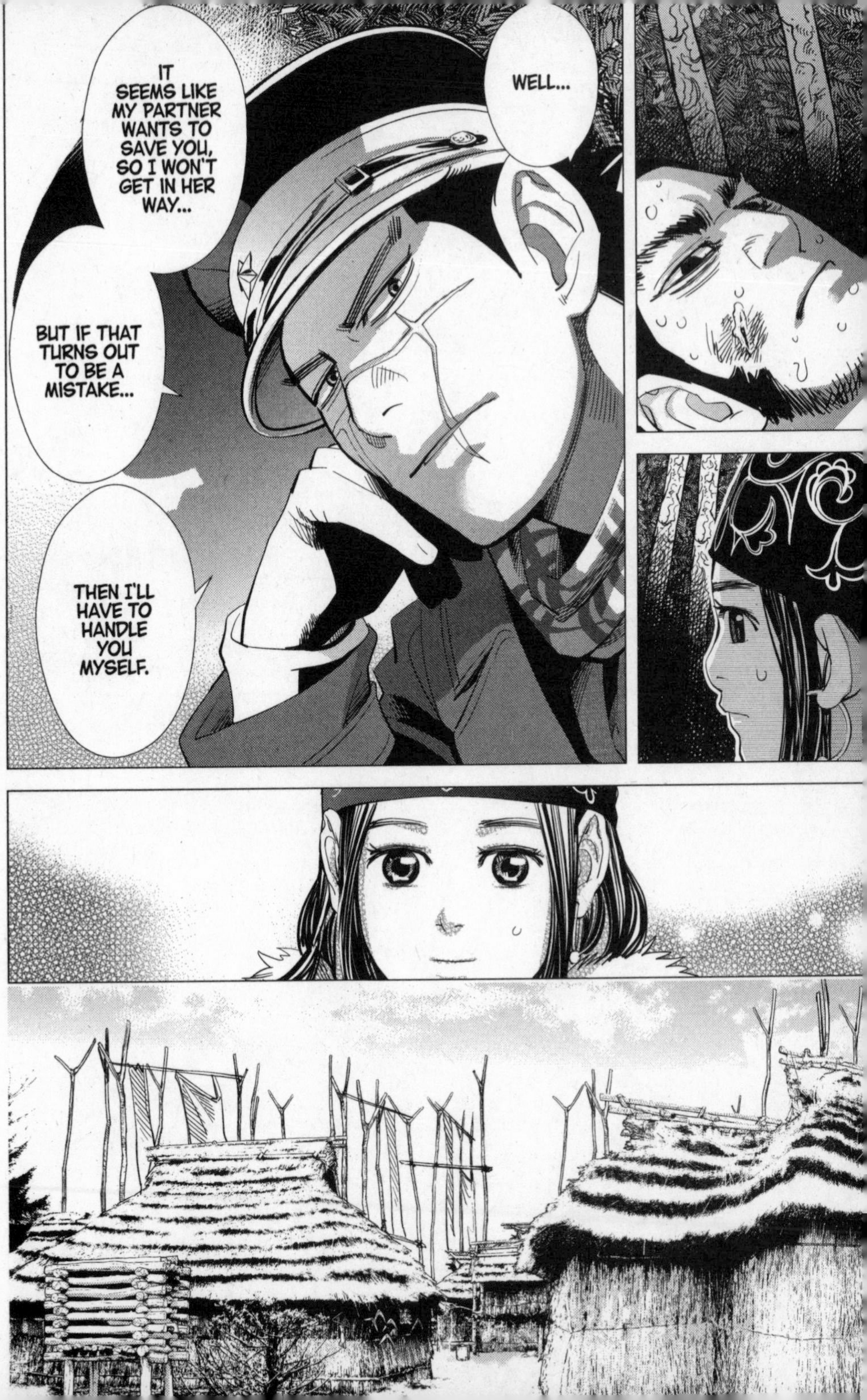
WELL...
IT SEEMS LIKE MY PARTNER WANTS TO SAVE YOU, SO I WON'T GET IN HER WAY...
BUT IF THAT TURNS OUT TO BE A MISTAKE...
THEN I'LL HAVE TO HANDLE YOU MYSELF.

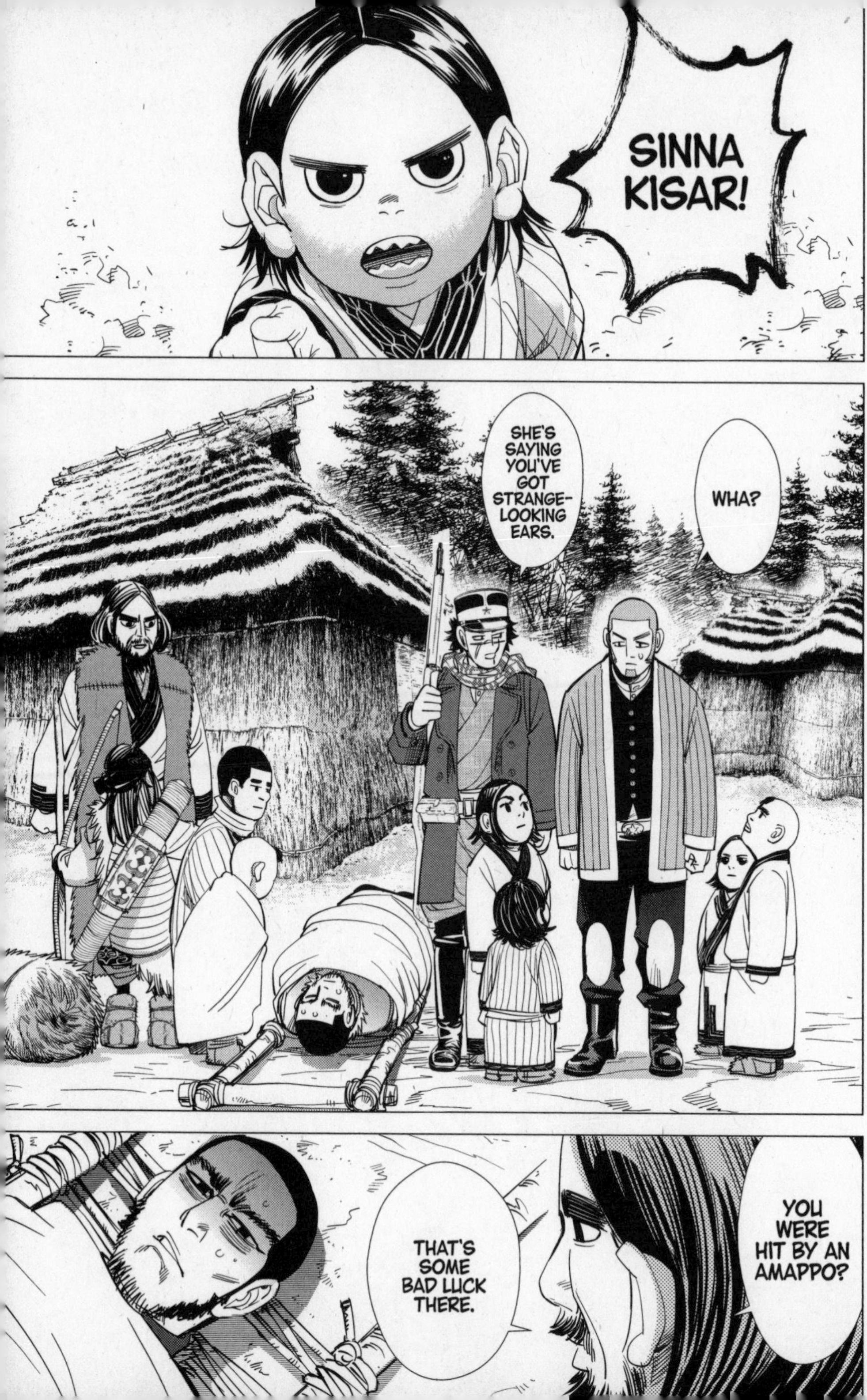
SINNA KISAR!
WHA?
SHE'S SAYING YOU'VE GOT STRANGE-LOOKING EARS.
YOU WERE HIT BY AN AMAPPO?
THAT'S SOME BAD LUCK THERE.

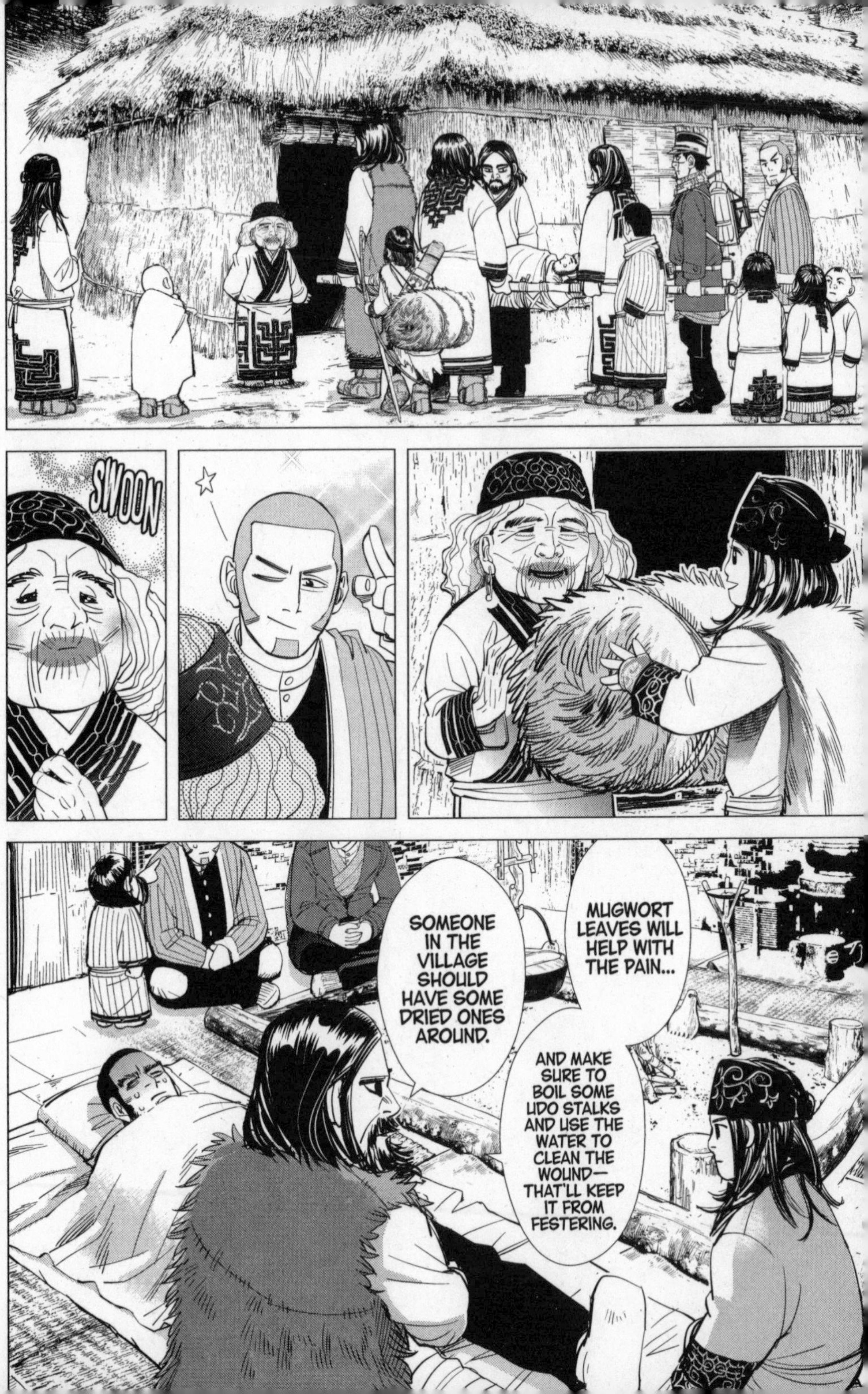
SWOON
MUGWORT LEAVES WILL HELP WITH THE PAIN...
SOMEONE IN THE VILLAGE SHOULD HAVE SOME DRIED ONES AROUND.
AND MAKE SURE TO BOIL SOME UDO STALKS AND USE THE WATER TO CLEAN THE WOUND— THAT'LL KEEP IT FROM FESTERING.

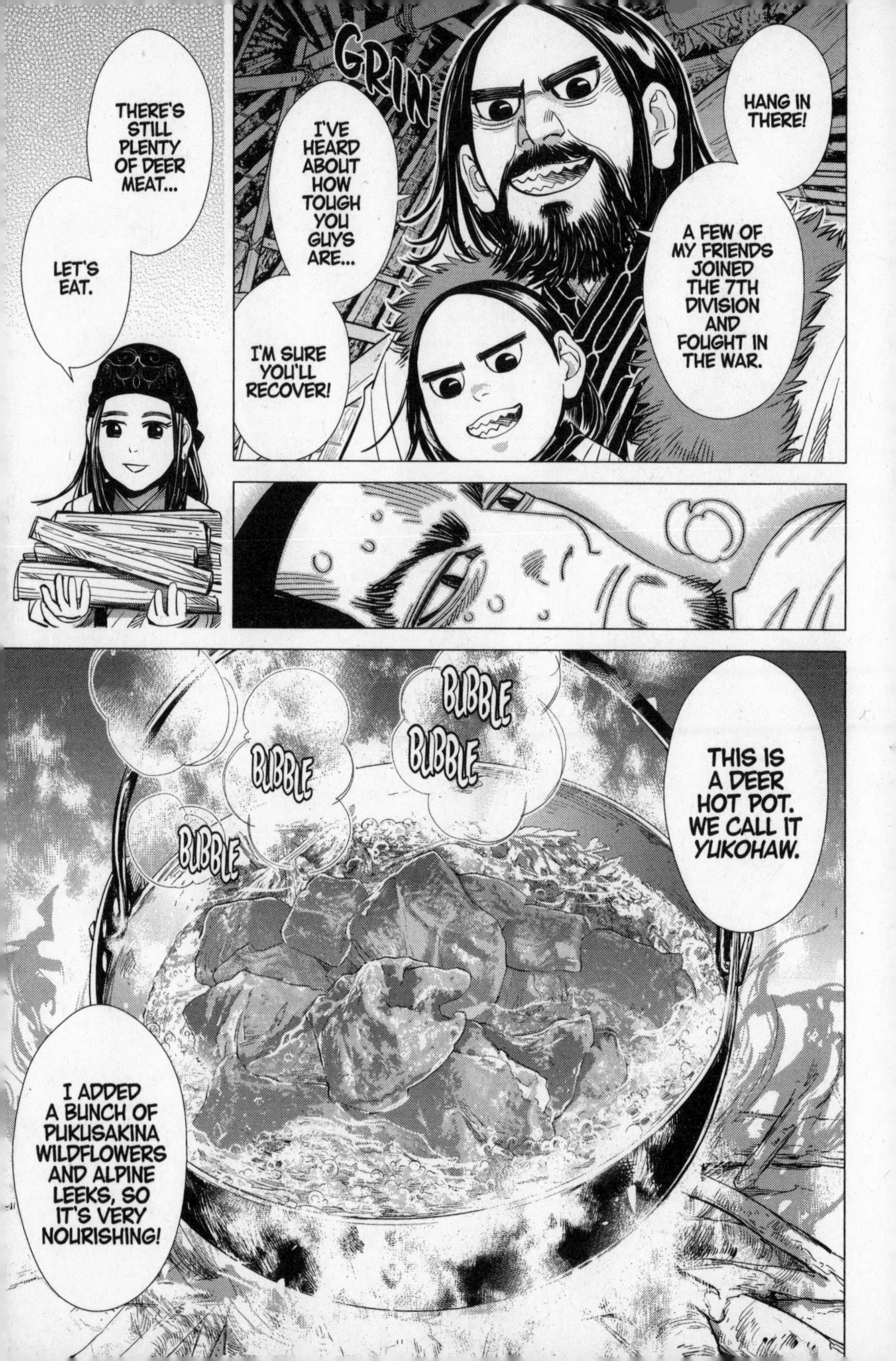
HANG IN THERE!
A FEW OF MY FRIENDS JOINED THE 7TH DIVISION AND FOUGHT IN THE WAR.
GRIN
I'VE HEARD ABOUT HOW TOUGH YOU GUYS ARE...
I'M SURE YOU'LL RECOVER!
THERE'S STILL PLENTY OF DEER MEAT...
LET'S EAT.
THIS IS A DEER HOT POT. WE CALL IT YUKOHAW.
BUBBLE
BUBBLE
BUBBLE
BUBBLE
I ADDED A BUNCH OF PUKUSAKINA WILDFLOWERS AND ALPINE LEEKS, SO IT'S VERY NOURISHING!

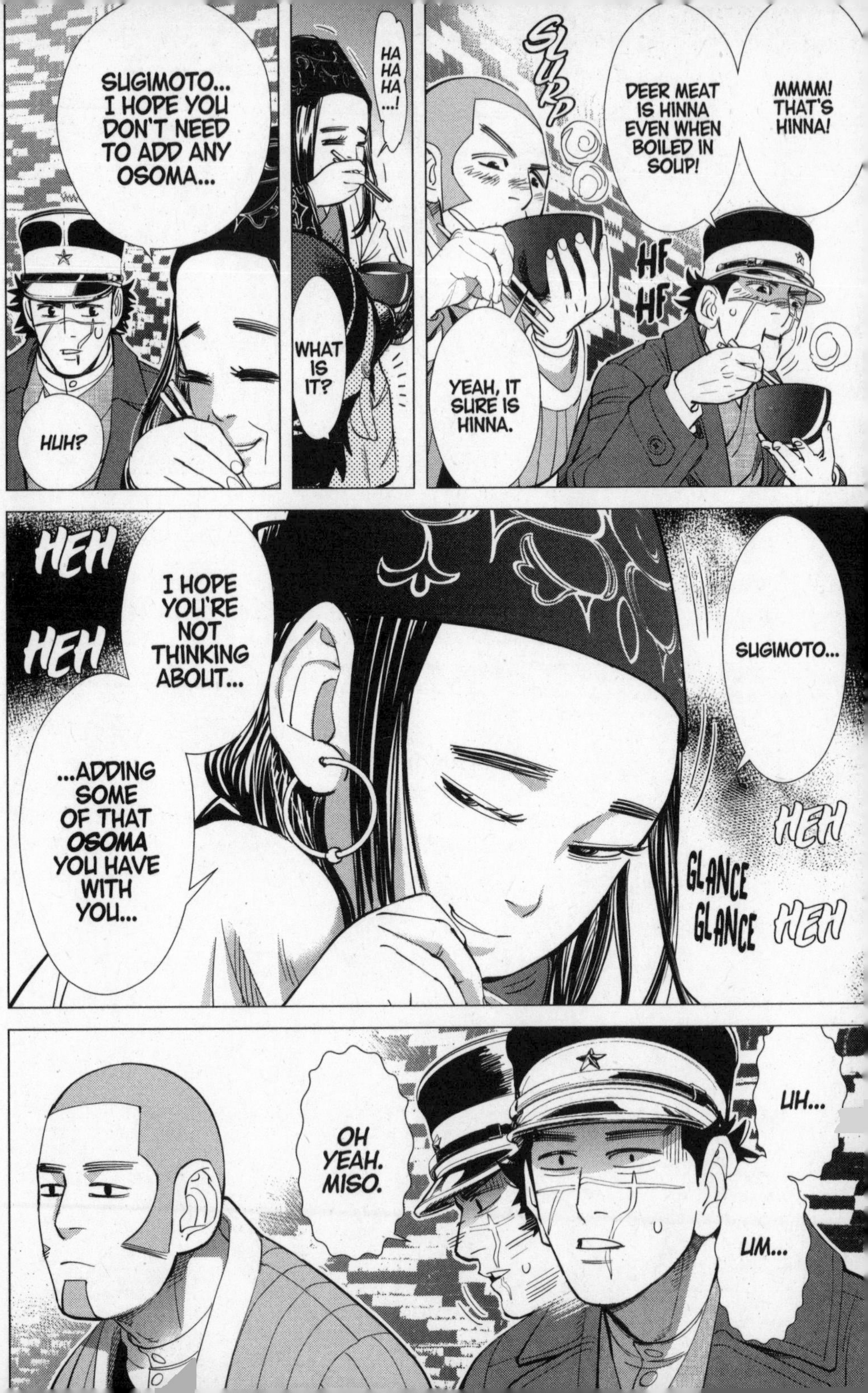
MMMM! THAT'S HINNA!
DEER MEAT IS HINNA EVEN WHEN BOILED IN SOUP!
HF HF
SLURP
YEAH, IT SURE IS HINNA.
HA HA HA ...!
WHAT IS IT?
SUGIMOTO... I HOPE YOU DON'T NEED TO ADD ANY OSOMA...
HUH?
SUGIMOTO...
HEH HEH
GLANCE GLANCE
I HOPE YOU'RE NOT THINKING ABOUT...
...ADDING SOME OF THAT OSOMA YOU HAVE WITH YOU...
HEH HEH
UH...
UM...
OH YEAH. MISO.

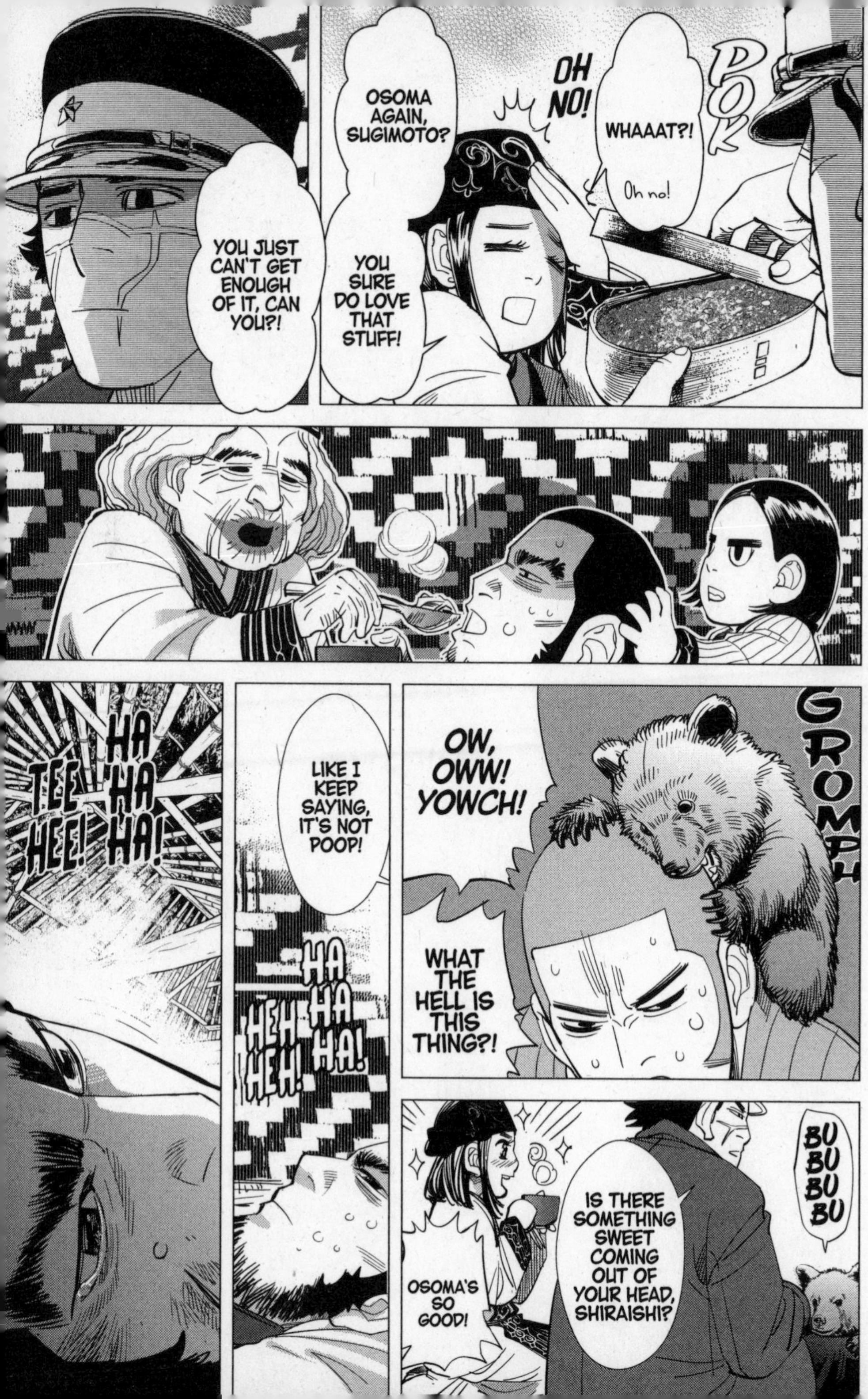
POK
WHAAAT?!
Oh no!
OH NO!
OSOMA AGAIN, SUGIMOTO?
YOU SURE DO LOVE THAT STUFF!
YOU JUST CAN'T GET ENOUGH OF IT, CAN YOU?!
GROMPH
OW, OWW! YOWCH!
WHAT THE HELL IS THIS THING?!
BUBUBUBU
IS THERE SOMETHING SWEET COMING OUT OF YOUR HEAD, SHIRAISHI?
OSOMA'S SO GOOD!
LIKE I KEEP SAYING, IT'S NOT POOP!
HA HA HA! HEH HEH!
HA HA HA! TEE HEE!

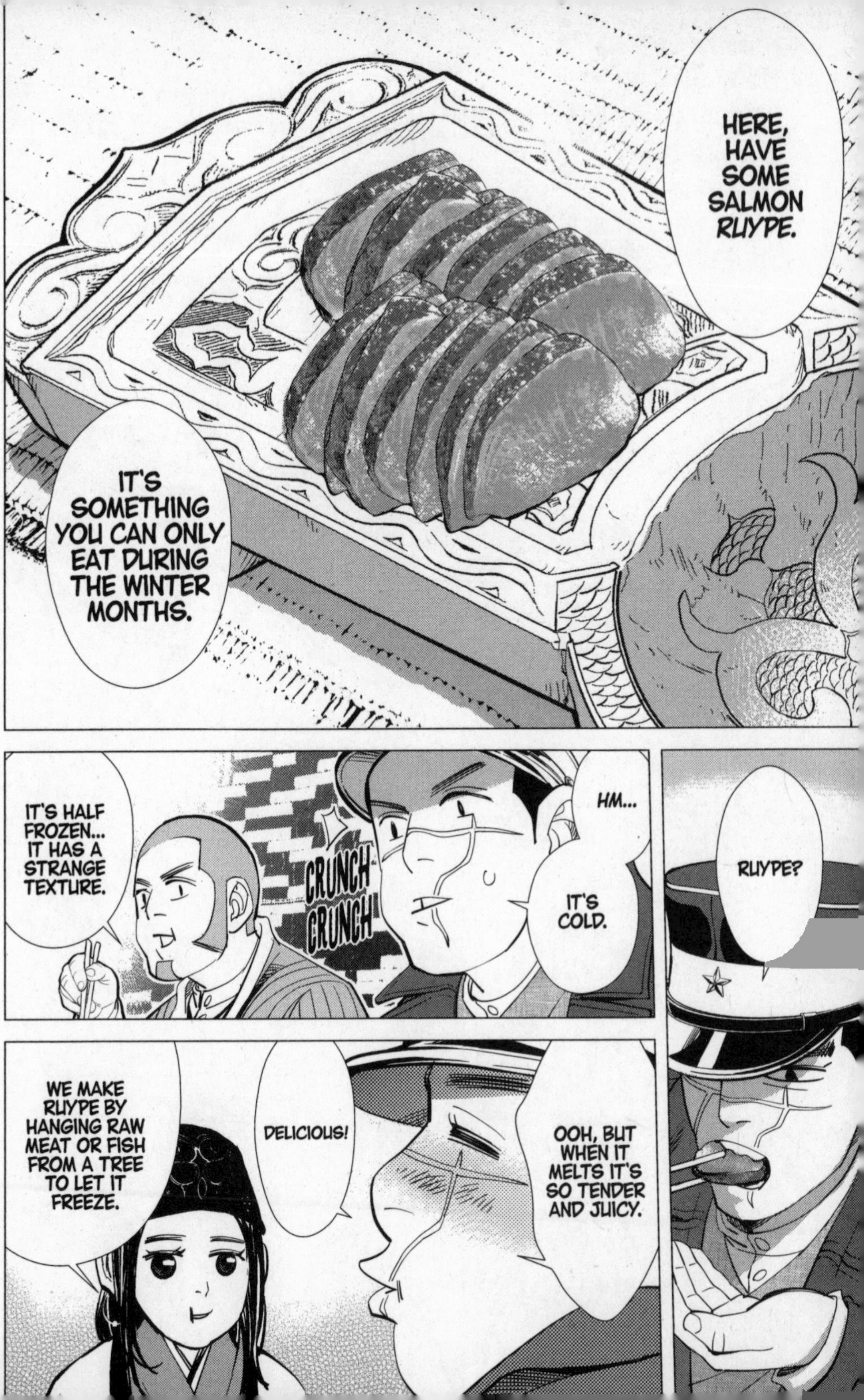
HERE, HAVE SOME SALMON RUYPE.
IT'S SOMETHING YOU CAN ONLY EAT DURING THE WINTER MONTHS.
RUYPE?
HM...
IT'S COLD.
CRUNCH CRUNCH
IT'S HALF FROZEN... IT HAS A STRANGE TEXTURE.
OOH, BUT WHEN IT MELTS IT'S SO TENDER AND JUICY.
DELICIOUS!
WE MAKE RUYPE BY HANGING RAW MEAT OR FISH FROM A TREE TO LET IT FREEZE.

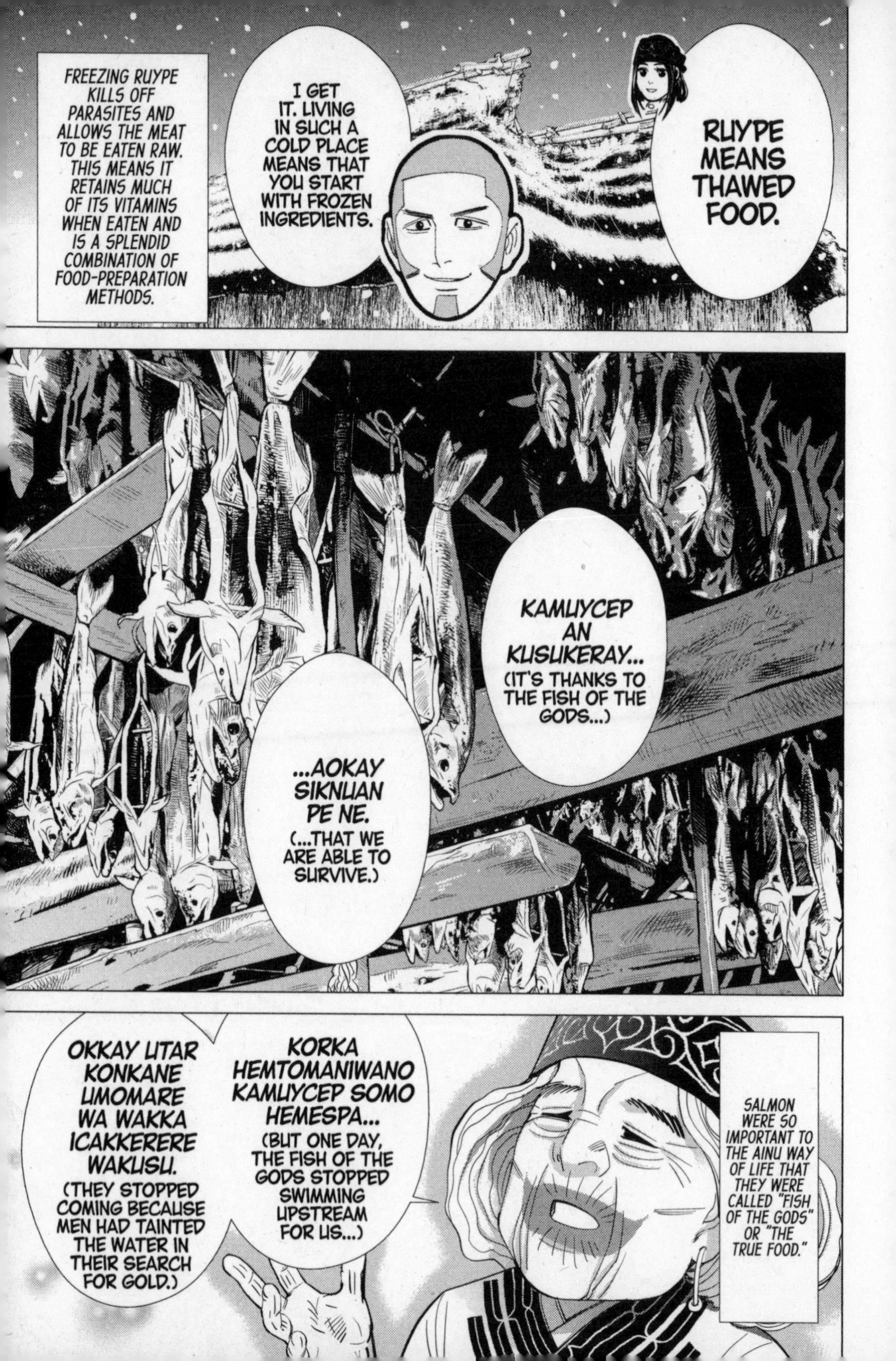
RUYPE MEANS THAWED FOOD.
I GET IT. LIVING IN SUCH A COLD PLACE MEANS THAT YOU START WITH FROZEN INGREDIENTS.
FREEZING RUYPE KILLS OFF PARASITES AND ALLOWS THE MEAT TO BE EATEN RAW. THIS MEANS IT RETAINS MUCH OF ITS VITAMINS WHEN EATEN AND IS A SPLENDID COMBINATION OF FOOD-PREPARATION METHODS.
KAMUYCEP AN KUSUKERAY... (IT'S THANKS TO THE FISH OF THE GODS...)
...AOKAY SIKNUAN PE NE. (...THAT WE ARE ABLE TO SURVIVE.)
SALMON WERE SO IMPORTANT TO THE AINU WAY OF LIFE THAT THEY WERE CALLED "FISH OF THE GODS" OR "THE TRUE FOOD."
KORKA HEMTOMANIWANO KAMUYCEP SOMO HEMESPA... (BUT ONE DAY, THE FISH OF THE GODS STOPPED SWIMMING UPSTREAM FOR US...)
OKKAY UTAR KONKANE UMOMARE WA WAKKA ICAKKERERE WAKUSU. (THEY STOPPED COMING BECAUSE MEN HAD TAINTED THE WATER IN THEIR SEARCH FOR GOLD.)

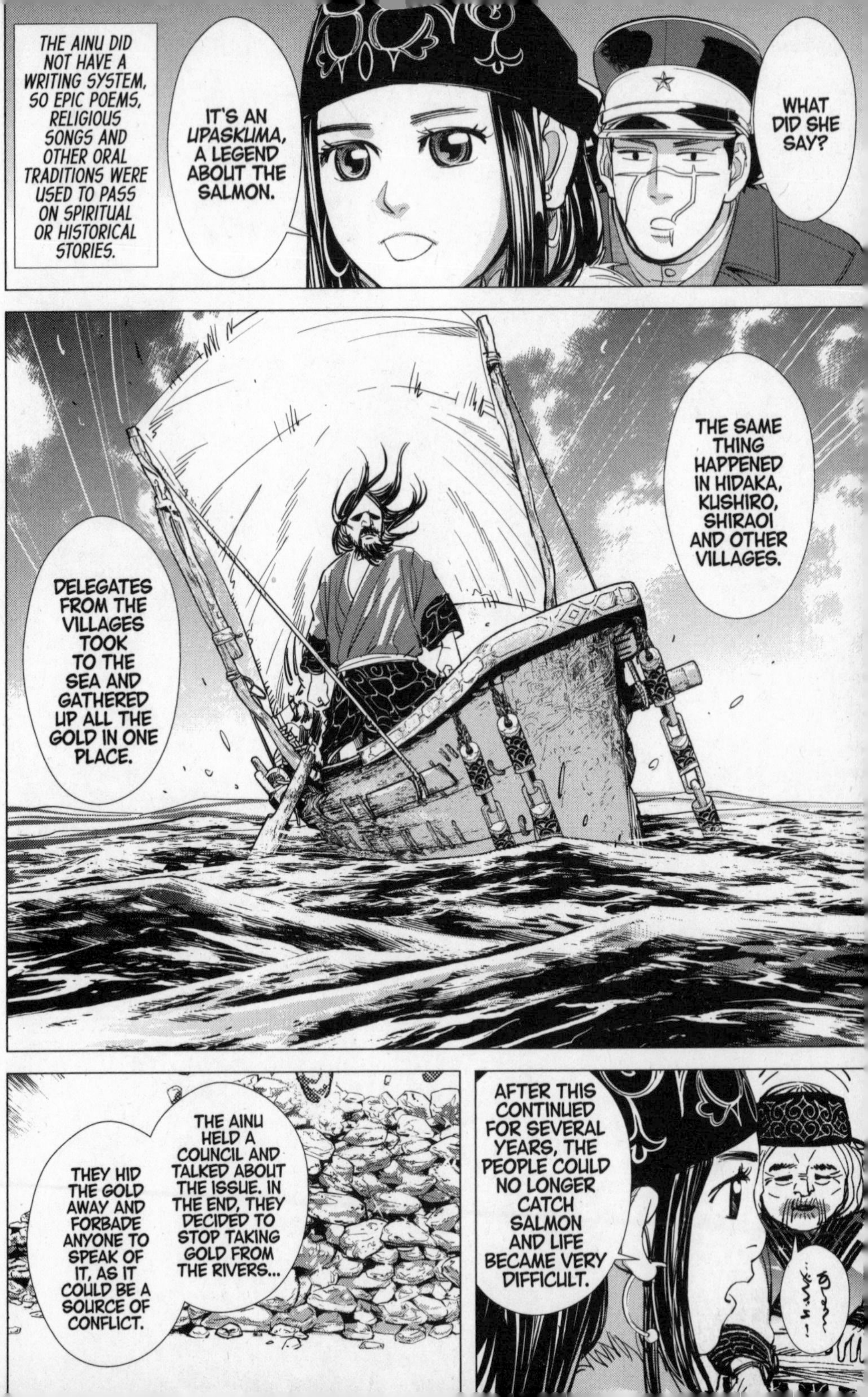
WHAT DID SHE SAY?
IT'S AN UPASKUMA, A LEGEND ABOUT THE SALMON.
THE AINU DID NOT HAVE A WRITING SYSTEM, SO EPIC POEMS, RELIGIOUS SONGS AND OTHER ORAL TRADITIONS WERE USED TO PASS ON SPIRITUAL OR HISTORICAL STORIES.
THE SAME THING HAPPENED IN HIDAKA, KUSHIRO, SHIRAOI AND OTHER VILLAGES.
DELEGATES FROM THE VILLAGES TOOK TO THE SEA AND GATHERED UP ALL THE GOLD IN ONE PLACE.
AFTER THIS CONTINUED FOR SEVERAL YEARS, THE PEOPLE COULD NO LONGER CATCH SALMON AND LIFE BECAME VERY DIFFICULT.
THE AINU HELD A COUNCIL AND TALKED ABOUT THE ISSUE. IN THE END, THEY DECIDED TO STOP TAKING GOLD FROM THE RIVERS...
THEY HID THE GOLD AWAY AND FORBADE ANYONE TO SPEAK OF IT, AS IT COULD BE A SOURCE OF CONFLICT.

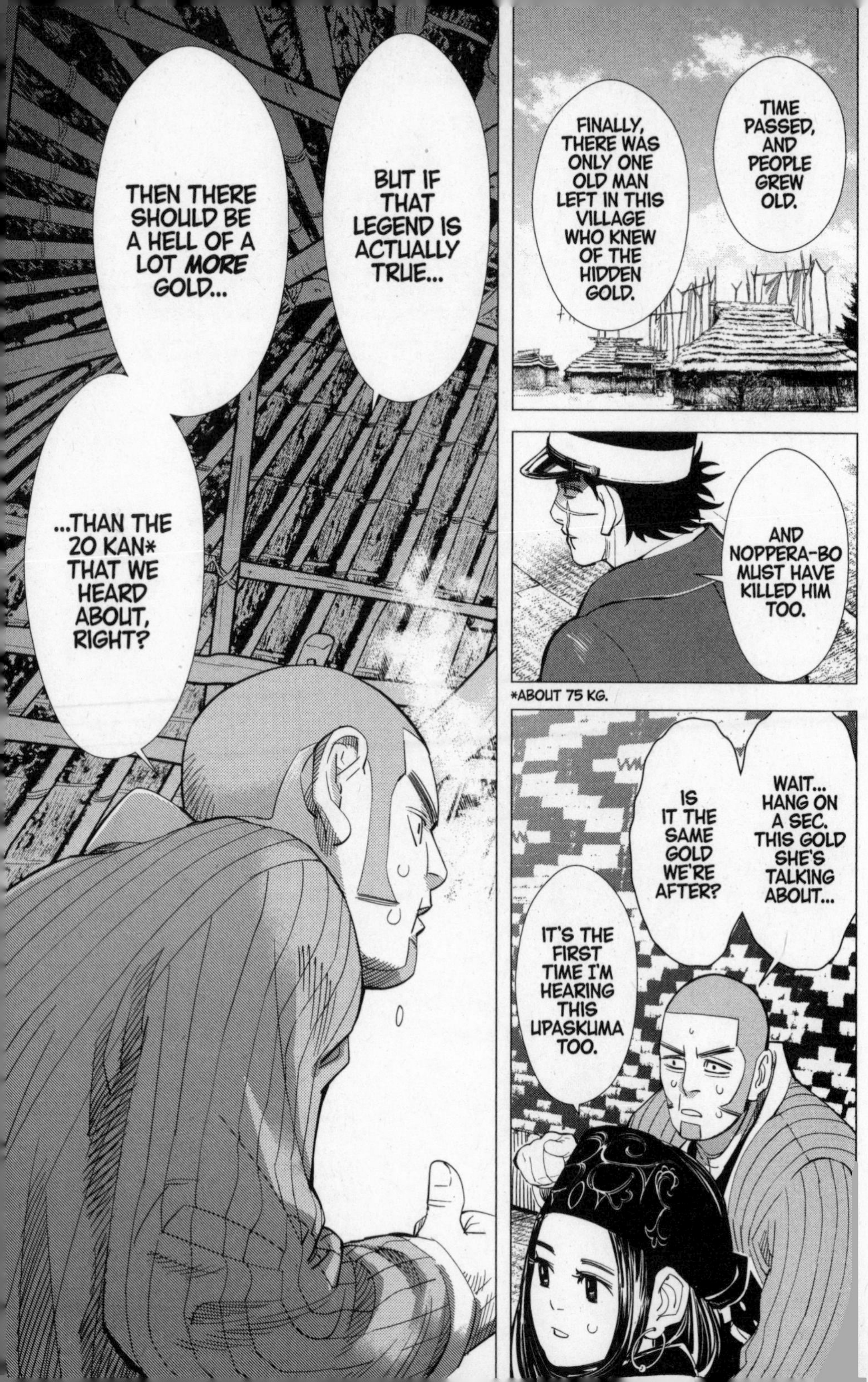
TIME PASSED, AND PEOPLE GREW OLD.
FINALLY, THERE WAS ONLY ONE OLD MAN LEFT IN THIS VILLAGE WHO KNEW OF THE HIDDEN GOLD.
AND NOPPERA-BO MUST HAVE KILLED HIM TOO.
WAIT... HANG ON A SEC. THIS GOLD SHE'S TALKING ABOUT...
IS IT THE SAME GOLD WE'RE AFTER?
IT'S THE FIRST TIME I'M HEARING THIS UPASKUMA TOO.
BUT IF THAT LEGEND IS ACTUALLY TRUE...
THEN THERE SHOULD BE A HELL OF A LOT *MORE* GOLD...
...THAN THE 20 KAN* THAT WE HEARD ABOUT, RIGHT?
*ABOUT 75 KG.

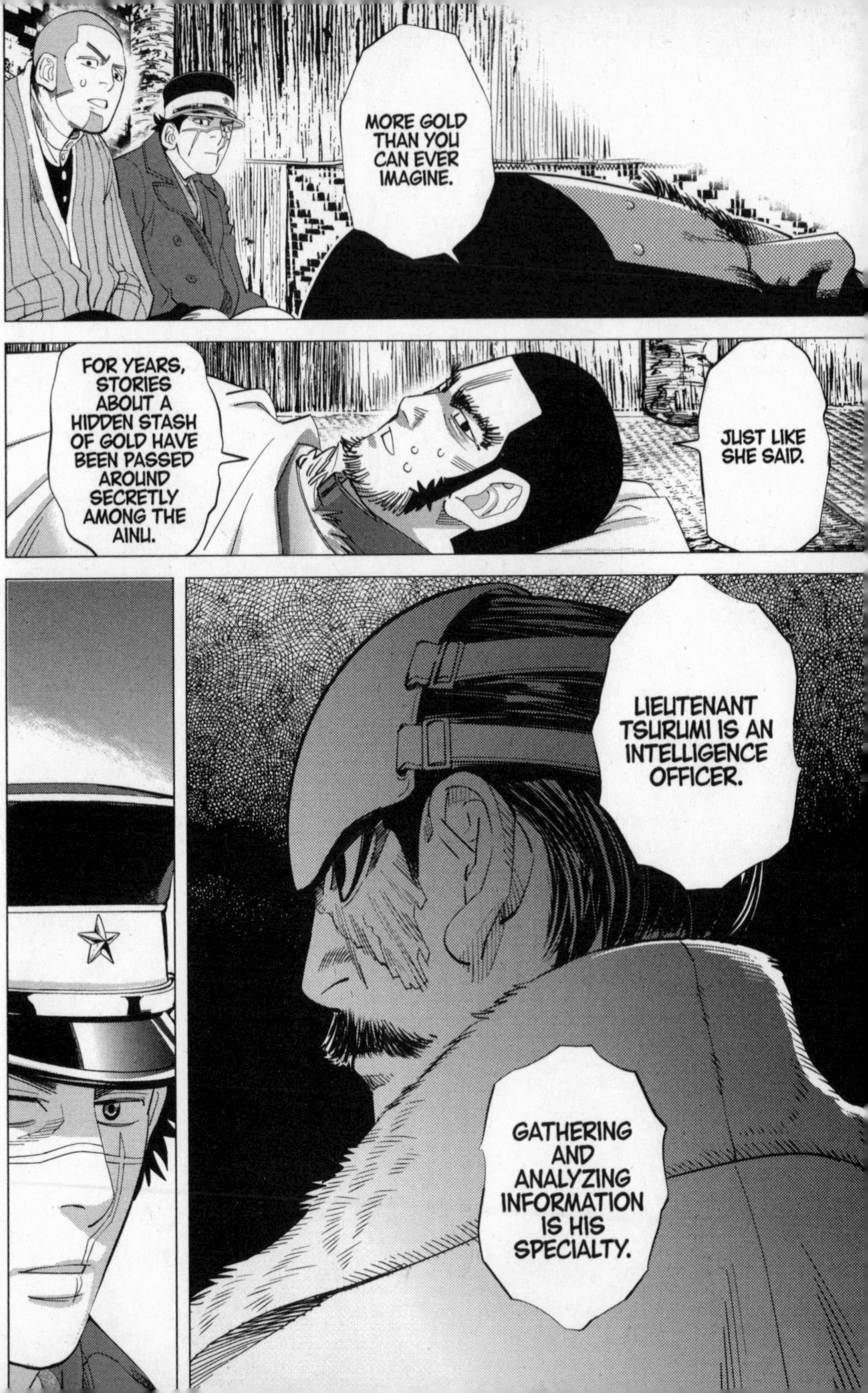
MORE GOLD THAN YOU CAN EVER IMAGINE.
JUST LIKE SHE SAID.
FOR YEARS, STORIES ABOUT A HIDDEN STASH OF GOLD HAVE BEEN PASSED AROUND SECRETLY AMONG THE AINU.
LIEUTENANT TSURUMI IS AN INTELLIGENCE OFFICER.
GATHERING AND ANALYZING INFORMATION IS HIS SPECIALTY.

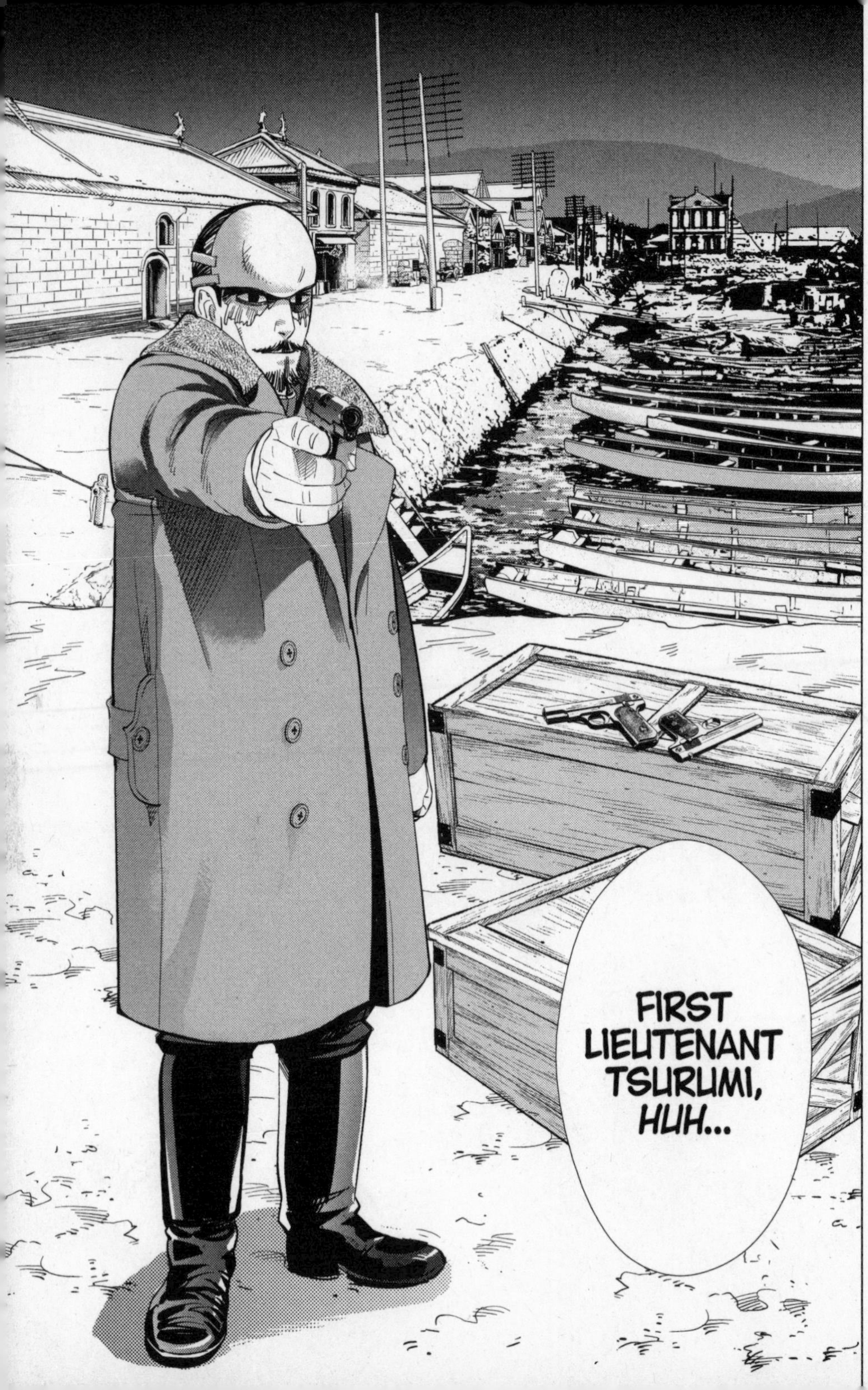
FIRST LIEUTENANT TSURUMI, HUH...

NOPPERA-BO MADE IT SO THAT...
...NO ONE COULD RETRACE HIS STEPS AND GUESS THE LOCATION OF THE GOLD.
TO MAKE SURE, HE EVEN SPREAD FALSE INFORMA-TION...
AND PEOPLE BELIEVED HIM, BECAUSE 20 KAN OF GOLD IS STILL AN AMOUNT ONE MAN CAN TRANSPORT HIMSELF.
BUT, IN REALITY, THERE WAS SO MUCH GOLD THAT HE COULDN'T POSSIBLY CARRY IT ALL.
IF LIEUTENANT TSURUMI'S SUSPICIONS ARE CORRECT...
THEN THE REAL AMOUNT OF GOLD IS A THOUSAND TIMES MORE THAN WHAT HE TOLD THE CONVICTS.
THUD

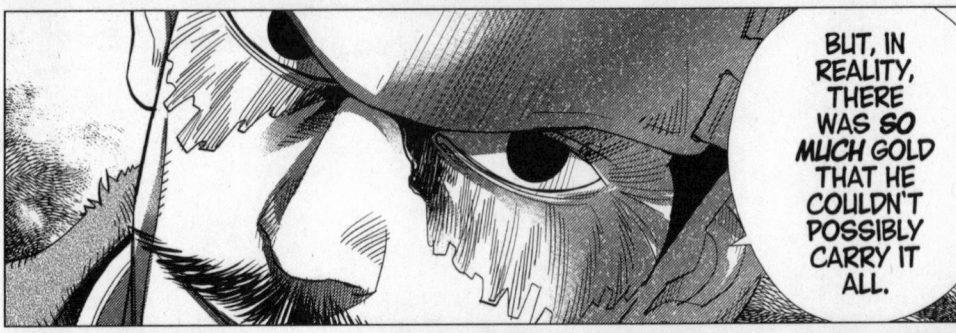

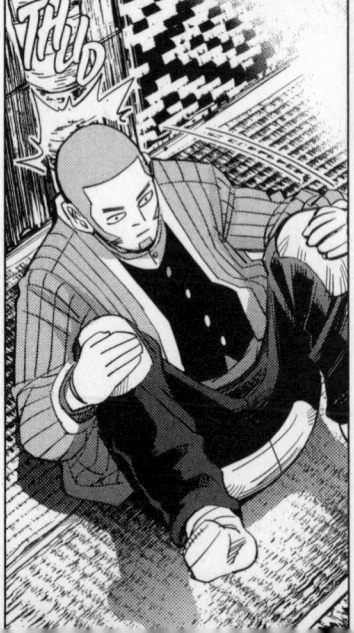

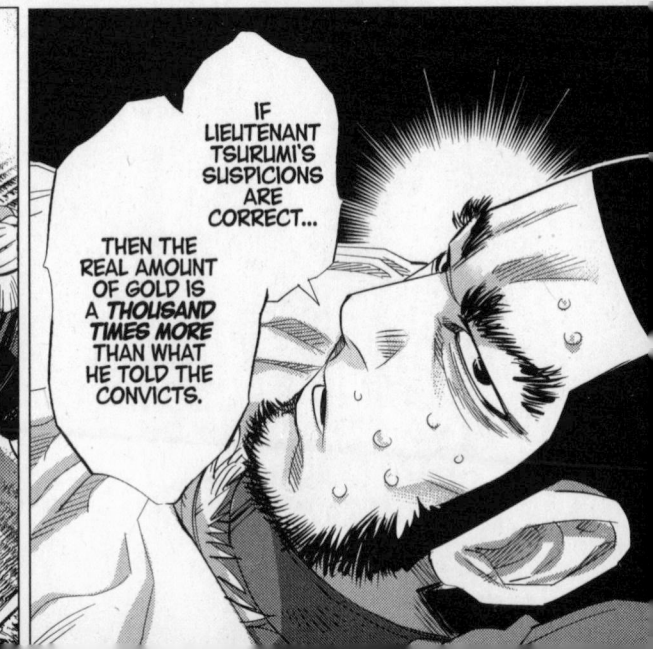

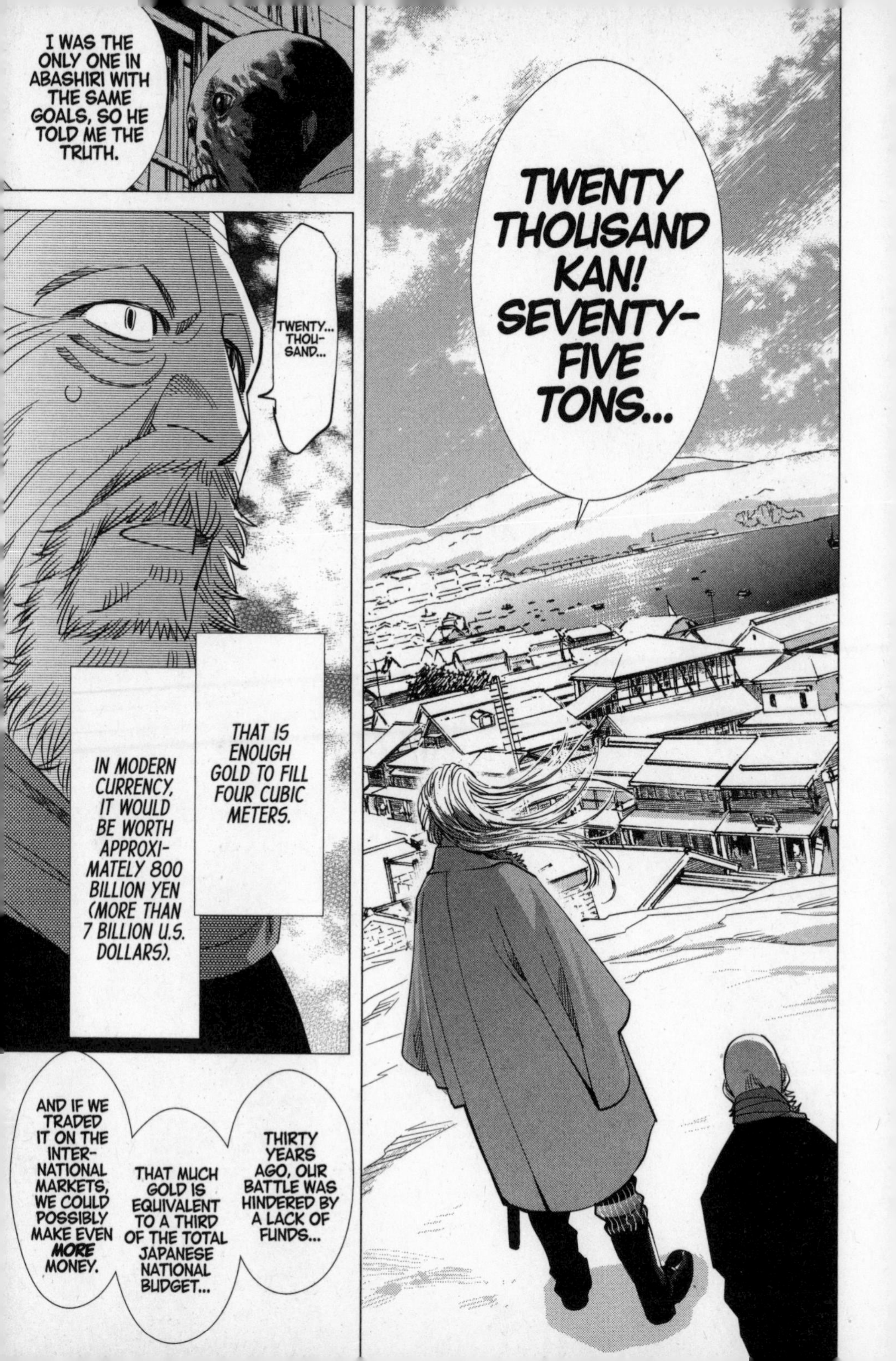
TWENTY THOUSAND KAN! SEVENTY-FIVE TONS...
I WAS THE ONLY ONE IN ABASHIRI WITH THE SAME GOALS, SO HE TOLD ME THE TRUTH.
TWENTY... THOU-SAND...
THAT IS ENOUGH GOLD TO FILL FOUR CUBIC METERS.
IN MODERN CURRENCY, IT WOULD BE WORTH APPROXI-MATELY 800 BILLION YEN (MORE THAN 7 BILLION U.S. DOLLARS).
THIRTY YEARS AGO, OUR BATTLE WAS HINDERED BY A LACK OF FUNDS...
THAT MUCH GOLD IS EQUIVALENT TO A THIRD OF THE TOTAL JAPANESE NATIONAL BUDGET...
AND IF WE TRADED IT ON THE INTER-NATIONAL MARKETS, WE COULD POSSIBLY MAKE EVEN *MORE* MONEY.

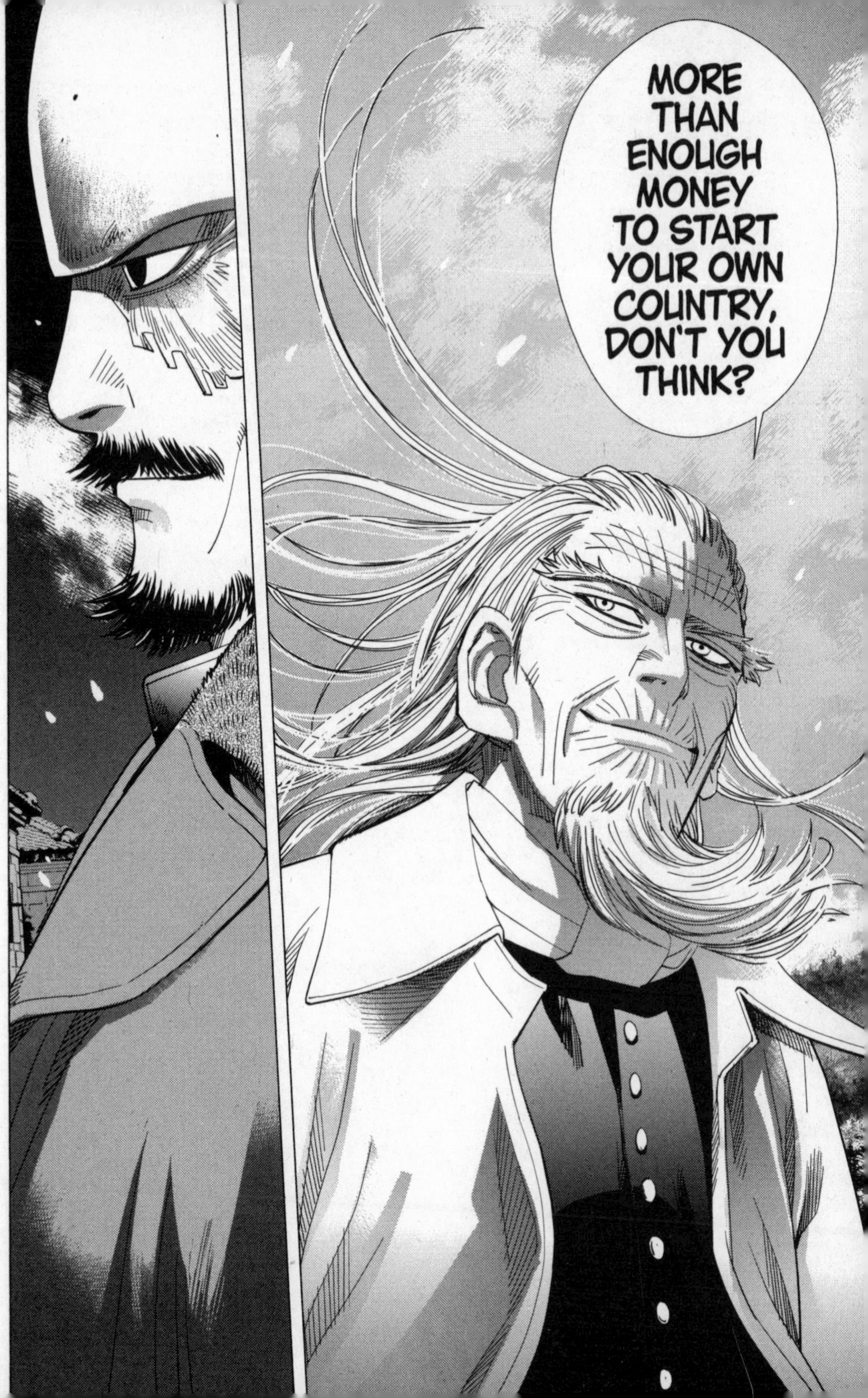
MORE THAN ENOUGH MONEY TO START YOUR OWN COUNTRY, DON'T YOU THINK?

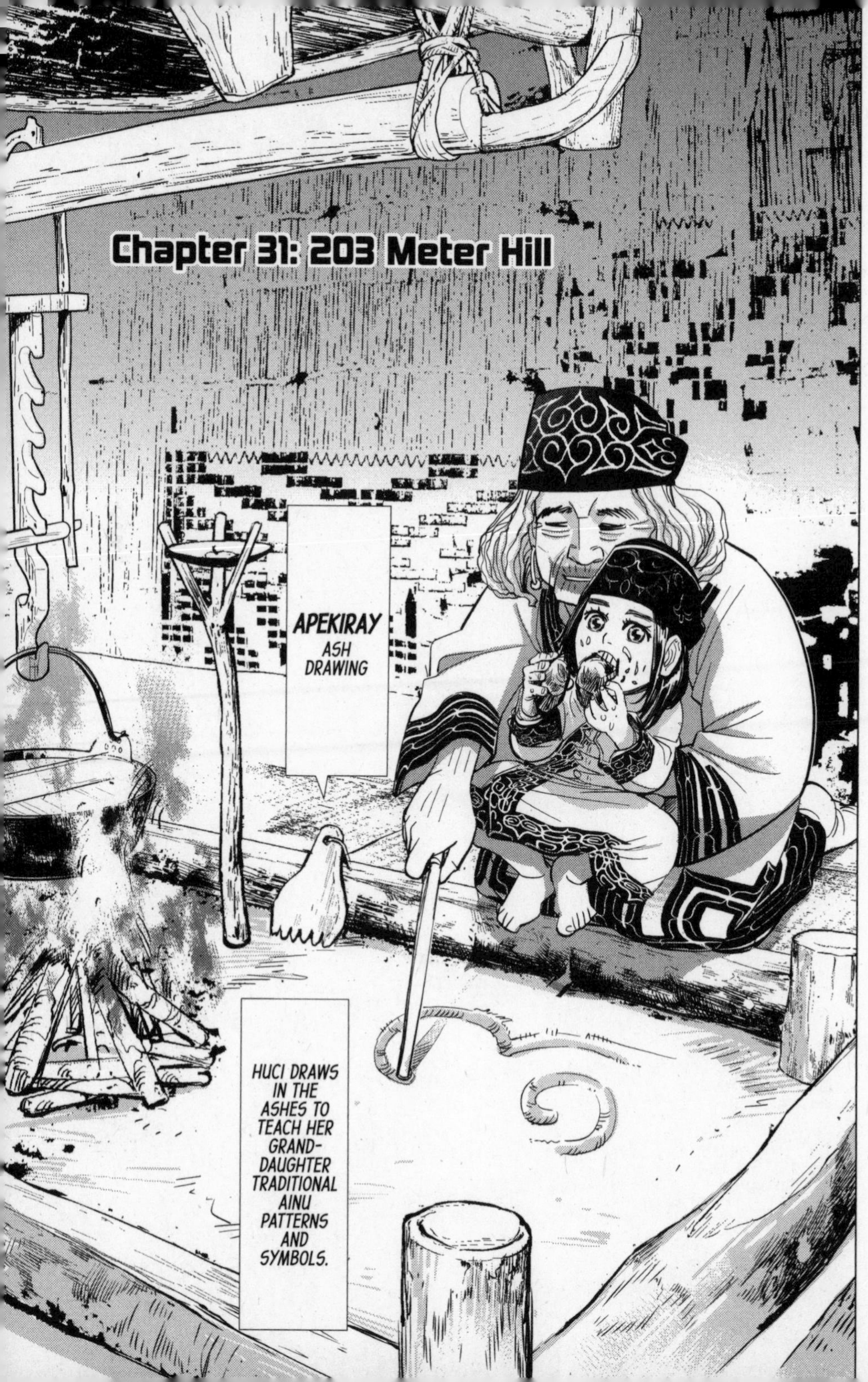
Chapter 31: 203 Meter Hill
APEKIRAY ASH DRAWING
HUCI DRAWS IN THE ASHES TO TEACH HER GRAND-DAUGHTER TRADITIONAL AINU PATTERNS AND SYMBOLS.

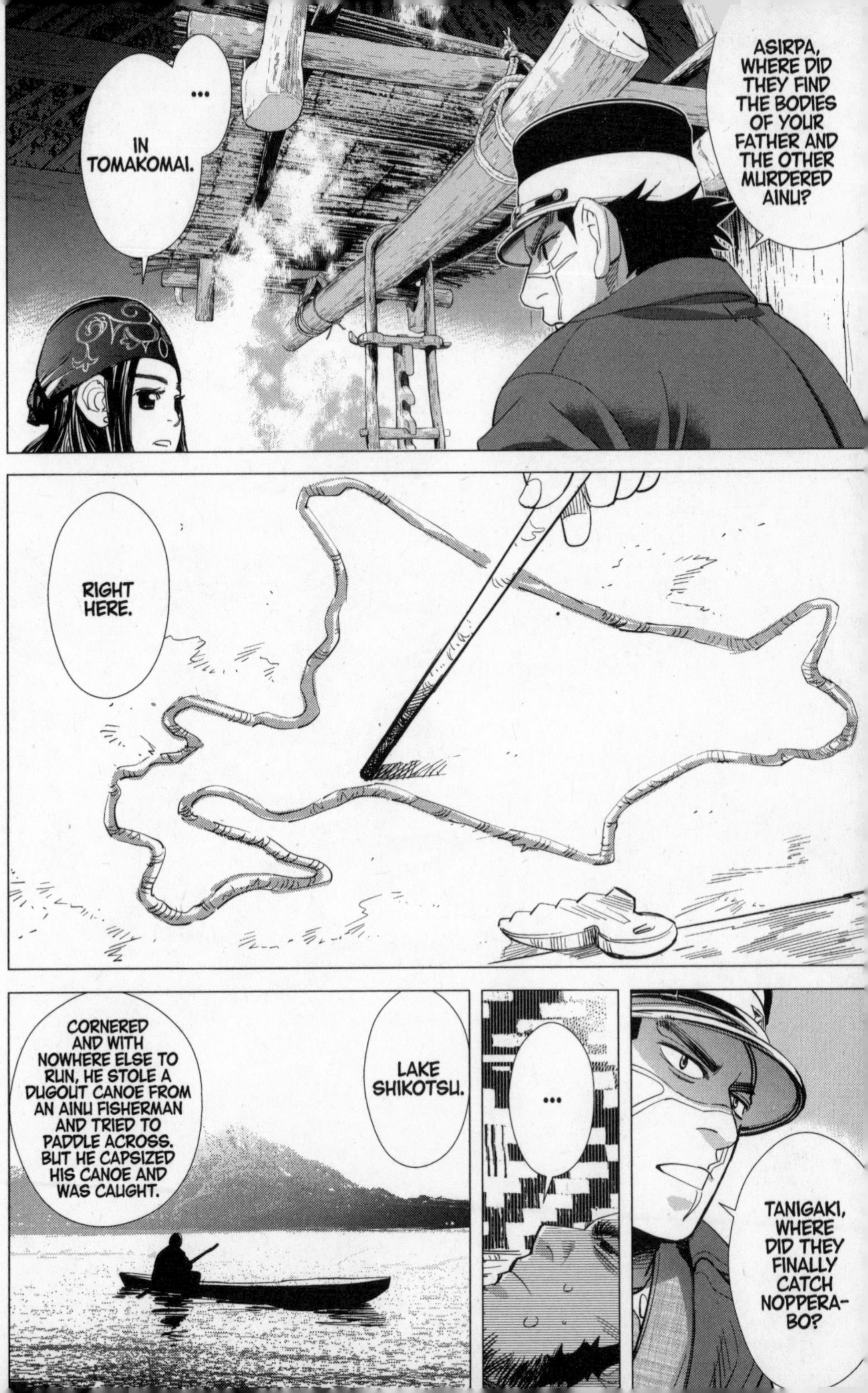
ASIRPA, WHERE DID THEY FIND THE BODIES OF YOUR FATHER AND THE OTHER MURDERED AINU?
...
IN TOMAKOMAI.
RIGHT HERE.
TANIGAKI, WHERE DID THEY FINALLY CATCH NOPPERA-BO?
...
LAKE SHIKOTSU.
CORNERED AND WITH NOWHERE ELSE TO RUN, HE STOLE A DUGOUT CANOE FROM AN AINU FISHERMAN AND TRIED TO PADDLE ACROSS. BUT HE CAPSIZED HIS CANOE AND WAS CAUGHT.

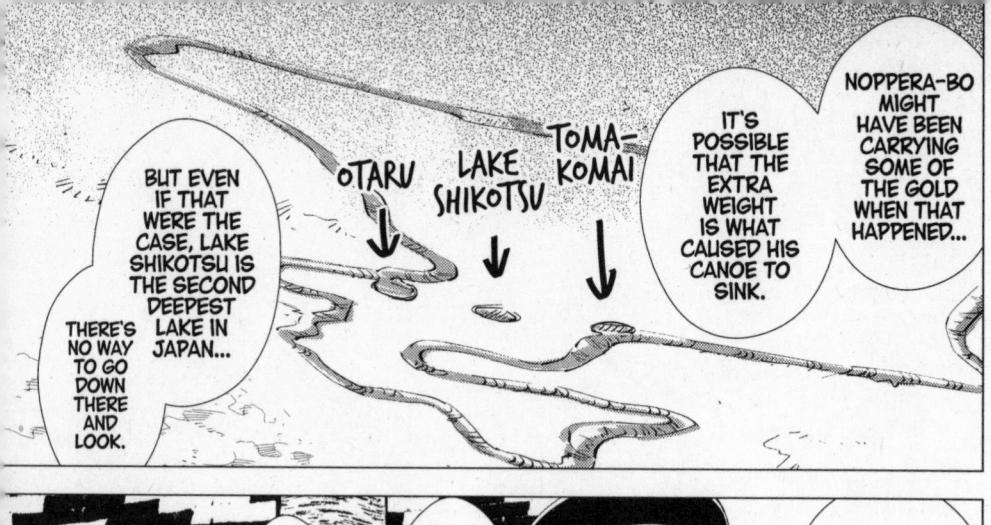

NOPPERA-BO MIGHT HAVE BEEN CARRYING SOME OF THE GOLD WHEN THAT HAPPENED...

IT'S POSSIBLE THAT THE EXTRA WEIGHT IS WHAT CAUSED HIS CANOE TO SINK.

OTARU

LAKE SHIKOTSU

TOMA- KOMAI

BUT EVEN IF THAT WERE THE CASE, LAKE SHIKOTSU IS THE SECOND DEEPEST LAKE IN JAPAN...

THERE'S NO WAY TO GO DOWN THERE AND LOOK.

SO, THIS...

...HAS TO BE A MAP, RIGHT?

MAYBE?

I KNOW THESE CHARAC- TERS...

THAT SKIN'S FROM AN OLD GUY NAMED GOTO.

HE WAS SENT TO ABASHIRI FOR GETTING DRUNK AND STABBING HIS WIFE AND KID TO DEATH. PATHETIC.

AND THIS OTHER SKIN WE HAVE...

I DON'T RECOGNIZE IT. HE MUST HAVE BEEN A NOBODY.

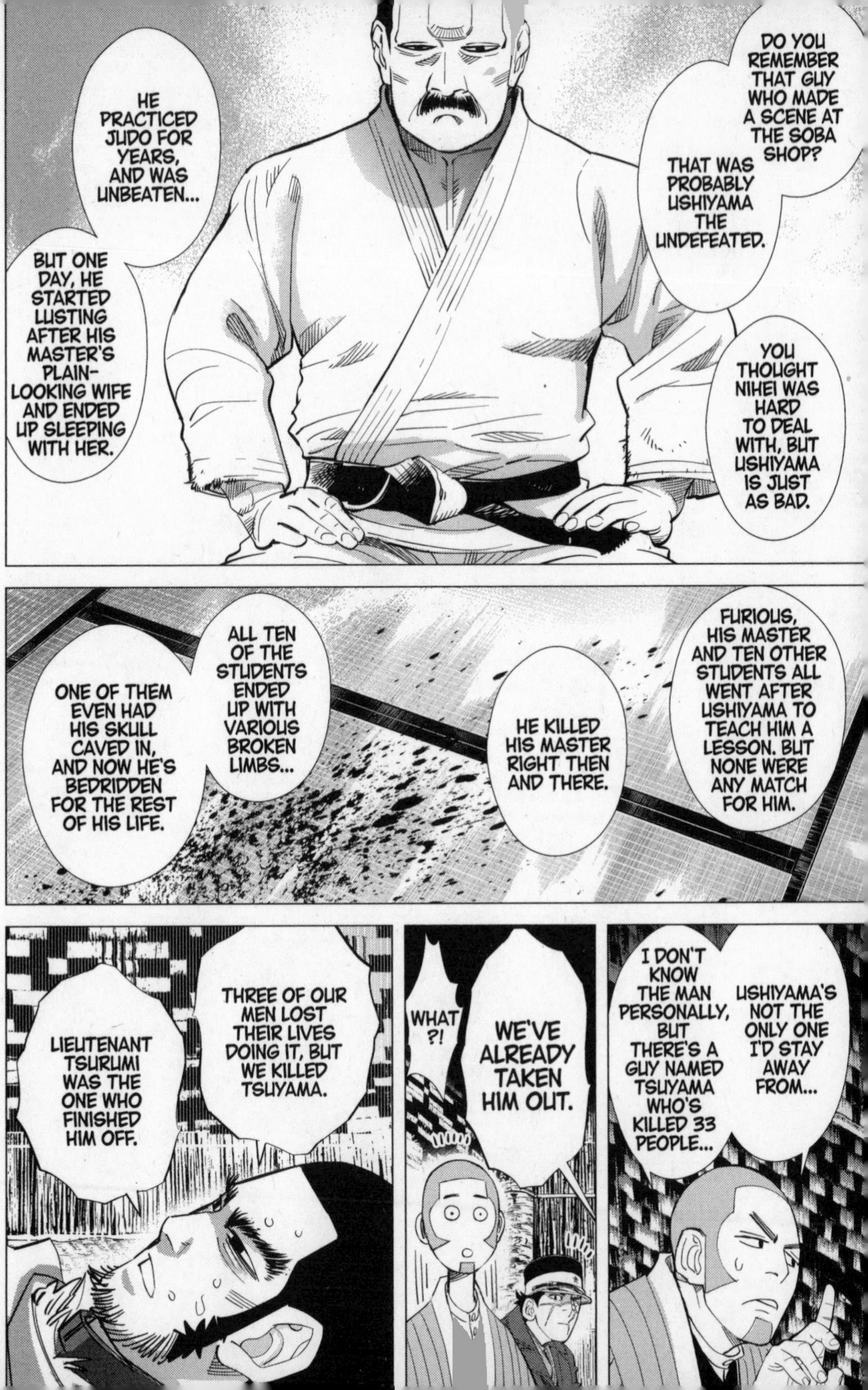
DO YOU REMEMBER THAT GUY WHO MADE A SCENE AT THE SOBA SHOP?
THAT WAS PROBABLY USHIYAMA THE UNDEFEATED.
HE PRACTICED JUDO FOR YEARS, AND WAS UNBEATEN...
BUT ONE DAY, HE STARTED LUSTING AFTER HIS MASTER'S PLAIN-LOOKING WIFE AND ENDED UP SLEEPING WITH HER.
YOU THOUGHT NIHEI WAS HARD TO DEAL WITH, BUT USHIYAMA IS JUST AS BAD.
FURIOUS, HIS MASTER AND TEN OTHER STUDENTS ALL WENT AFTER USHIYAMA TO TEACH HIM A LESSON. BUT NONE WERE ANY MATCH FOR HIM.
HE KILLED HIS MASTER RIGHT THEN AND THERE.
ALL TEN OF THE STUDENTS ENDED UP WITH VARIOUS BROKEN LIMBS...
ONE OF THEM EVEN HAD HIS SKULL CAVED IN, AND NOW HE'S BEDRIDDEN FOR THE REST OF HIS LIFE.
I DON'T KNOW THE MAN PERSONALLY, BUT THERE'S A GUY NAMED TSUYAMA WHO'S KILLED 33 PEOPLE...
USHIYAMA'S NOT THE ONLY ONE I'D STAY AWAY FROM...
WE'VE ALREADY TAKEN HIM OUT.
WHAT?!
THREE OF OUR MEN LOST THEIR LIVES DOING IT, BUT WE KILLED TSUYAMA.
LIEUTENANT TSURUMI WAS THE ONE WHO FINISHED HIM OFF.

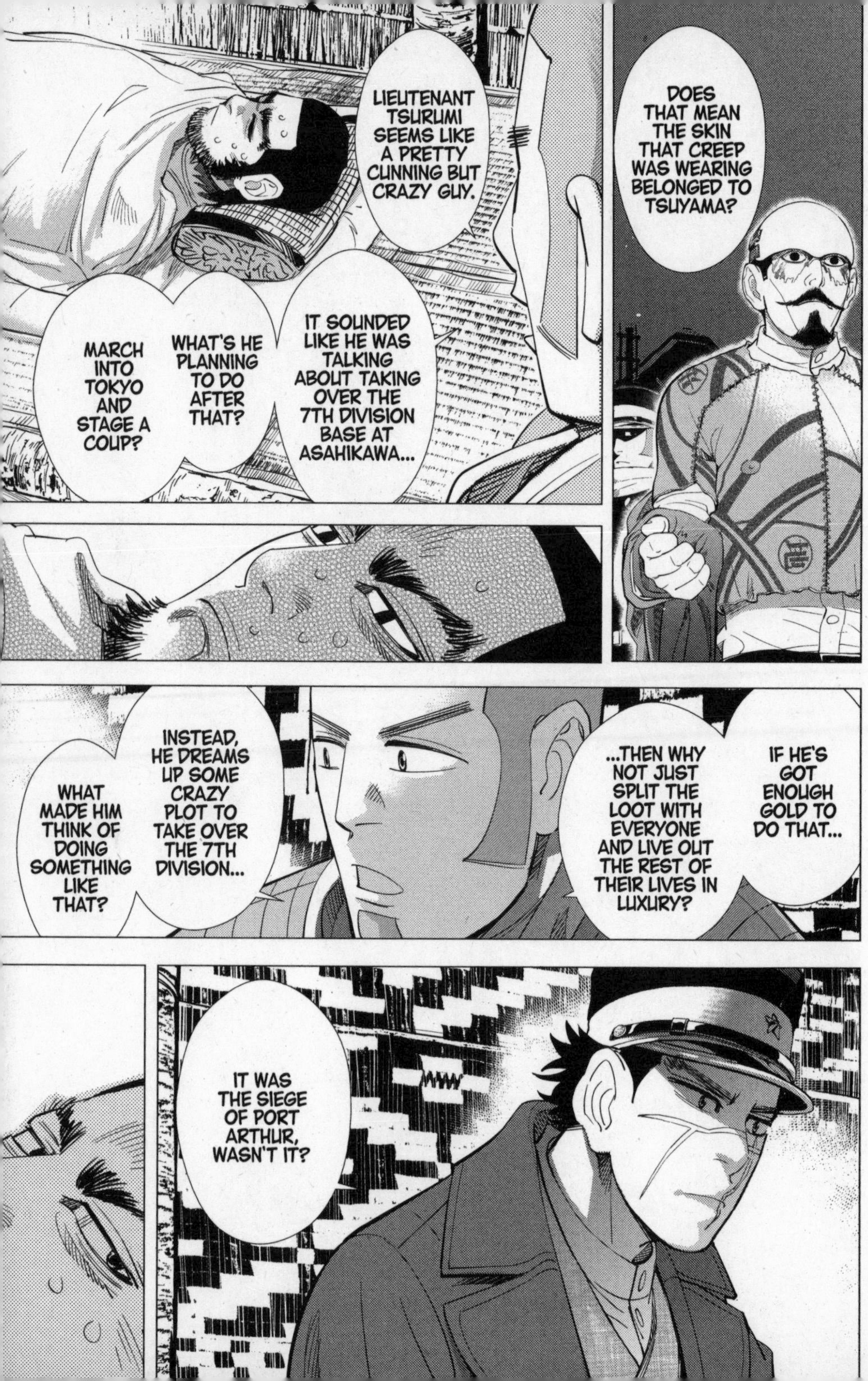
DOES THAT MEAN THE SKIN THAT CREEP WAS WEARING BELONGED TO TSUYAMA?
LIEUTENANT TSURUMI SEEMS LIKE A PRETTY CUNNING BUT CRAZY GUY.
IT SOUNDED LIKE HE WAS TALKING ABOUT TAKING OVER THE 7TH DIVISION BASE AT ASAHIKAWA...
WHAT'S HE PLANNING TO DO AFTER THAT?
MARCH INTO TOKYO AND STAGE A COUP?
IF HE'S GOT ENOUGH GOLD TO DO THAT...
...THEN WHY NOT JUST SPLIT THE LOOT WITH EVERYONE AND LIVE OUT THE REST OF THEIR LIVES IN LUXURY?
INSTEAD, HE DREAMS UP SOME CRAZY PLOT TO TAKE OVER THE 7TH DIVISION...
WHAT MADE HIM THINK OF DOING SOMETHING LIKE THAT?
IT WAS THE SIEGE OF PORT ARTHUR, WASN'T IT?

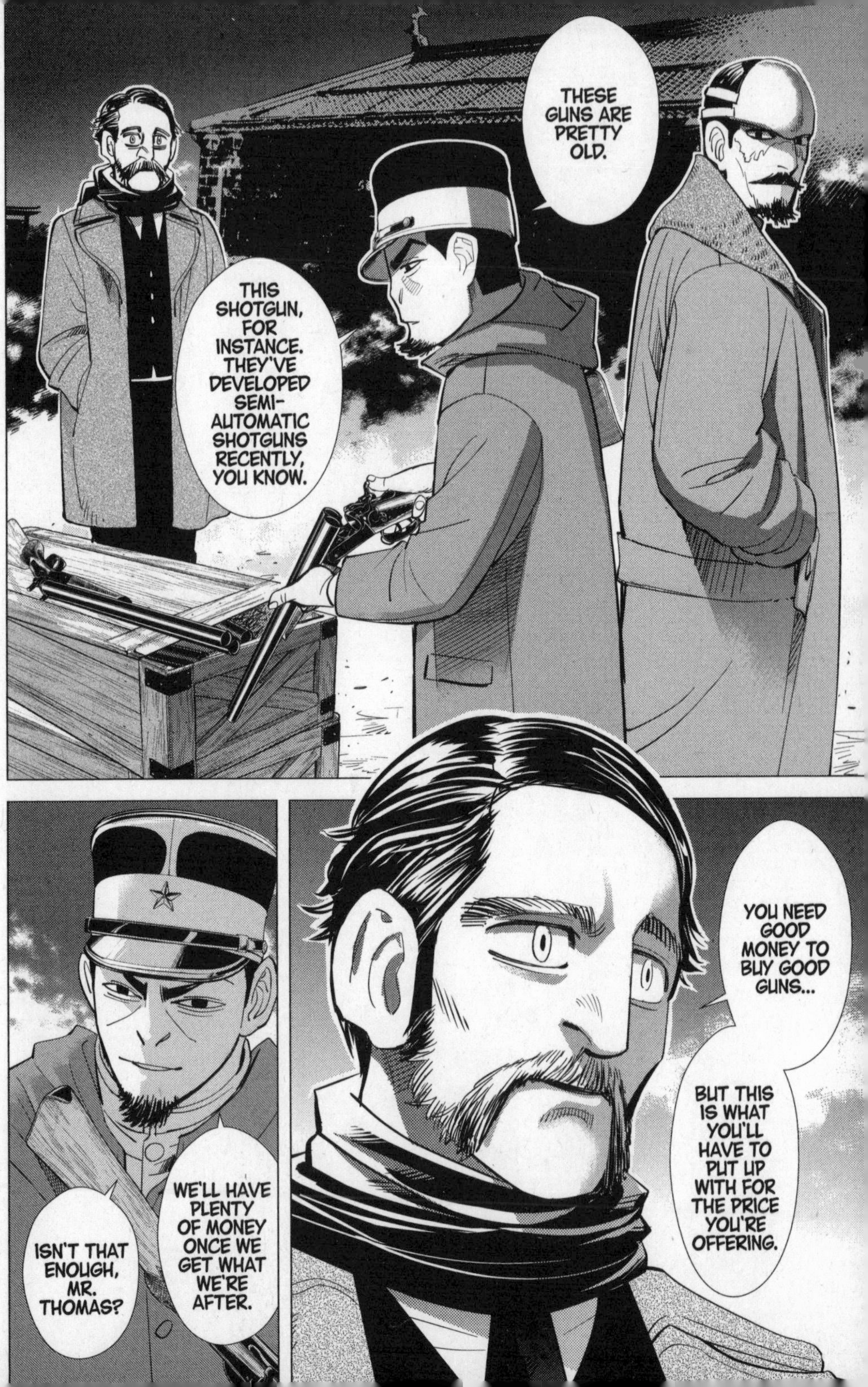
THESE GUNS ARE PRETTY OLD.
THIS SHOTGUN, FOR INSTANCE. THEY'VE DEVELOPED SEMI-AUTOMATIC SHOTGUNS RECENTLY, YOU KNOW.
YOU NEED GOOD MONEY TO BUY GOOD GUNS...
BUT THIS IS WHAT YOU'LL HAVE TO PUT UP WITH FOR THE PRICE YOU'RE OFFERING.
WE'LL HAVE PLENTY OF MONEY ONCE WE GET WHAT WE'RE AFTER.
ISN'T THAT ENOUGH, MR. THOMAS?

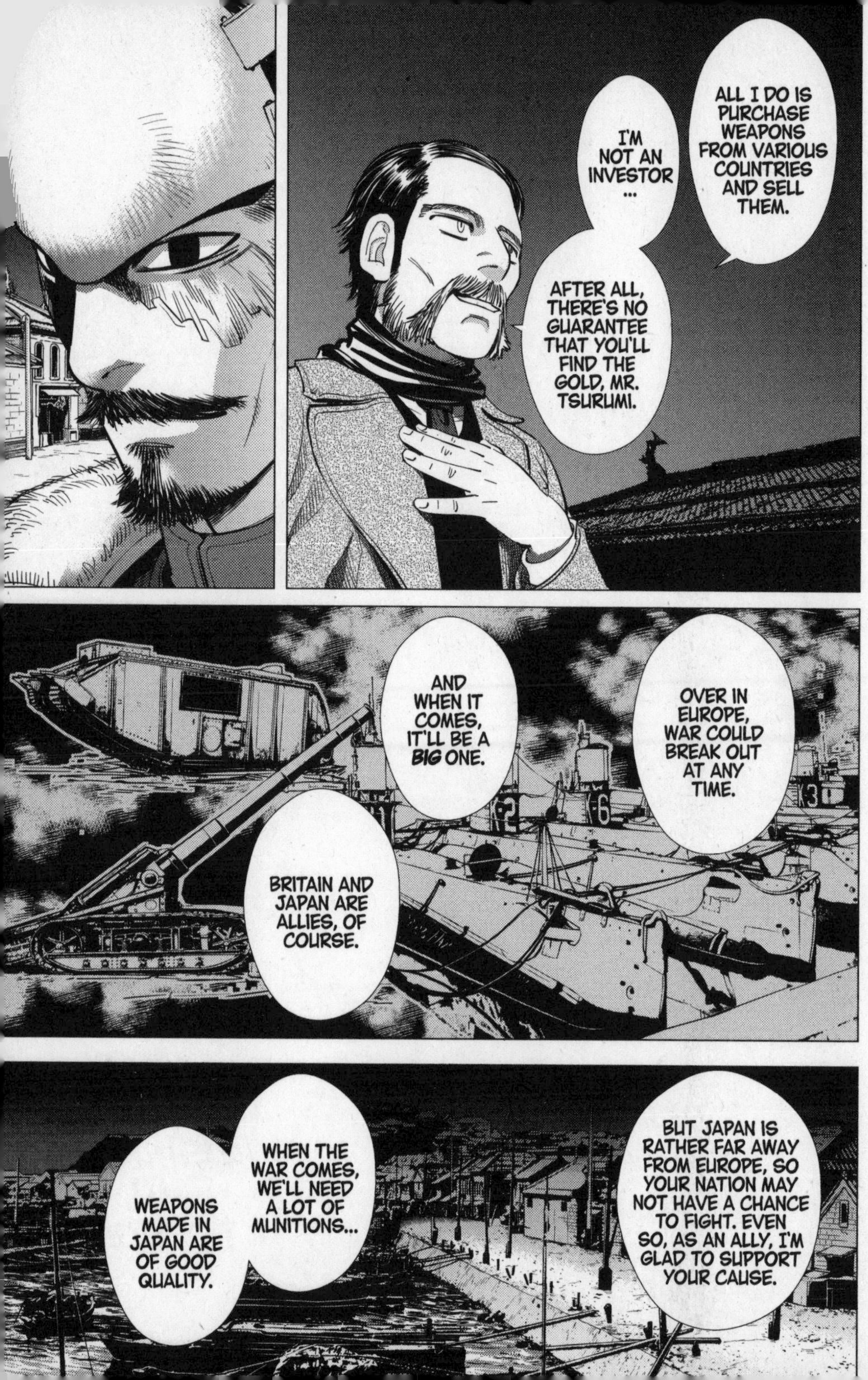
ALL I DO IS PURCHASE WEAPONS FROM VARIOUS COUNTRIES AND SELL THEM.
I'M NOT AN INVESTOR ...
AFTER ALL, THERE'S NO GUARANTEE THAT YOU'LL FIND THE GOLD, MR. TSURUMI.
OVER IN EUROPE, WAR COULD BREAK OUT AT ANY TIME.
AND WHEN IT COMES, IT'LL BE A **BIG** ONE.
BRITAIN AND JAPAN ARE ALLIES, OF COURSE.
BUT JAPAN IS RATHER FAR AWAY FROM EUROPE, SO YOUR NATION MAY NOT HAVE A CHANCE TO FIGHT. EVEN SO, AS AN ALLY, I'M GLAD TO SUPPORT YOUR CAUSE.
WHEN THE WAR COMES, WE'LL NEED A LOT OF MUNITIONS...
WEAPONS MADE IN JAPAN ARE OF GOOD QUALITY.

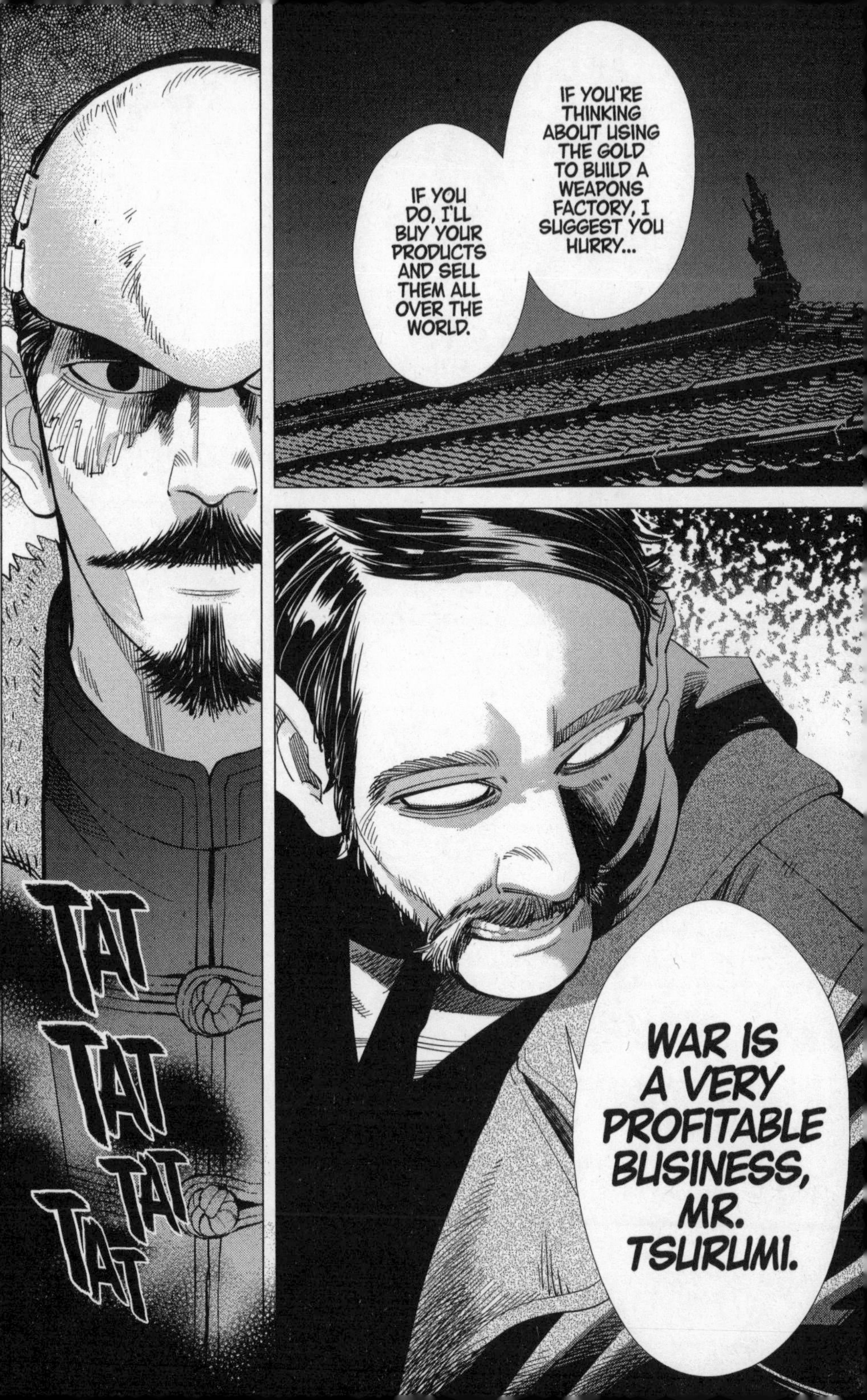
IF YOU'RE THINKING ABOUT USING THE GOLD TO BUILD A WEAPONS FACTORY, I SUGGEST YOU HURRY...
IF YOU DO, I'LL BUY YOUR PRODUCTS AND SELL THEM ALL OVER THE WORLD.
WAR IS A VERY PROFITABLE BUSINESS, MR. TSURUMI.
TAT TAT TAT TAT

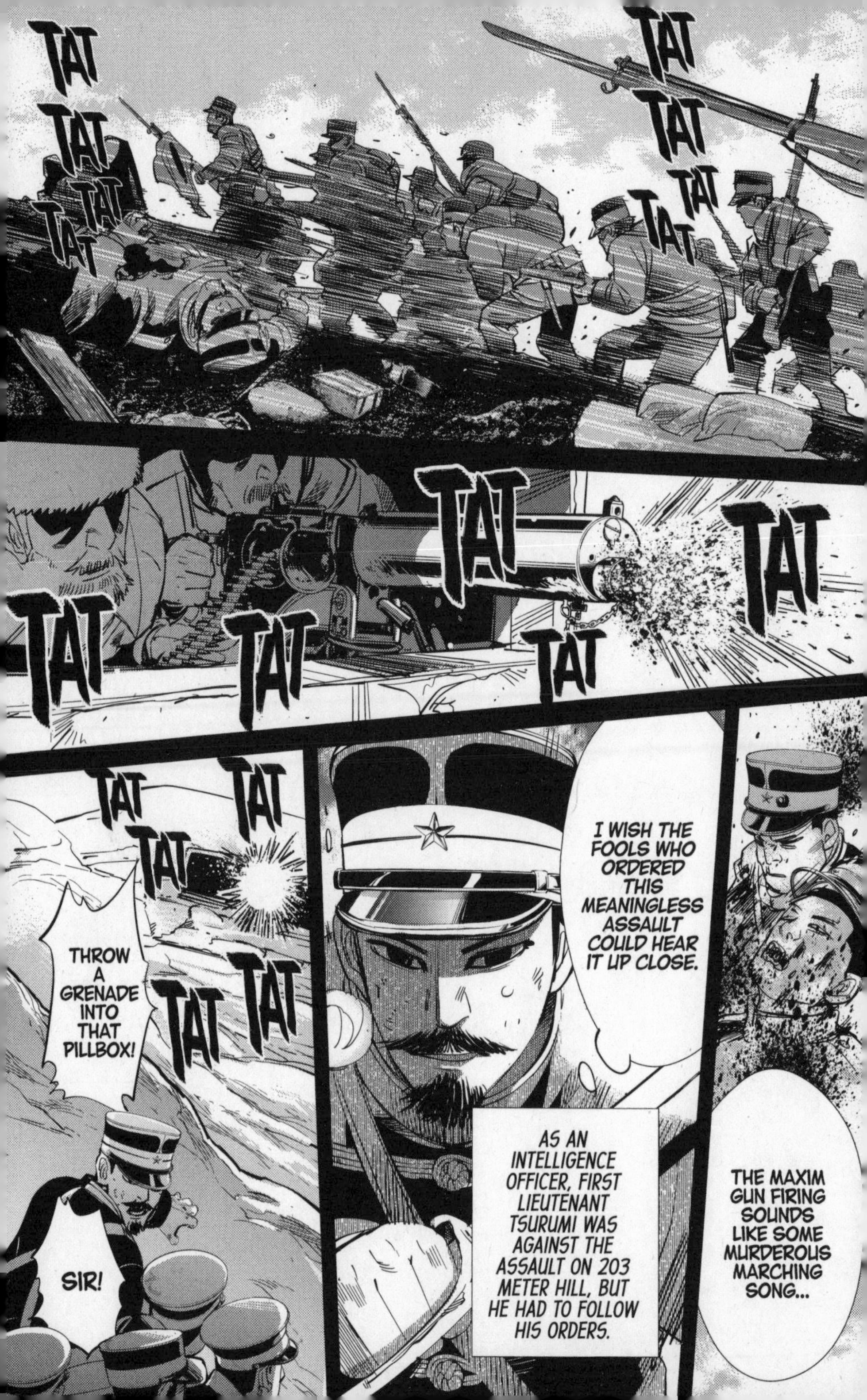
TAT TAT TAT TAT
TAT TAT TAT TAT
TAT TAT TAT TAT
THE MAXIM GUN FIRING SOUNDS LIKE SOME MURDEROUS MARCHING SONG...
I WISH THE FOOLS WHO ORDERED THIS MEANINGLESS ASSAULT COULD HEAR IT UP CLOSE.
AS AN INTELLIGENCE OFFICER, FIRST LIEUTENANT TSURUMI WAS AGAINST THE ASSAULT ON 203 METER HILL, BUT HE HAD TO FOLLOW HIS ORDERS.
TAT TAT TAT TAT TAT
THROW A GRENADE INTO THAT PILLBOX!
SIR!

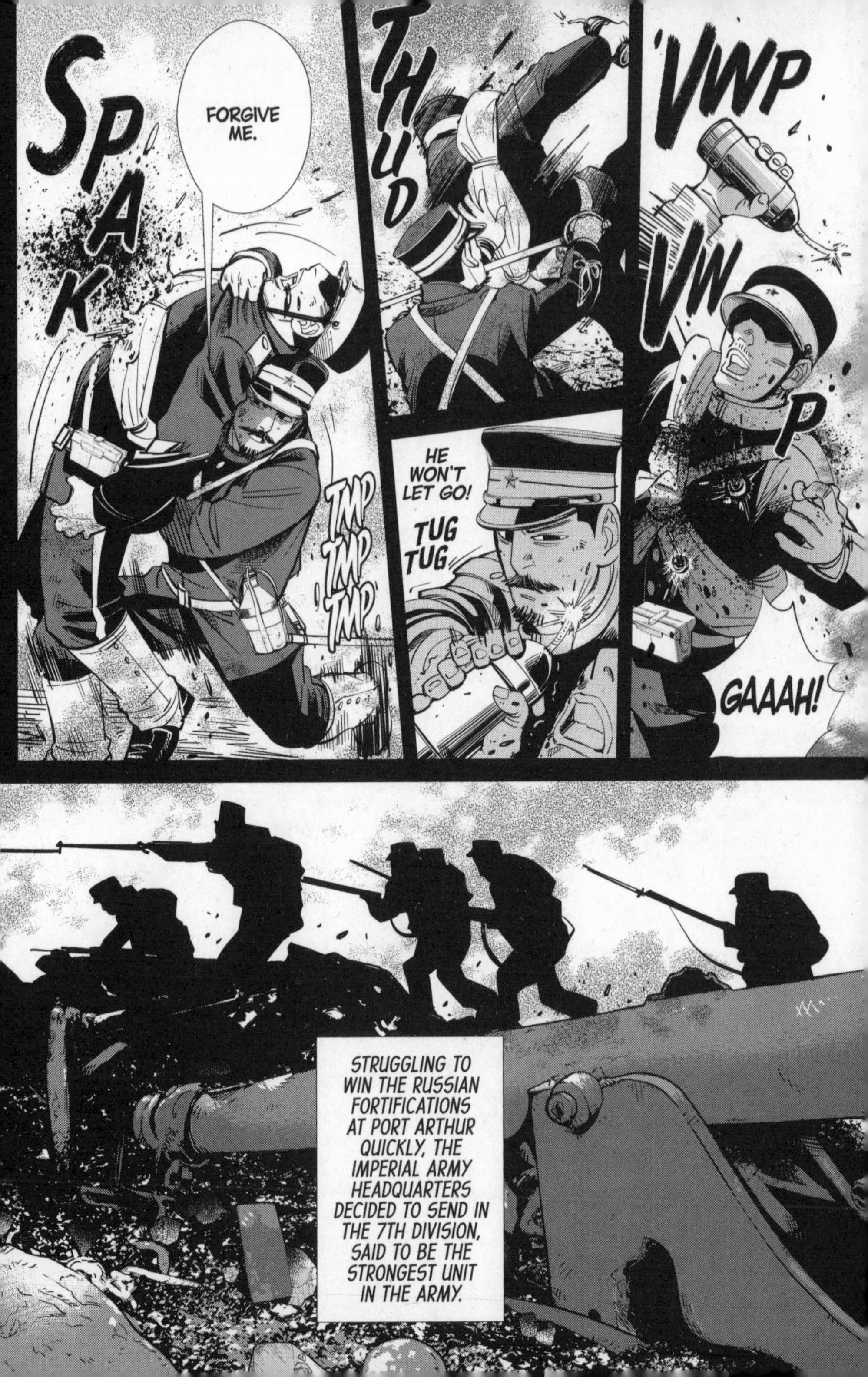
'VWP
VWP
GAAAH!
THUD
HE WON'T LET GO!
TUG TUG
SPAK
FORGIVE ME.
TMP TMP TMP
STRUGGLING TO WIN THE RUSSIAN FORTIFICATIONS AT PORT ARTHUR QUICKLY, THE IMPERIAL ARMY HEADQUARTERS DECIDED TO SEND IN THE 7TH DIVISION, SAID TO BE THE STRONGEST UNIT IN THE ARMY.

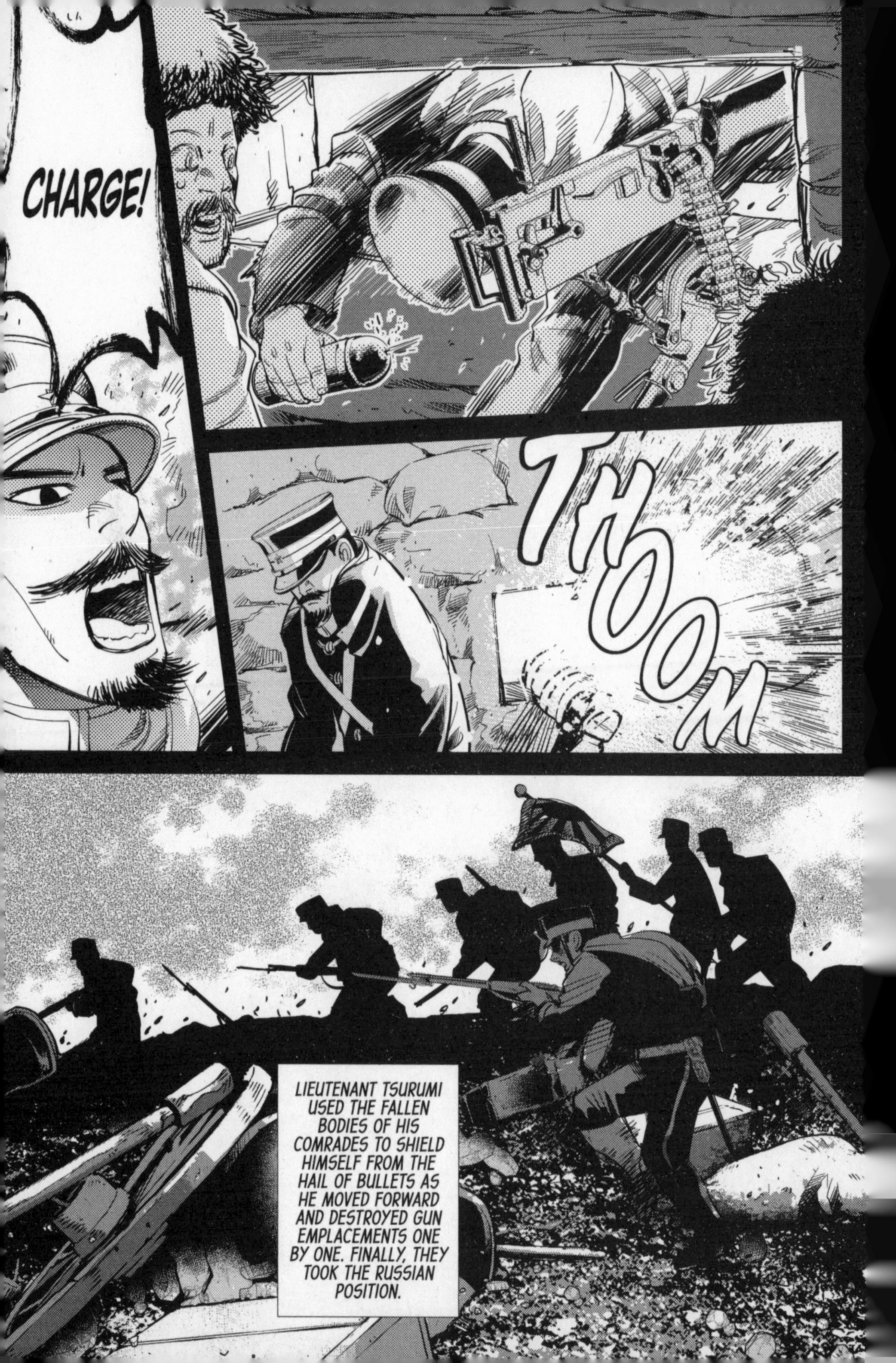
THOOM
CHARGE!
LIEUTENANT TSURUMI USED THE FALLEN BODIES OF HIS COMRADES TO SHIELD HIMSELF FROM THE HAIL OF BULLETS AS HE MOVED FORWARD AND DESTROYED GUN EMPLACEMENTS ONE BY ONE. FINALLY, THEY TOOK THE RUSSIAN POSITION.

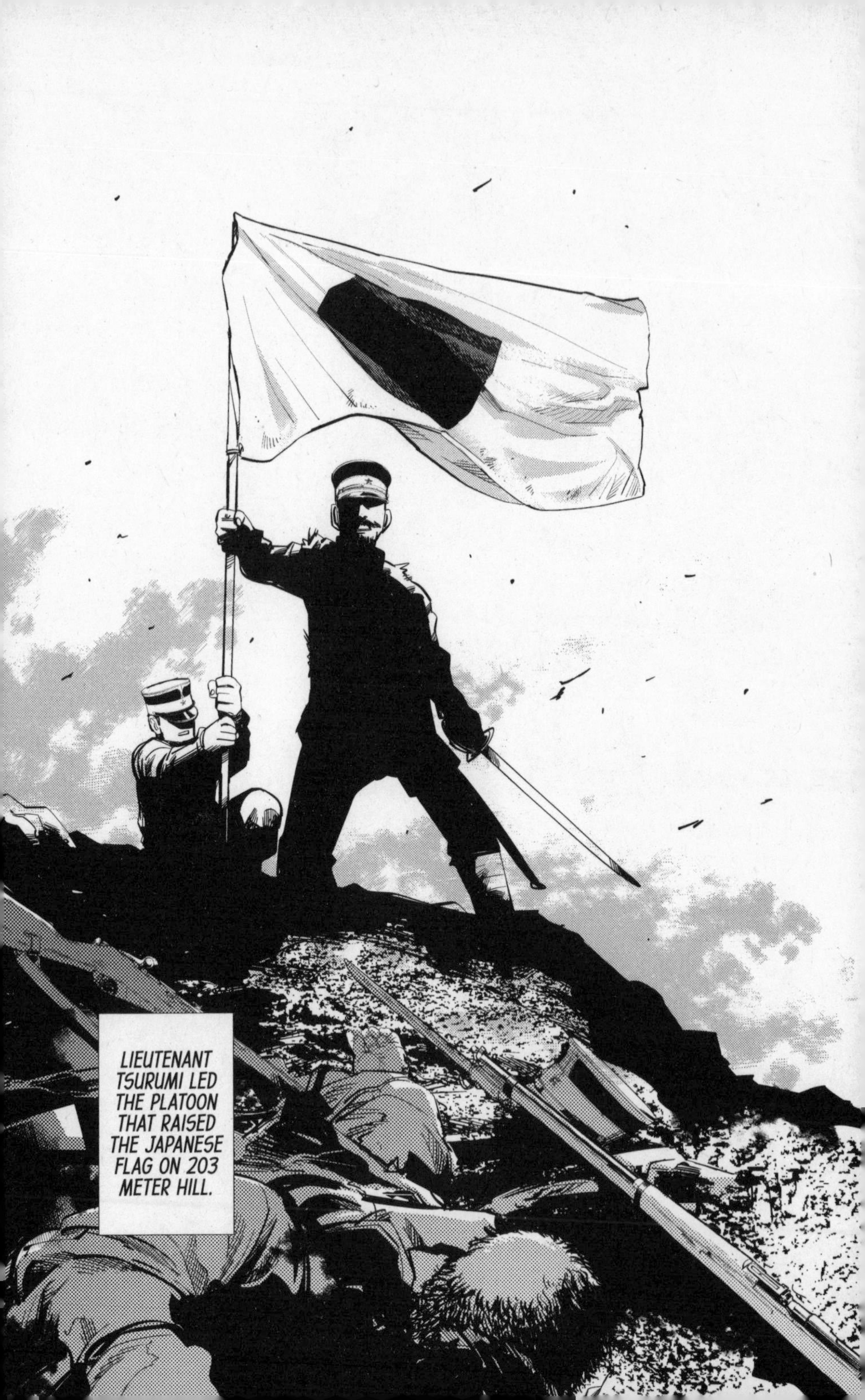
LIEUTENANT TSURUMI LED THE PLATOON THAT RAISED THE JAPANESE FLAG ON 203 METER HILL.

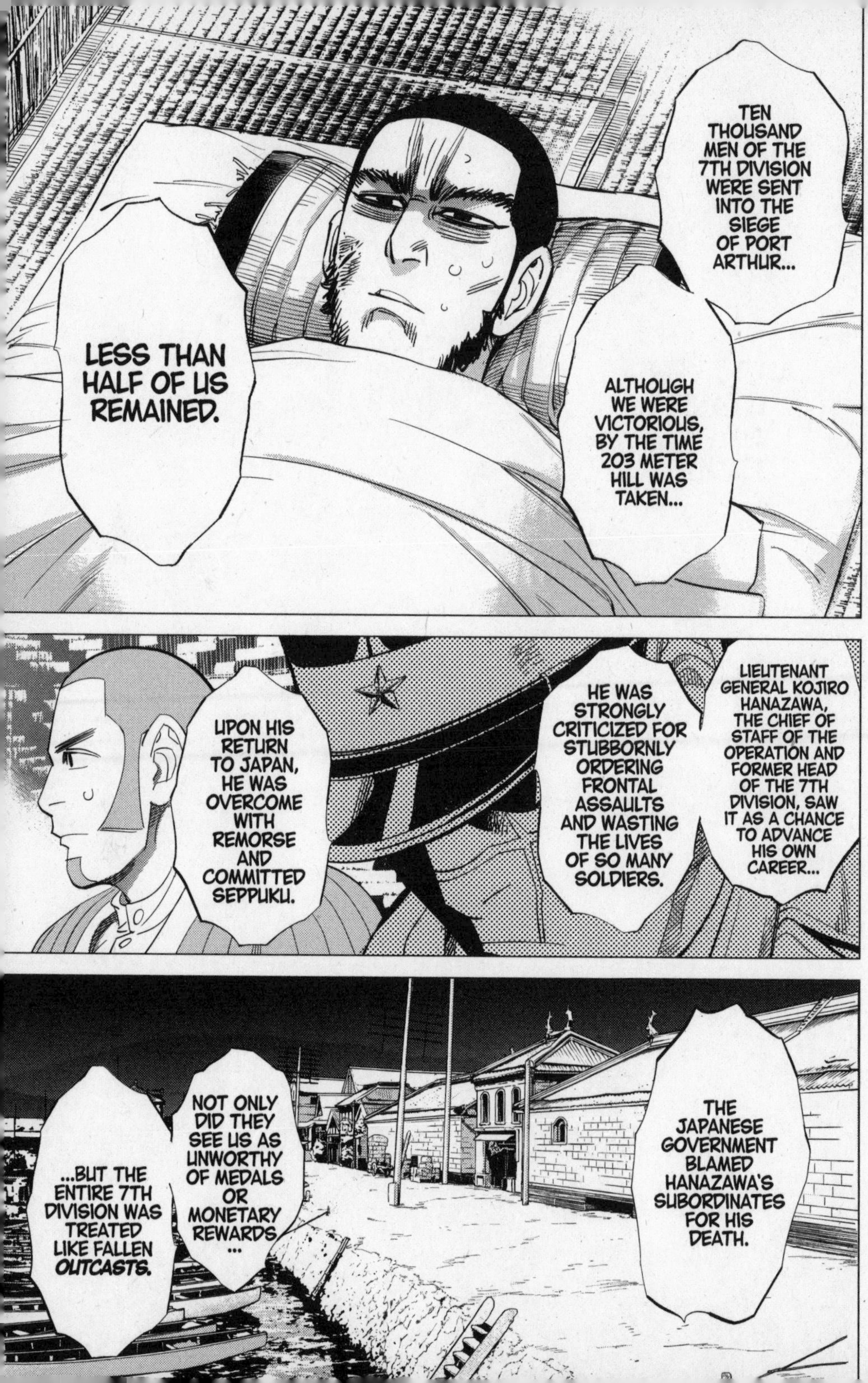
TEN THOUSAND MEN OF THE 7TH DIVISION WERE SENT INTO THE SIEGE OF PORT ARTHUR...
ALTHOUGH WE WERE VICTORIOUS, BY THE TIME 203 METER HILL WAS TAKEN...
LESS THAN HALF OF US REMAINED.
LIEUTENANT GENERAL KOJIRO HANAZAWA, THE CHIEF OF STAFF OF THE OPERATION AND FORMER HEAD OF THE 7TH DIVISION, SAW IT AS A CHANCE TO ADVANCE HIS OWN CAREER...
HE WAS STRONGLY CRITICIZED FOR STUBBORNLY ORDERING FRONTAL ASSAULTS AND WASTING THE LIVES OF SO MANY SOLDIERS.
UPON HIS RETURN TO JAPAN, HE WAS OVERCOME WITH REMORSE AND COMMITTED SEPPUKU.
THE JAPANESE GOVERNMENT BLAMED HANAZAWA'S SUBORDINATES FOR HIS DEATH.
NOT ONLY DID THEY SEE US AS UNWORTHY OF MEDALS OR MONETARY REWARDS...
...BUT THE ENTIRE 7TH DIVISION WAS TREATED LIKE FALLEN OUTCASTS.

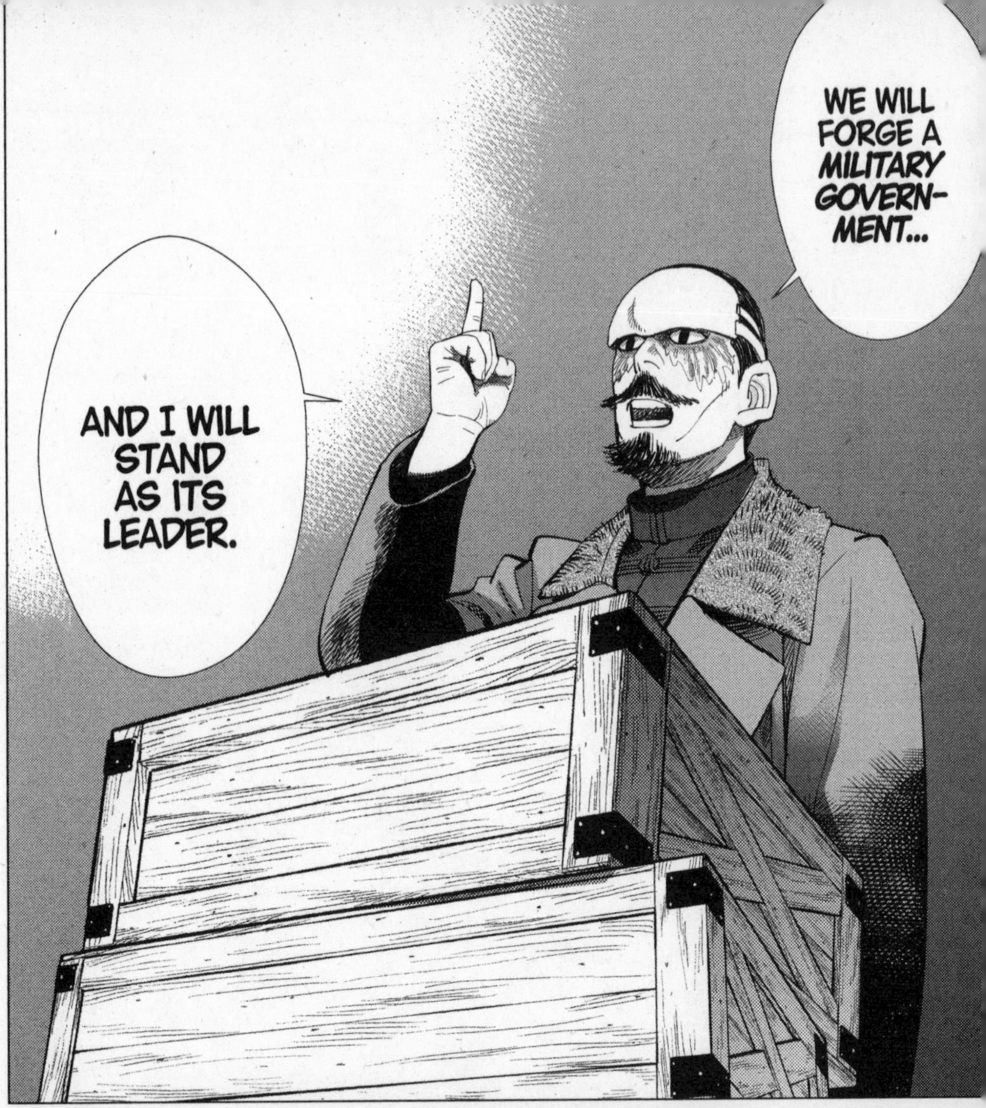
WE WILL FORGE A MILITARY GOVERNMENT...
AND I WILL STAND AS ITS LEADER.
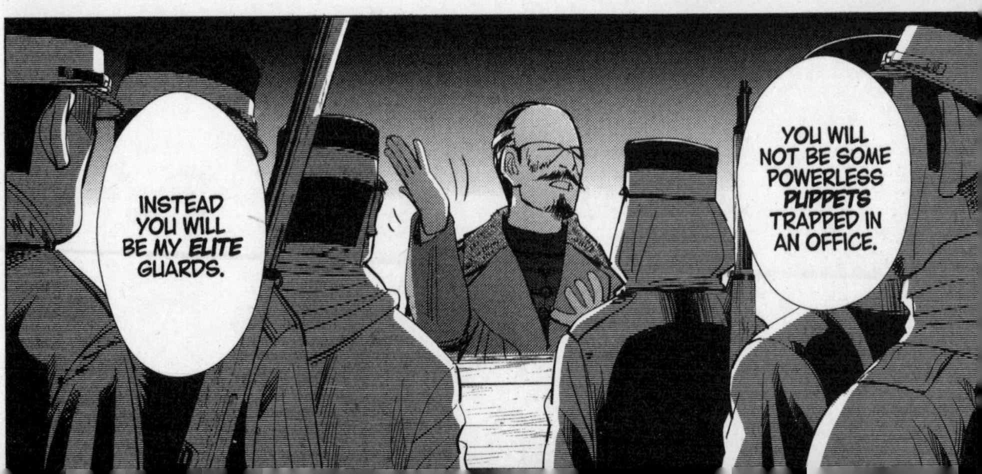
YOU WILL NOT BE SOME POWERLESS PUPPETS TRAPPED IN AN OFFICE.
INSTEAD YOU WILL BE MY ELITE GUARDS.

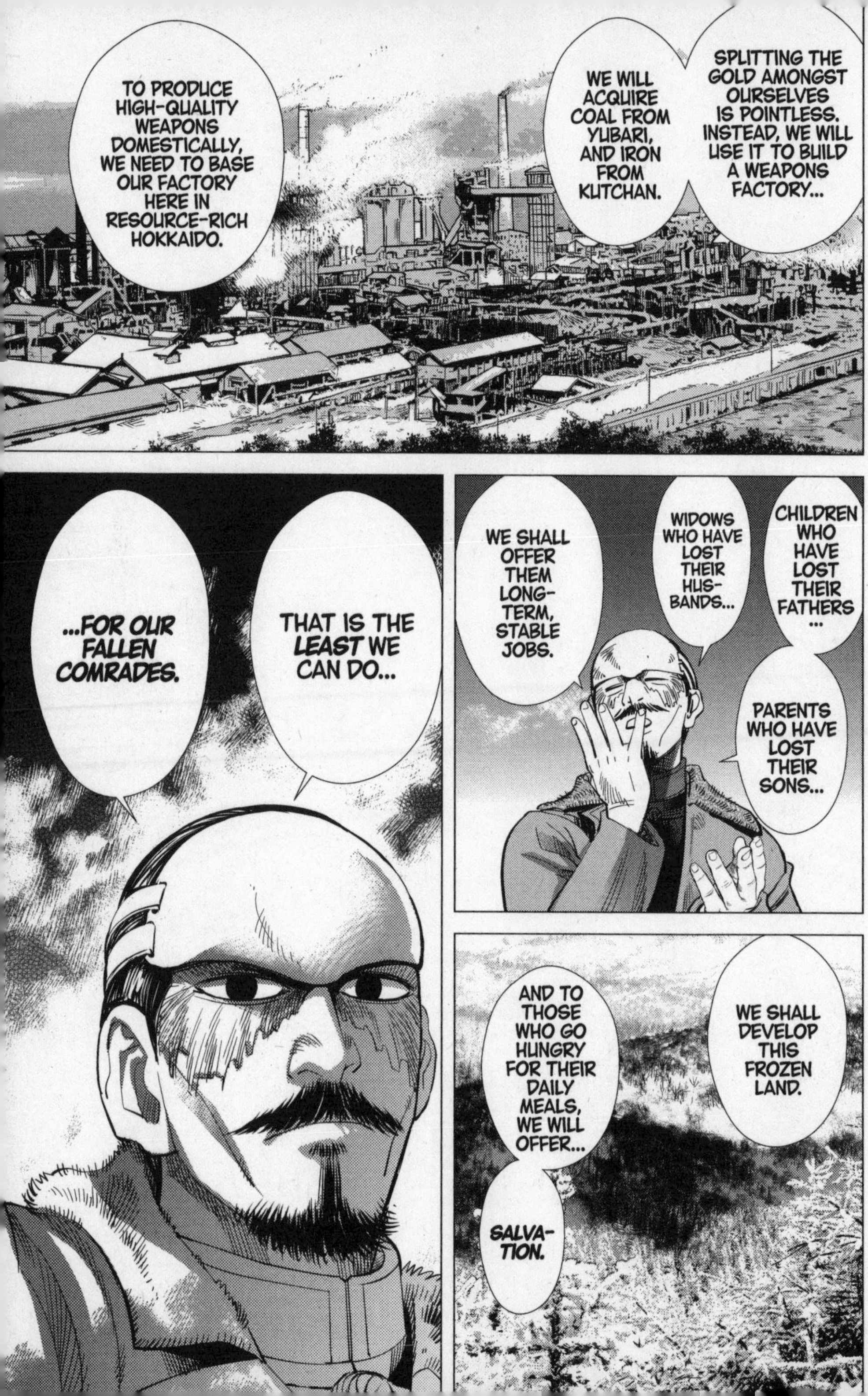
SPLITTING THE GOLD AMONGST OURSELVES IS POINTLESS. INSTEAD, WE WILL USE IT TO BUILD A WEAPONS FACTORY...
WE WILL ACQUIRE COAL FROM YUBARI, AND IRON FROM KUTCHAN.
TO PRODUCE HIGH-QUALITY WEAPONS DOMESTICALLY, WE NEED TO BASE OUR FACTORY HERE IN RESOURCE-RICH HOKKAIDO.
CHILDREN WHO HAVE LOST THEIR FATHERS ...
WIDOWS WHO HAVE LOST THEIR HUS-BANDS...
WE SHALL OFFER THEM LONG-TERM, STABLE JOBS.
PARENTS WHO HAVE LOST THEIR SONS...
WE SHALL DEVELOP THIS FROZEN LAND.
AND TO THOSE WHO GO HUNGRY FOR THEIR DAILY MEALS, WE WILL OFFER...
SALVA-TION.
THAT IS THE LEAST WE CAN DO...
...FOR OUR FALLEN COMRADES.

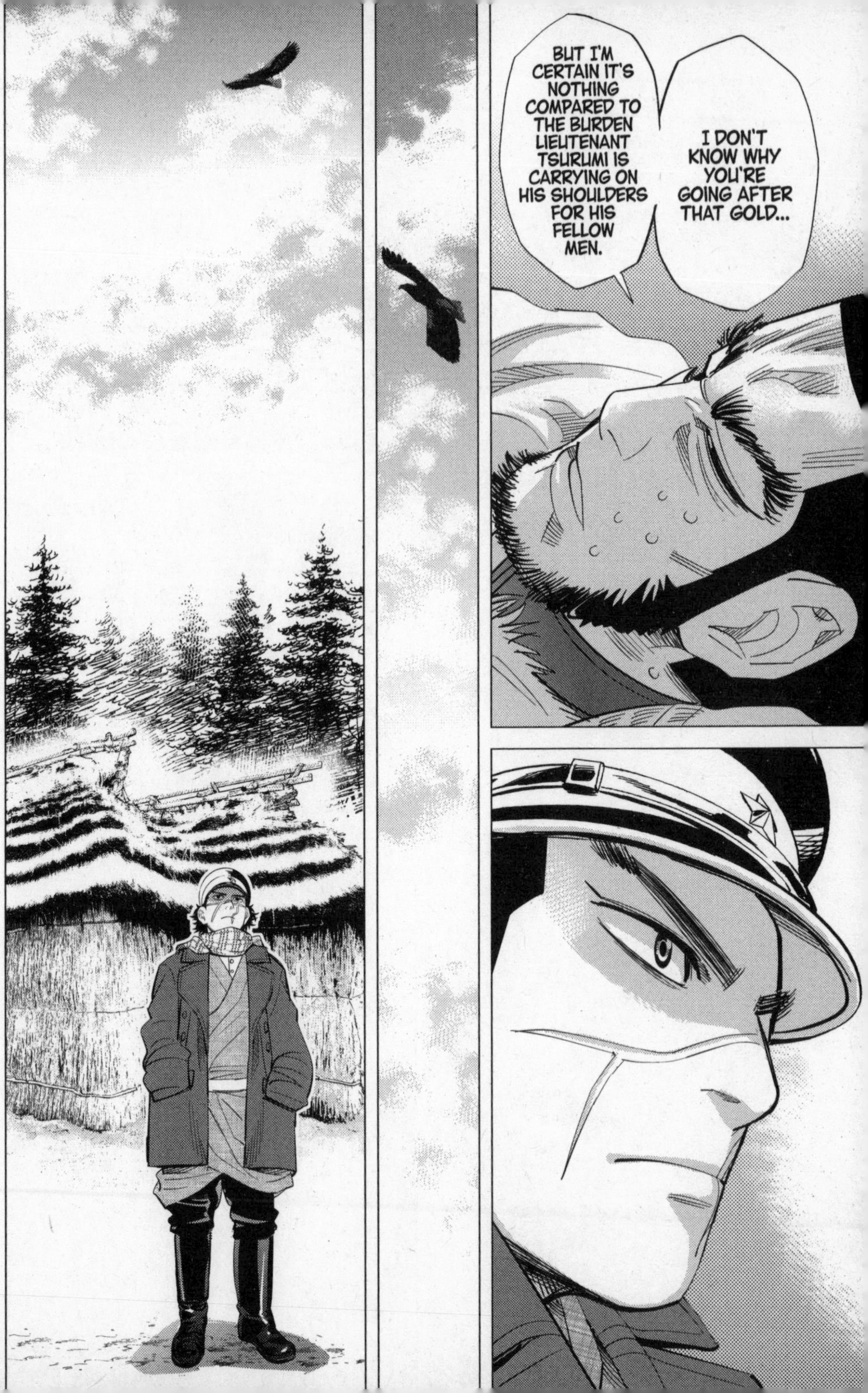
I DON'T KNOW WHY YOU'RE GOING AFTER THAT GOLD...
BUT I'M CERTAIN IT'S NOTHING COMPARED TO THE BURDEN LIEUTENANT TSURUMI IS CARRYING ON HIS SHOULDERS FOR HIS FELLOW MEN.

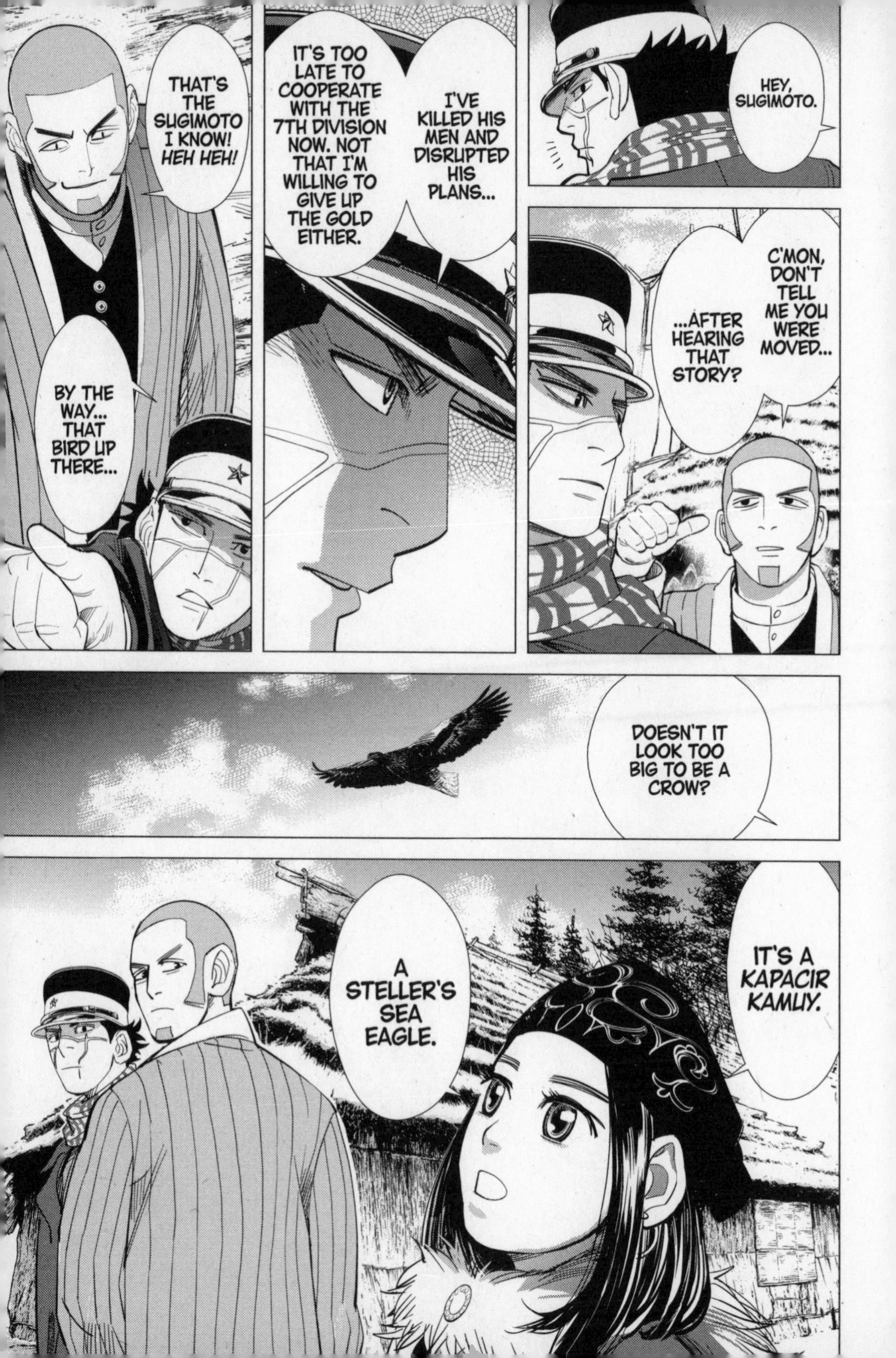
HEY, SUGIMOTO.
C'MON, DON'T TELL ME YOU WERE MOVED...
...AFTER HEARING THAT STORY?
I'VE KILLED HIS MEN AND DISRUPTED HIS PLANS...
IT'S TOO LATE TO COOPERATE WITH THE 7TH DIVISION NOW. NOT THAT I'M WILLING TO GIVE UP THE GOLD EITHER.
THAT'S THE SUGIMOTO I KNOW! HEH HEH!
BY THE WAY... THAT BIRD UP THERE...
DOESN'T IT LOOK TOO BIG TO BE A CROW?
IT'S A KAPACIR KAMUY.
A STELLER'S SEA EAGLE.

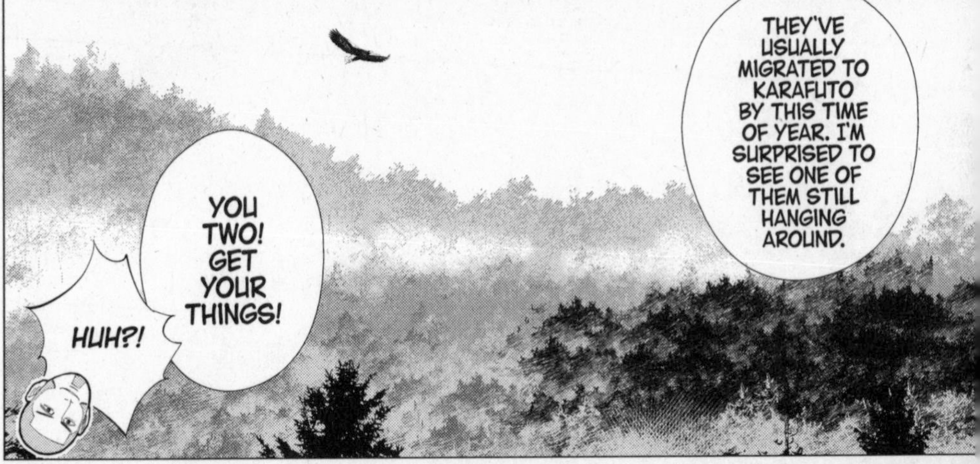
THEY'VE USUALLY MIGRATED TO KARAFUTO BY THIS TIME OF YEAR. I'M SURPRISED TO SEE ONE OF THEM STILL HANGING AROUND.
YOU TWO! GET YOUR THINGS!
HUH?!
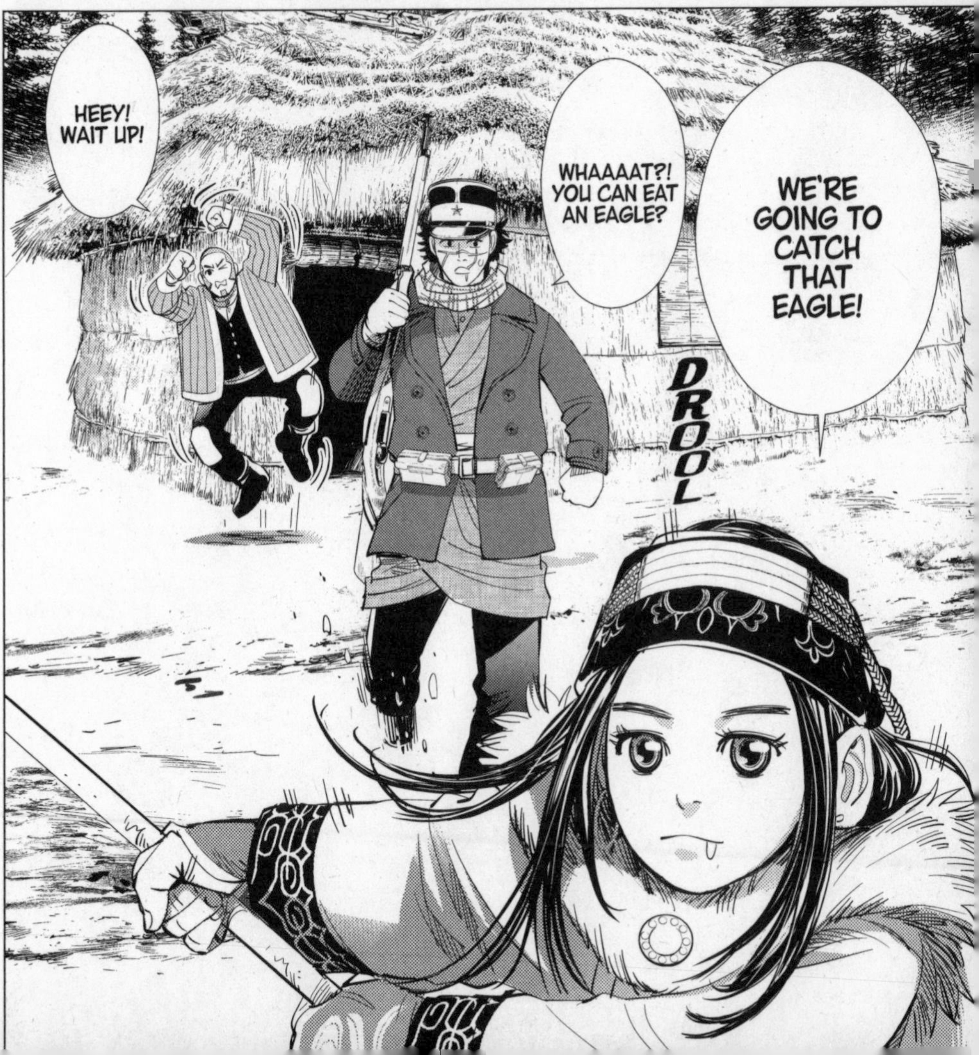
WE'RE GOING TO CATCH THAT EAGLE!
DROOL
WHAAAAT?! YOU CAN EAT AN EAGLE?
HEEY! WAIT UP!

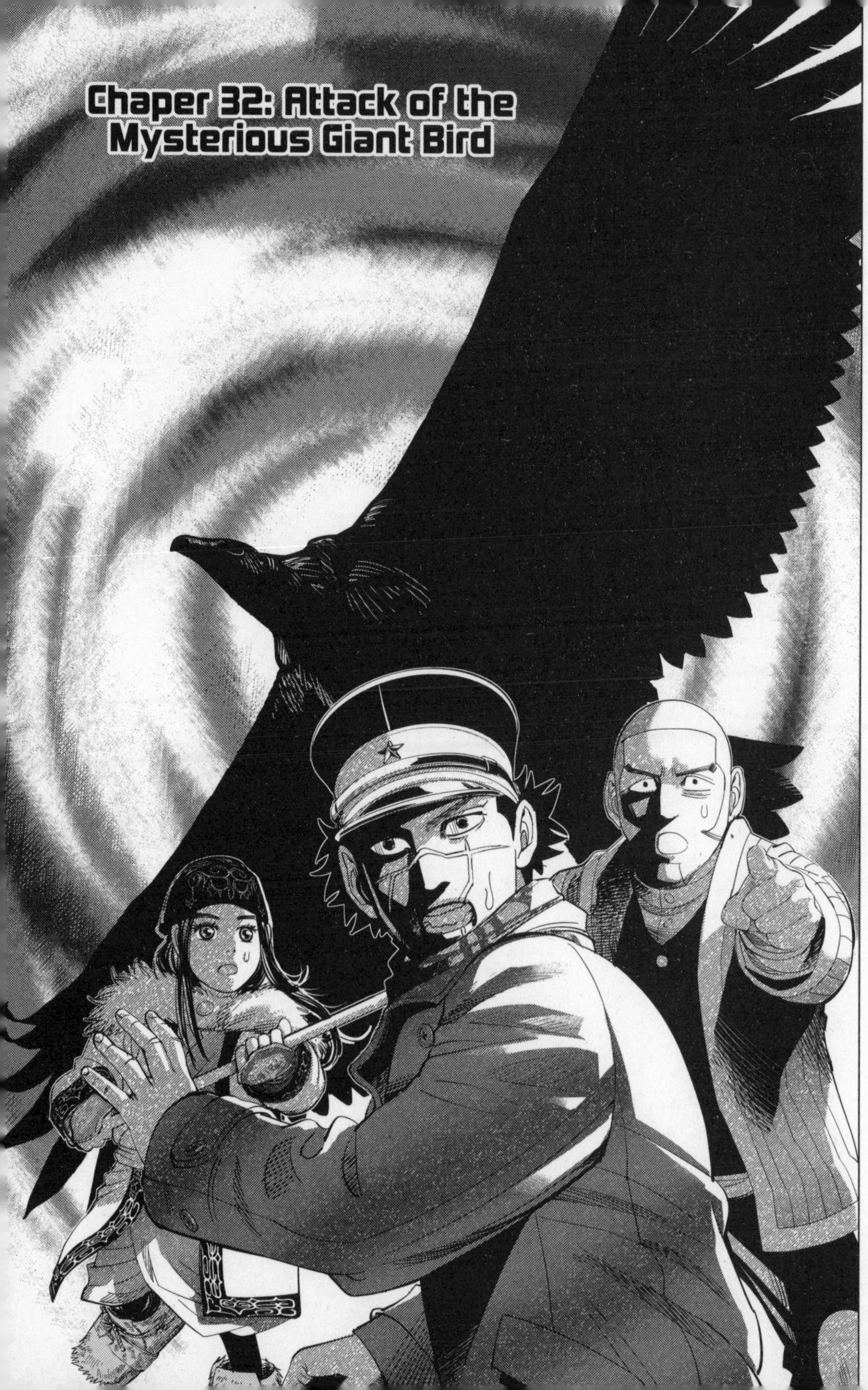
Chaper 32: Attack of the
Mysterious Giant Bird

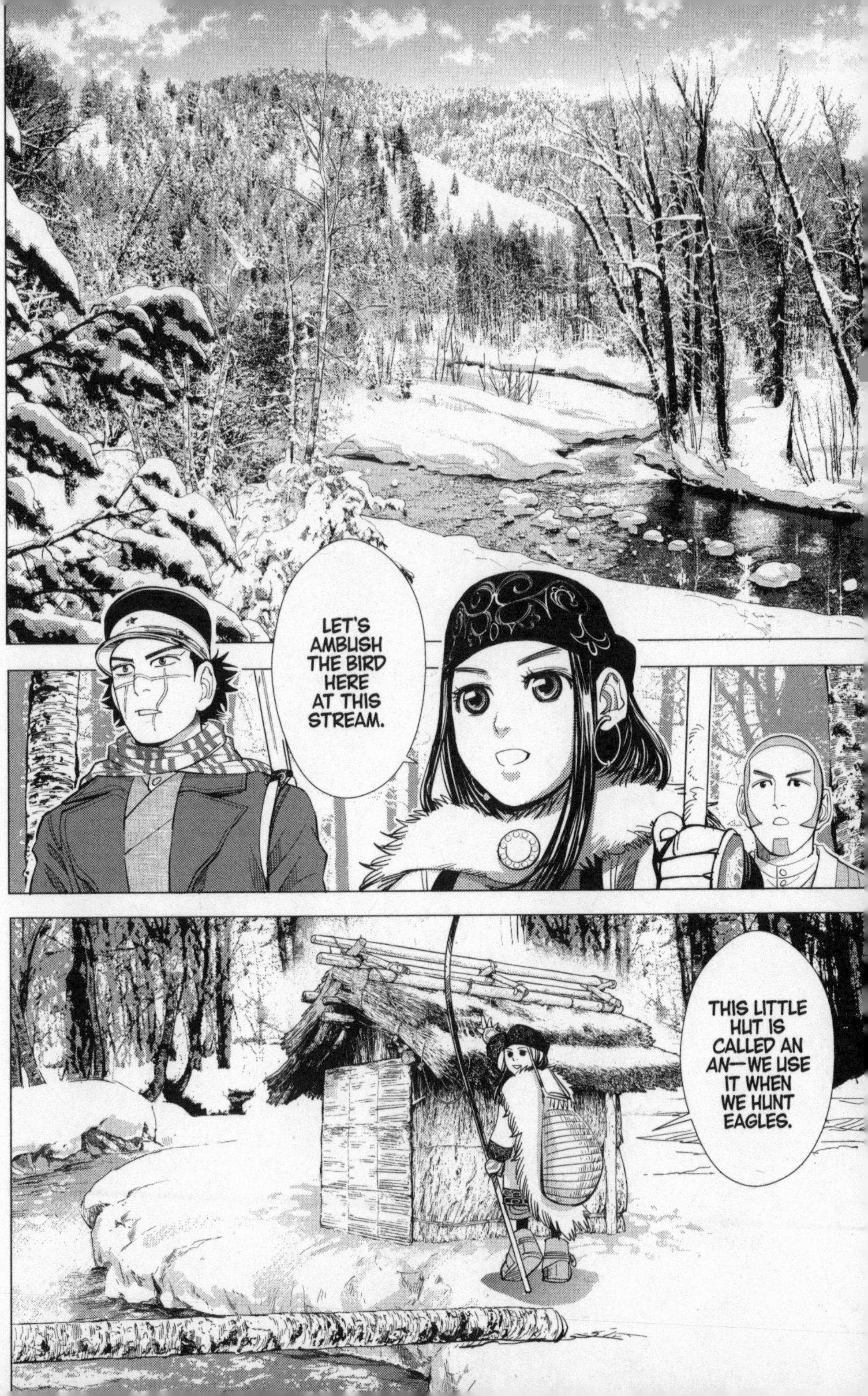
LET'S AMBUSH THE BIRD HERE AT THIS STREAM.
THIS LITTLE HUT IS CALLED AN AN—WE USE IT WHEN WE HUNT EAGLES.

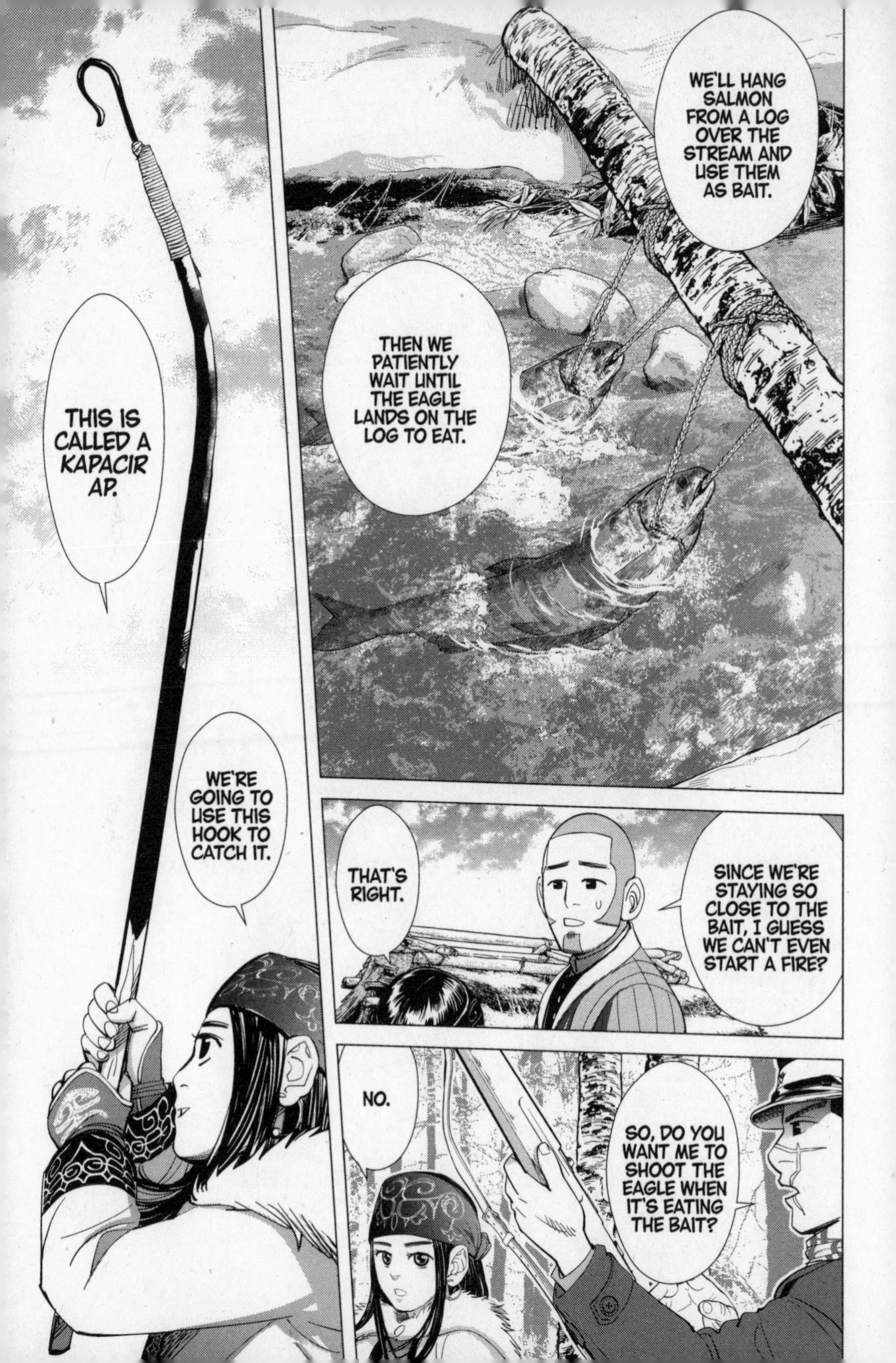
WE'LL HANG SALMON FROM A LOG OVER THE STREAM AND USE THEM AS BAIT.
THEN WE PATIENTLY WAIT UNTIL THE EAGLE LANDS ON THE LOG TO EAT.
SINCE WE'RE STAYING SO CLOSE TO THE BAIT, I GUESS WE CAN'T EVEN START A FIRE?
THAT'S RIGHT.
SO, DO YOU WANT ME TO SHOOT THE EAGLE WHEN IT'S EATING THE BAIT?
NO.
THIS IS CALLED A KAPACIR AP.
WE'RE GOING TO USE THIS HOOK TO CATCH IT.

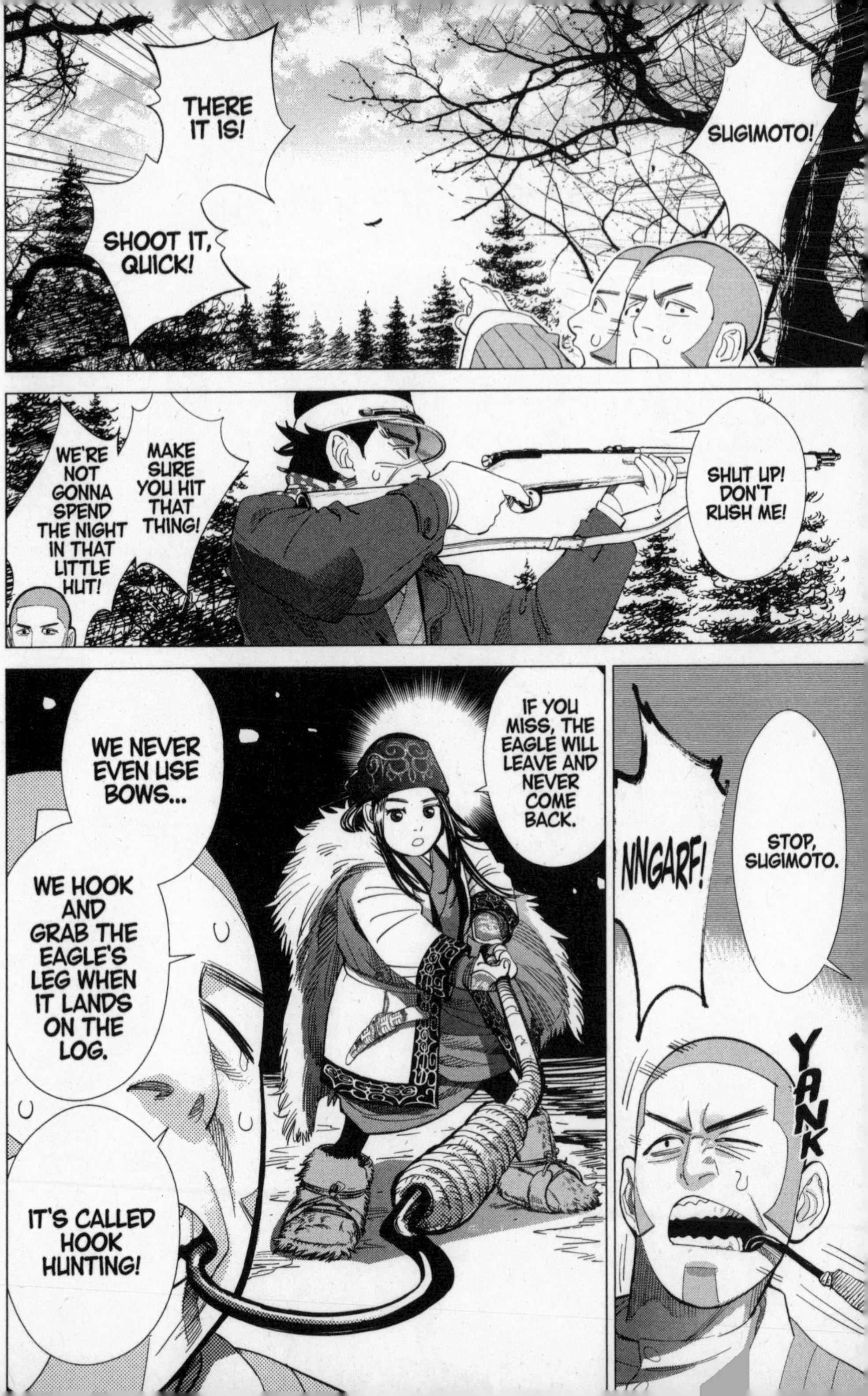
THERE IT IS!
SHOOT IT, QUICK!
SUGIMOTO!
MAKE SURE YOU HIT THAT THING!
WE'RE NOT GONNA SPEND THE NIGHT IN THAT LITTLE HUT!
SHUT UP! DON'T RUSH ME!
STOP, SUGIMOTO.
NNGARF!
YANK
IF YOU MISS, THE EAGLE WILL LEAVE AND NEVER COME BACK.
WE NEVER EVEN USE BOWS...
WE HOOK AND GRAB THE EAGLE'S LEG WHEN IT LANDS ON THE LOG.
IT'S CALLED HOOK HUNTING!

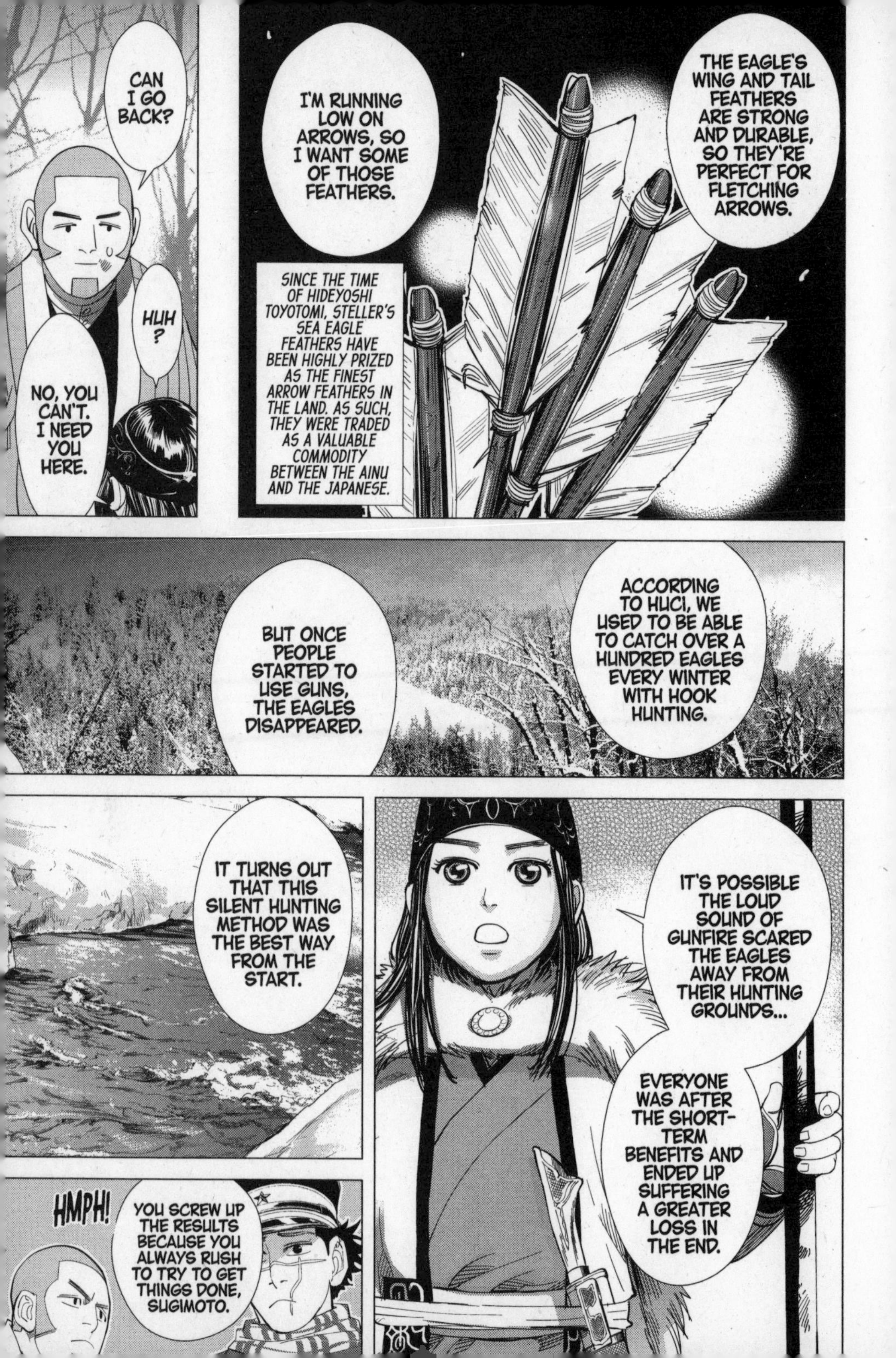
THE EAGLE'S WING AND TAIL FEATHERS ARE STRONG AND DURABLE, SO THEY'RE PERFECT FOR FLETCHING ARROWS.
I'M RUNNING LOW ON ARROWS, SO I WANT SOME OF THOSE FEATHERS.
SINCE THE TIME OF HIDEYOSHI TOYOTOMI, STELLER'S SEA EAGLE FEATHERS HAVE BEEN HIGHLY PRIZED AS THE FINEST ARROW FEATHERS IN THE LAND. AS SUCH, THEY WERE TRADED AS A VALUABLE COMMODITY BETWEEN THE AINU AND THE JAPANESE.
CAN I GO BACK?
HUH?
NO, YOU CAN'T. I NEED YOU HERE.
ACCORDING TO HUCI, WE USED TO BE ABLE TO CATCH OVER A HUNDRED EAGLES EVERY WINTER WITH HOOK HUNTING.
BUT ONCE PEOPLE STARTED TO USE GUNS, THE EAGLES DISAPPEARED.
IT'S POSSIBLE THE LOUD SOUND OF GUNFIRE SCARED THE EAGLES AWAY FROM THEIR HUNTING GROUNDS...
EVERYONE WAS AFTER THE SHORT-TERM BENEFITS AND ENDED UP SUFFERING A GREATER LOSS IN THE END.
IT TURNS OUT THAT THIS SILENT HUNTING METHOD WAS THE BEST WAY FROM THE START.
YOU SCREW UP THE RESULTS BECAUSE YOU ALWAYS RUSH TO TRY TO GET THINGS DONE, SUGIMOTO.
HMPH!

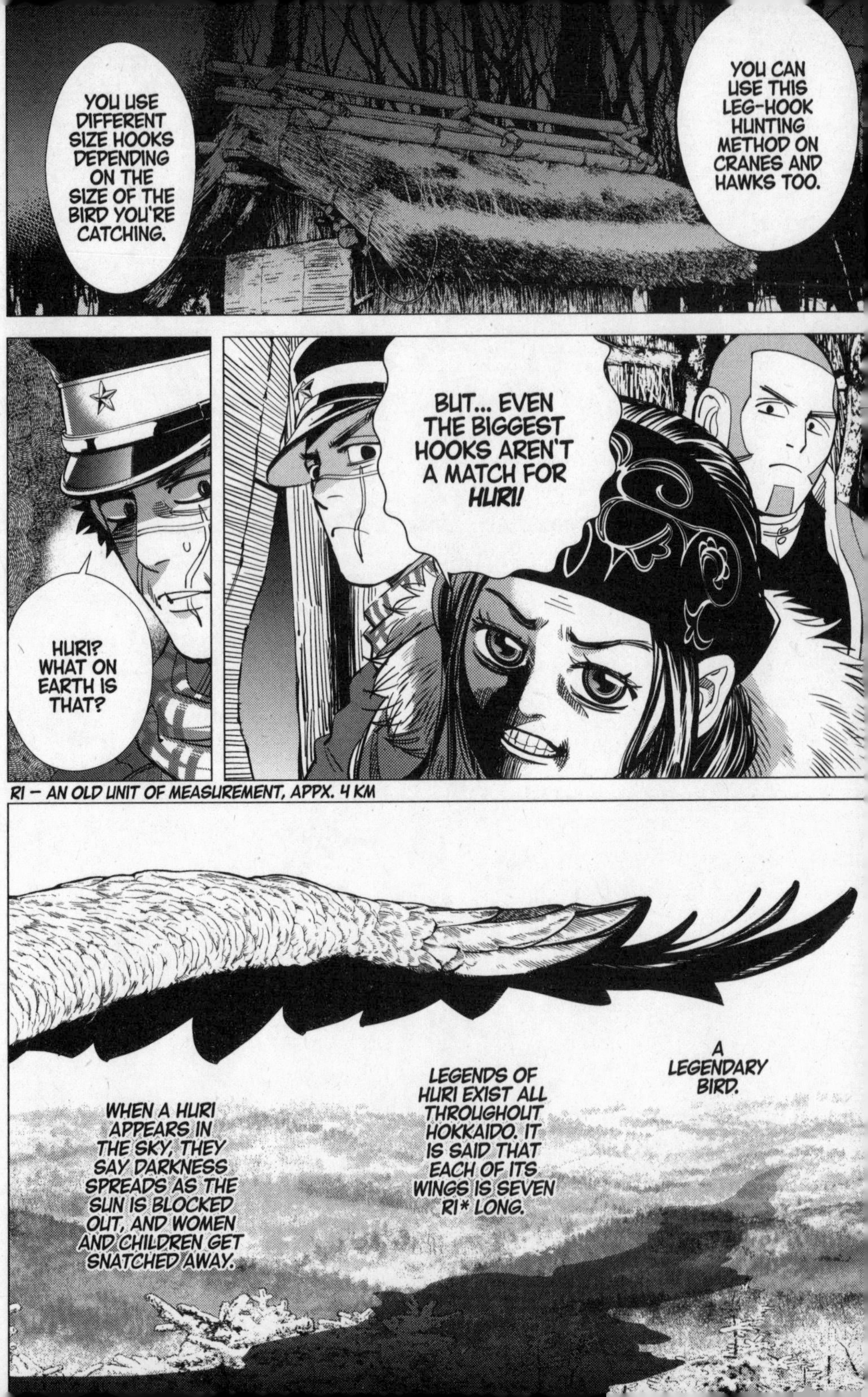
YOU CAN USE THIS LEG-HOOK HUNTING METHOD ON CRANES AND HAWKS TOO.
YOU USE DIFFERENT SIZE HOOKS DEPENDING ON THE SIZE OF THE BIRD YOU'RE CATCHING.
BUT... EVEN THE BIGGEST HOOKS AREN'T A MATCH FOR HURI!
HURI? WHAT ON EARTH IS THAT?
RI – AN OLD UNIT OF MEASUREMENT, APPX. 4 KM
A LEGENDARY BIRD.
LEGENDS OF HURI EXIST ALL THROUGHOUT HOKKAIDO. IT IS SAID THAT EACH OF ITS WINGS IS SEVEN RI* LONG.
WHEN A HURI APPEARS IN THE SKY, THEY SAY DARKNESS SPREADS AS THE SUN IS BLOCKED OUT, AND WOMEN AND CHILDREN GET SNATCHED AWAY.

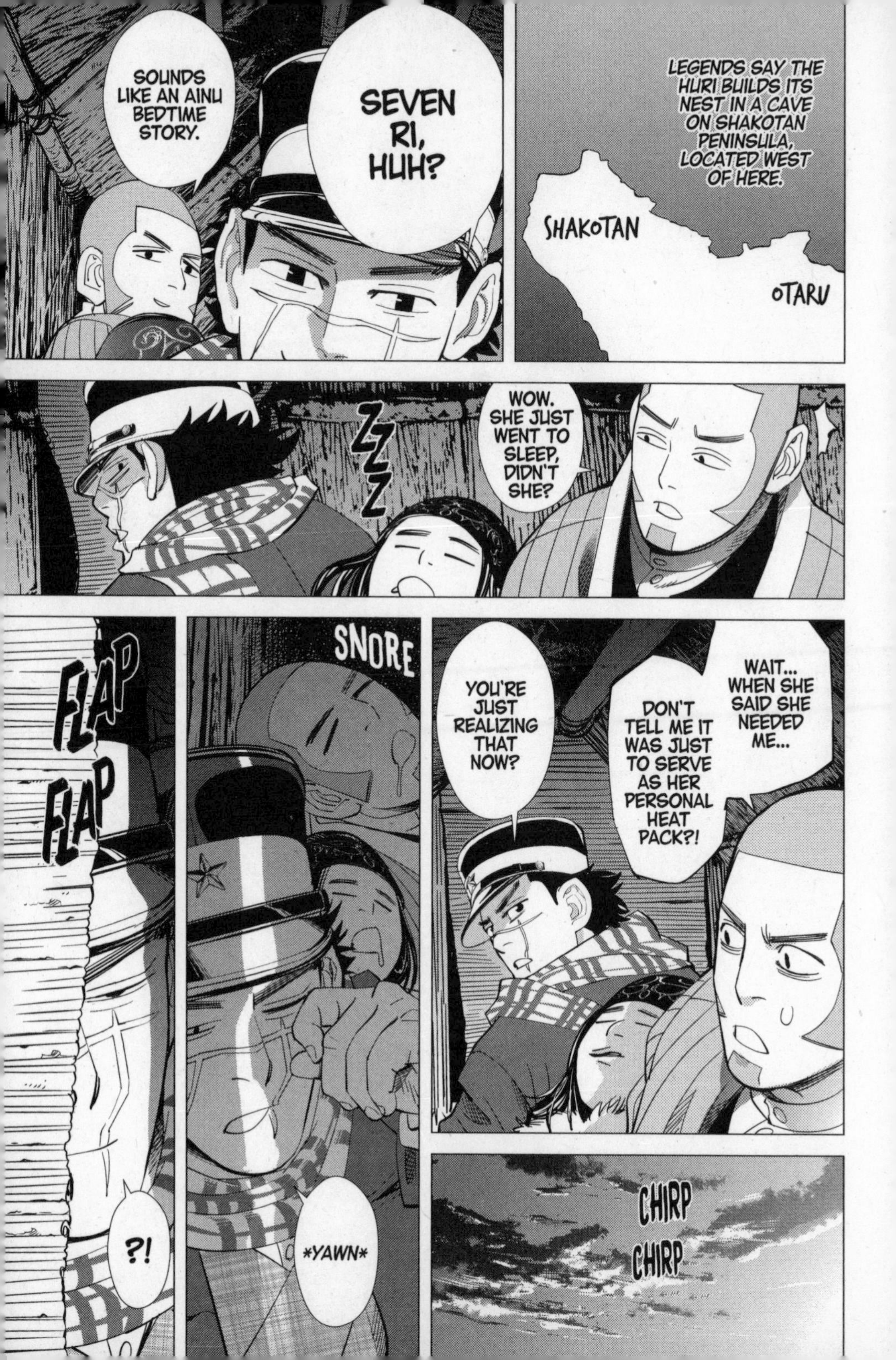
LEGENDS SAY THE HURI BUILDS ITS NEST IN A CAVE ON SHAKOTAN PENINSULA, LOCATED WEST OF HERE.
SHAKOTAN
OTARU
SEVEN RI, HUH?
SOUNDS LIKE AN AINU BEDTIME STORY.
WOW. SHE JUST WENT TO SLEEP, DIDN'T SHE?
ZZZ
WAIT... WHEN SHE SAID SHE NEEDED ME...
DON'T TELL ME IT WAS JUST TO SERVE AS HER PERSONAL HEAT PACK?!
YOU'RE JUST REALIZING THAT NOW?
CHIRP
CHIRP
SNORE
YAWN
FLAP
FLAP
?!

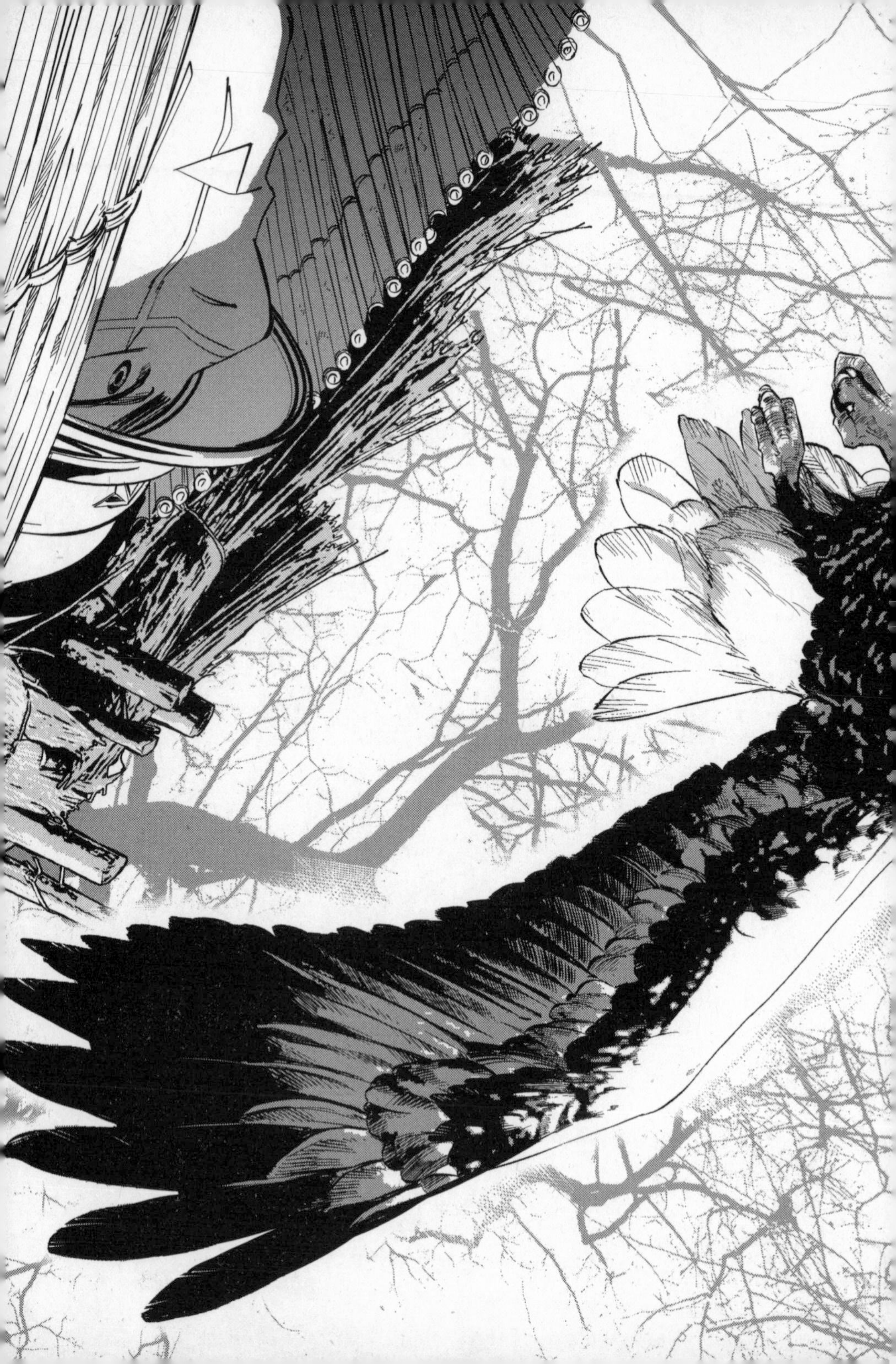

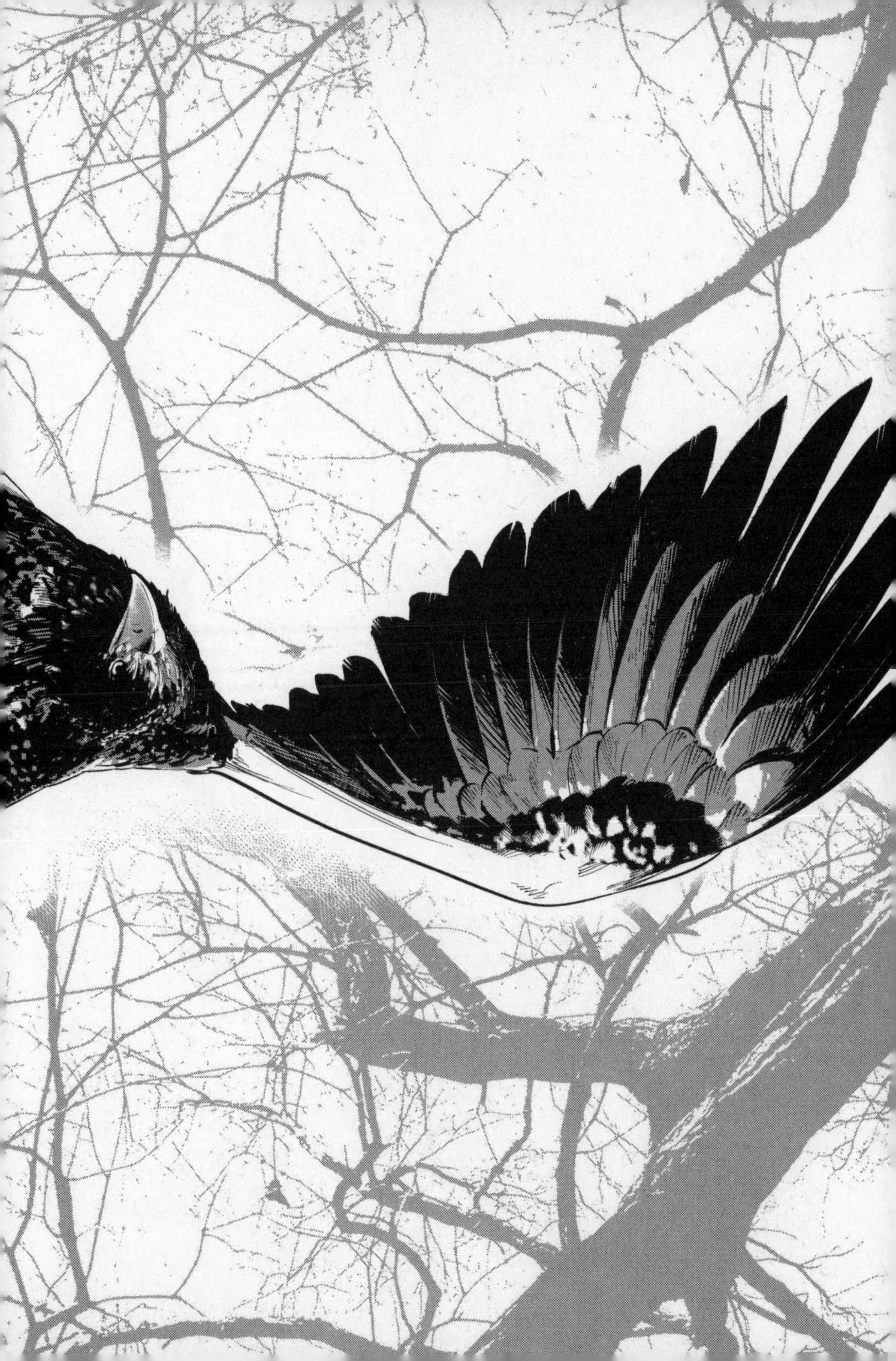

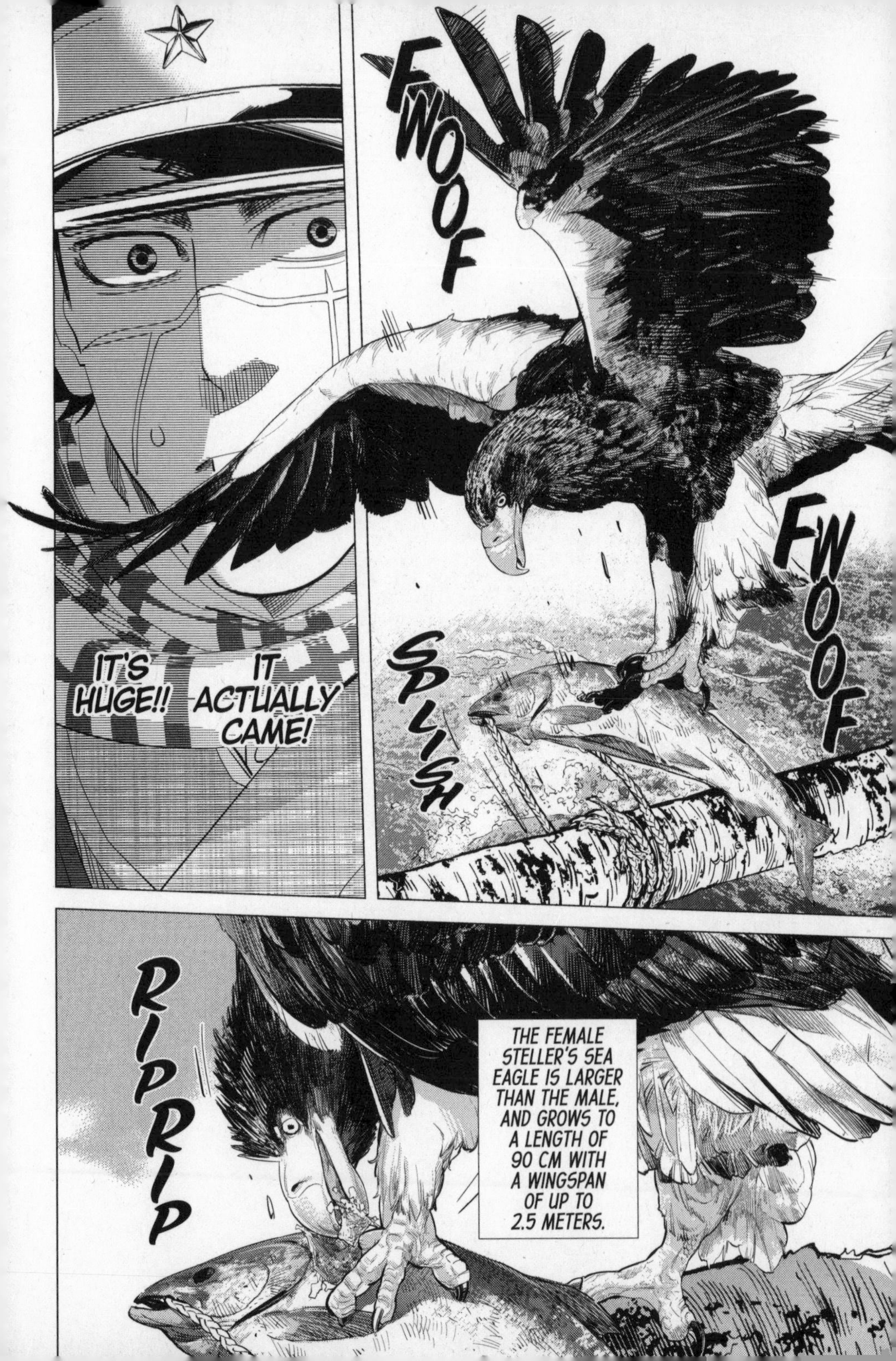
FWOOF
FWOOF
SPLISH
IT ACTUALLY CAME!
IT'S HUGE!!
THE FEMALE STELLER'S SEA EAGLE IS LARGER THAN THE MALE, AND GROWS TO A LENGTH OF 90 CM WITH A WINGSPAN OF UP TO 2.5 METERS.
RIPRIP

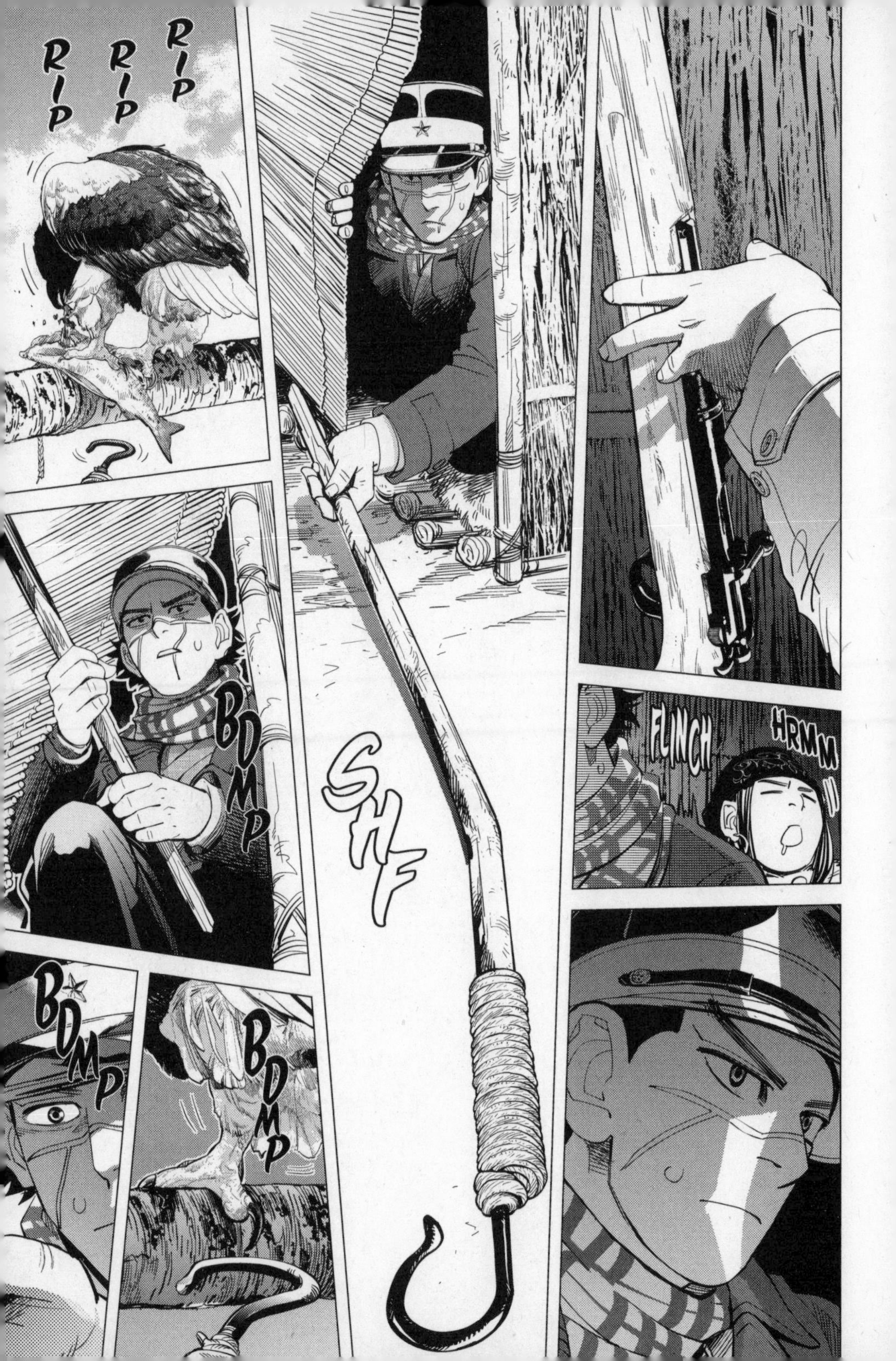
HRMM
FLINCH
SHF
RIP RIP RIP
BDMP
BDMP
BDMP

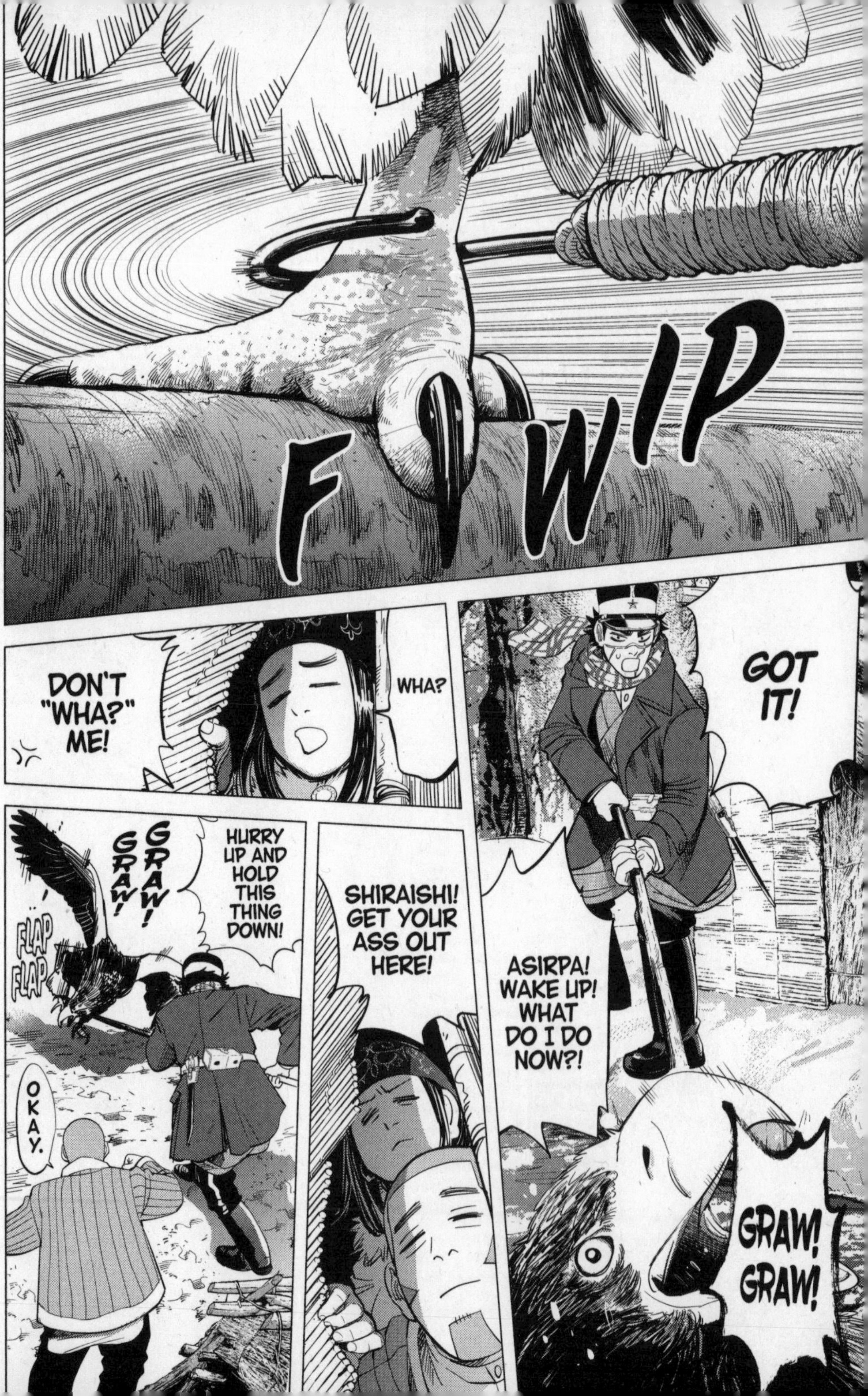
FWIP
GOT IT!
ASIRPA! WAKE UP! WHAT DO I DO NOW?!
GRAW! GRAW!
WHA?
DON'T "WHA?" ME!
SHIRAISHI! GET YOUR ASS OUT HERE!
HURRY UP AND HOLD THIS THING DOWN!
GRAW! GRAW!
FLAP FLAP
OKAY.

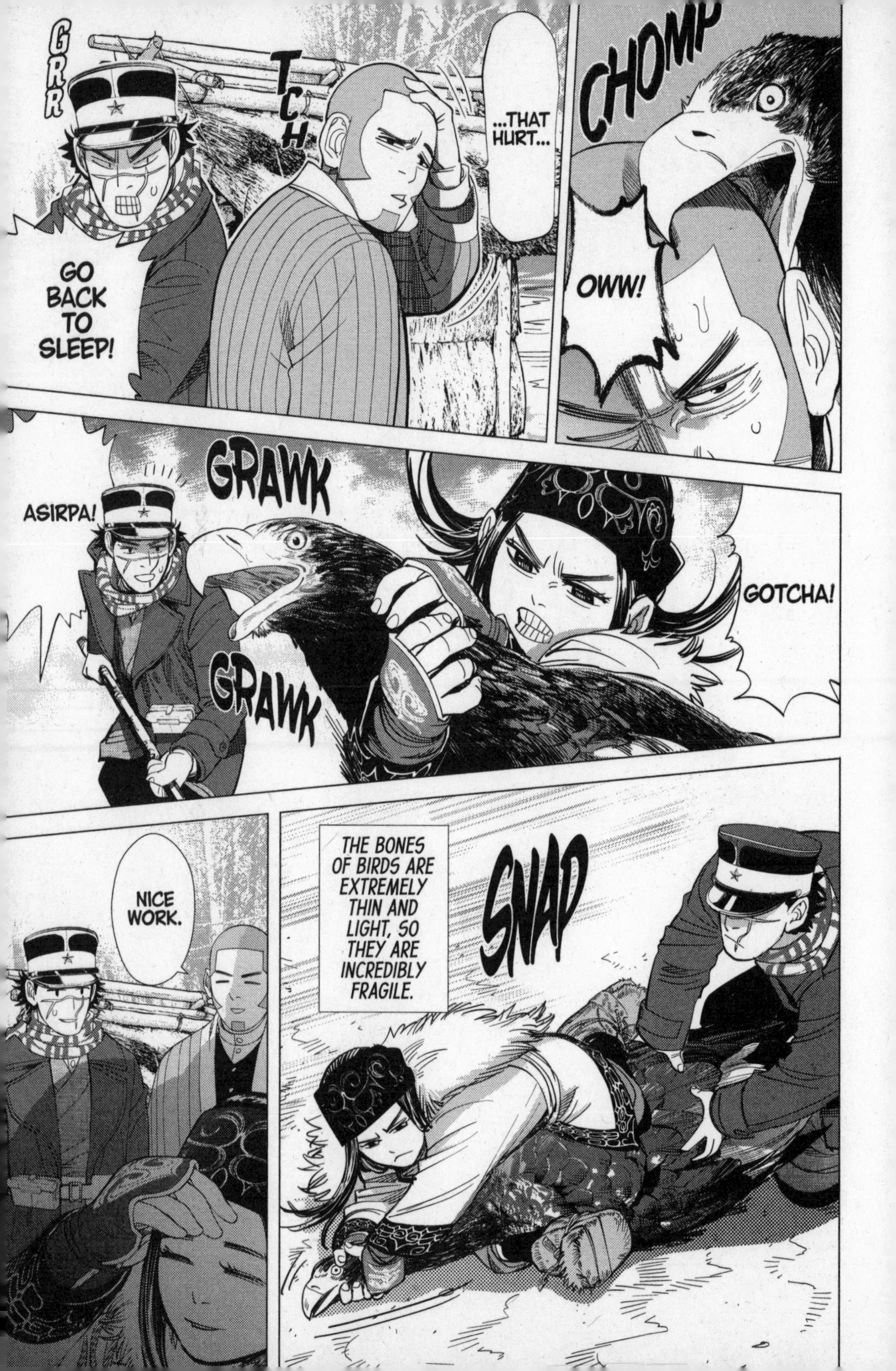
CHOMP
OWW!
...THAT HURT...
TCH
GRR
GO BACK TO SLEEP!
GOTCHA!
GRAWK
GRAWK
ASIRPA!
THE BONES OF BIRDS ARE EXTREMELY THIN AND LIGHT, SO THEY ARE INCREDIBLY FRAGILE.
SNAP
NICE WORK.

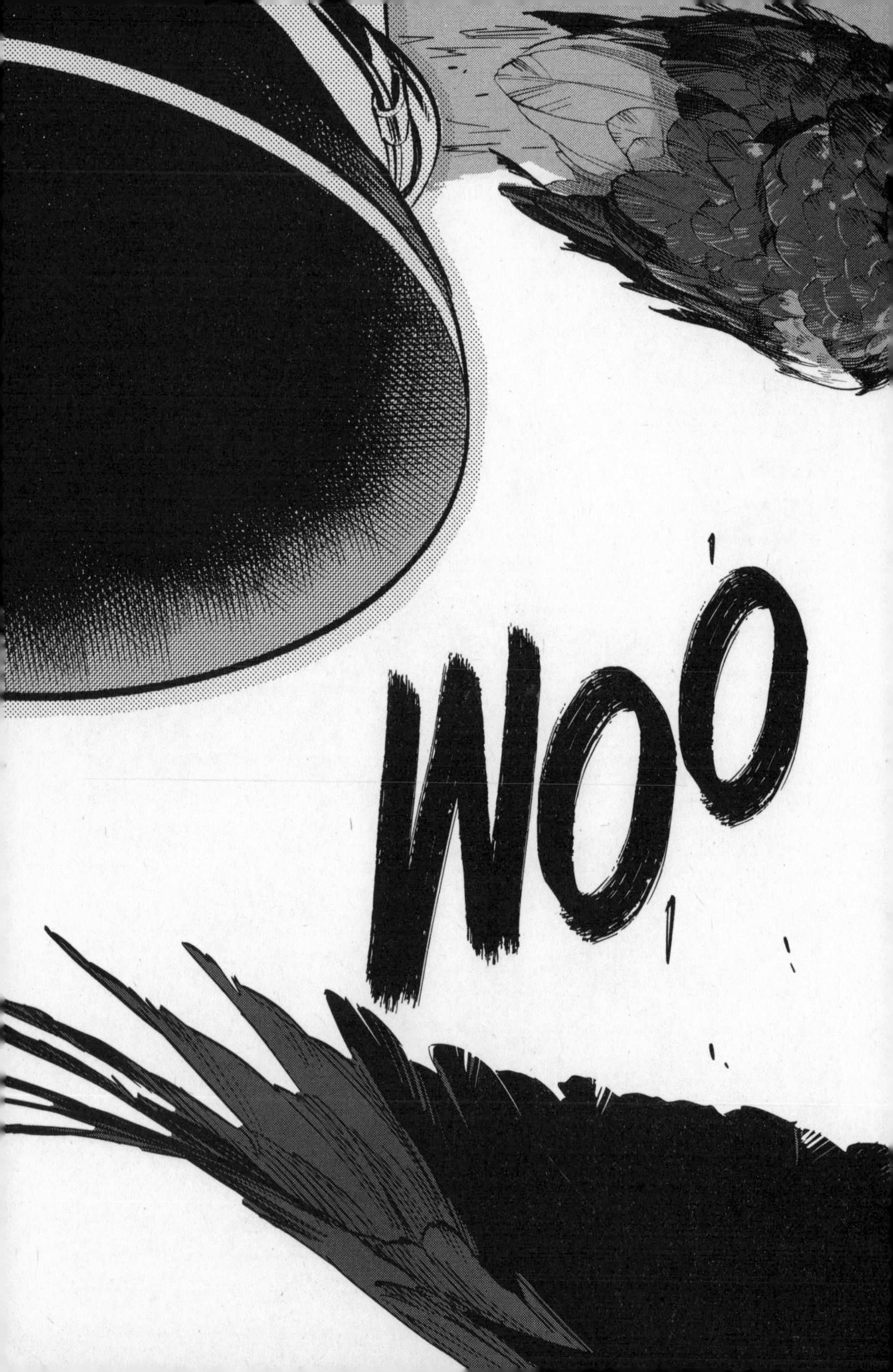
WOOO

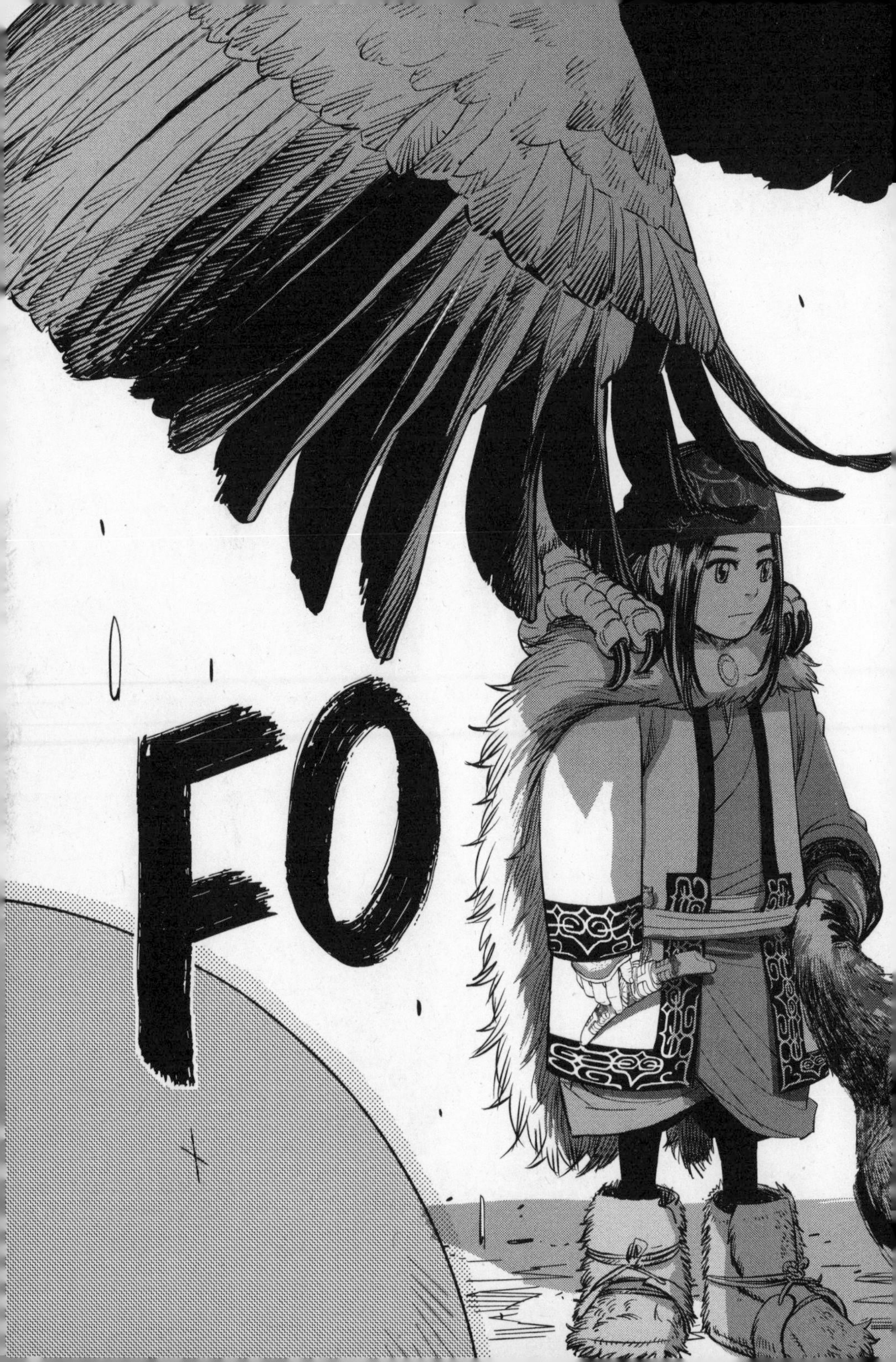
FO

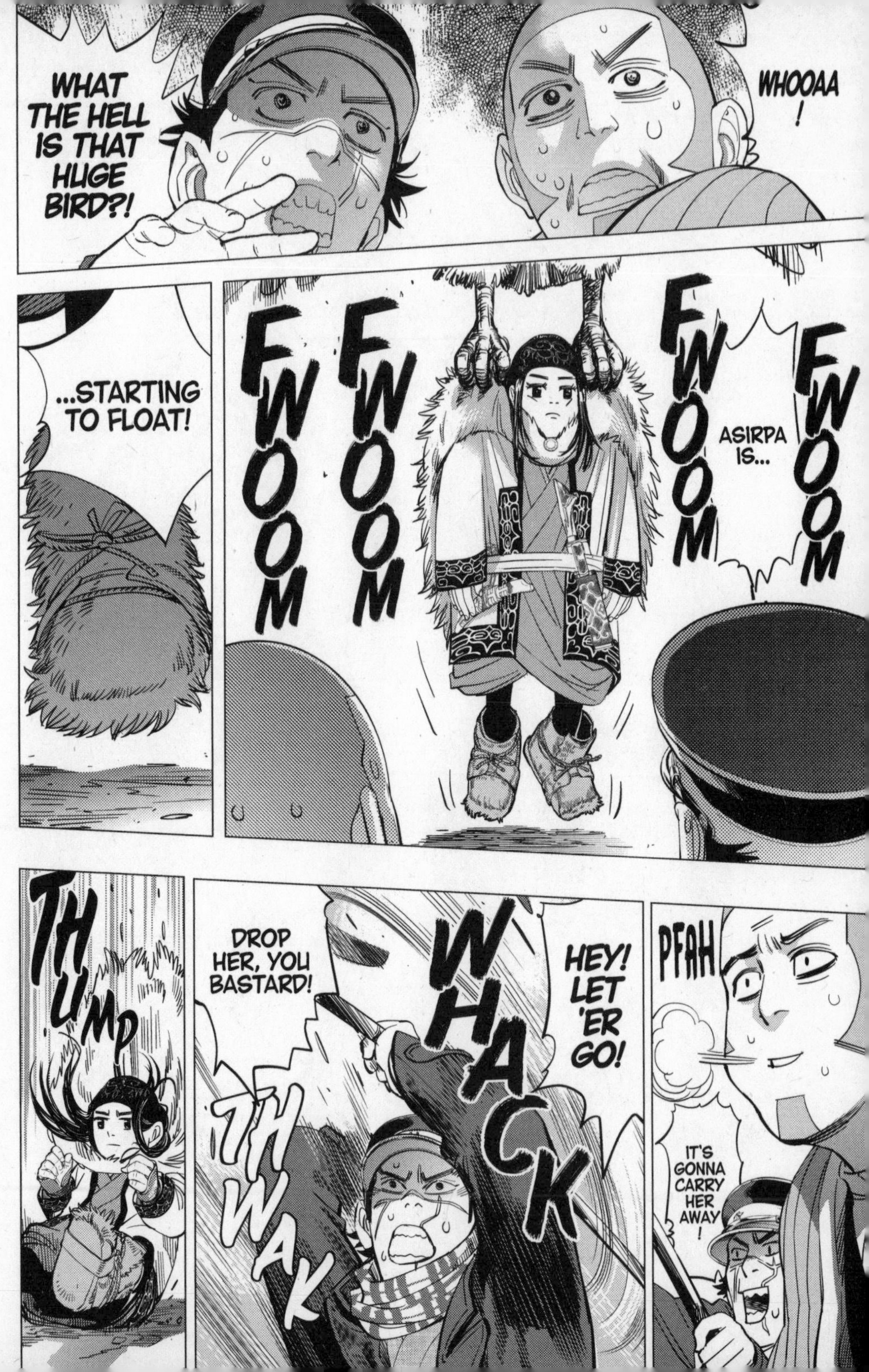
WHOOAA!
WHAT THE HELL IS THAT HUGE BIRD?!
FWOOM
ASIRPA IS...
FWOOM
FWOOM
FWOOM
...STARTING TO FLOAT!
PFAH
IT'S GONNA CARRY HER AWAY!
HEY! LET 'ER GO!
WHACK
DROP HER, YOU BASTARD!
THWAK
THUMP

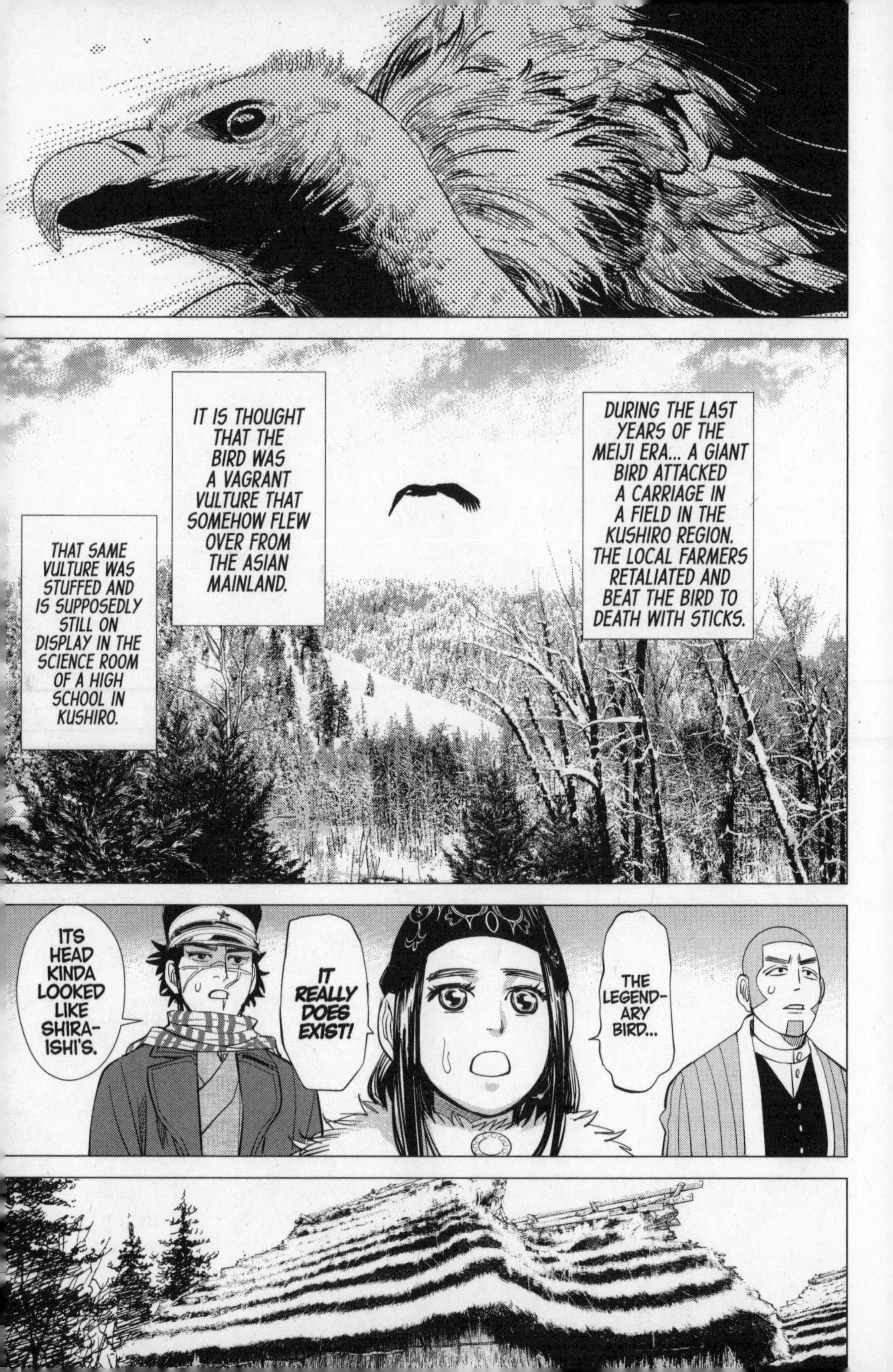
DURING THE LAST YEARS OF THE MEIJI ERA... A GIANT BIRD ATTACKED A CARRIAGE IN A FIELD IN THE KUSHIRO REGION. THE LOCAL FARMERS RETALIATED AND BEAT THE BIRD TO DEATH WITH STICKS.
IT IS THOUGHT THAT THE BIRD WAS A VAGRANT VULTURE THAT SOMEHOW FLEW OVER FROM THE ASIAN MAINLAND.
THAT SAME VULTURE WAS STUFFED AND IS SUPPOSEDLY STILL ON DISPLAY IN THE SCIENCE ROOM OF A HIGH SCHOOL IN KUSHIRO.
THE LEGENDARY BIRD...
IT REALLY DOES EXIST!
ITS HEAD KINDA LOOKED LIKE SHIRAISHI'S.

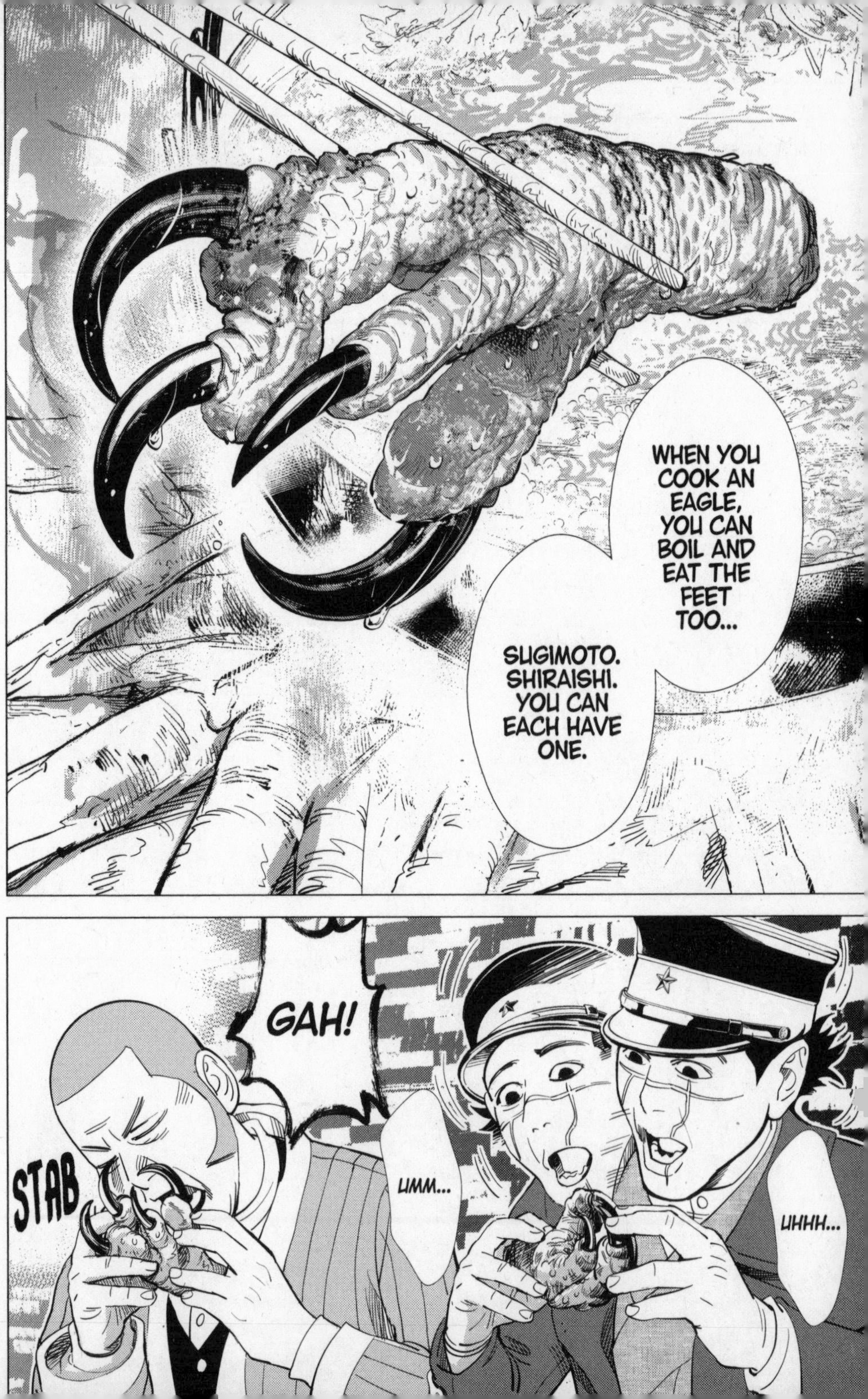
WHEN YOU COOK AN EAGLE, YOU CAN BOIL AND EAT THE FEET TOO...
SUGIMOTO. SHIRAISHI. YOU CAN EACH HAVE ONE.
UHHH...
UMM...
GAH!
STAB

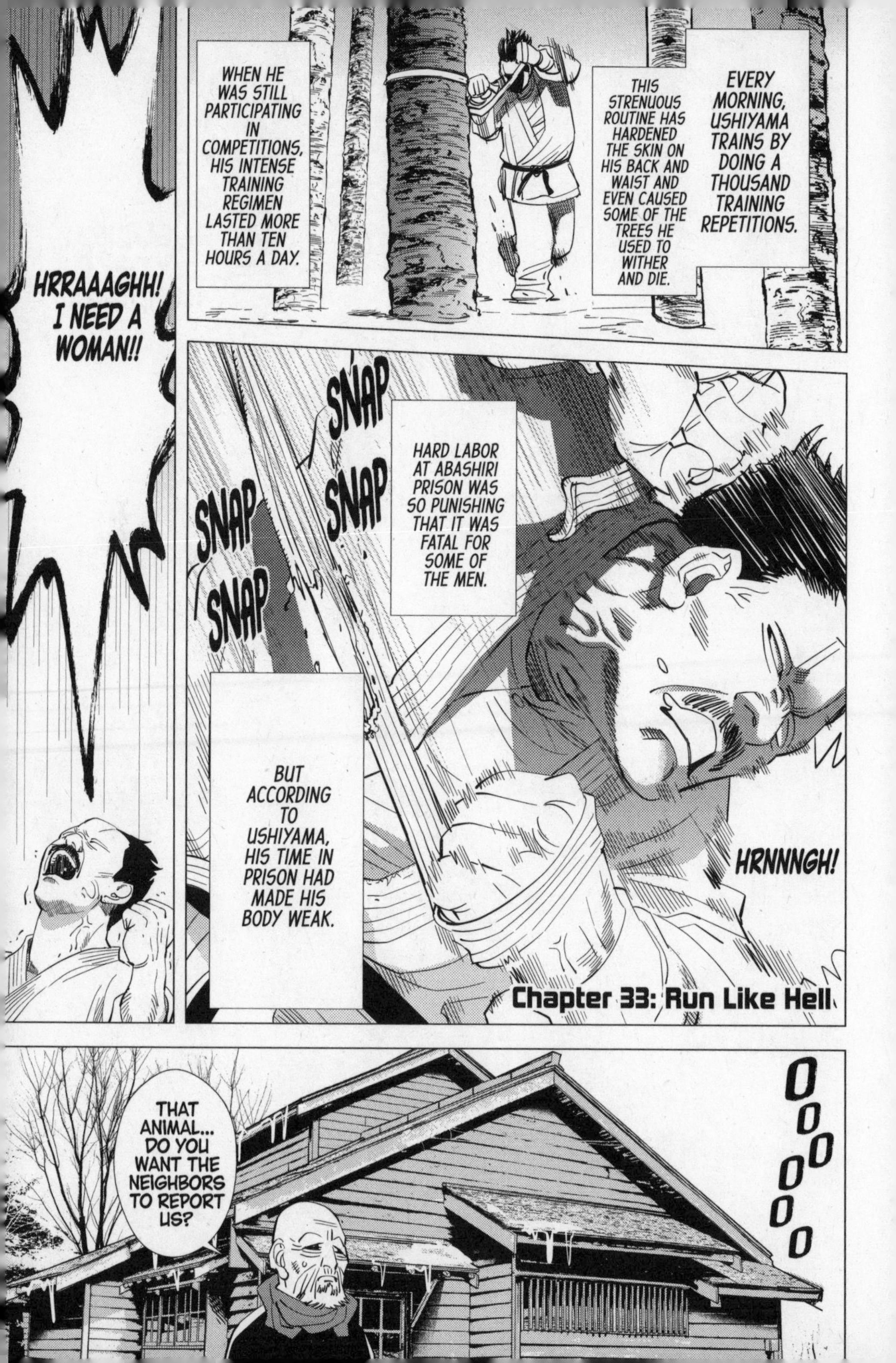
EVERY MORNING, USHIYAMA TRAINS BY DOING A THOUSAND TRAINING REPETITIONS.
THIS STRENUOUS ROUTINE HAS HARDENED THE SKIN ON HIS BACK AND WAIST AND EVEN CAUSED SOME OF THE TREES HE USED TO WITHER AND DIE.
WHEN HE WAS STILL PARTICIPATING IN COMPETITIONS, HIS INTENSE TRAINING REGIMEN LASTED MORE THAN TEN HOURS A DAY.
HRRAAAGHH! I NEED A WOMAN!!
HRNNNGH!
HARD LABOR AT ABASHIRI PRISON WAS SO PUNISHING THAT IT WAS FATAL FOR SOME OF THE MEN.
SNAP SNAP
SNAP SNAP
BUT ACCORDING TO USHIYAMA, HIS TIME IN PRISON HAD MADE HIS BODY WEAK.
Chapter 33: Run Like Hell
OOOOOOO
THAT ANIMAL... DO YOU WANT THE NEIGHBORS TO REPORT US?

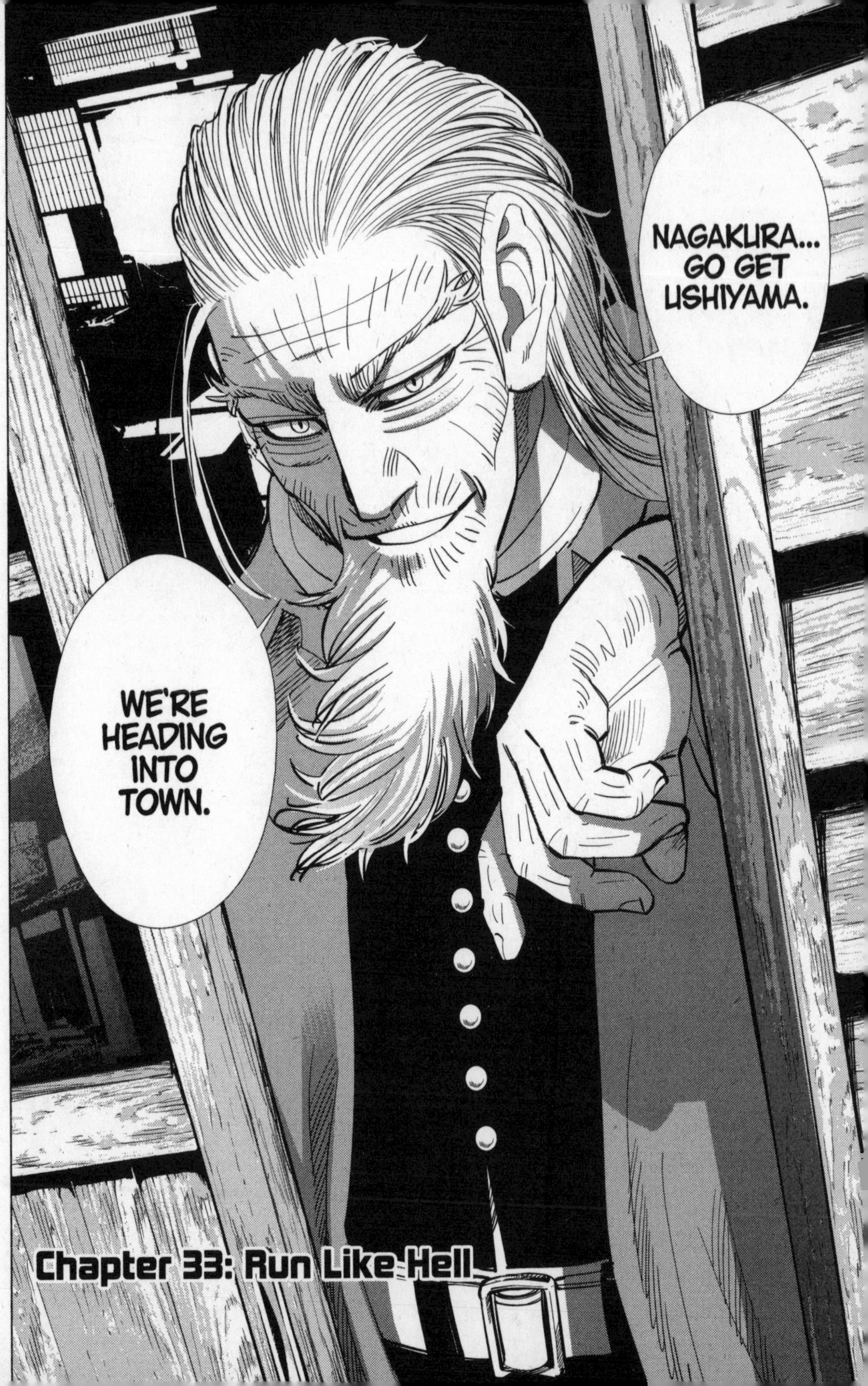
NAGAKURA... GO GET USHIYAMA.
WE'RE HEADING INTO TOWN.
Chapter 33: Run Like Hell

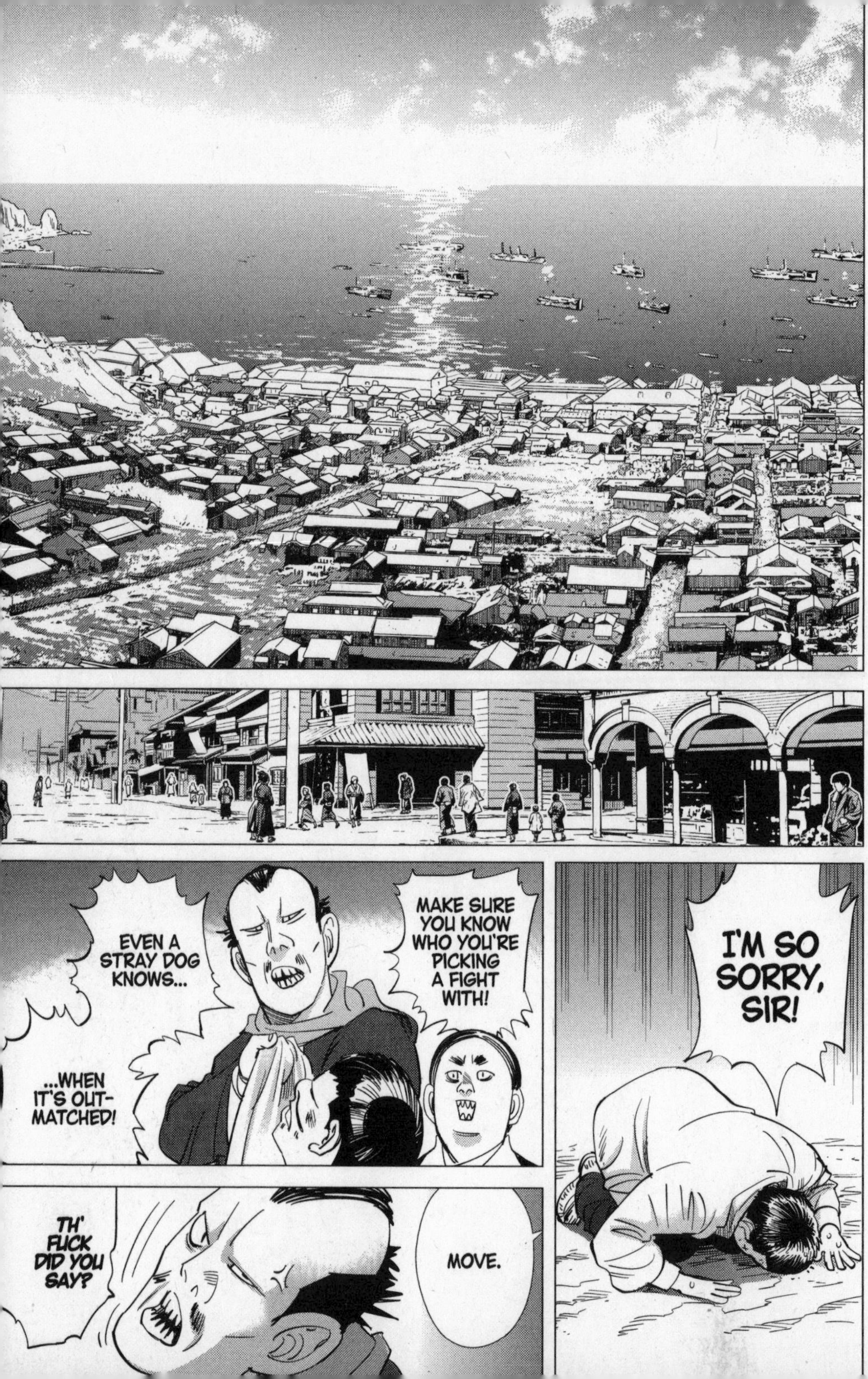
I'M SO SORRY, SIR!
MAKE SURE YOU KNOW WHO YOU'RE PICKING A FIGHT WITH!
EVEN A STRAY DOG KNOWS...
...WHEN IT'S OUT-MATCHED!
MOVE.
TH' FUCK DID YOU SAY?

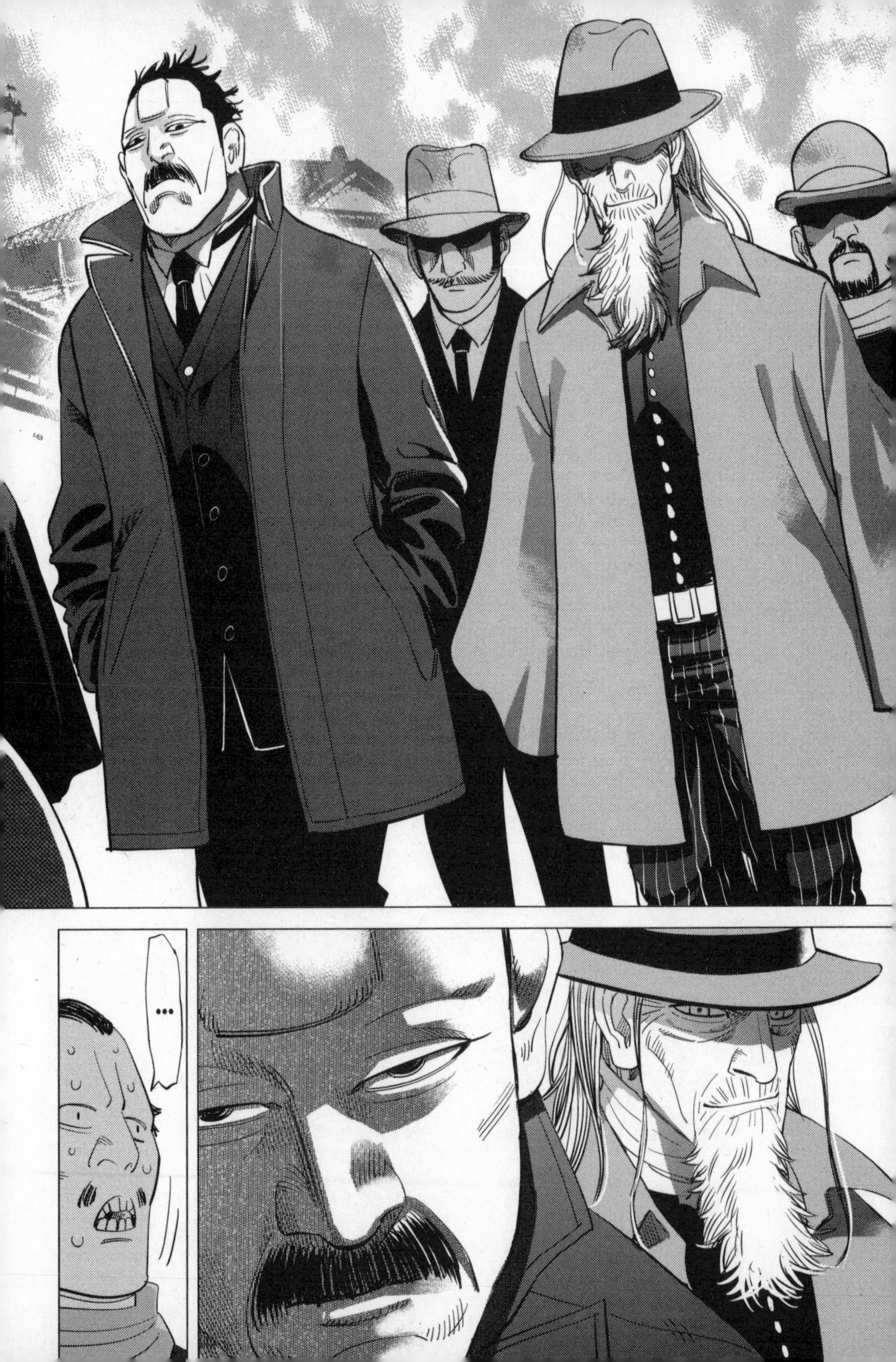
...

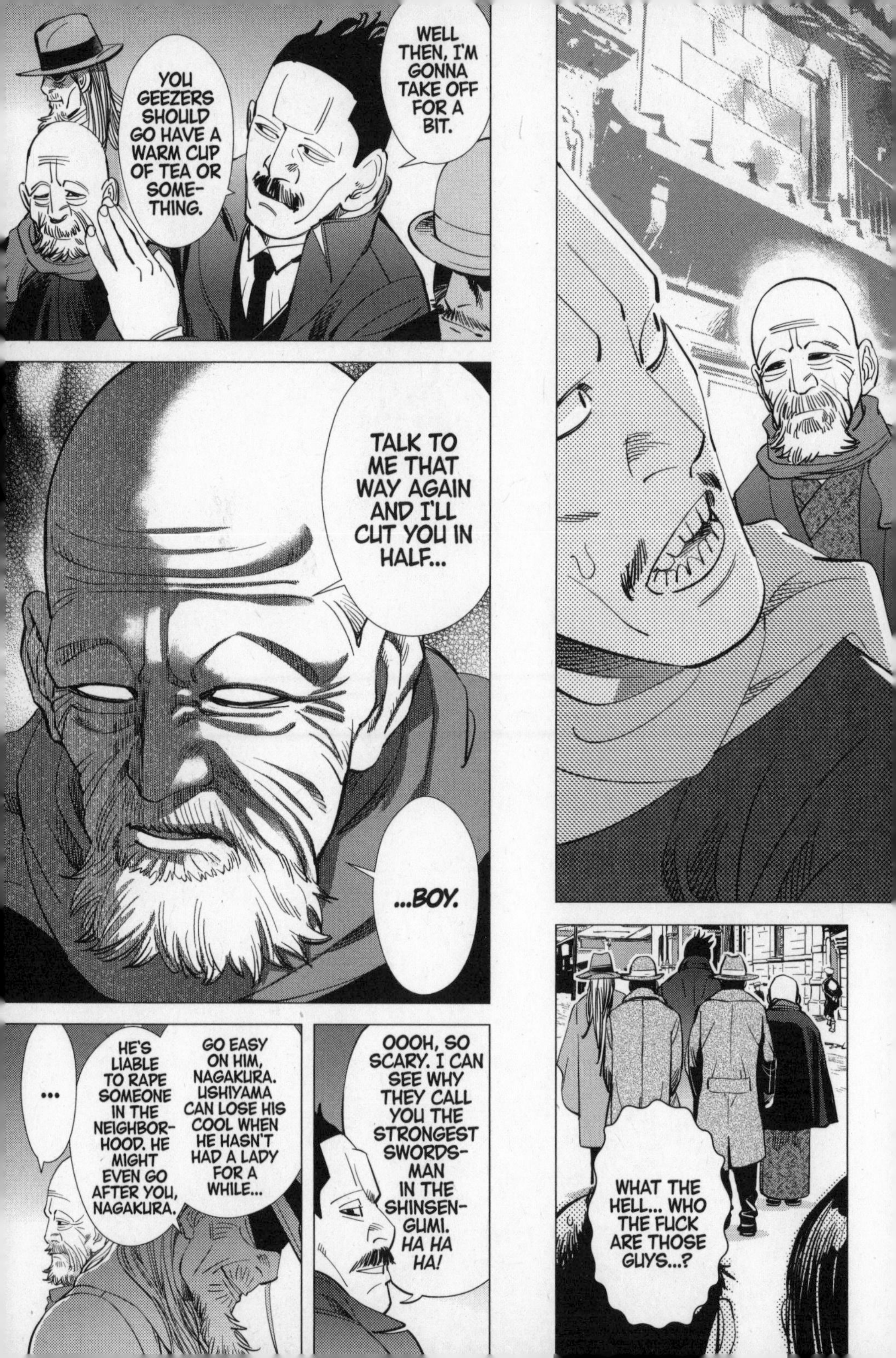
WHAT THE HELL... WHO THE FUCK ARE THOSE GUYS...?
WELL THEN, I'M GONNA TAKE OFF FOR A BIT.
YOU GEEZERS SHOULD GO HAVE A WARM CUP OF TEA OR SOME-THING.
TALK TO ME THAT WAY AGAIN AND I'LL CUT YOU IN HALF...
...BOY.
OOOH, SO SCARY. I CAN SEE WHY THEY CALL YOU THE STRONGEST SWORDS-MAN IN THE SHINSEN-GUMI. HA HA HA!
GO EASY ON HIM, NAGAKURA. USHIYAMA CAN LOSE HIS COOL WHEN HE HASN'T HAD A LADY FOR A WHILE...
HE'S LIABLE TO RAPE SOMEONE IN THE NEIGHBOR-HOOD. HE MIGHT EVEN GO AFTER YOU, NAGAKURA.
...

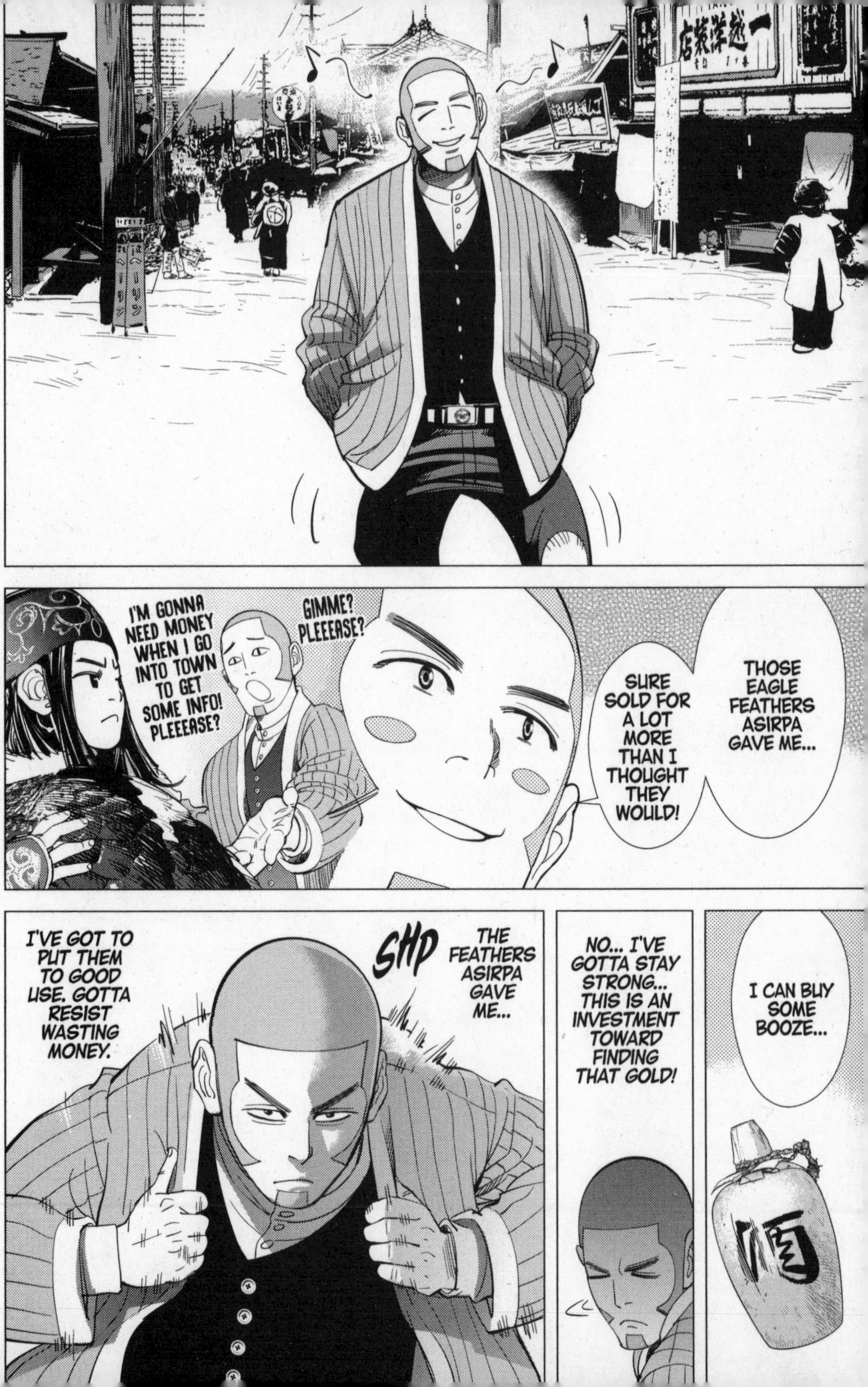
THOSE EAGLE FEATHERS ASIRPA GAVE ME...
SURE SOLD FOR A LOT MORE THAN I THOUGHT THEY WOULD!
GIMME? PLEEEASE?
I'M GONNA NEED MONEY WHEN I GO INTO TOWN TO GET SOME INFO! PLEEEASE?
I CAN BUY SOME BOOZE...
NO... I'VE GOTTA STAY STRONG... THIS IS AN INVESTMENT TOWARD FINDING THAT GOLD!
THE FEATHERS ASIRPA GAVE ME...
SHP
I'VE GOT TO PUT THEM TO GOOD USE. GOTTA RESIST WASTING MONEY.

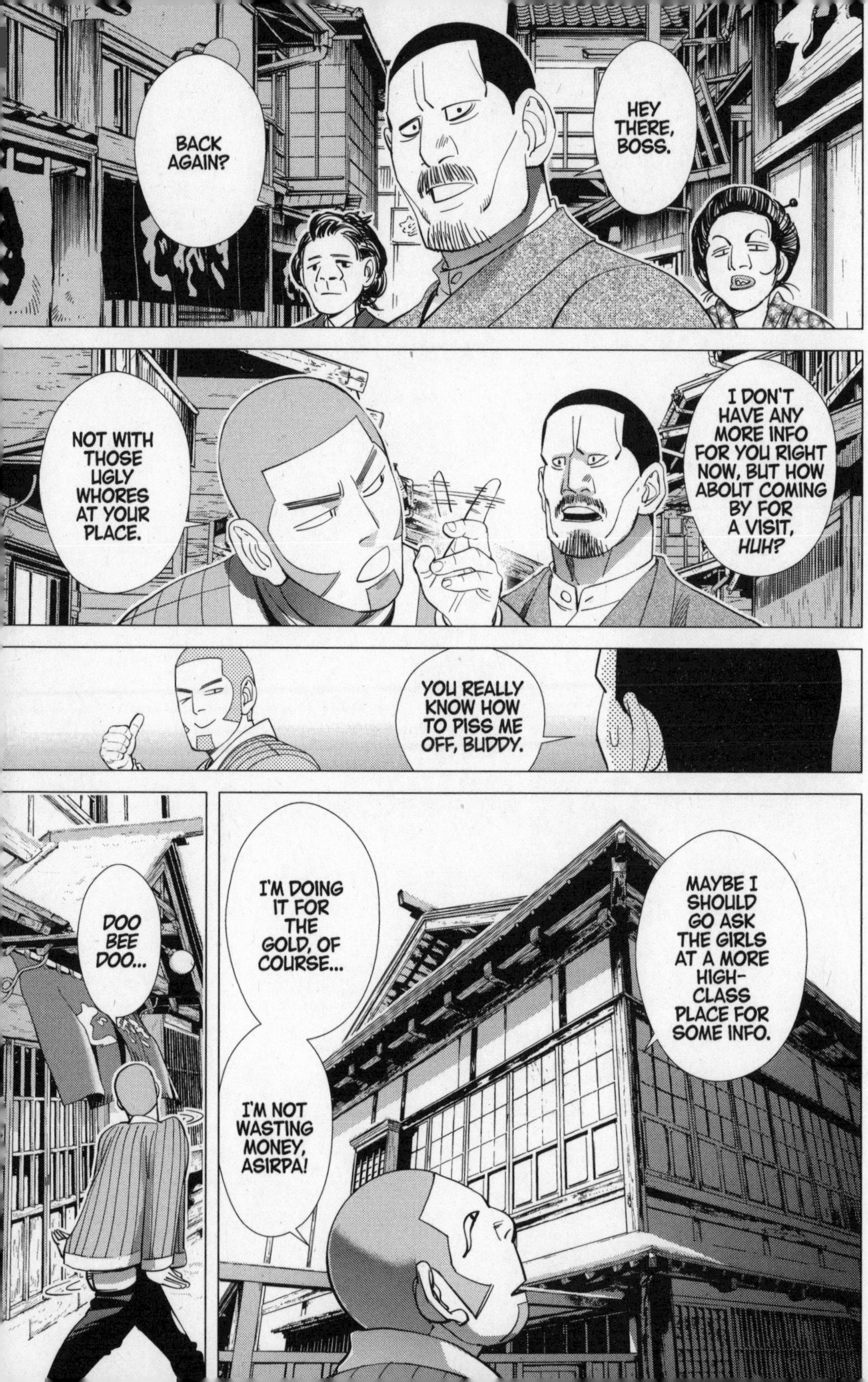
HEY THERE, BOSS.
BACK AGAIN?
I DON'T HAVE ANY MORE INFO FOR YOU RIGHT NOW, BUT HOW ABOUT COMING BY FOR A VISIT, HUH?
NOT WITH THOSE UGLY WHORES AT YOUR PLACE.
YOU REALLY KNOW HOW TO PISS ME OFF, BUDDY.
MAYBE I SHOULD GO ASK THE GIRLS AT A MORE HIGH-CLASS PLACE FOR SOME INFO.
I'M DOING IT FOR THE GOLD, OF COURSE...
I'M NOT WASTING MONEY, ASIRPA!
DOO BEE DOO...

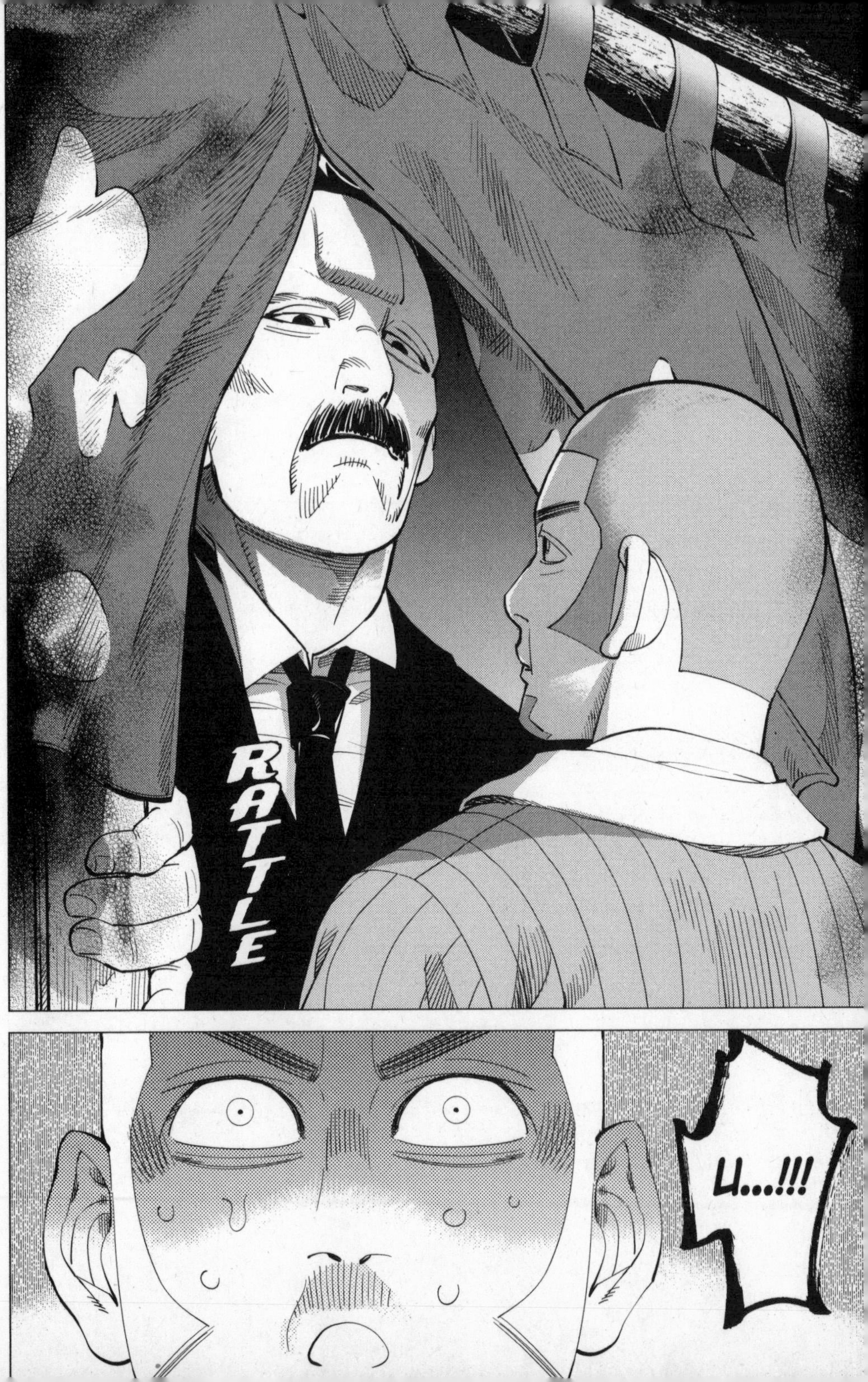
RATTLE
U...!!!

HEY THERE, YOSHITAKE SHIRAISHI.

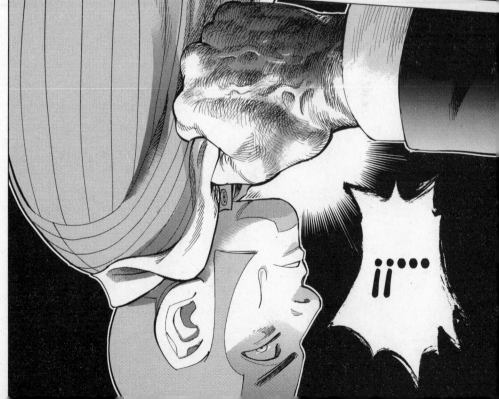

¡¡...!!

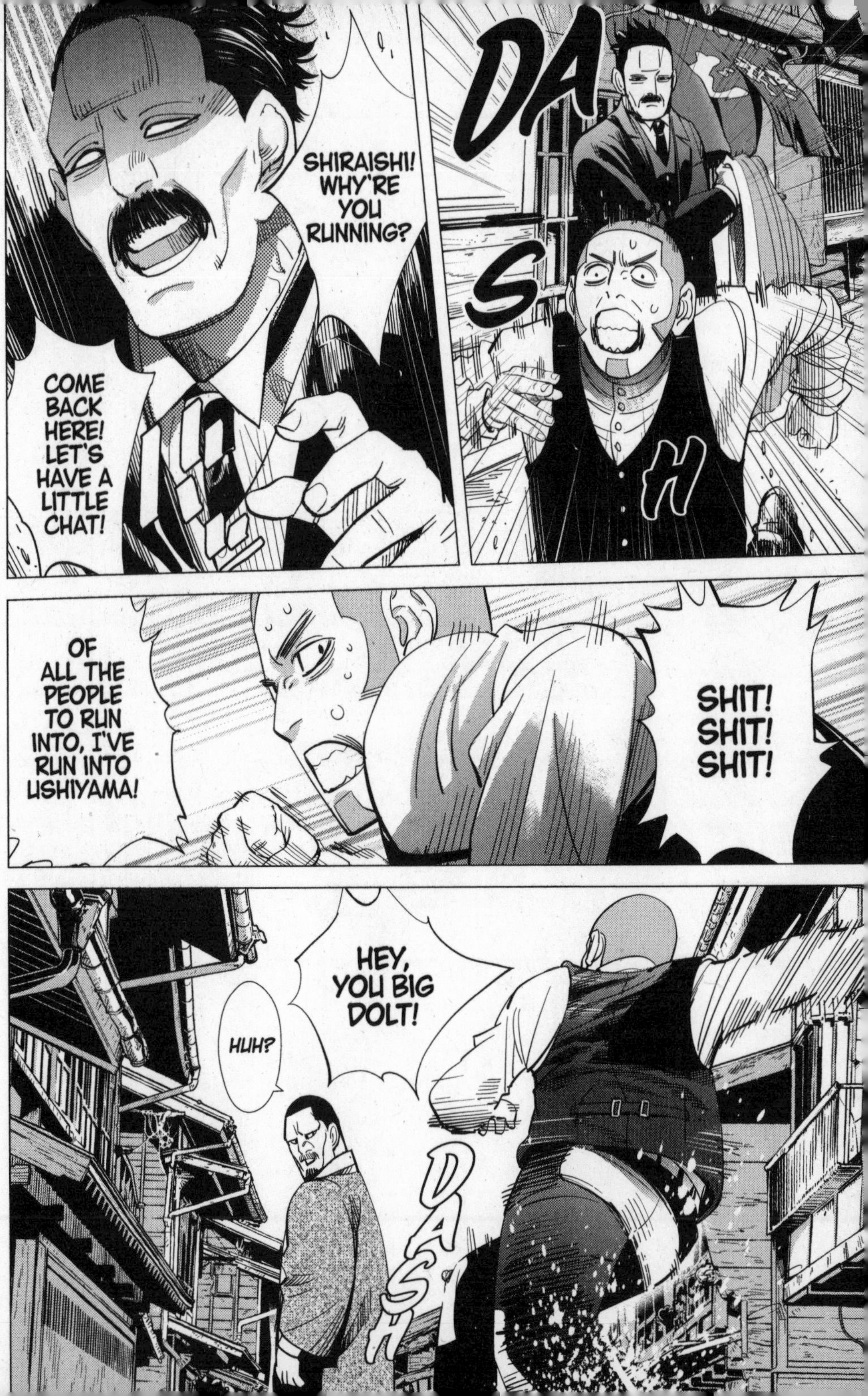
DA
S
H
SHIRAISHI! WHY'RE YOU RUNNING?
COME BACK HERE! LET'S HAVE A LITTLE CHAT!
SHIT! SHIT! SHIT!
OF ALL THE PEOPLE TO RUN INTO, I'VE RUN INTO USHIYAMA!
HEY, YOU BIG DOLT!
HUH?
DASH

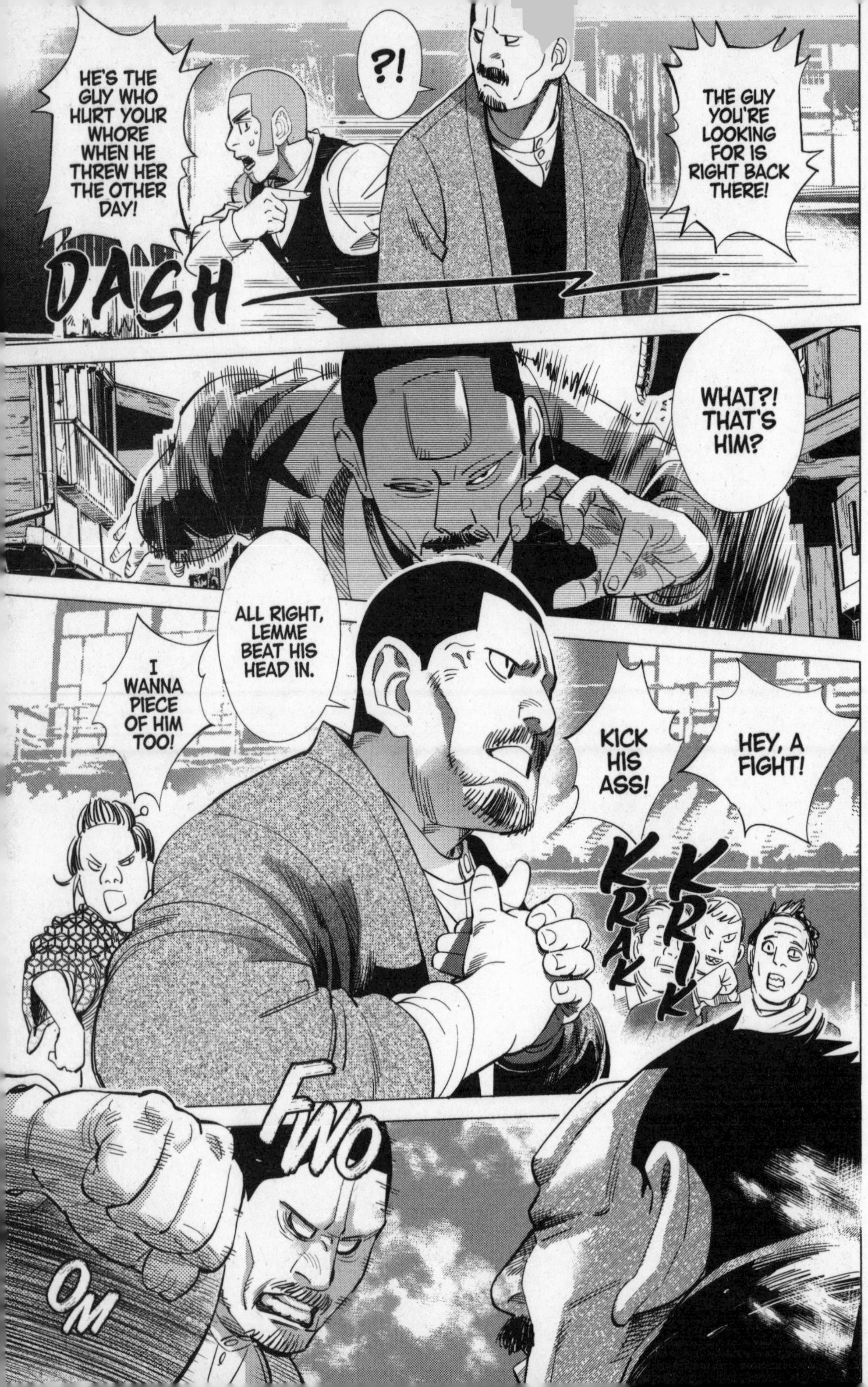
THE GUY YOU'RE LOOKING FOR IS RIGHT BACK THERE!
?!
HE'S THE GUY WHO HURT YOUR WHORE WHEN HE THREW HER THE OTHER DAY!
DASH
WHAT?! THAT'S HIM?
HEY, A FIGHT!
KICK HIS ASS!
KRIK
KRAK
ALL RIGHT, LEMME BEAT HIS HEAD IN.
I WANNA PIECE OF HIM TOO!
FWOOM

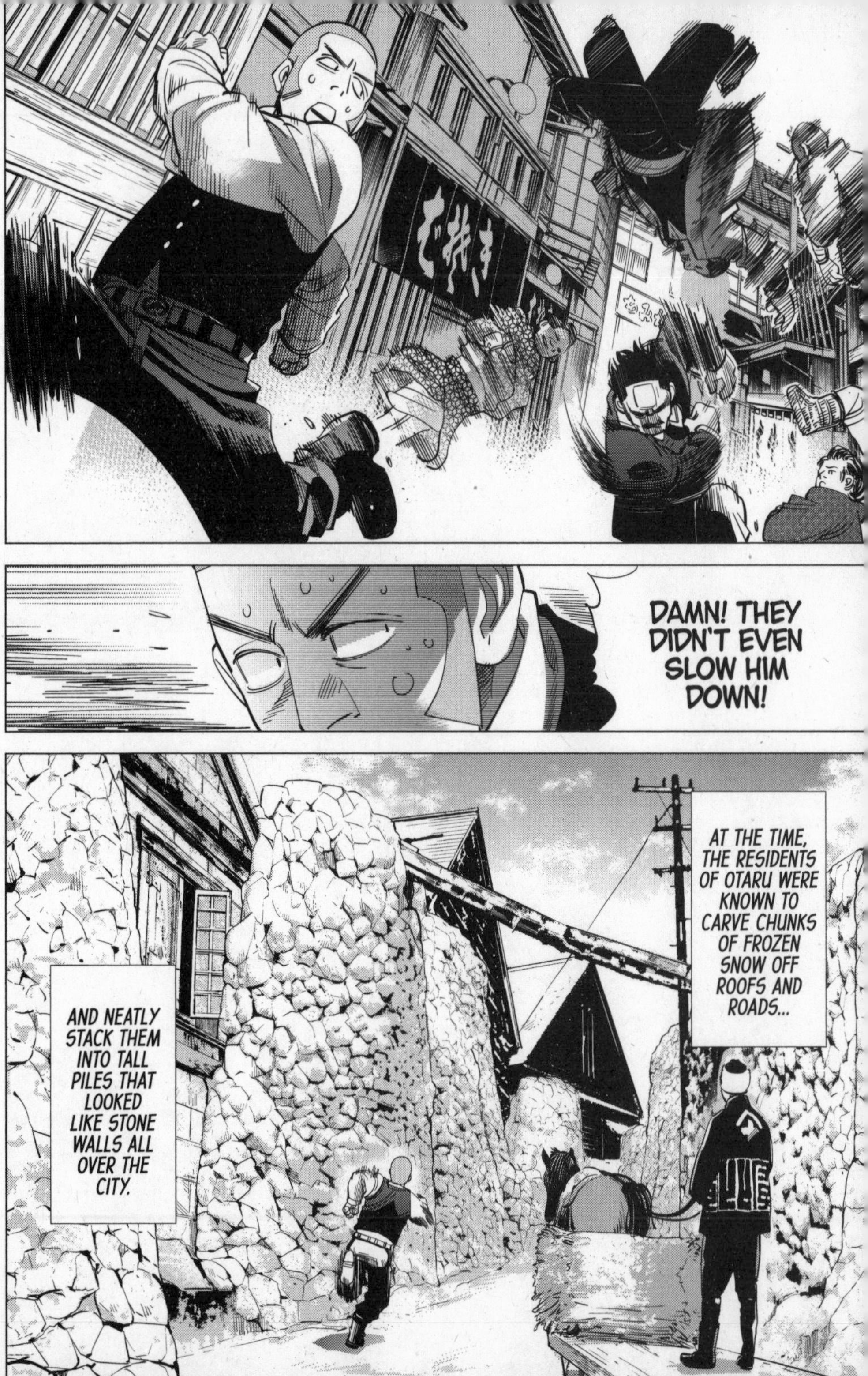
DAMN! THEY DIDN'T EVEN SLOW HIM DOWN!
AT THE TIME, THE RESIDENTS OF OTARU WERE KNOWN TO CARVE CHUNKS OF FROZEN SNOW OFF ROOFS AND ROADS...
AND NEATLY STACK THEM INTO TALL PILES THAT LOOKED LIKE STONE WALLS ALL OVER THE CITY.

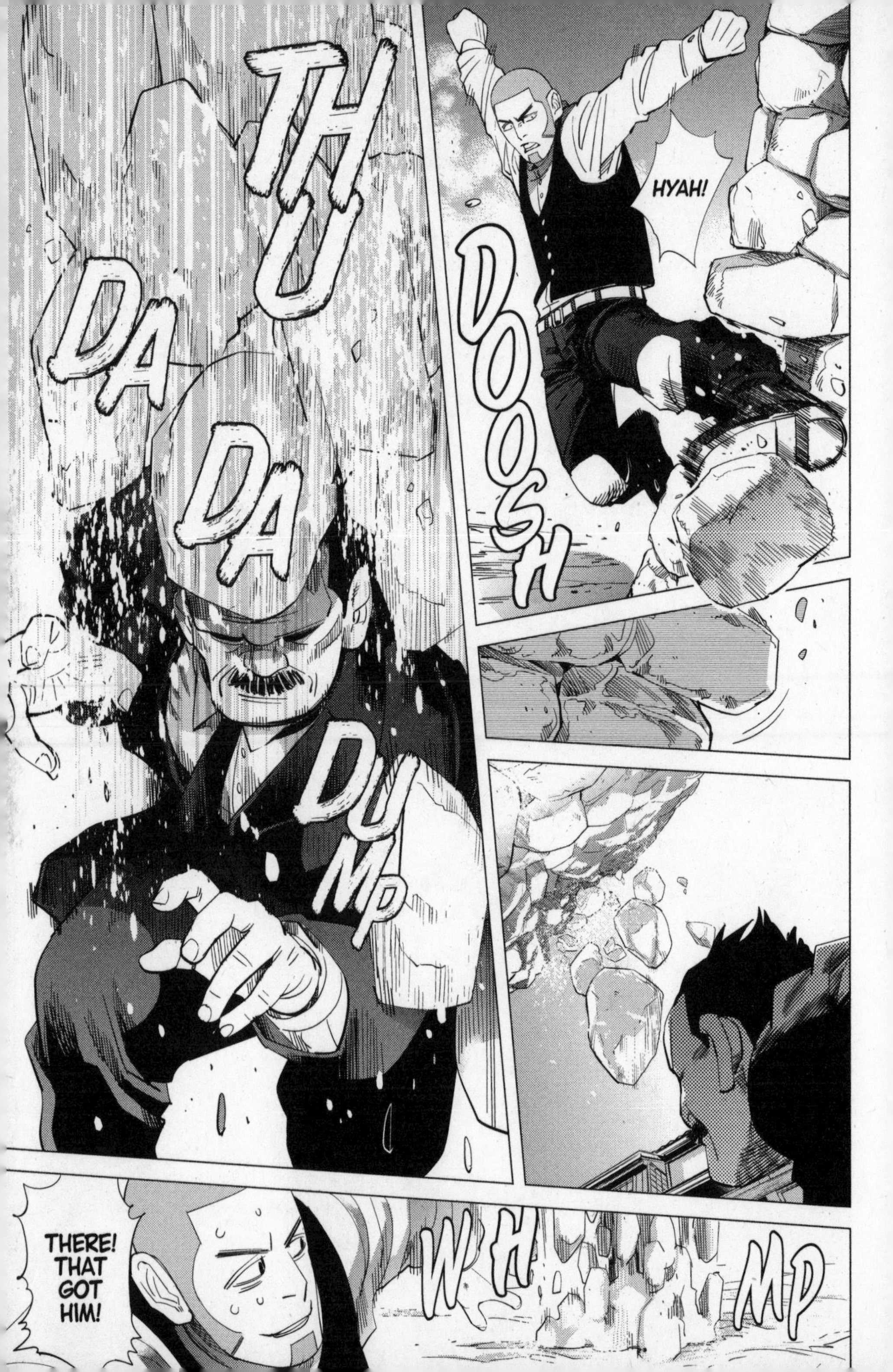
HYAH!
DOOOSH
THUDA DA DUMP
THERE! THAT GOT HIM!
WHMP

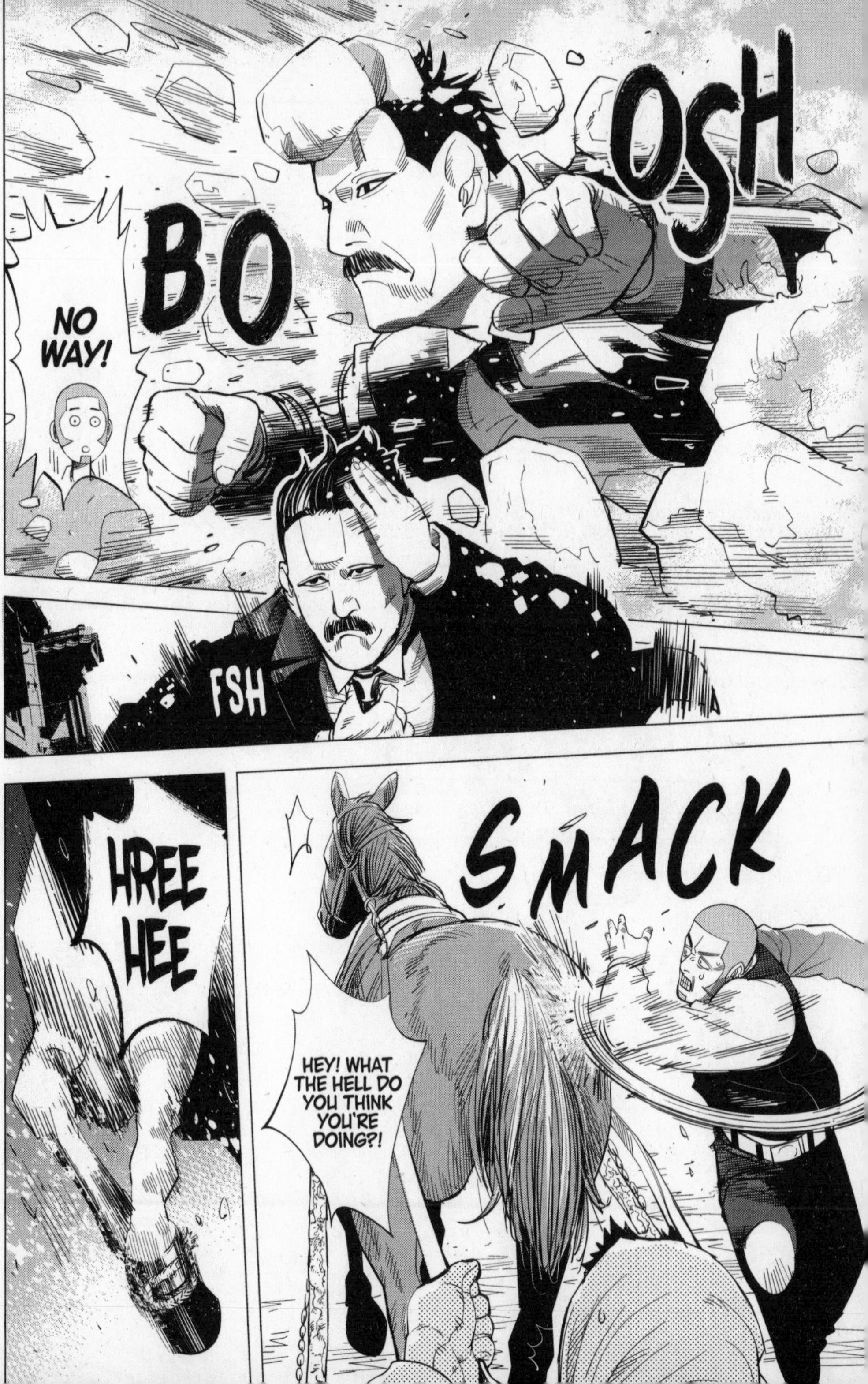
BOOSH
NO WAY!
FSH
SMACK
HEY! WHAT THE HELL DO YOU THINK YOU'RE DOING?!
HREE HEE

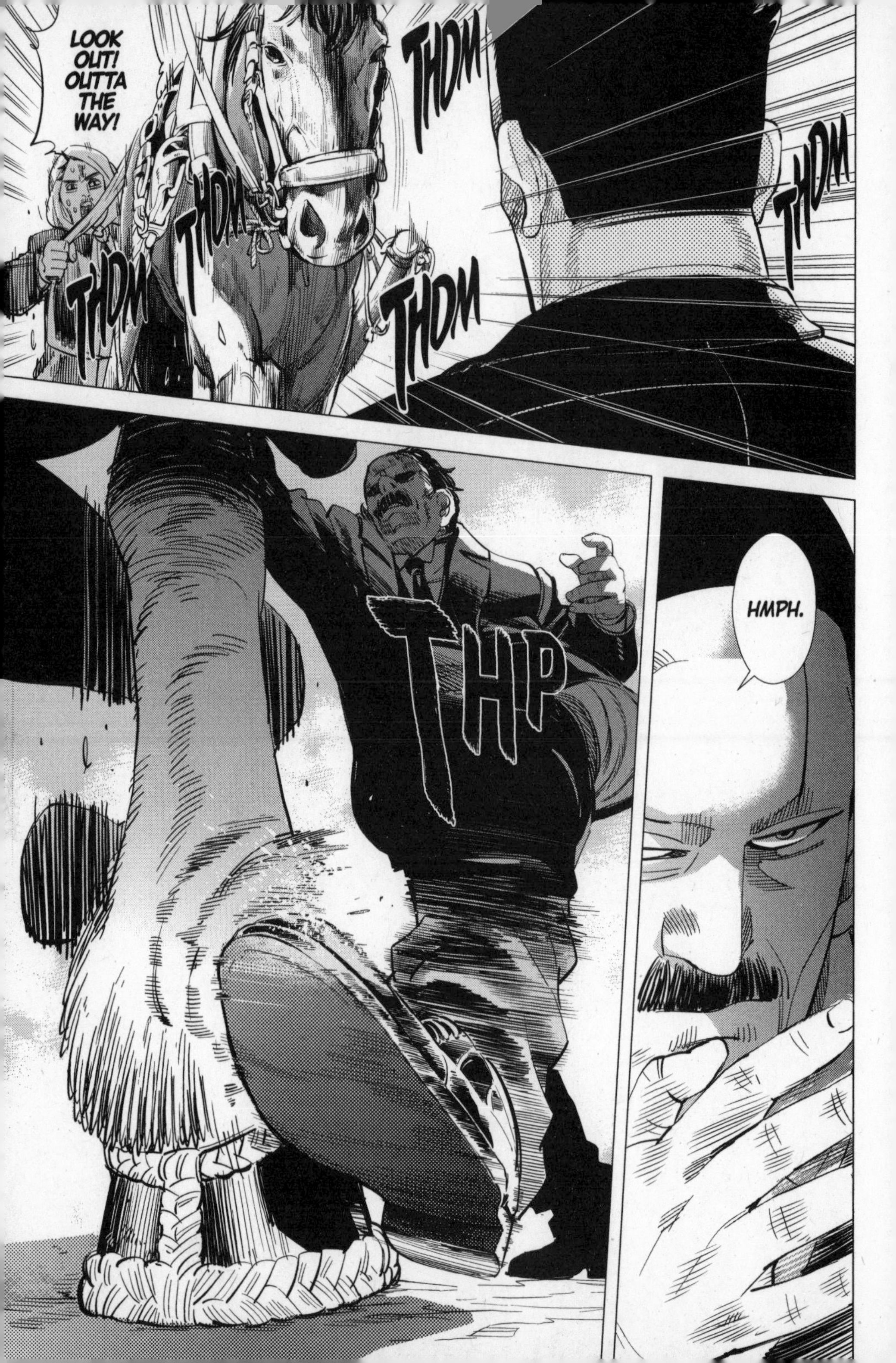
THOM
THOM
THOM
THOM
THOM
THOM
LOOK OUT! OUTTA THE WAY!
HMPH.
THP

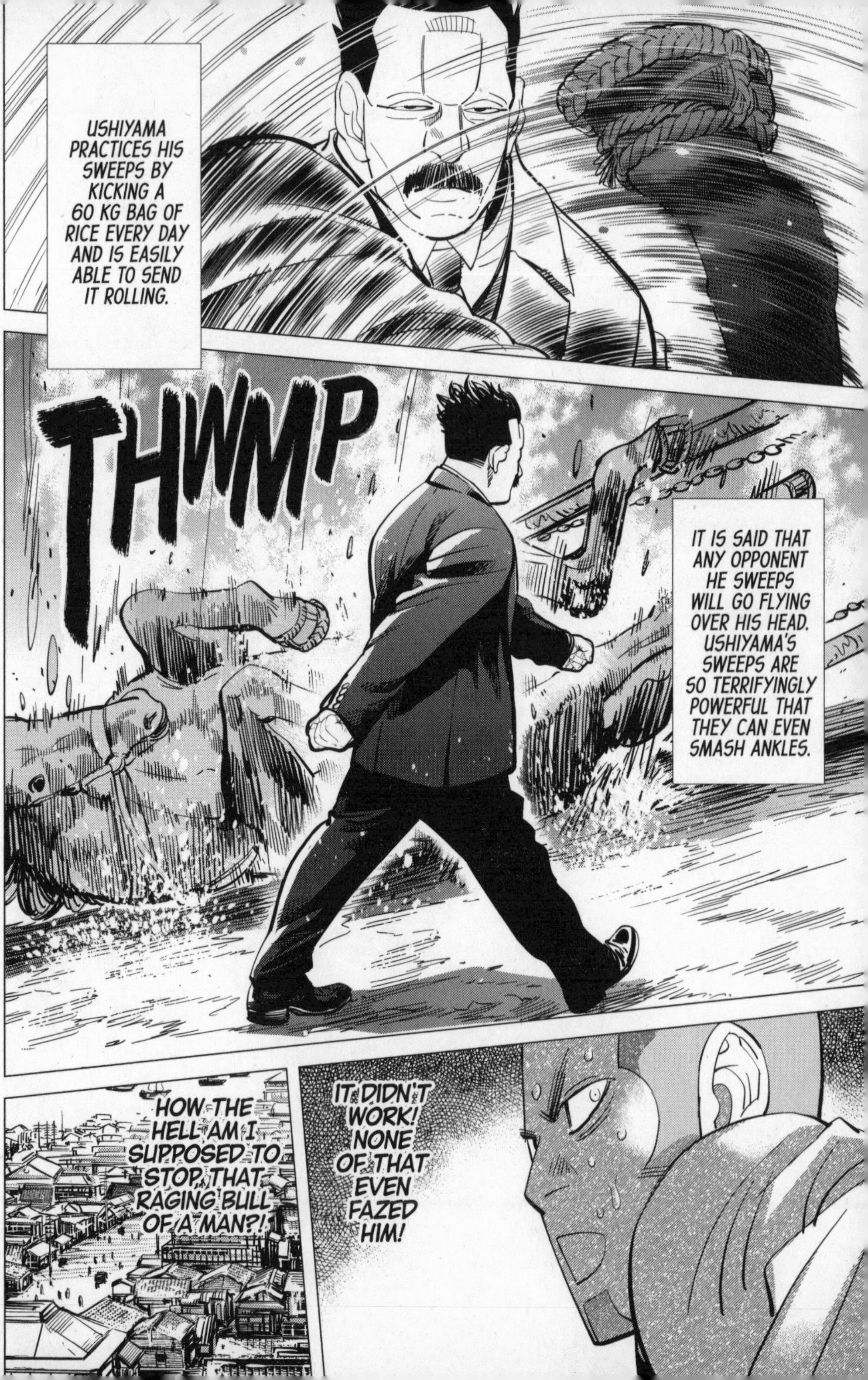
USHIYAMA PRACTICES HIS SWEEPS BY KICKING A 60 KG BAG OF RICE EVERY DAY AND IS EASILY ABLE TO SEND IT ROLLING.
IT IS SAID THAT ANY OPPONENT HE SWEEPS WILL GO FLYING OVER HIS HEAD. USHIYAMA'S SWEEPS ARE SO TERRIFYINGLY POWERFUL THAT THEY CAN EVEN SMASH ANKLES.
THWMP
IT DIDN'T WORK! NONE OF THAT EVEN FAZED HIM!
HOW THE HELL AM I SUPPOSED TO STOP THAT RAGING BULL OF A MAN?!

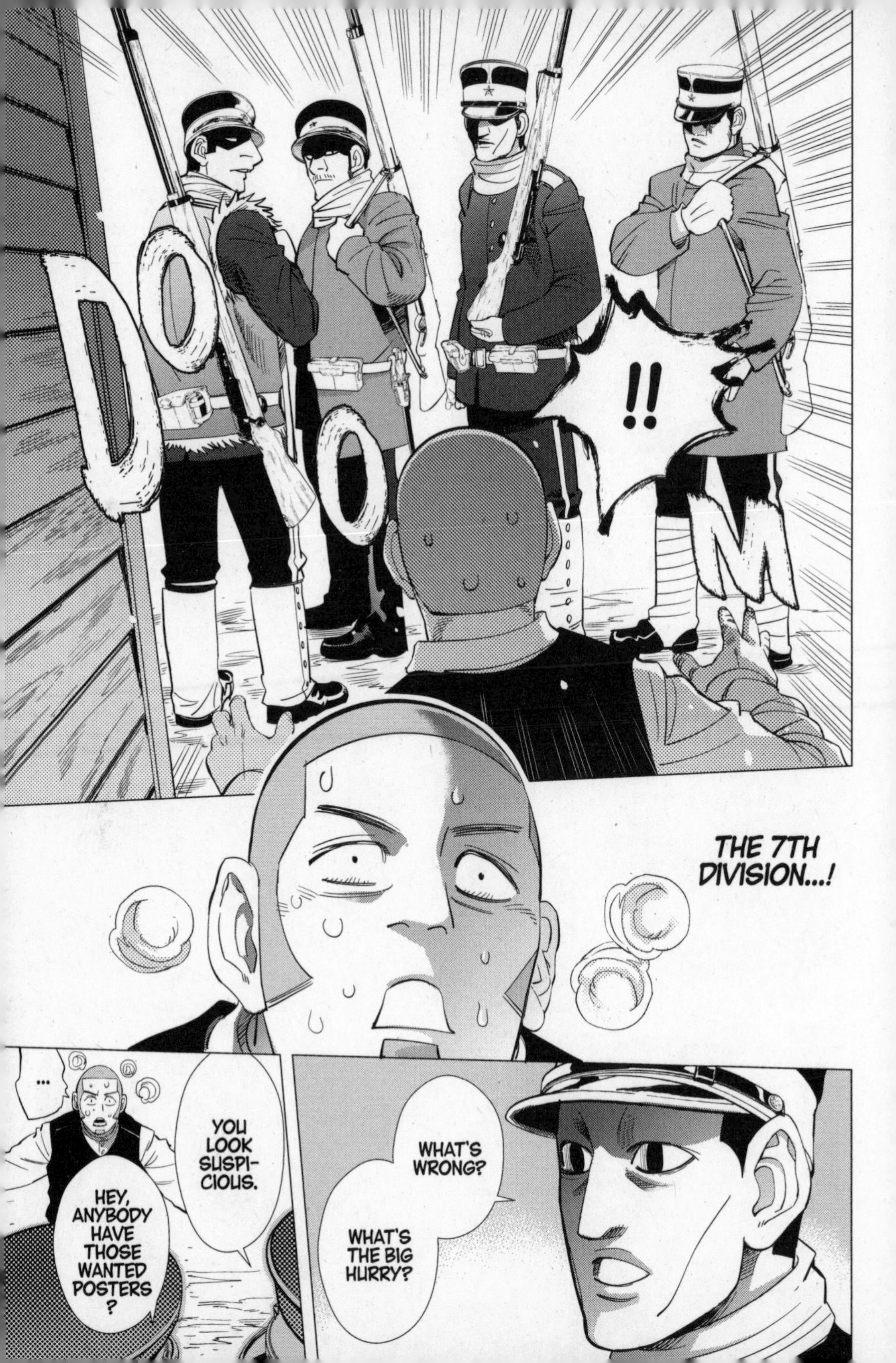
DOOOM
!!
THE 7TH DIVISION...!
WHAT'S WRONG?
WHAT'S THE BIG HURRY?
YOU LOOK SUSPICIOUS.
HEY, ANYBODY HAVE THOSE WANTED POSTERS?
...

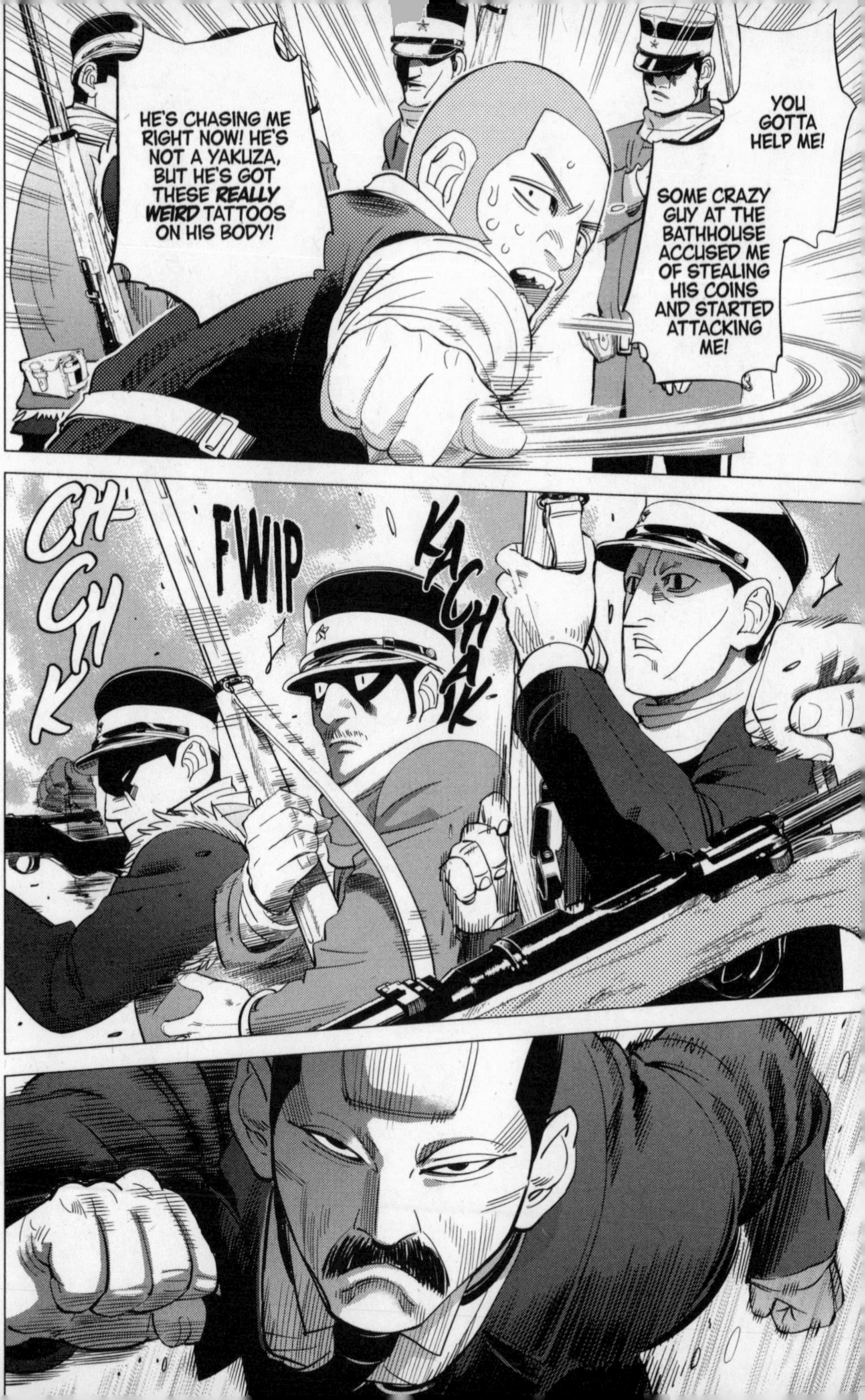
YOU GOTTA HELP ME!
SOME CRAZY GUY AT THE BATHHOUSE ACCUSED ME OF STEALING HIS COINS AND STARTED ATTACKING ME!
HE'S CHASING ME RIGHT NOW! HE'S NOT A YAKUZA, BUT HE'S GOT THESE **REALLY WEIRD** TATTOOS ON HIS BODY!
KACHAK
FWIP
CH CH CH K

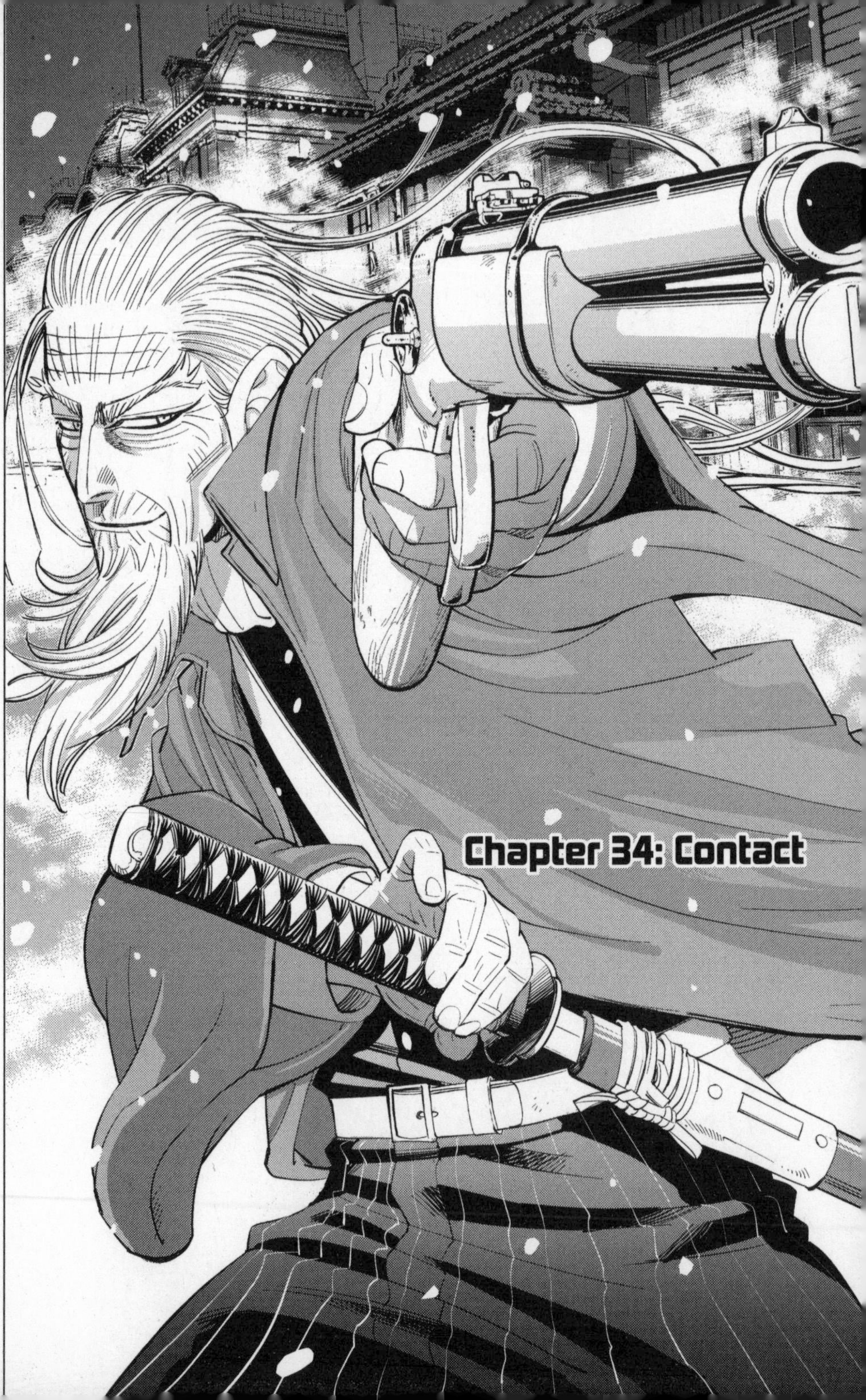
Chapter 34: Contact

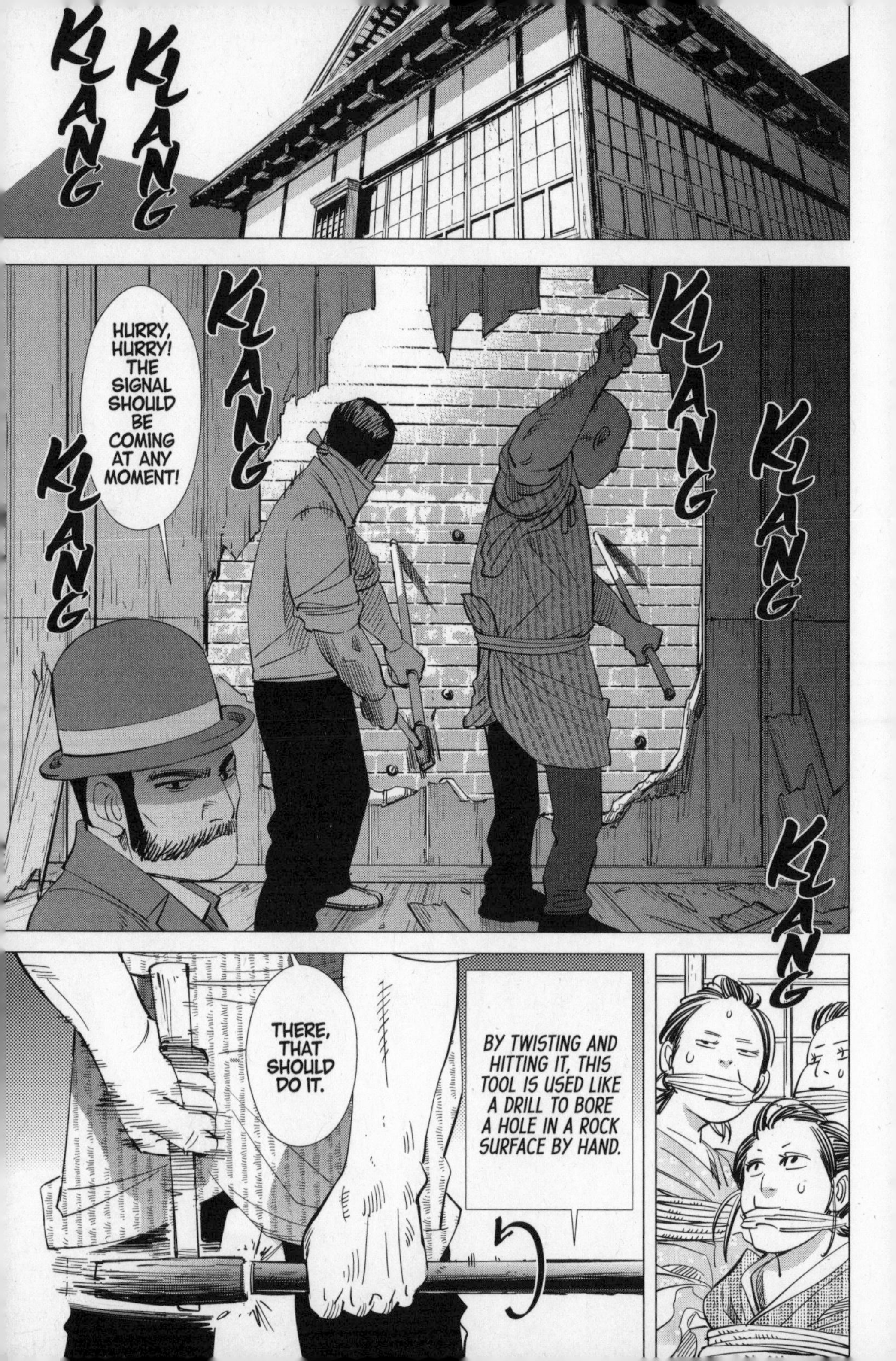
KLANG
KLANG
KLANG
KLANG
KLANG
HURRY, HURRY! THE SIGNAL SHOULD BE COMING AT ANY MOMENT!
KLANG
KLANG
BY TWISTING AND HITTING IT, THIS TOOL IS USED LIKE A DRILL TO BORE A HOLE IN A ROCK SURFACE BY HAND.
THERE, THAT SHOULD DO IT.

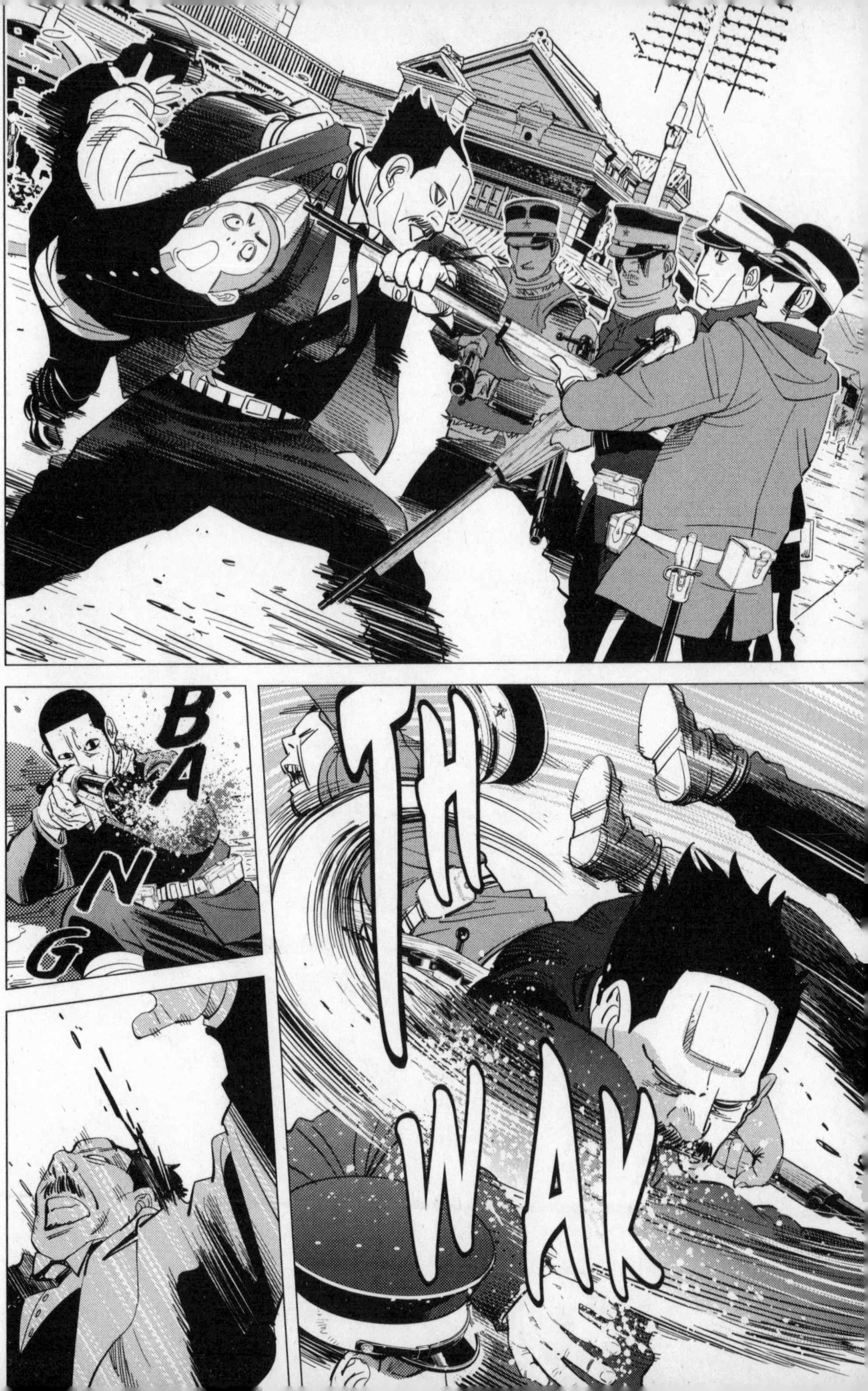
THWAK
BANG

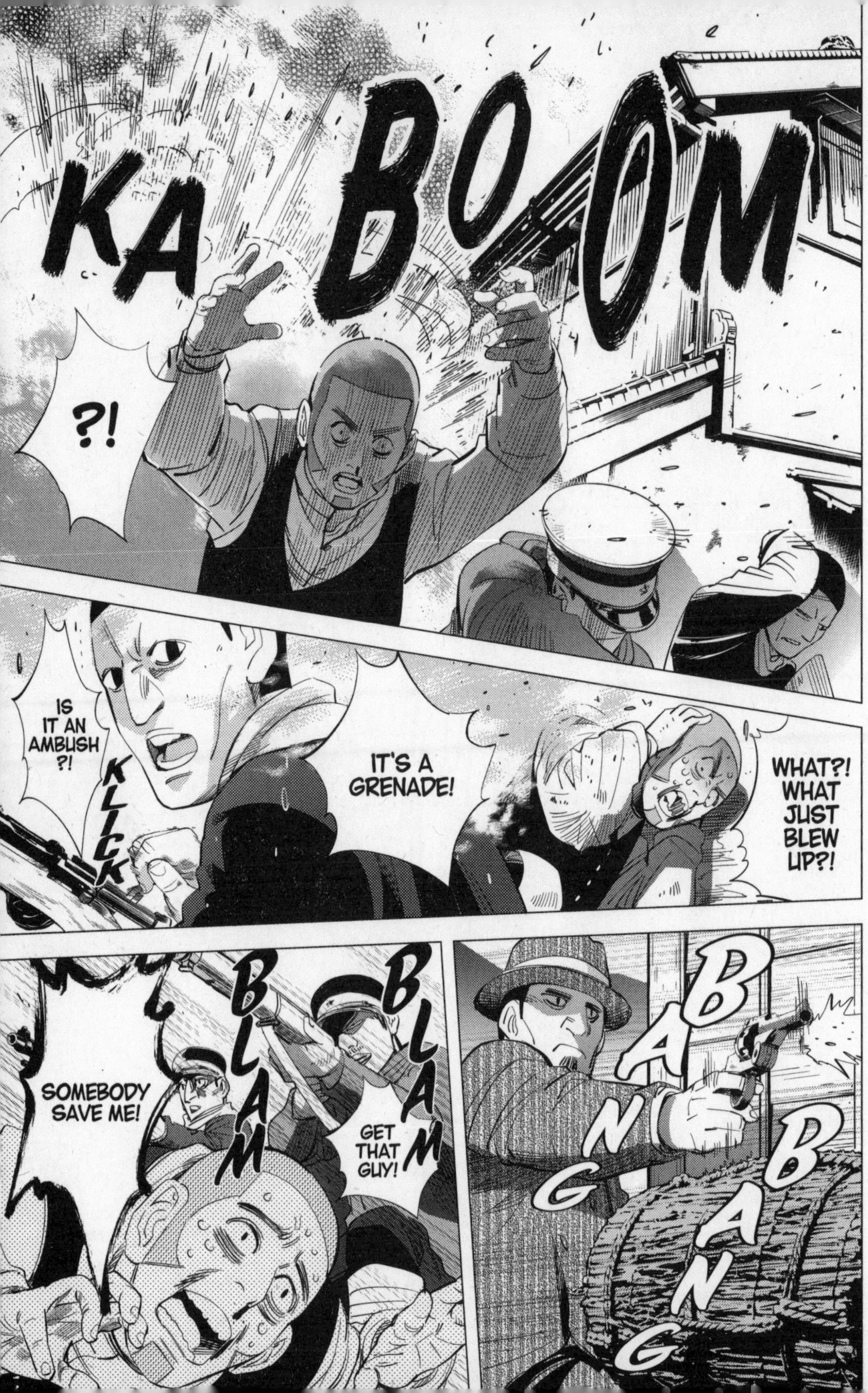
KA-BOOM
?!
WHAT?! WHAT JUST BLEW UP?!
IT'S A GRENADE!
IS IT AN AMBUSH ?!
KLICK
BANG
BANG
BLAM
GET THAT GUY!
BLAM
SOMEBODY SAVE ME!

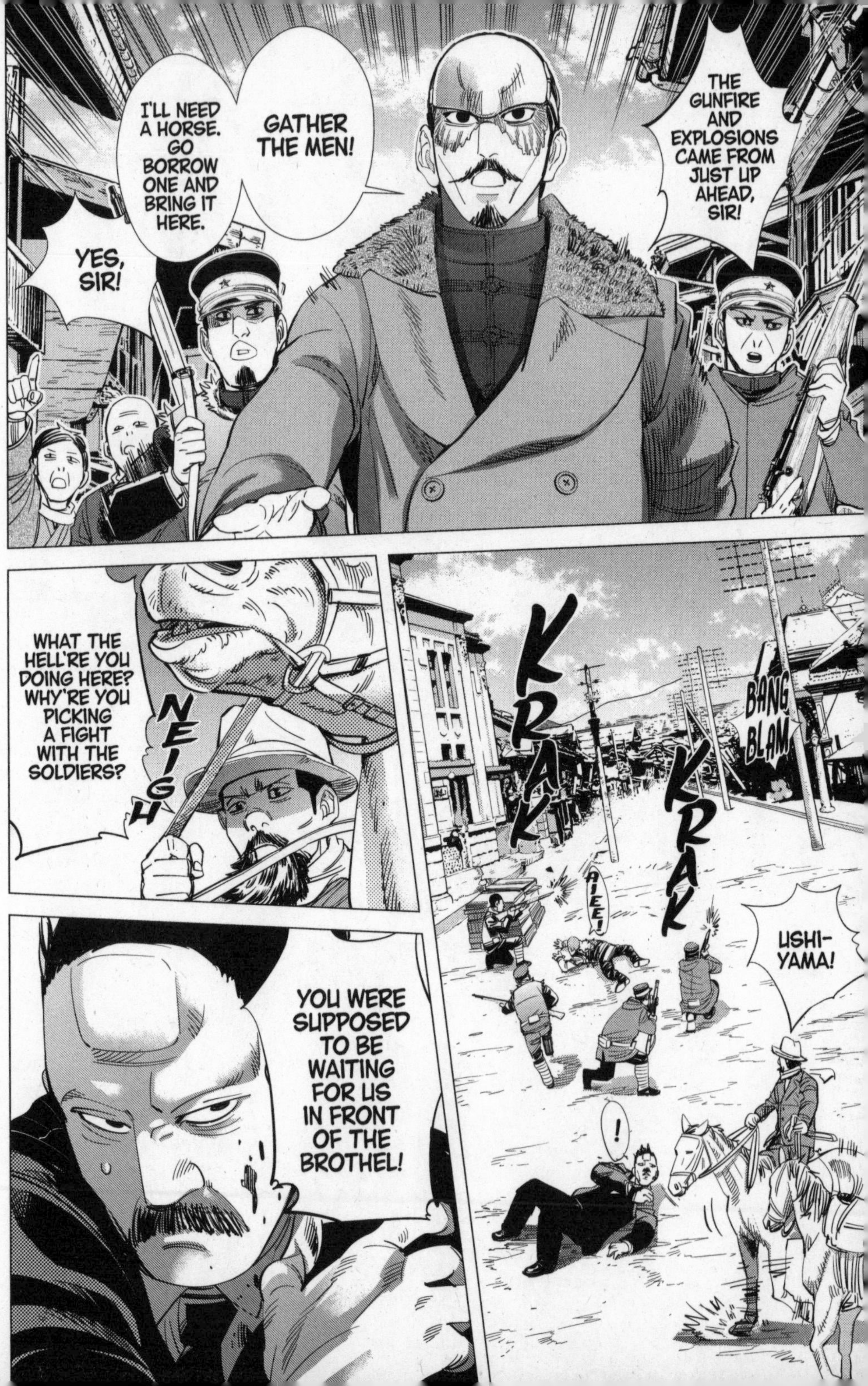
THE GUNFIRE AND EXPLOSIONS CAME FROM JUST UP AHEAD, SIR!
GATHER THE MEN!
I'LL NEED A HORSE. GO BORROW ONE AND BRING IT HERE.
YES, SIR!
BANG BLAM
KRAK
KRAK
AIEE!
USHI-YAMA!
!
NEIGH
WHAT THE HELL'RE YOU DOING HERE? WHY'RE YOU PICKING A FIGHT WITH THE SOLDIERS?
YOU WERE SUPPOSED TO BE WAITING FOR US IN FRONT OF THE BROTHEL!

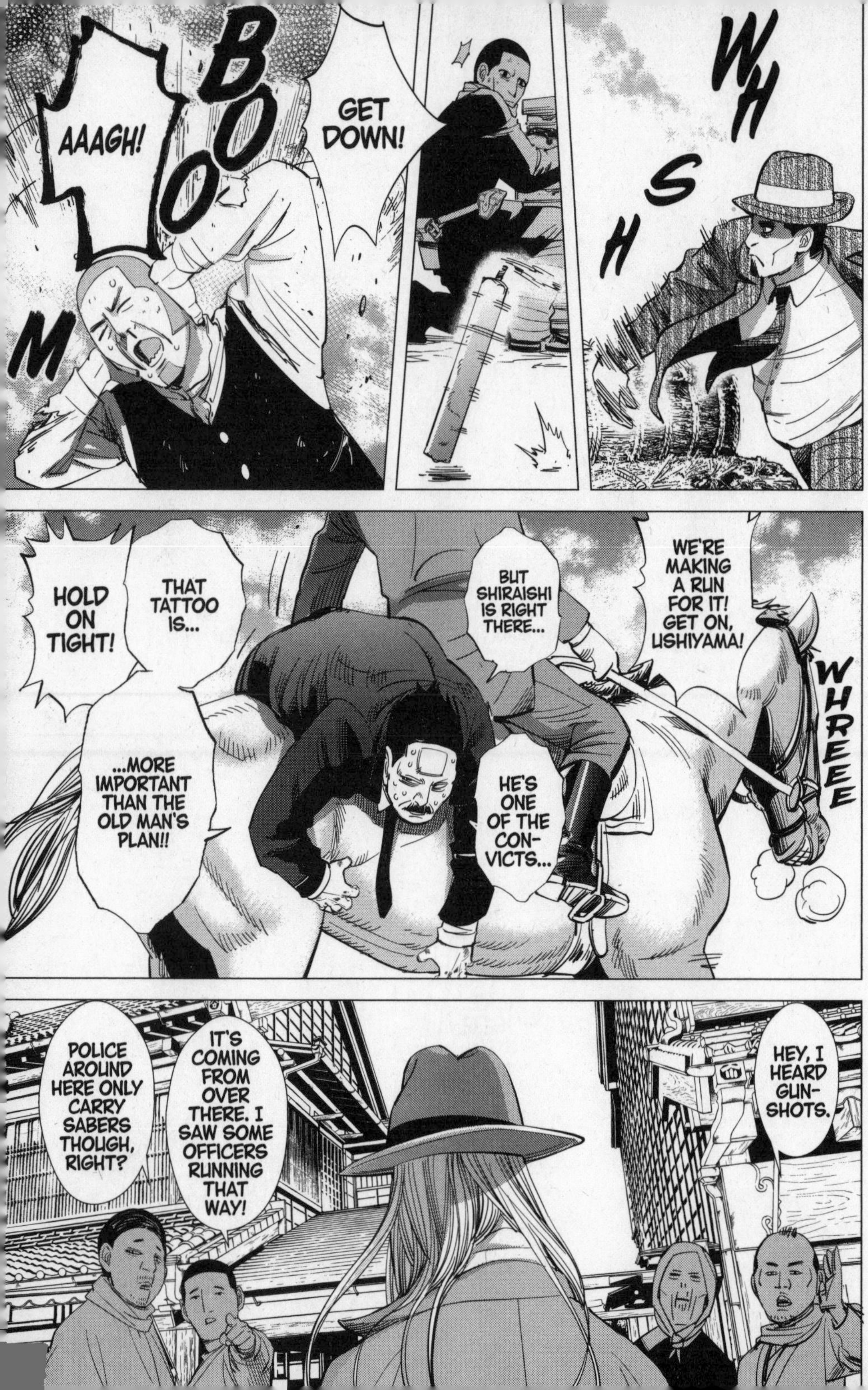
WHSH
GET DOWN!
BOOM
AAAGH!
WE'RE MAKING A RUN FOR IT! GET ON, USHIYAMA!
WHREEE
BUT SHIRAISHI IS RIGHT THERE...
HE'S ONE OF THE CON-VICTS...
THAT TATTOO IS...
...MORE IMPORTANT THAN THE OLD MAN'S PLAN!!
HOLD ON TIGHT!
HEY, I HEARD GUN-SHOTS.
IT'S COMING FROM OVER THERE. I SAW SOME OFFICERS RUNNING THAT WAY!
POLICE AROUND HERE ONLY CARRY SABERS THOUGH, RIGHT?

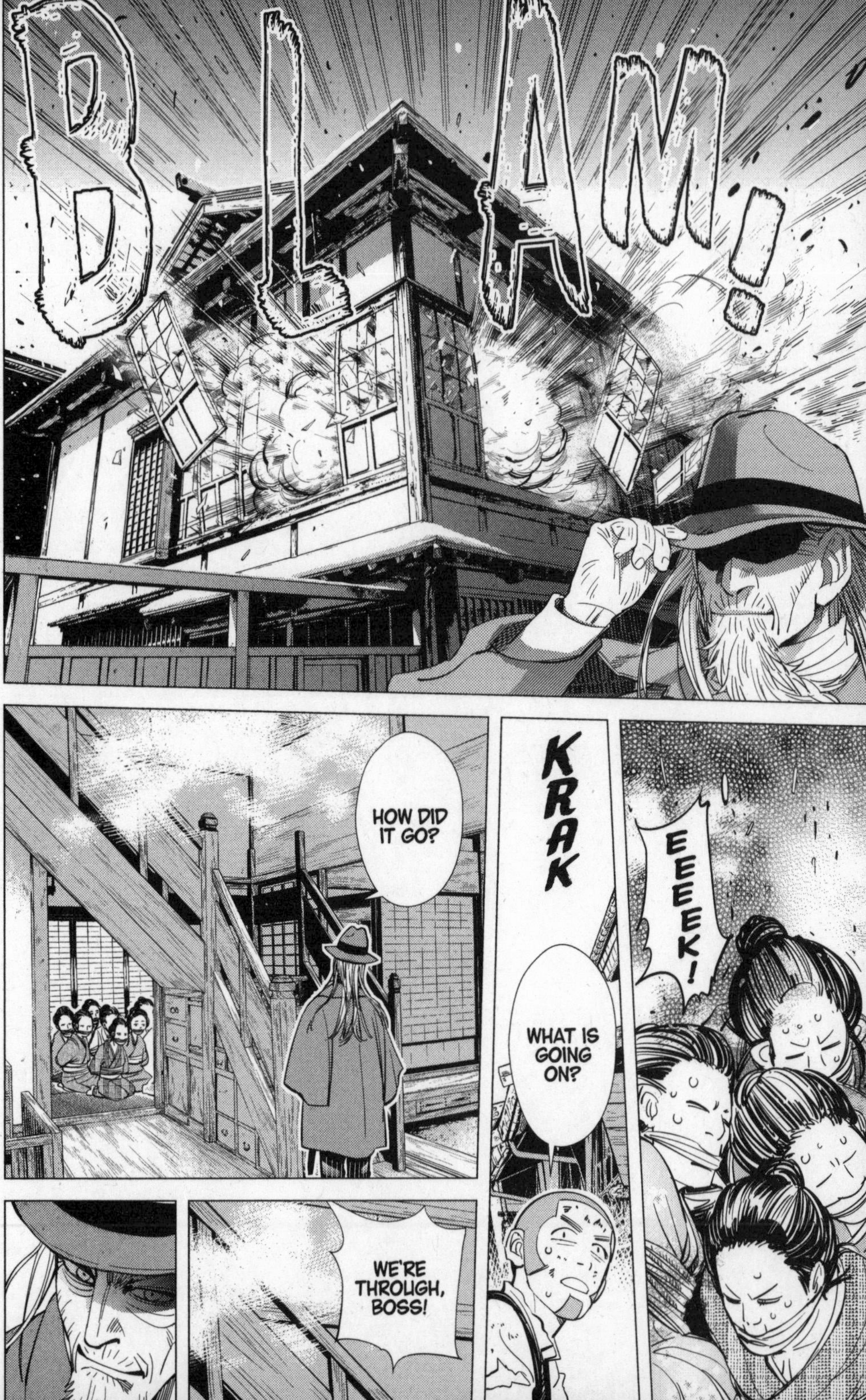
DLAM!
EEEEK!
WHAT IS GOING ON?
KRAK
HOW DID IT GO?
WE'RE THROUGH, BOSS!

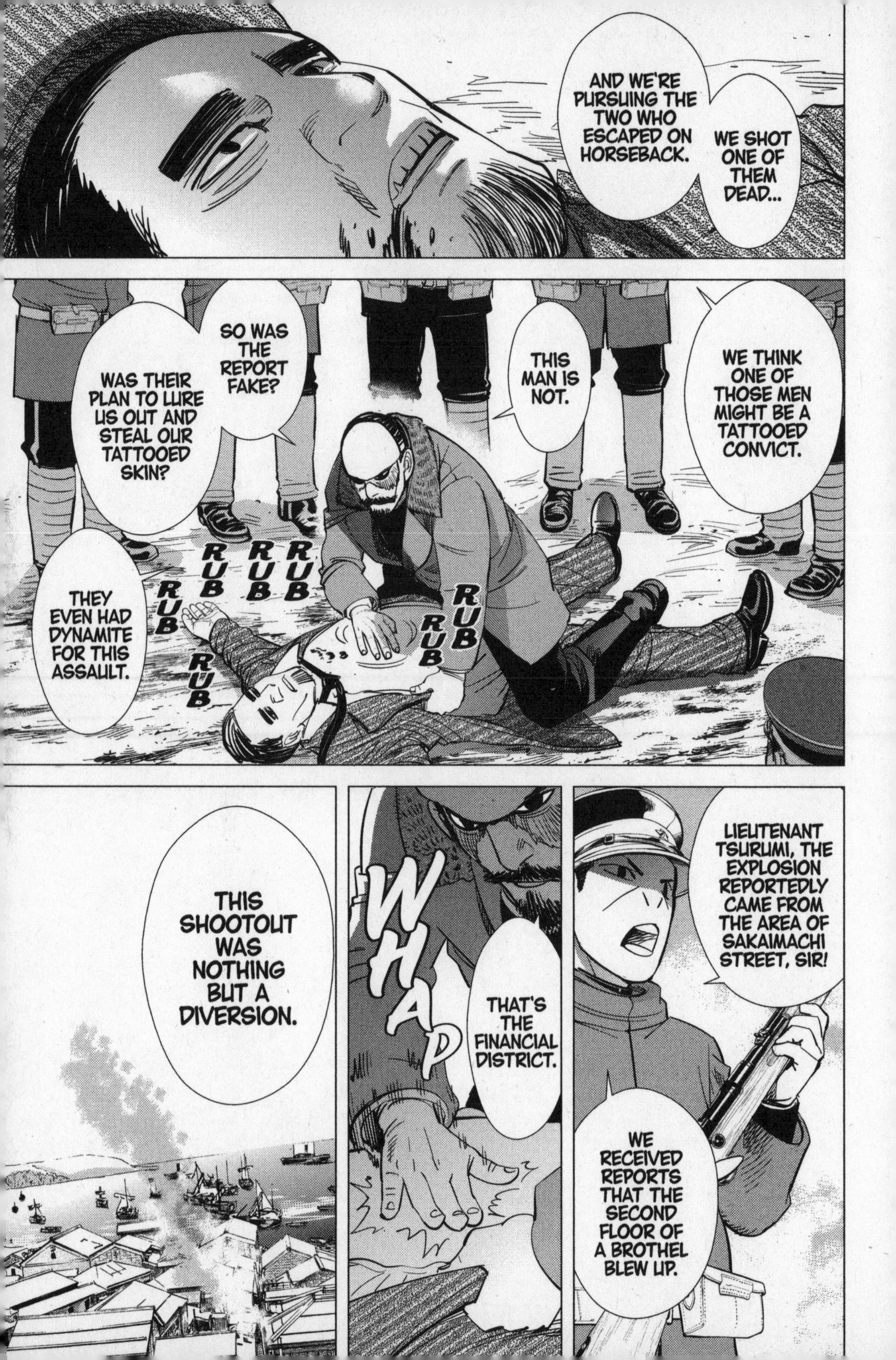
AND WE'RE PURSUING THE TWO WHO ESCAPED ON HORSEBACK.
WE SHOT ONE OF THEM DEAD...
WE THINK ONE OF THOSE MEN MIGHT BE A TATTOOED CONVICT.
THIS MAN IS NOT.
SO WAS THE REPORT FAKE?
WAS THEIR PLAN TO LURE US OUT AND STEAL OUR TATTOOED SKIN?
RUB RUB RUB RUB RUB RUB RUB
THEY EVEN HAD DYNAMITE FOR THIS ASSAULT.
LIEUTENANT TSURUMI, THE EXPLOSION REPORTEDLY CAME FROM THE AREA OF SAKAIMACHI STREET, SIR!
WE RECEIVED REPORTS THAT THE SECOND FLOOR OF A BROTHEL BLEW UP.
WHAP
THAT'S THE FINANCIAL DISTRICT.
THIS SHOOTOUT WAS NOTHING BUT A DIVERSION.

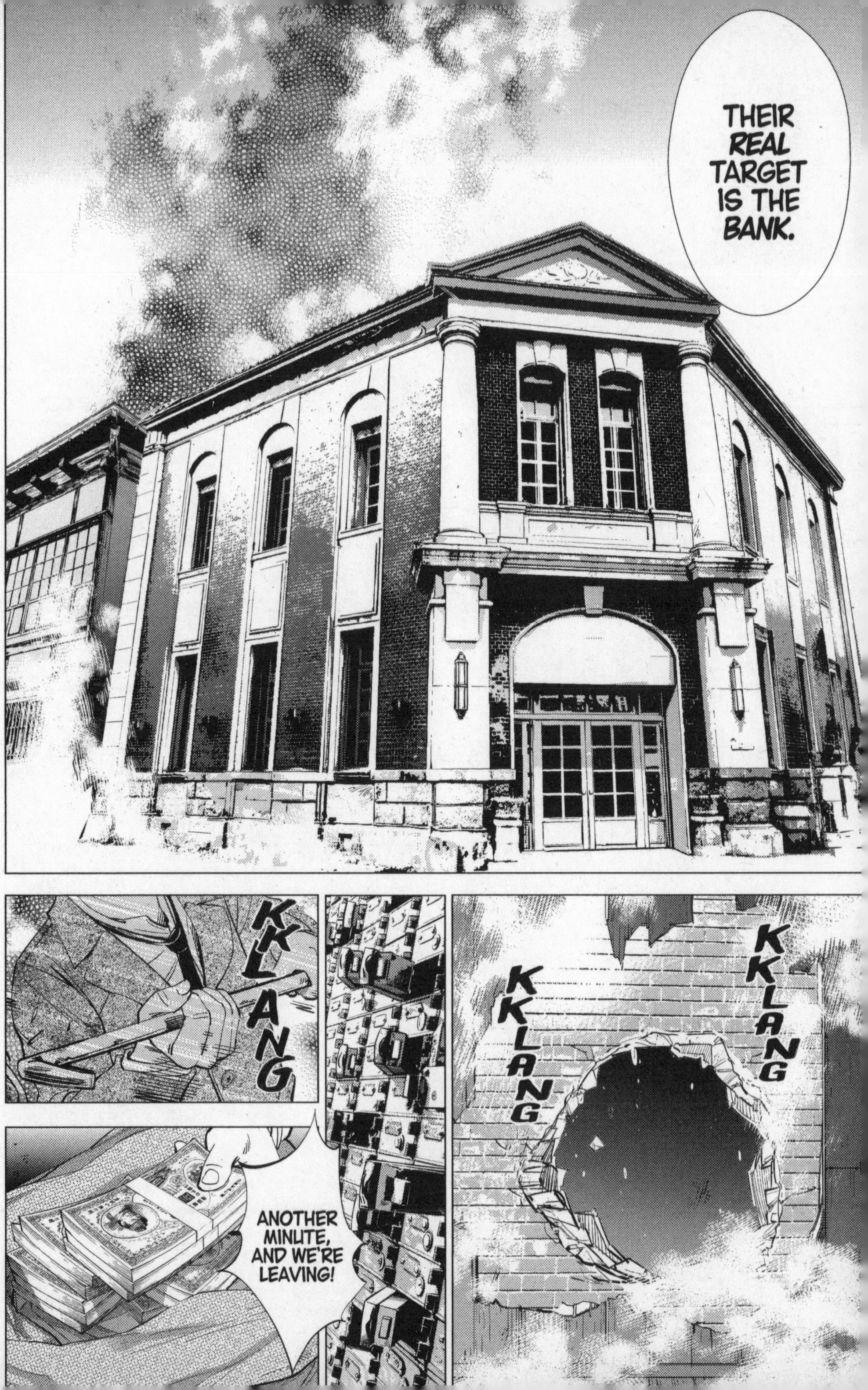
THEIR REAL TARGET IS THE BANK.
KKLANG
KKLANG
KKLANG
ANOTHER MINUTE, AND WE'RE LEAVING!

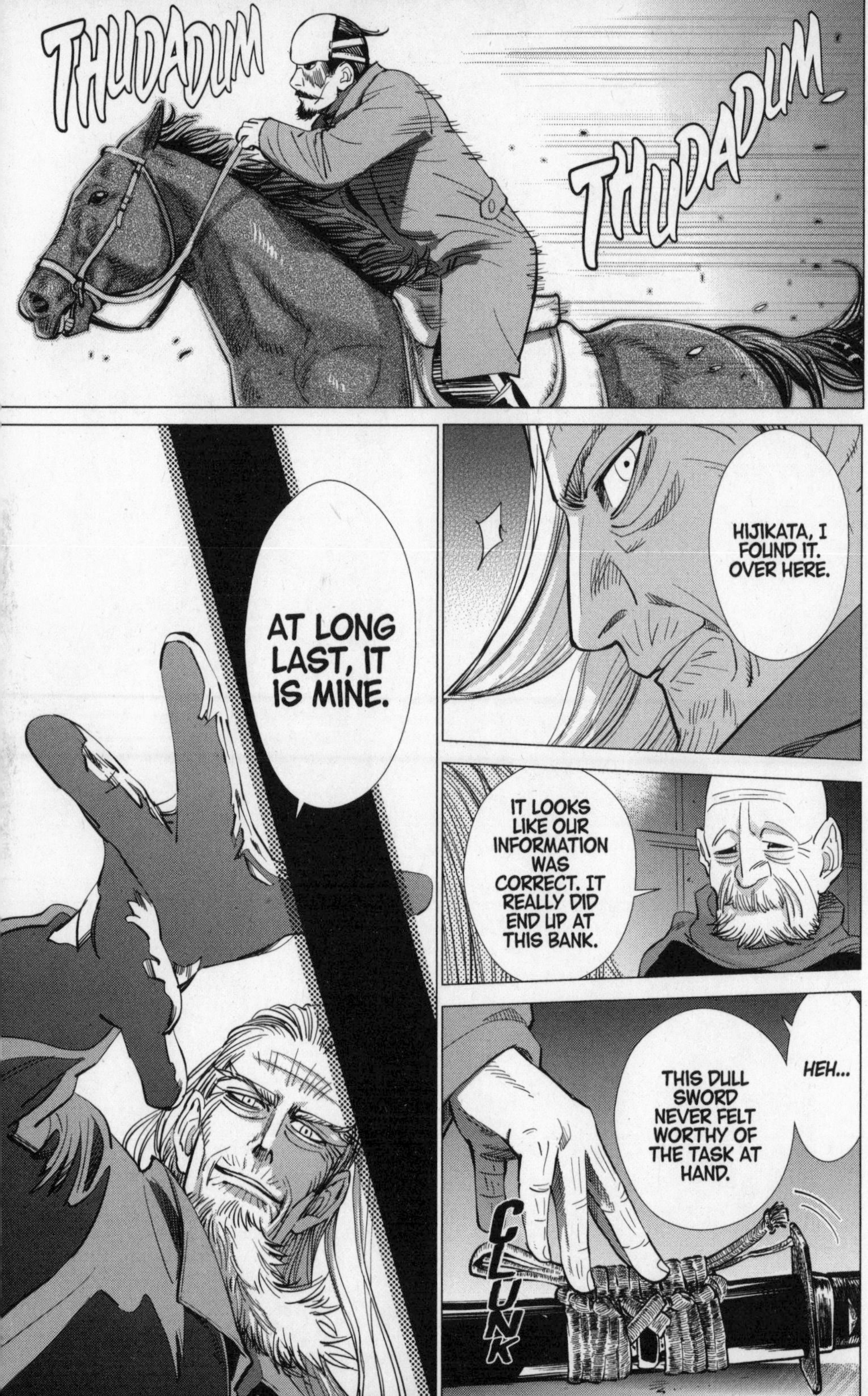
THUDADUM
THUDADUM
HIJIKATA, I FOUND IT. OVER HERE.
IT LOOKS LIKE OUR INFORMATION WAS CORRECT. IT REALLY DID END UP AT THIS BANK.
HEH...
THIS DULL SWORD NEVER FELT WORTHY OF THE TASK AT HAND.
CLUNK
AT LONG LAST, IT IS MINE.

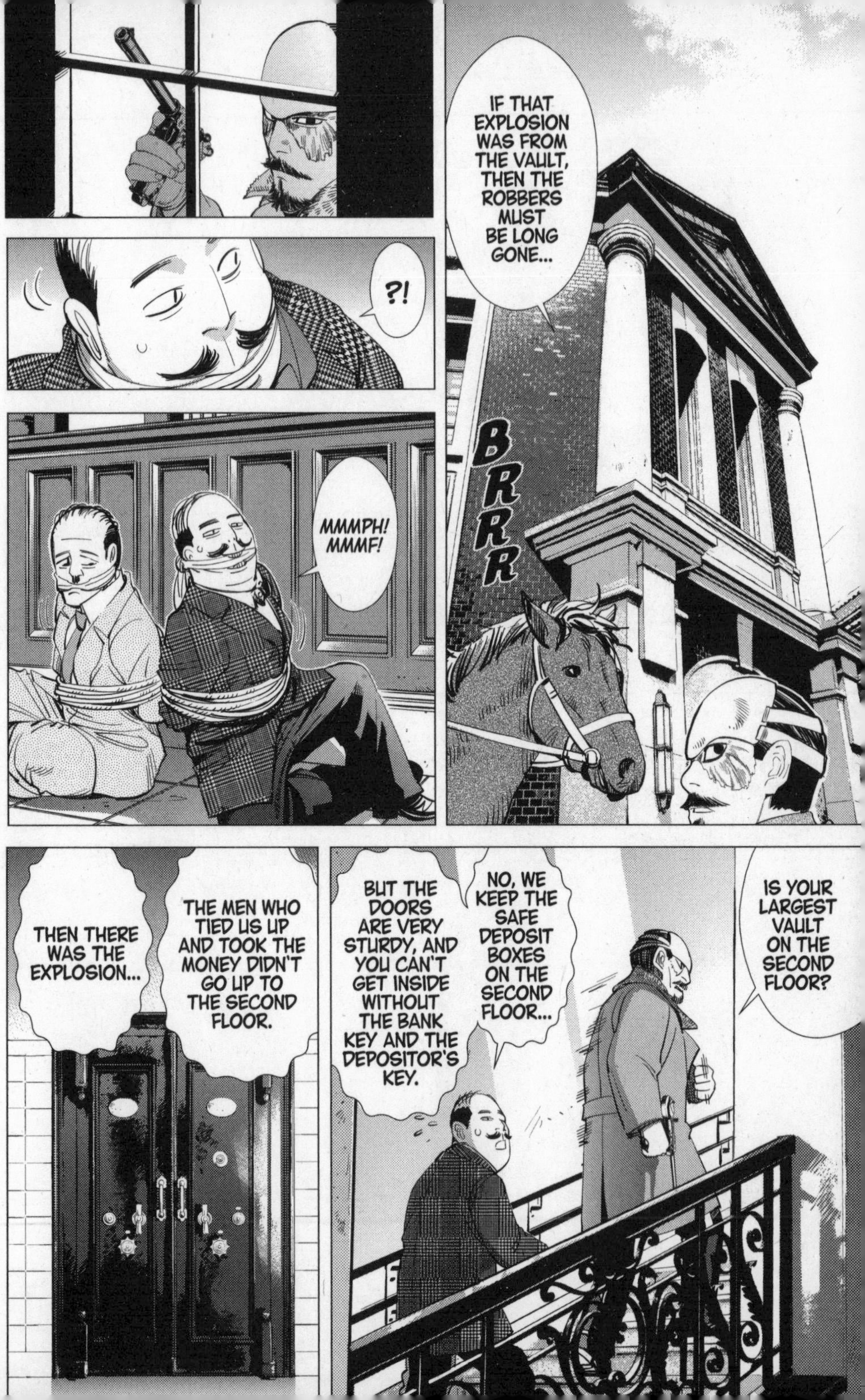
IF THAT EXPLOSION WAS FROM THE VAULT, THEN THE ROBBERS MUST BE LONG GONE...
BRRR
?!
MMMPH! MMMF!
IS YOUR LARGEST VAULT ON THE SECOND FLOOR?
NO, WE KEEP THE SAFE DEPOSIT BOXES ON THE SECOND FLOOR...
BUT THE DOORS ARE VERY STURDY, AND YOU CAN'T GET INSIDE WITHOUT THE BANK KEY AND THE DEPOSITOR'S KEY.
THE MEN WHO TIED US UP AND TOOK THE MONEY DIDN'T GO UP TO THE SECOND FLOOR.
THEN THERE WAS THE EXPLOSION...

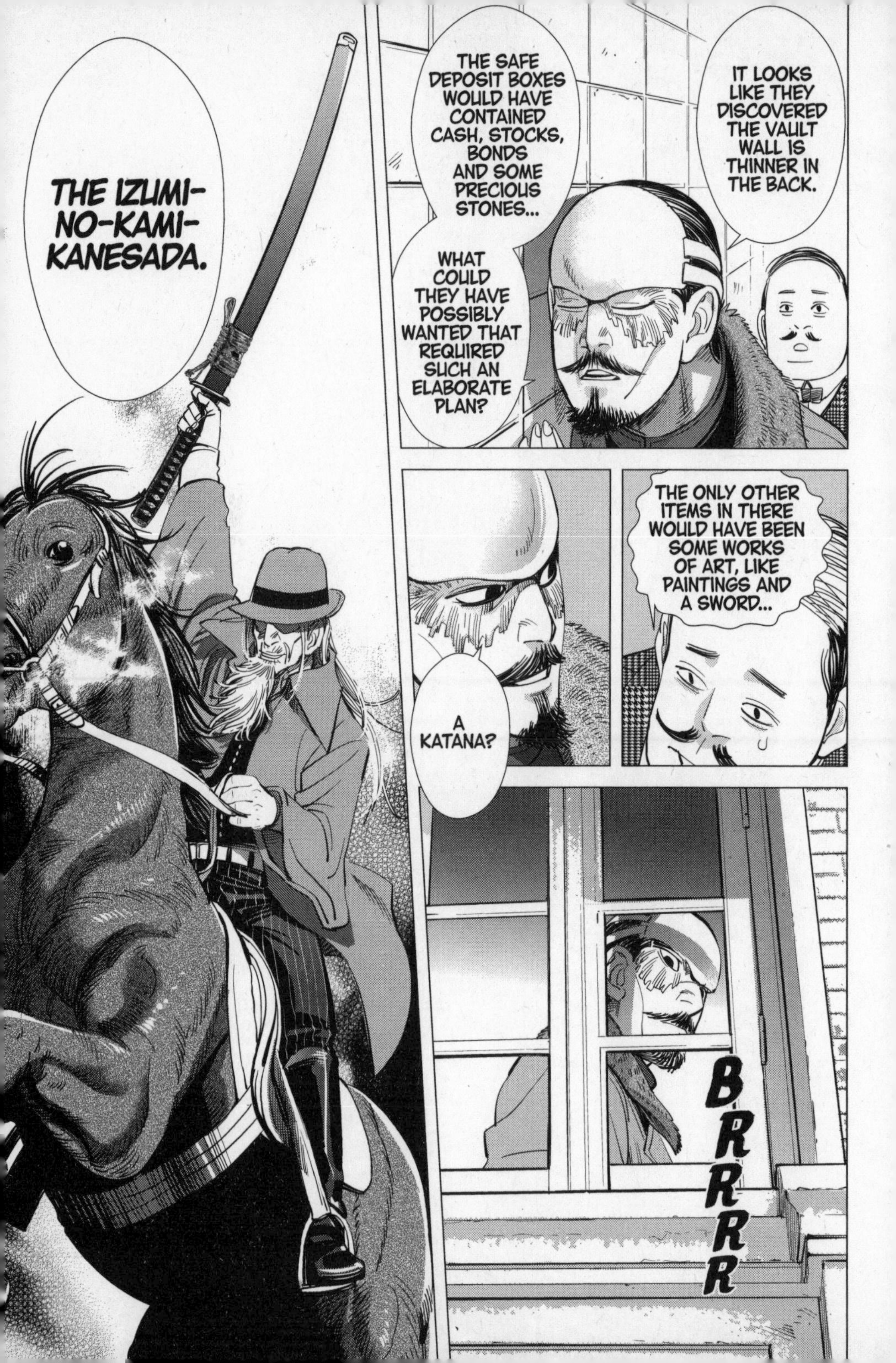
IT LOOKS LIKE THEY DISCOVERED THE VAULT WALL IS THINNER IN THE BACK.
THE SAFE DEPOSIT BOXES WOULD HAVE CONTAINED CASH, STOCKS, BONDS AND SOME PRECIOUS STONES...
WHAT COULD THEY HAVE POSSIBLY WANTED THAT REQUIRED SUCH AN ELABORATE PLAN?
THE ONLY OTHER ITEMS IN THERE WOULD HAVE BEEN SOME WORKS OF ART, LIKE PAINTINGS AND A SWORD...
A KATANA?
BRRRR
THE IZUMI-NO-KAMI-KANESADA.

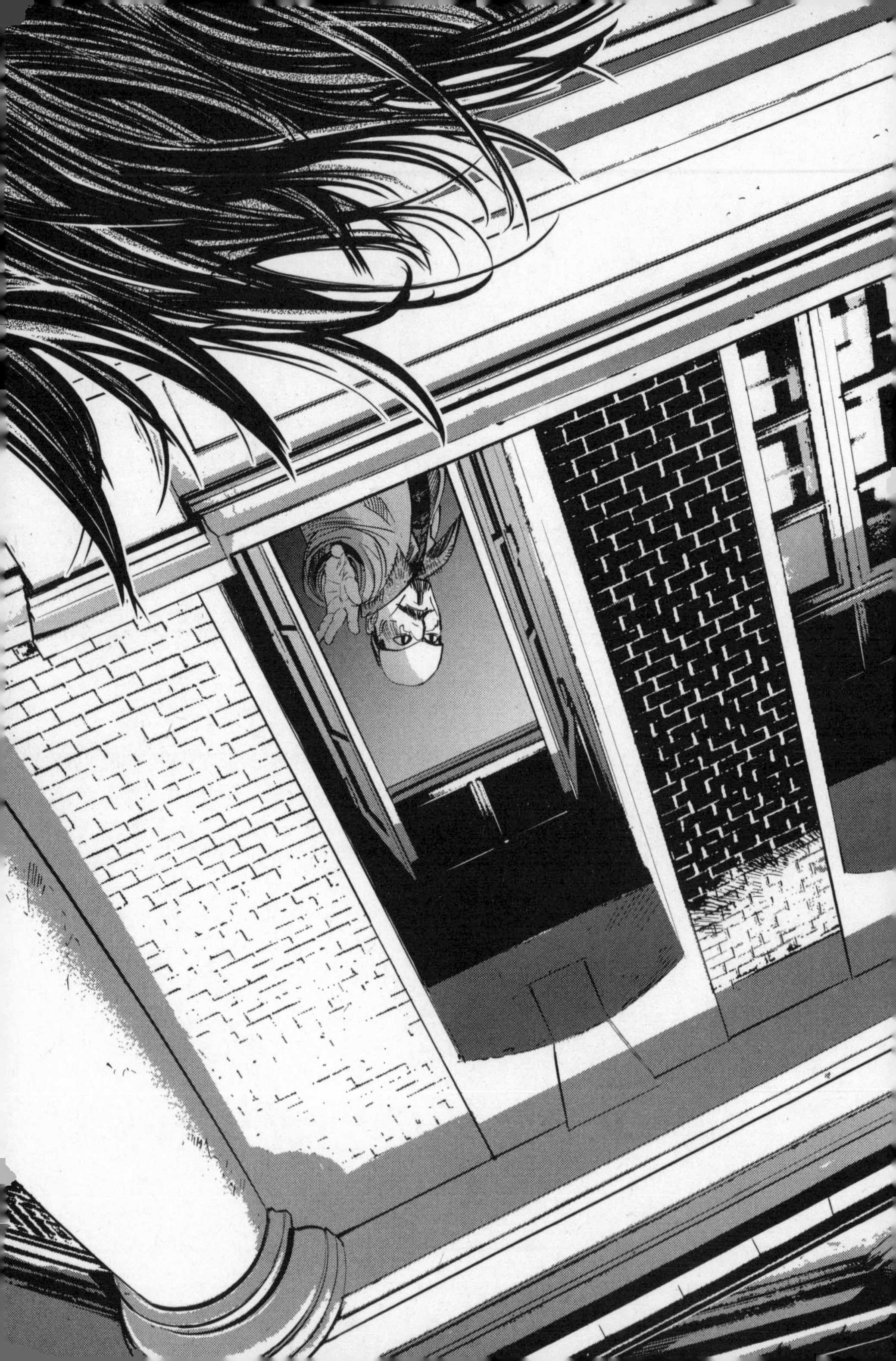

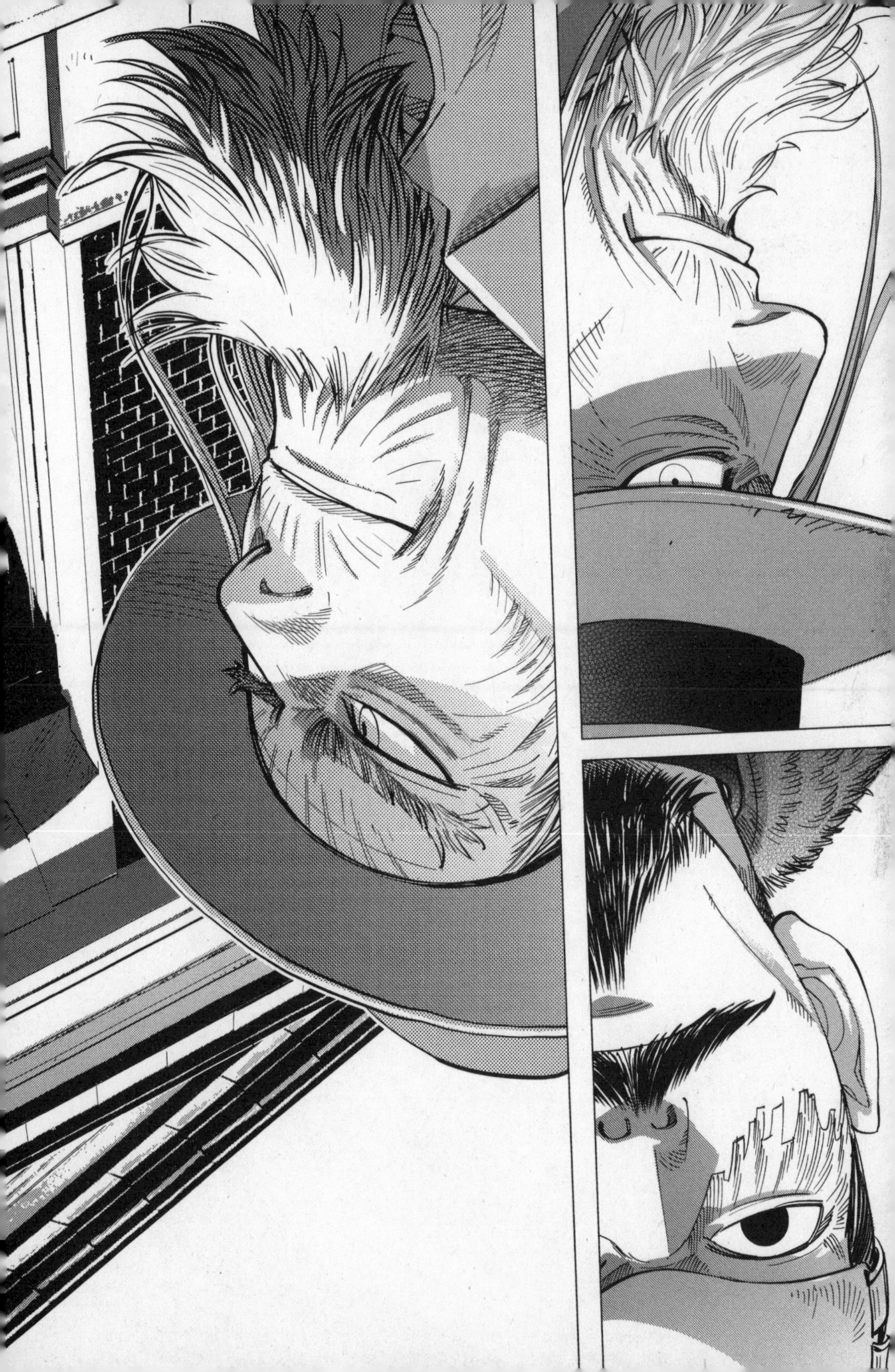

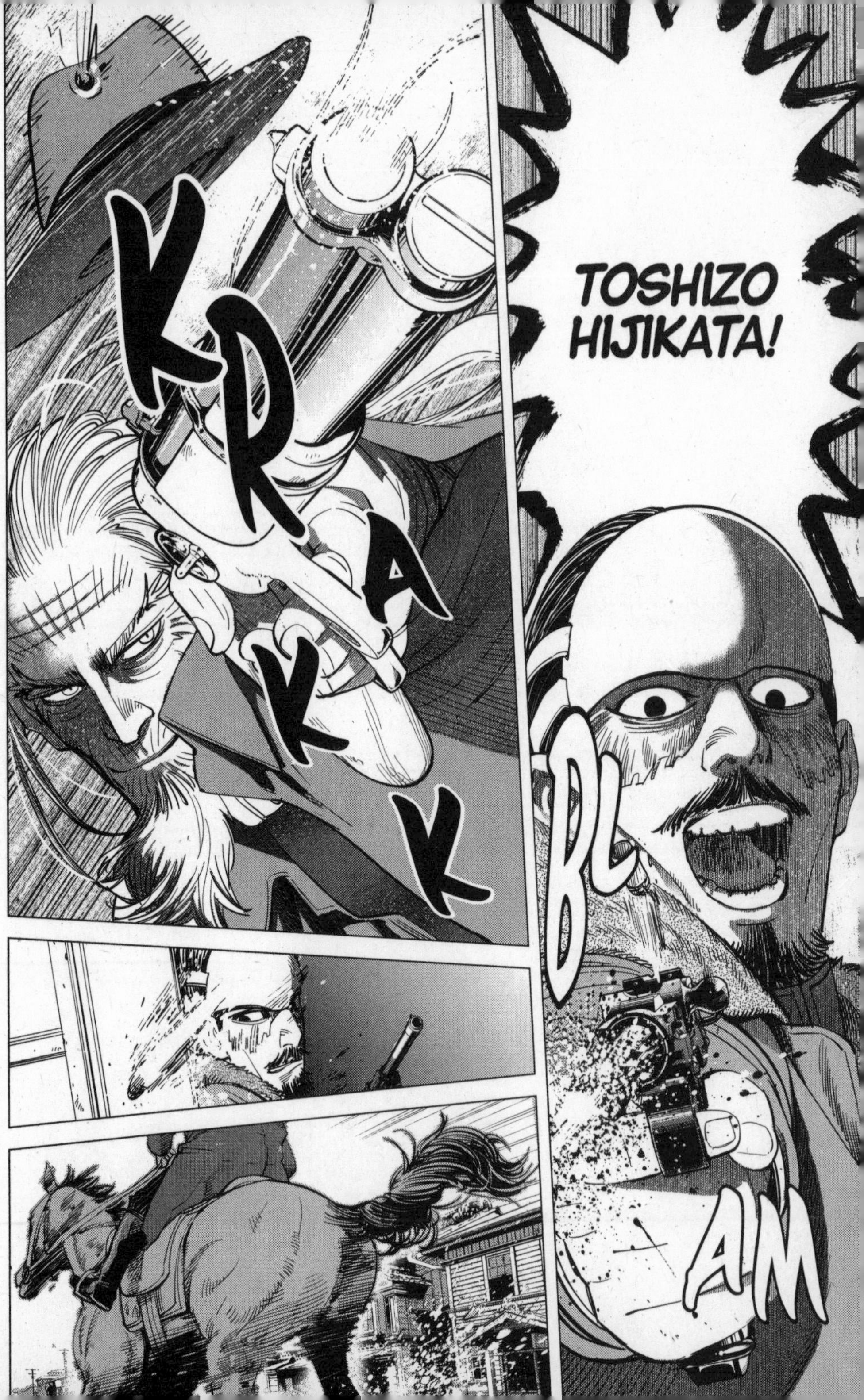
TOSHIZO HIJIKATA!
BLAM
KRAKK

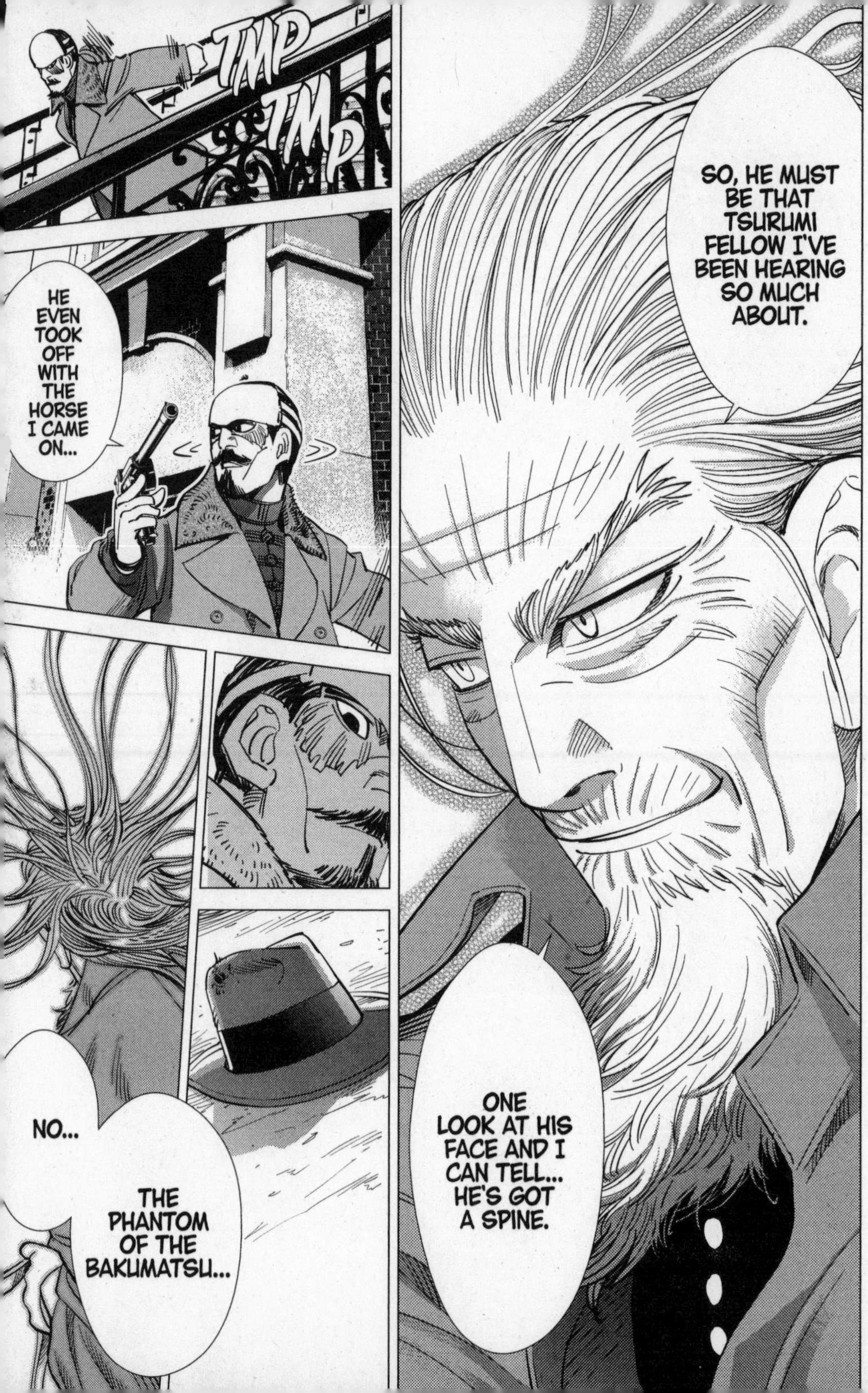
SO, HE MUST BE THAT TSURUMI FELLOW I'VE BEEN HEARING SO MUCH ABOUT.
ONE LOOK AT HIS FACE AND I CAN TELL... HE'S GOT A SPINE.
TMP
TMP
HE EVEN TOOK OFF WITH THE HORSE I CAME ON...
NO...
THE PHANTOM OF THE BAKUMATSU...

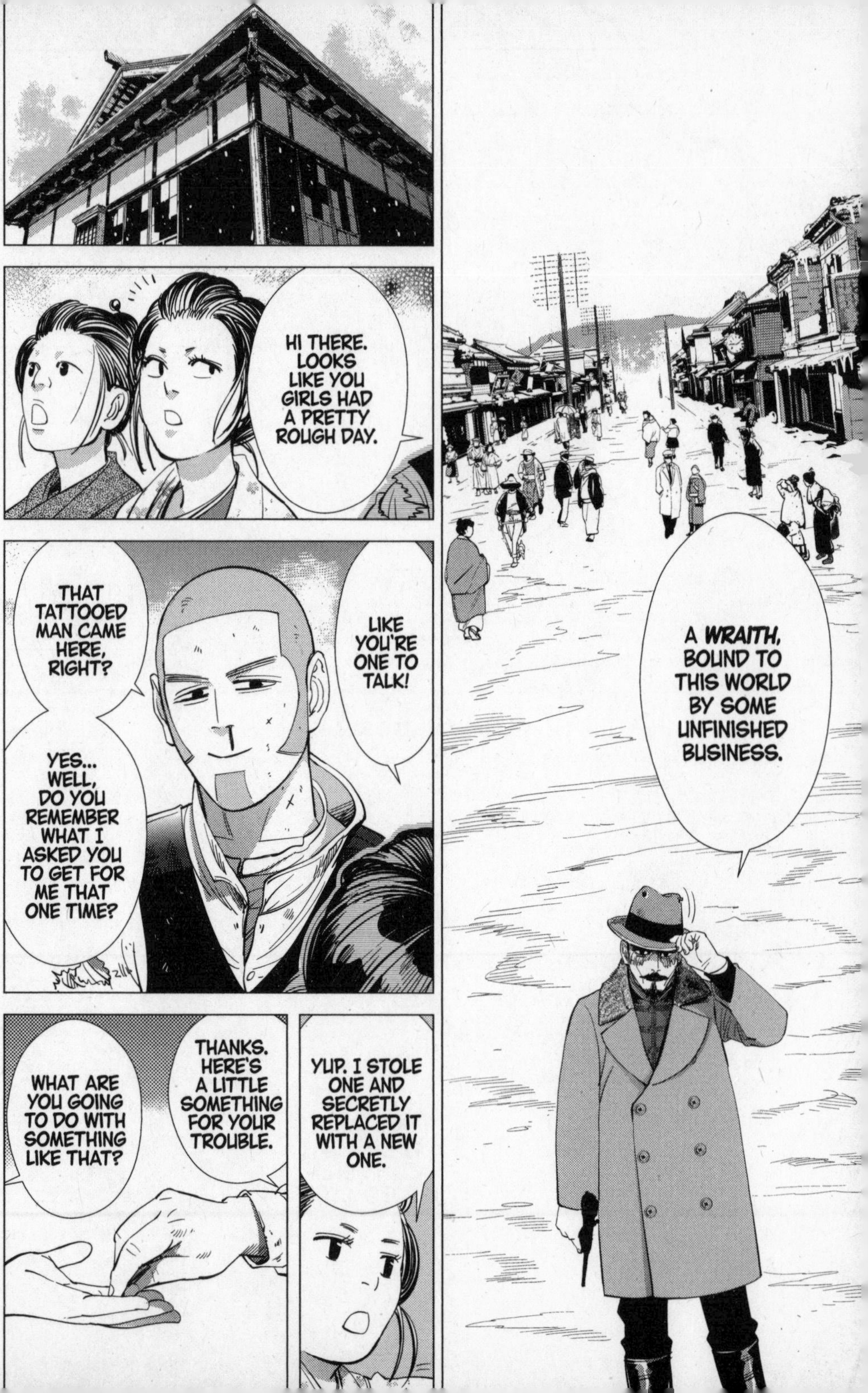
A WRAITH, BOUND TO THIS WORLD BY SOME UNFINISHED BUSINESS.
HI THERE. LOOKS LIKE YOU GIRLS HAD A PRETTY ROUGH DAY.
LIKE YOU'RE ONE TO TALK!
THAT TATTOOED MAN CAME HERE, RIGHT?
YES... WELL, DO YOU REMEMBER WHAT I ASKED YOU TO GET FOR ME THAT ONE TIME?
YUP. I STOLE ONE AND SECRETLY REPLACED IT WITH A NEW ONE.
THANKS. HERE'S A LITTLE SOMETHING FOR YOUR TROUBLE.
WHAT ARE YOU GOING TO DO WITH SOMETHING LIKE THAT?

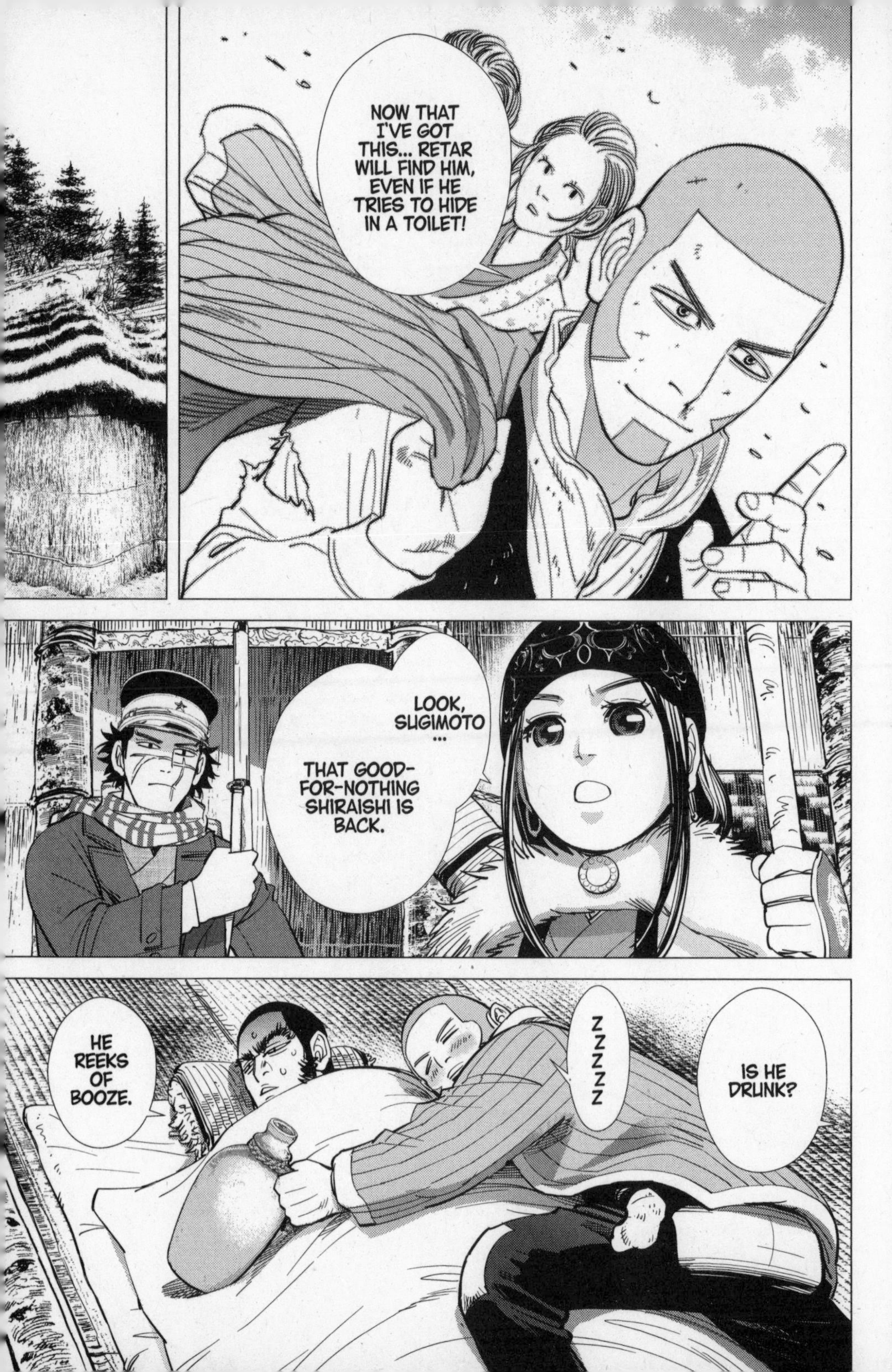
NOW THAT I'VE GOT THIS... RETAR WILL FIND HIM, EVEN IF HE TRIES TO HIDE IN A TOILET!
LOOK, SUGIMOTO ...
THAT GOOD-FOR-NOTHING SHIRAISHI IS BACK.
IS HE DRUNK?
ZZZZ
HE REEKS OF BOOZE.

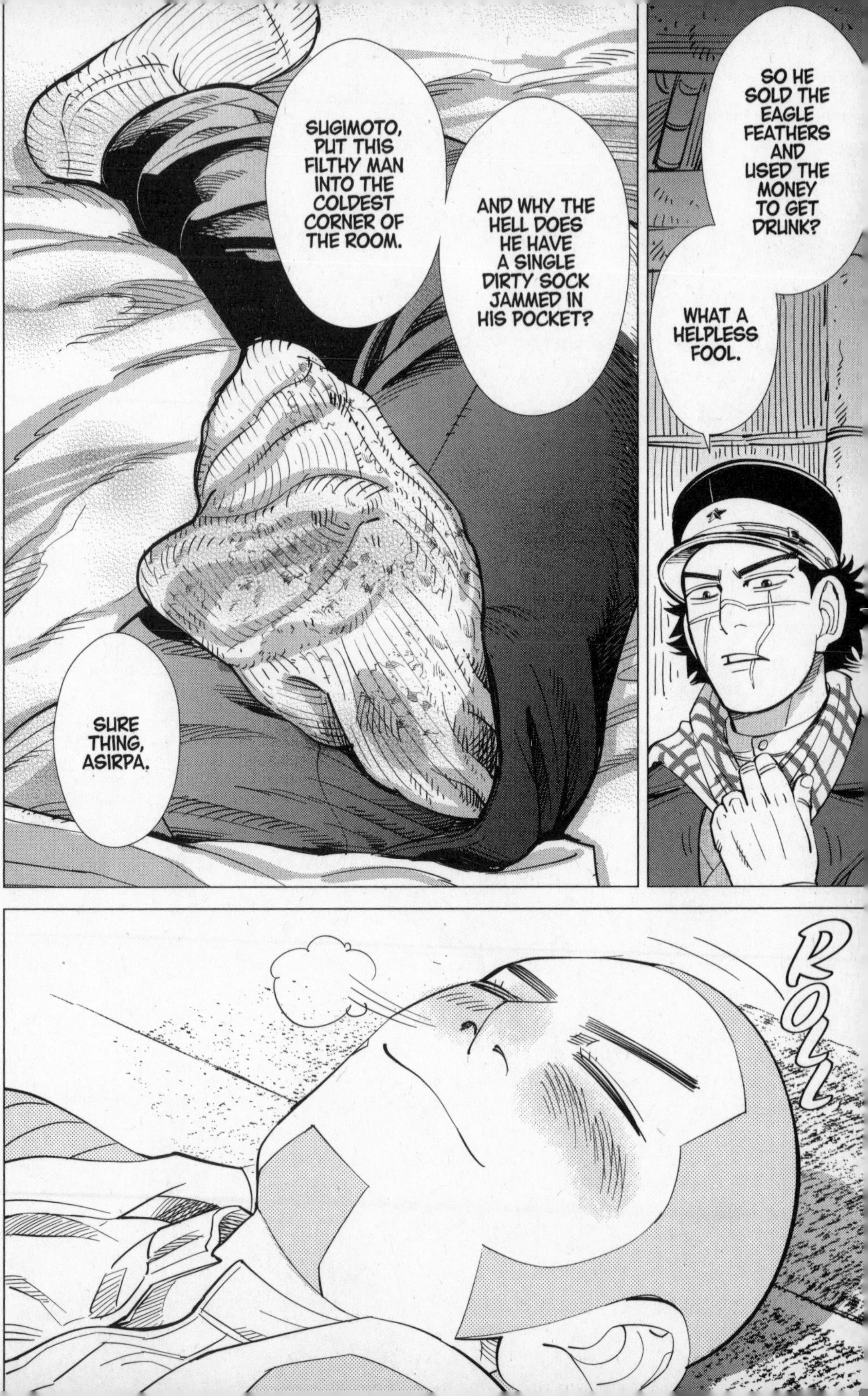
SO HE SOLD THE EAGLE FEATHERS AND USED THE MONEY TO GET DRUNK?
WHAT A HELPLESS FOOL.
SUGIMOTO, PUT THIS FILTHY MAN INTO THE COLDEST CORNER OF THE ROOM.
AND WHY THE HELL DOES HE HAVE A SINGLE DIRTY SOCK JAMMED IN HIS POCKET?
SURE THING, ASIRPA.
ROLL

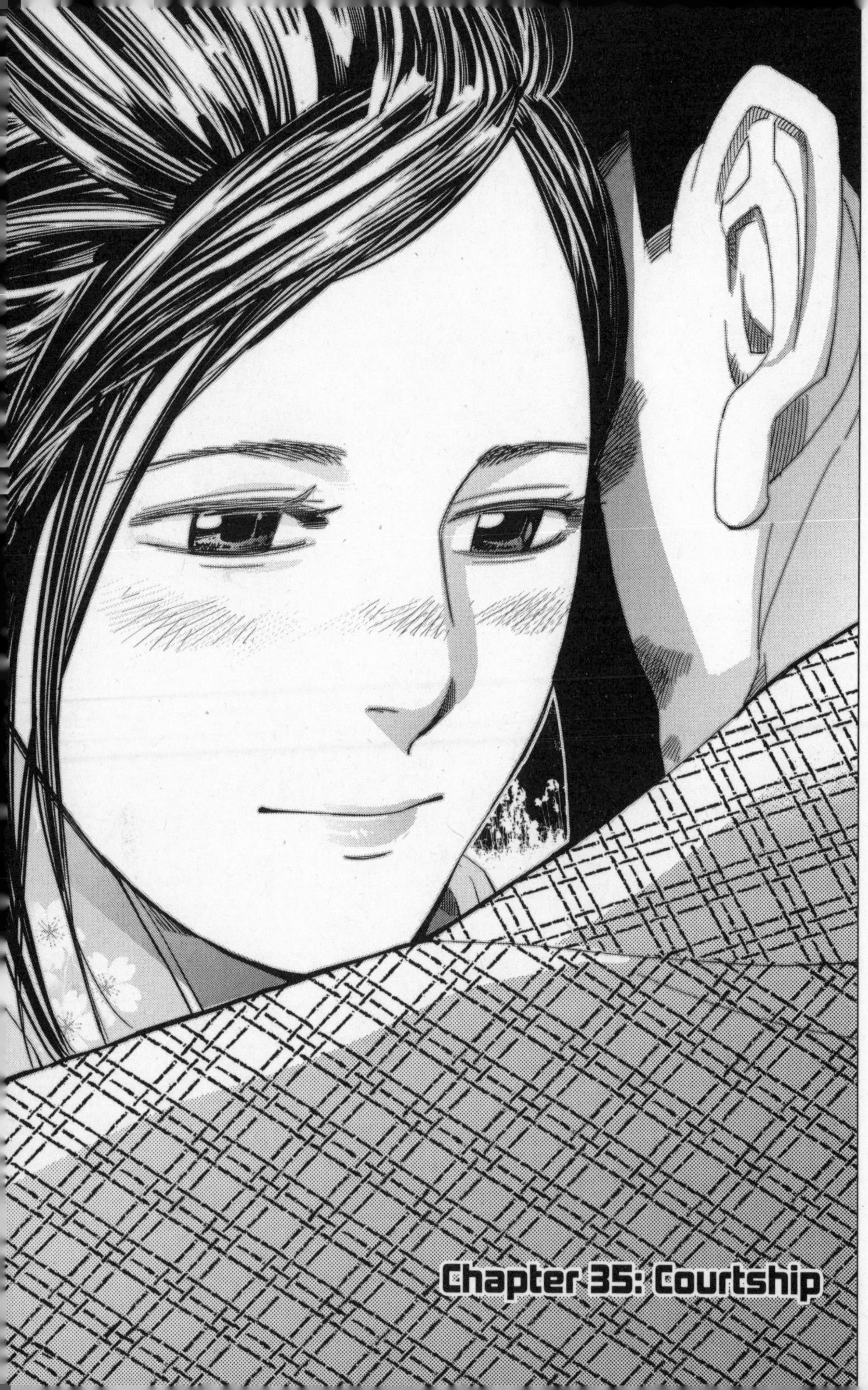
Chapter 35: Courtship

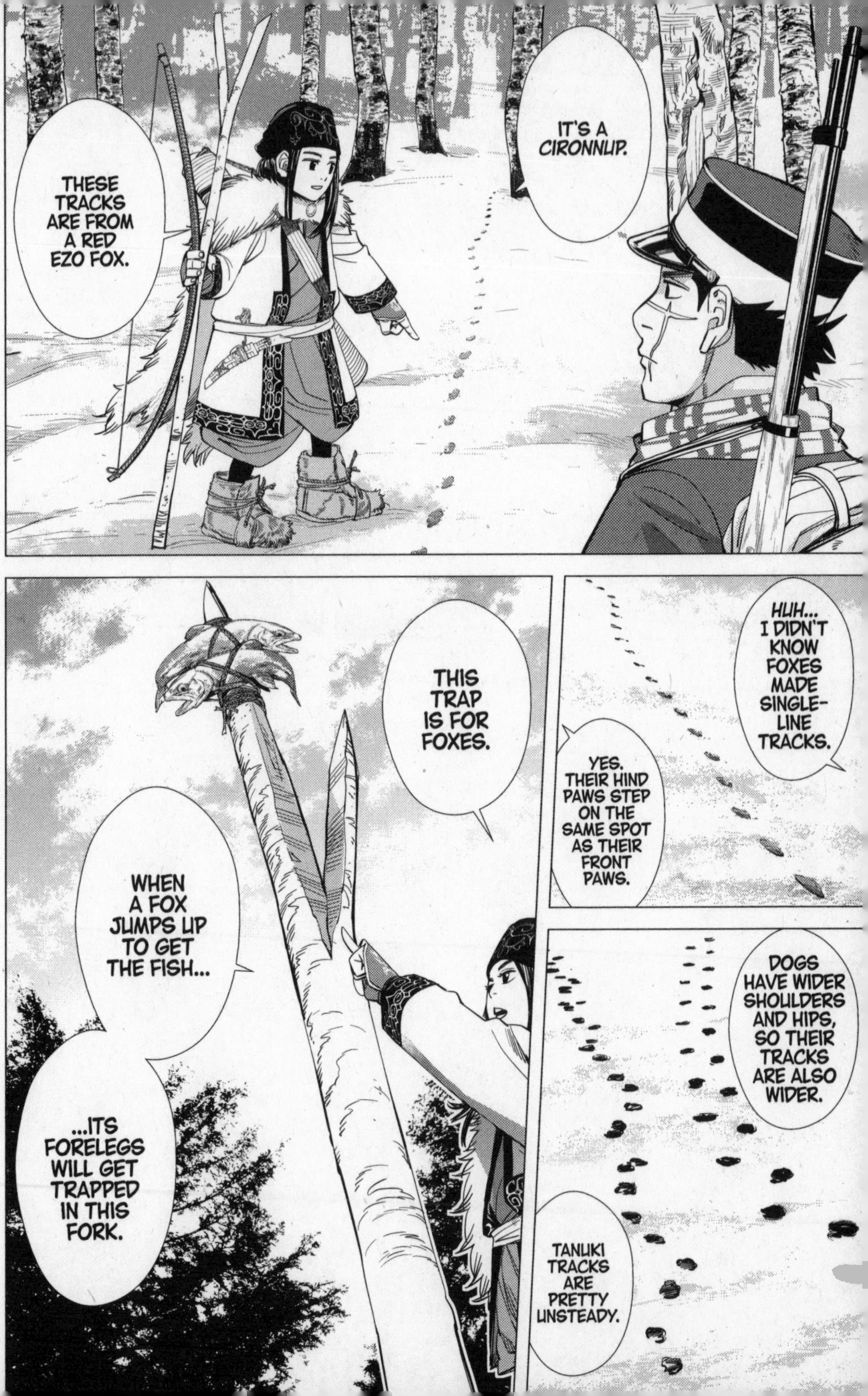
IT'S A CIRONNUP.
THESE TRACKS ARE FROM A RED EZO FOX.
HUH... I DIDN'T KNOW FOXES MADE SINGLE-LINE TRACKS.
YES. THEIR HIND PAWS STEP ON THE SAME SPOT AS THEIR FRONT PAWS.
DOGS HAVE WIDER SHOULDERS AND HIPS, SO THEIR TRACKS ARE ALSO WIDER.
TANUKI TRACKS ARE PRETTY UNSTEADY.
THIS TRAP IS FOR FOXES.
WHEN A FOX JUMPS UP TO GET THE FISH...
...ITS FORELEGS WILL GET TRAPPED IN THIS FORK.

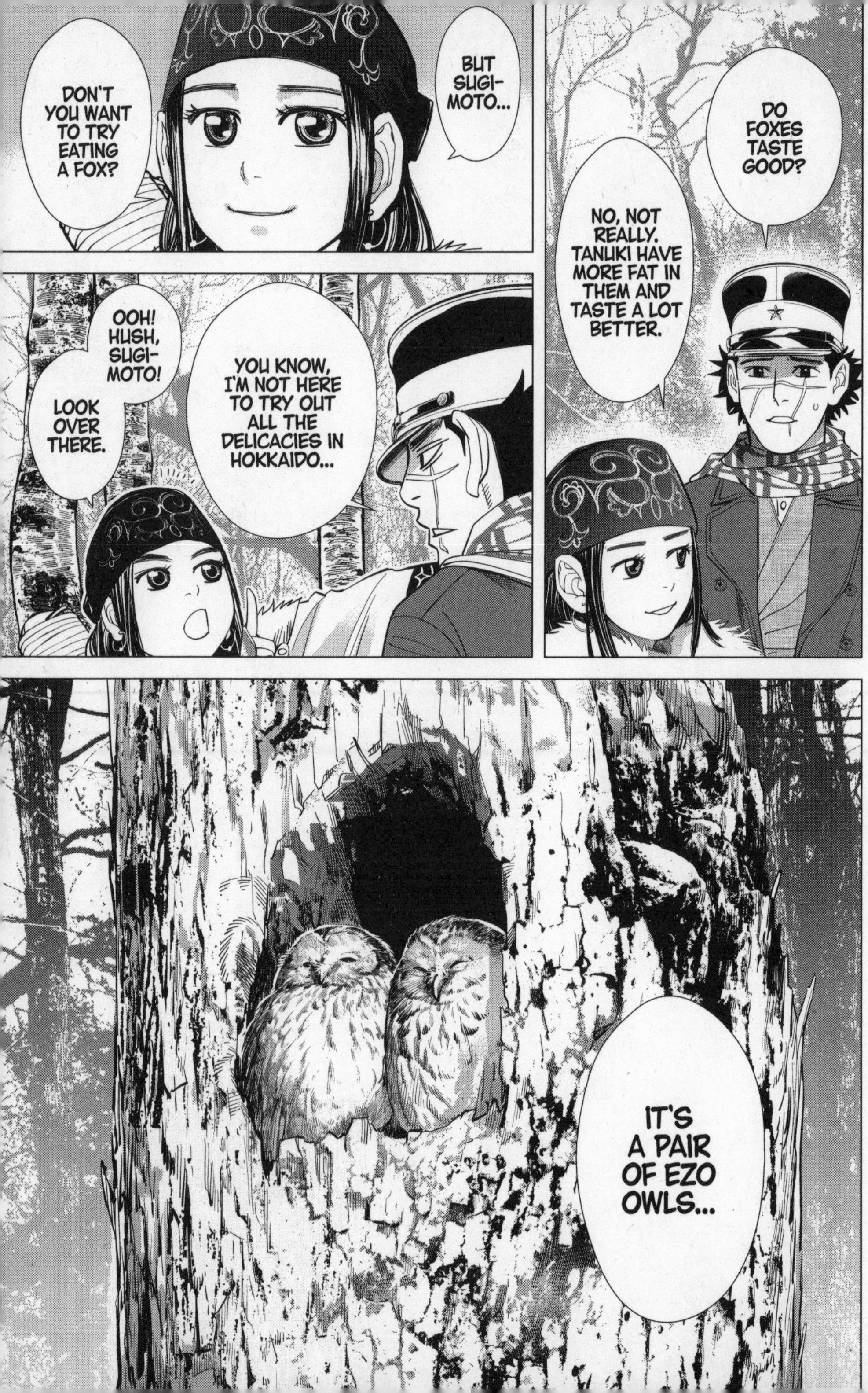
DO FOXES TASTE GOOD?
NO, NOT REALLY. TANUKI HAVE MORE FAT IN THEM AND TASTE A LOT BETTER.
DON'T YOU WANT TO TRY EATING A FOX?
BUT SUGI-MOTO...
YOU KNOW, I'M NOT HERE TO TRY OUT ALL THE DELICACIES IN HOKKAIDO...
OOH! HUSH, SUGI-MOTO!
LOOK OVER THERE.
IT'S A PAIR OF EZO OWLS...

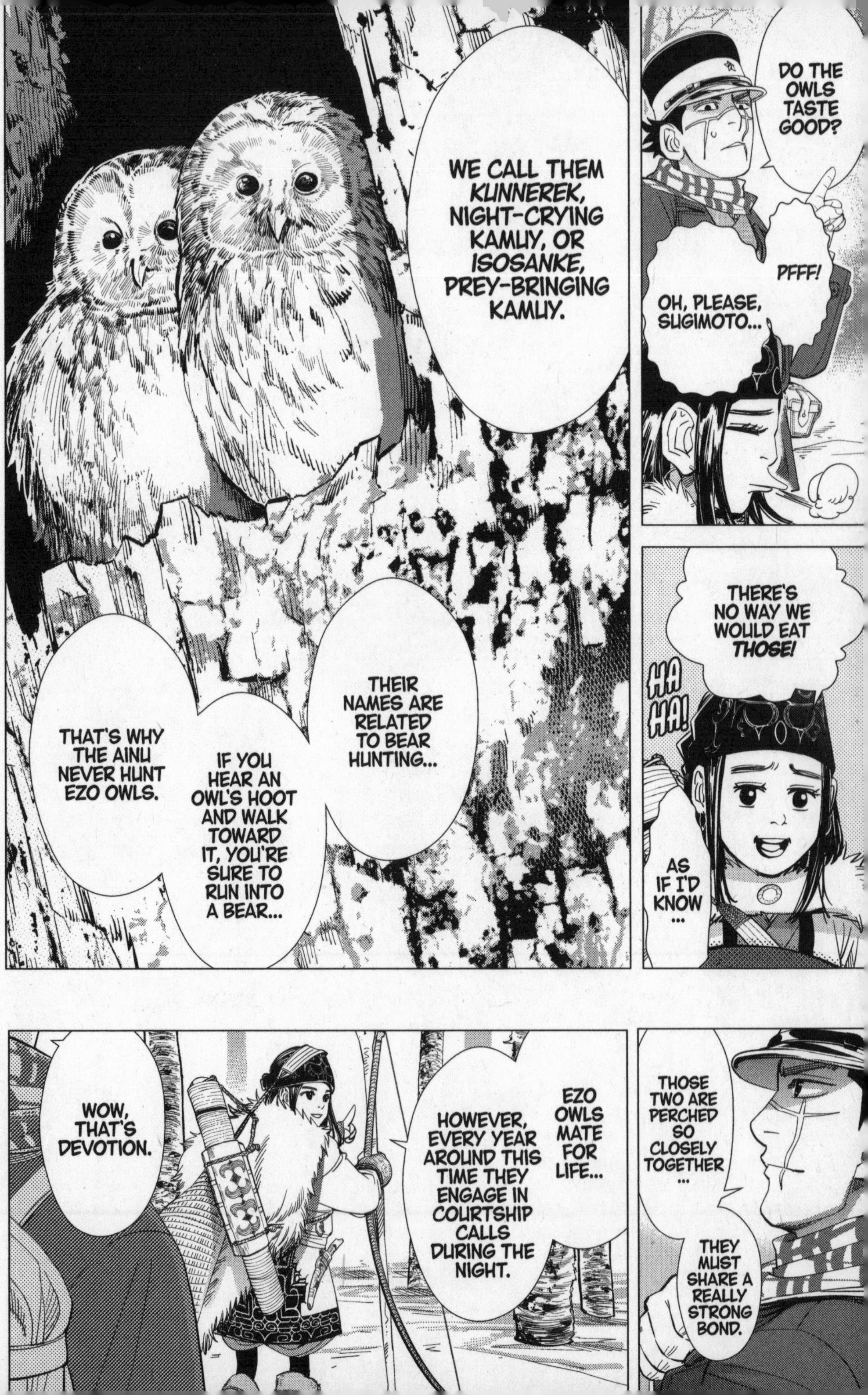
DO THE OWLS TASTE GOOD?
PFFF!
OH, PLEASE, SUGIMOTO...
THERE'S NO WAY WE WOULD EAT THOSE!
HA HA!
AS IF I'D KNOW...
WE CALL THEM KUNNEREK, NIGHT-CRYING KAMUY, OR ISOSANKE, PREY-BRINGING KAMUY.
THEIR NAMES ARE RELATED TO BEAR HUNTING...
IF YOU HEAR AN OWL'S HOOT AND WALK TOWARD IT, YOU'RE SURE TO RUN INTO A BEAR...
THAT'S WHY THE AINU NEVER HUNT EZO OWLS.
THOSE TWO ARE PERCHED SO CLOSELY TOGETHER...
THEY MUST SHARE A REALLY STRONG BOND.
EZO OWLS MATE FOR LIFE...
HOWEVER, EVERY YEAR AROUND THIS TIME THEY ENGAGE IN COURTSHIP CALLS DURING THE NIGHT.
WOW, THAT'S DEVOTION.

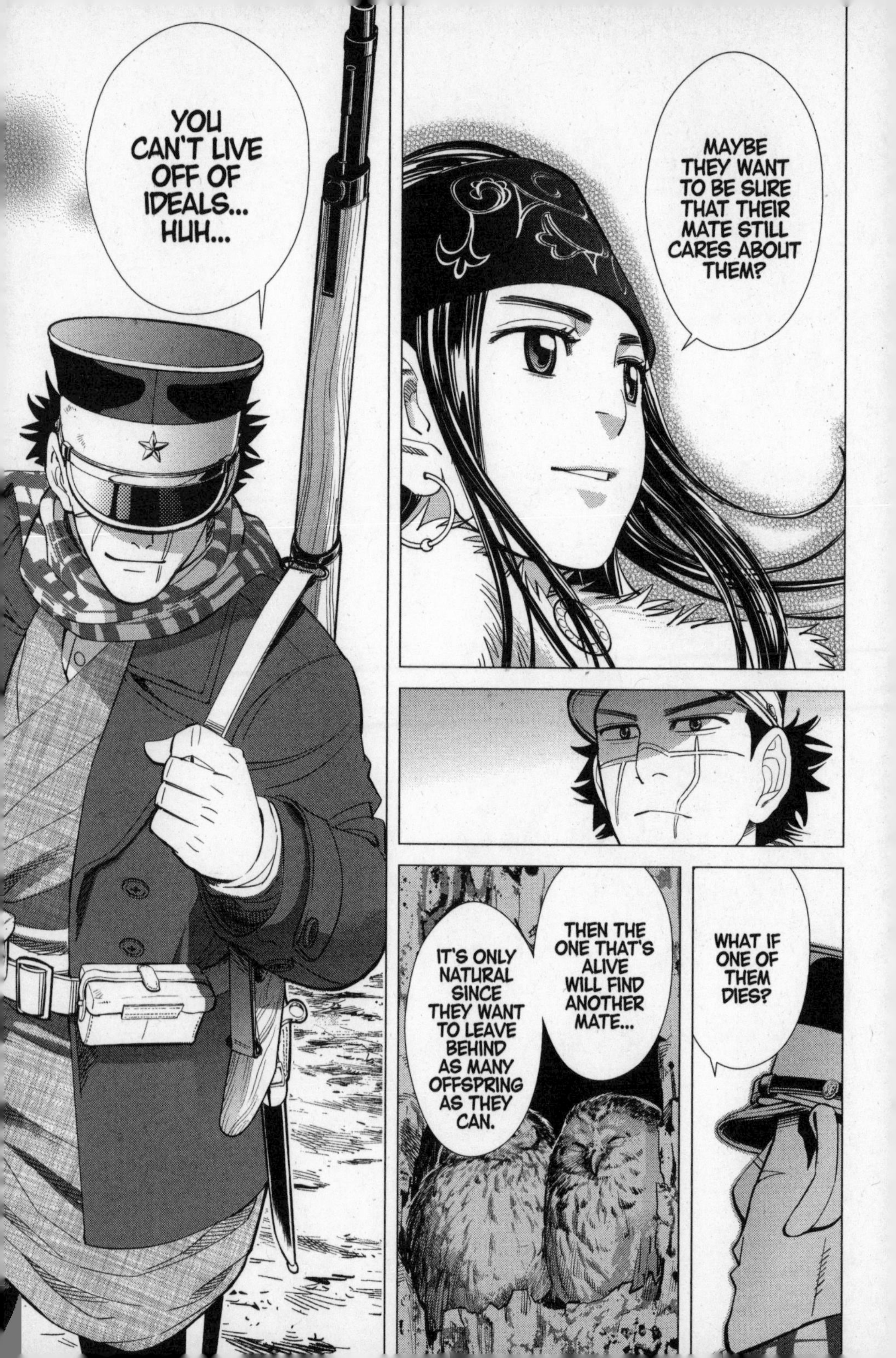
MAYBE THEY WANT TO BE SURE THAT THEIR MATE STILL CARES ABOUT THEM?
WHAT IF ONE OF THEM DIES?
THEN THE ONE THAT'S ALIVE WILL FIND ANOTHER MATE...
IT'S ONLY NATURAL SINCE THEY WANT TO LEAVE BEHIND AS MANY OFFSPRING AS THEY CAN.
YOU CAN'T LIVE OFF OF IDEALS... HUH...

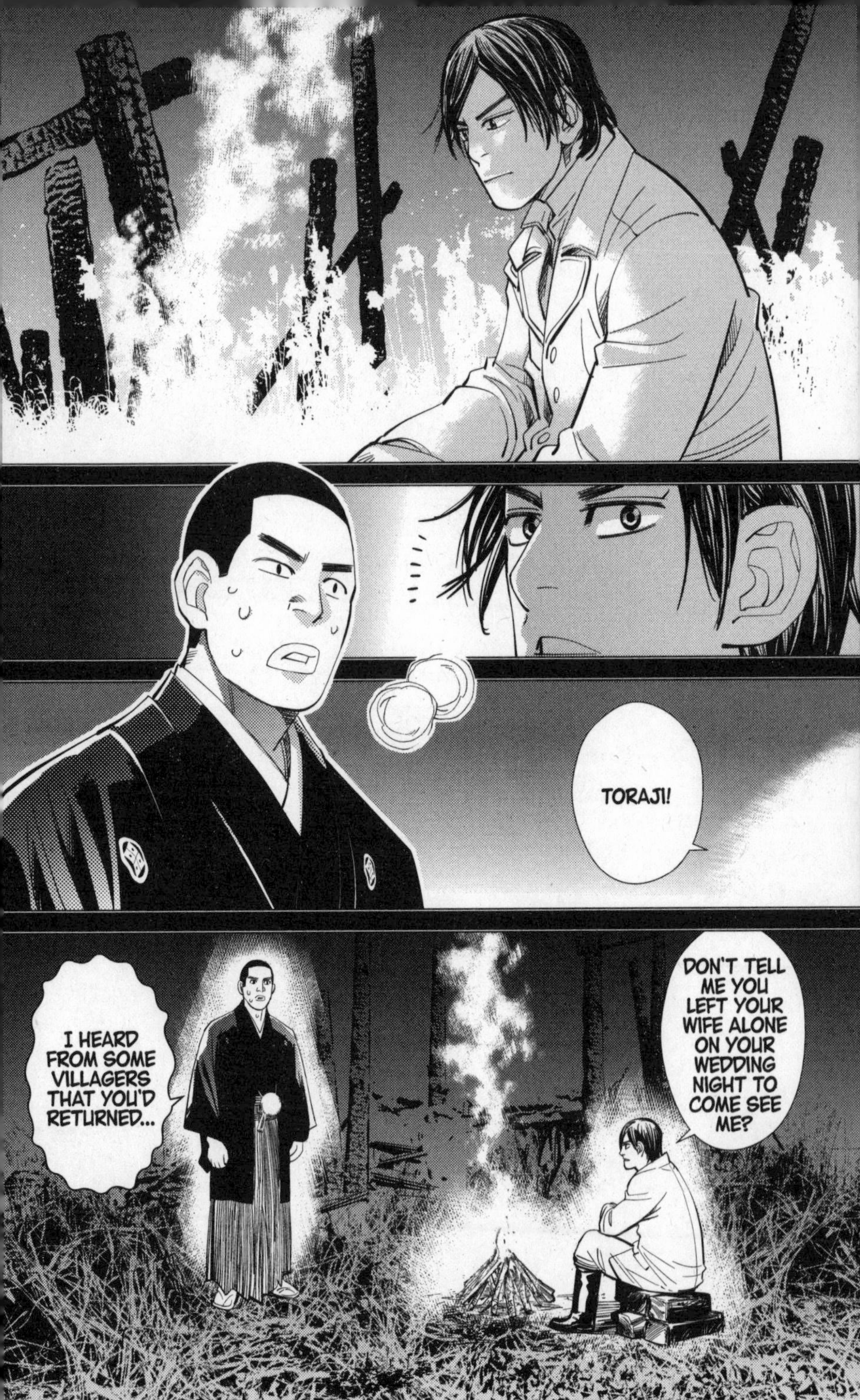
...
TORAJI!
DON'T TELL ME YOU LEFT YOUR WIFE ALONE ON YOUR WEDDING NIGHT TO COME SEE ME?
I HEARD FROM SOME VILLAGERS THAT YOU'D RETURNED...

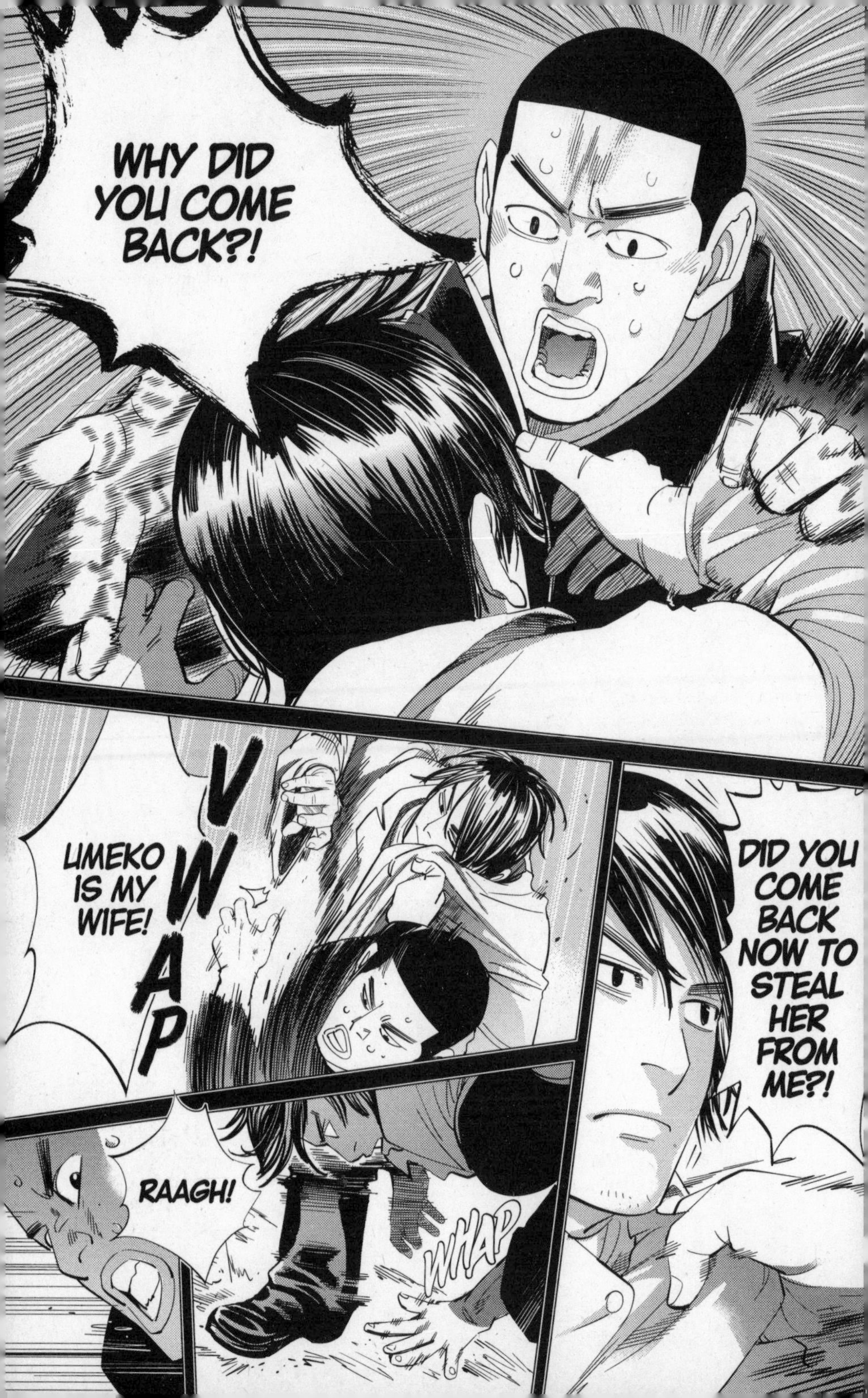
WHY DID YOU COME BACK?!
DID YOU COME BACK NOW TO STEAL HER FROM ME?!
UMEKO IS MY WIFE!
VWAP
RAAGH!
WHAP

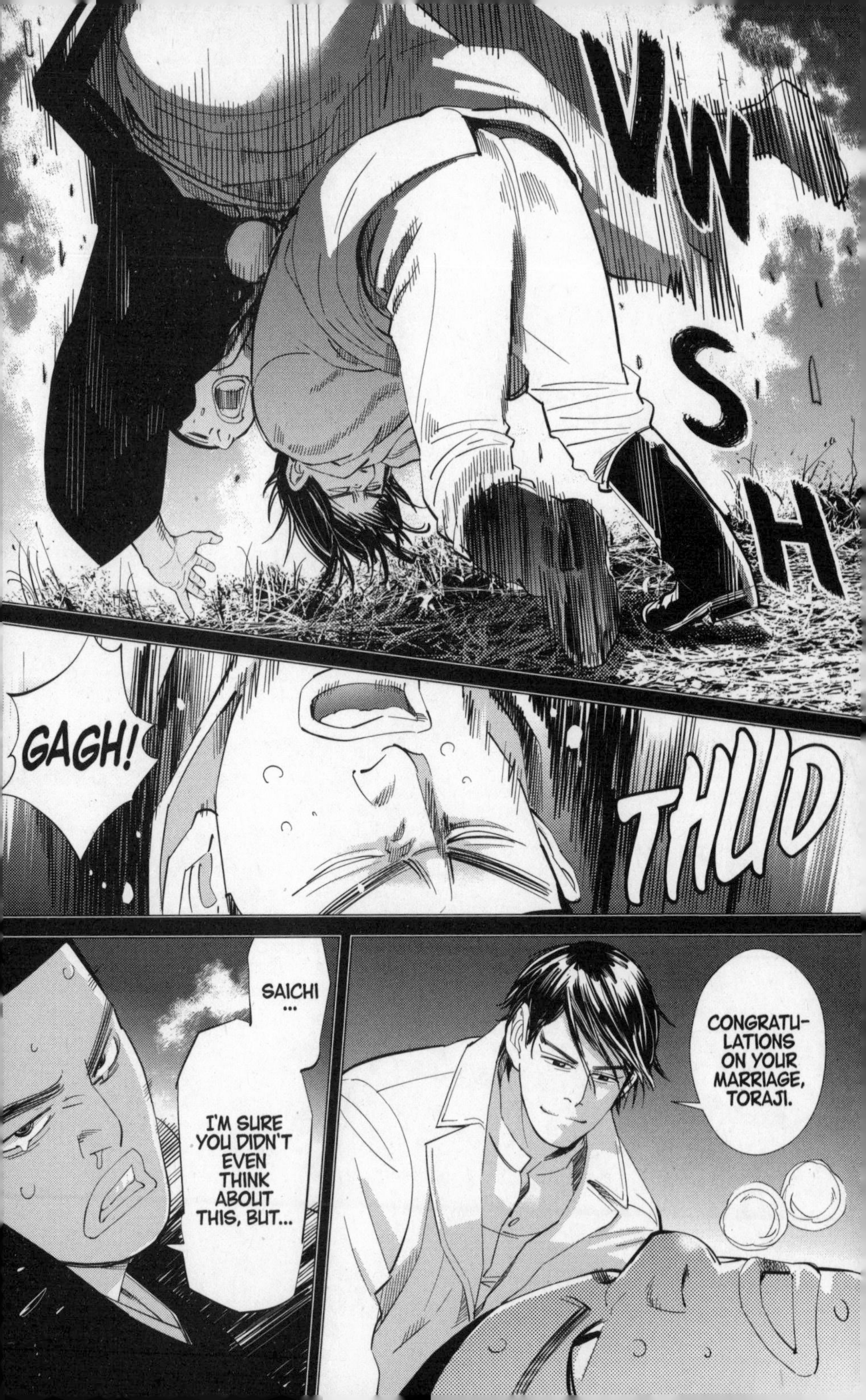
VWSH
THUD
GAGH!
CONGRATU-LATIONS ON YOUR MARRIAGE, TORAJI.
SAICHI ...
I'M SURE YOU DIDN'T EVEN THINK ABOUT THIS, BUT...

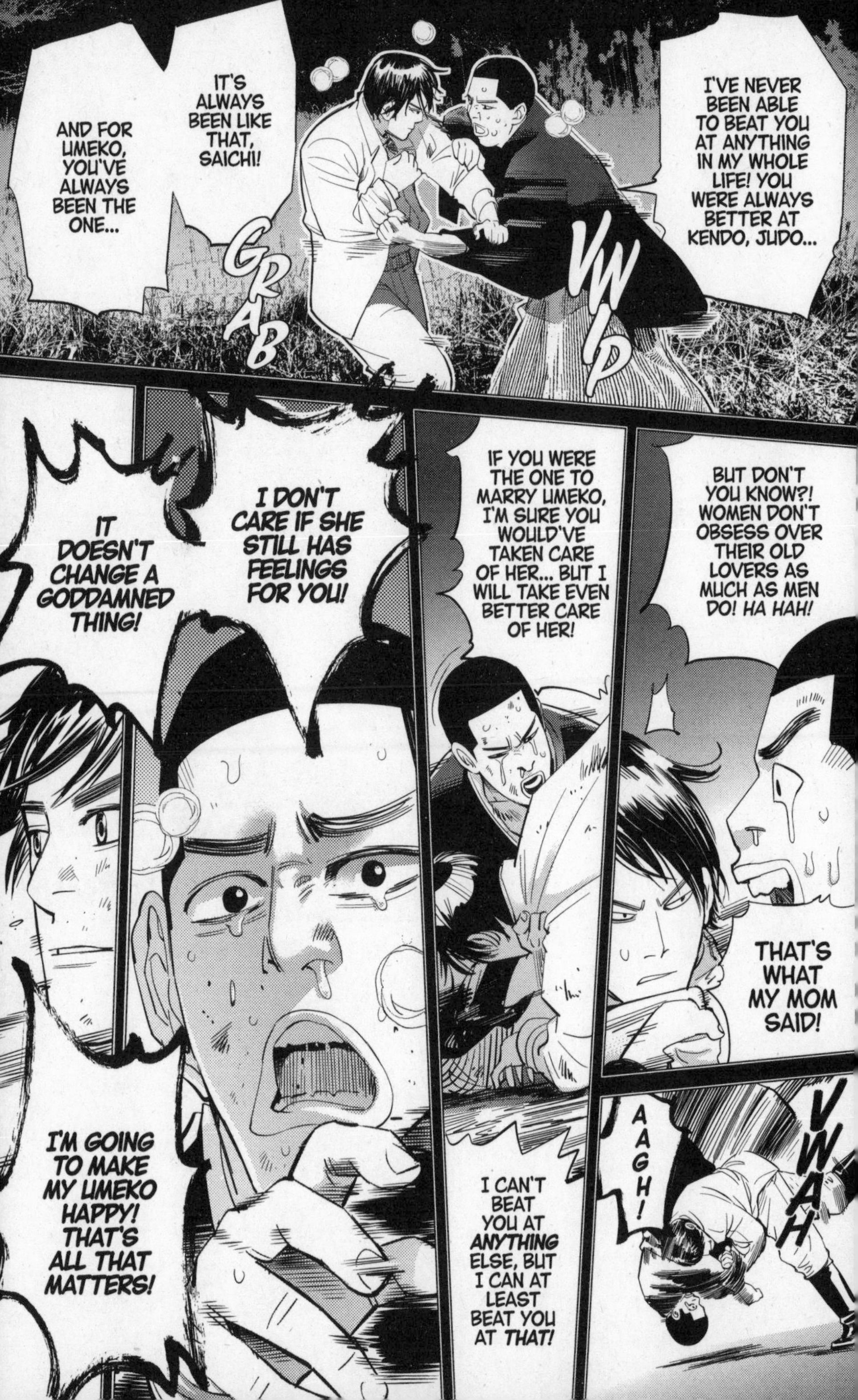
I'VE NEVER BEEN ABLE TO BEAT YOU AT ANYTHING IN MY WHOLE LIFE! YOU WERE ALWAYS BETTER AT KENDO, JUDO...
VWIP
IT'S ALWAYS BEEN LIKE THAT, SAICHI!
GRAB
AND FOR UMEKO, YOU'VE ALWAYS BEEN THE ONE...
BUT DON'T YOU KNOW?! WOMEN DON'T OBSESS OVER THEIR OLD LOVERS AS MUCH AS MEN DO! HA HAH!
THAT'S WHAT MY MOM SAID!
IF YOU WERE THE ONE TO MARRY UMEKO, I'M SURE YOU WOULD'VE TAKEN CARE OF HER... BUT I WILL TAKE EVEN BETTER CARE OF HER!
I DON'T CARE IF SHE STILL HAS FEELINGS FOR YOU!
IT DOESN'T CHANGE A GODDAMNED THING!
VWAH
AAGH!
I CAN'T BEAT YOU AT ANYTHING ELSE, BUT I CAN AT LEAST BEAT YOU AT THAT!
I'M GOING TO MAKE MY UMEKO HAPPY! THAT'S ALL THAT MATTERS!

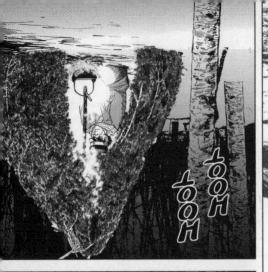

HOOT
HOOT

HOOT
HOOT

ZZZ

KRAK!

HOOT
HOOT

TO BE HONEST WITH YOU, IT STILL BOTHERED ME FOR A LONG TIME AFTERWARD.

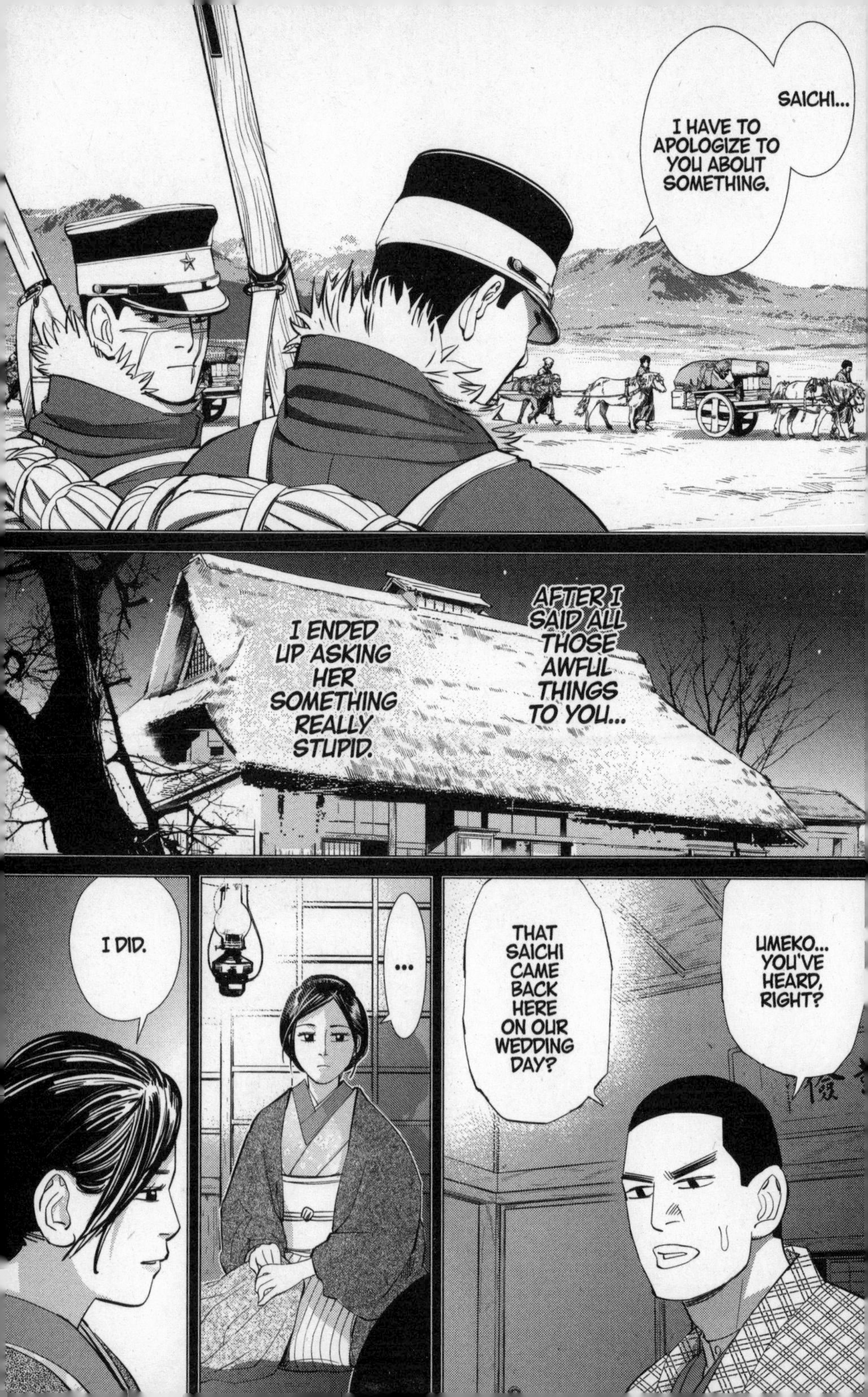
SAICHI...
I HAVE TO APOLOGIZE TO YOU ABOUT SOMETHING.
AFTER I SAID ALL THOSE AWFUL THINGS TO YOU...
I ENDED UP ASKING HER SOMETHING REALLY STUPID.
UMEKO... YOU'VE HEARD, RIGHT?
THAT SAICHI CAME BACK HERE ON OUR WEDDING DAY?
...
I DID.

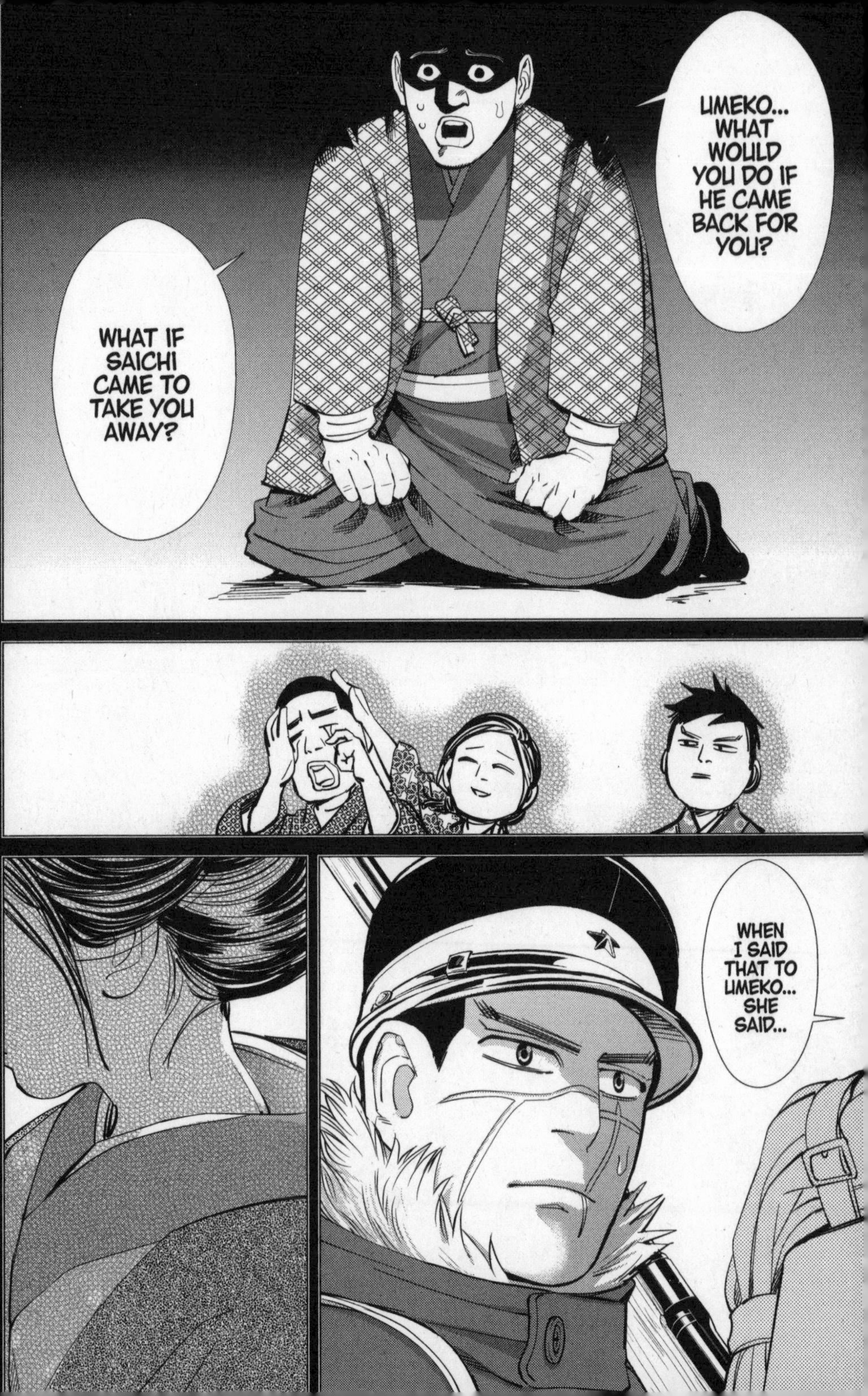
UMEKO... WHAT WOULD YOU DO IF HE CAME BACK FOR YOU?
WHAT IF SAICHI CAME TO TAKE YOU AWAY?
WHEN I SAID THAT TO UMEKO... SHE SAID...

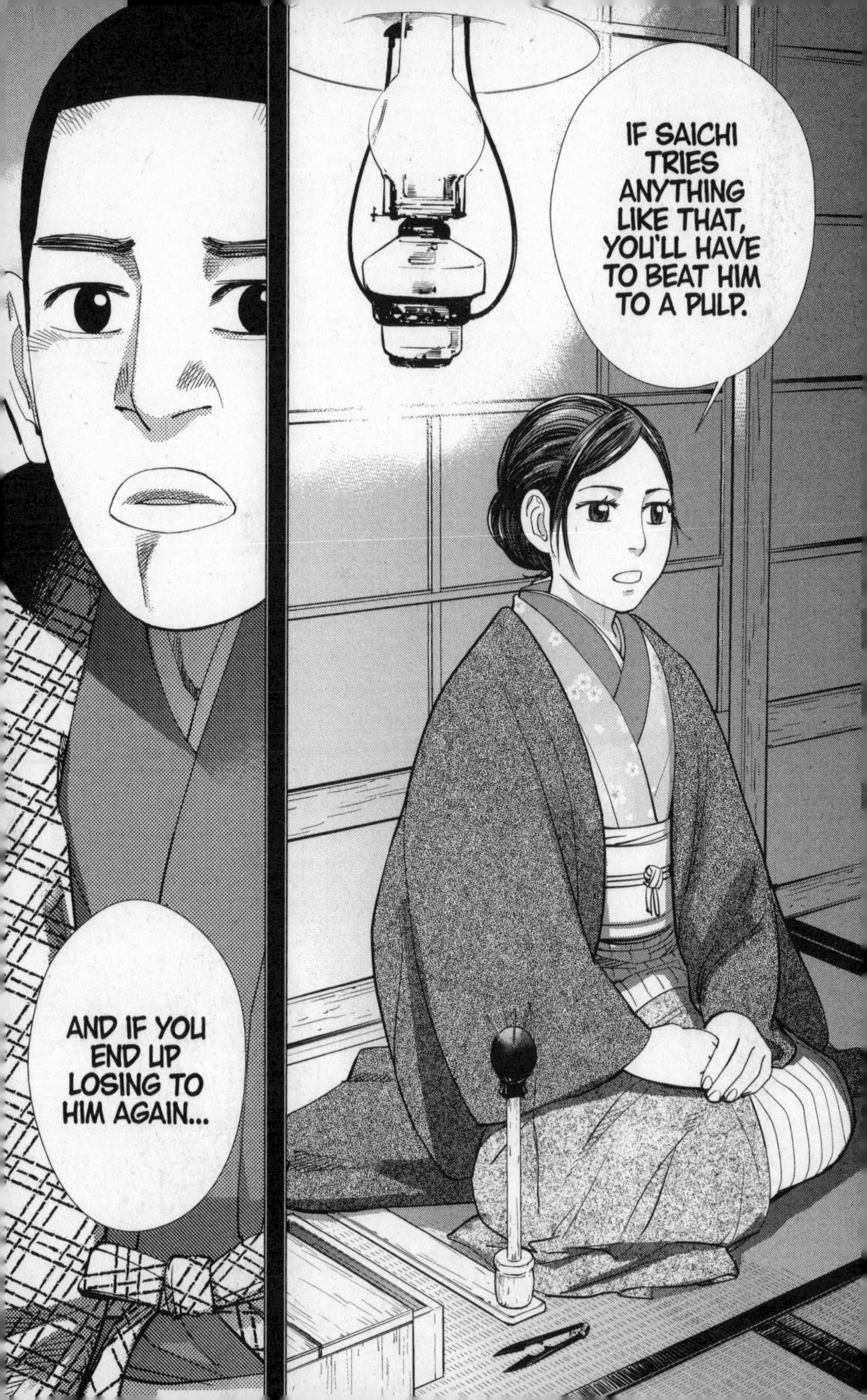
IF SAICHI TRIES ANYTHING LIKE THAT, YOU'LL HAVE TO BEAT HIM TO A PULP.
AND IF YOU END UP LOSING TO HIM AGAIN...

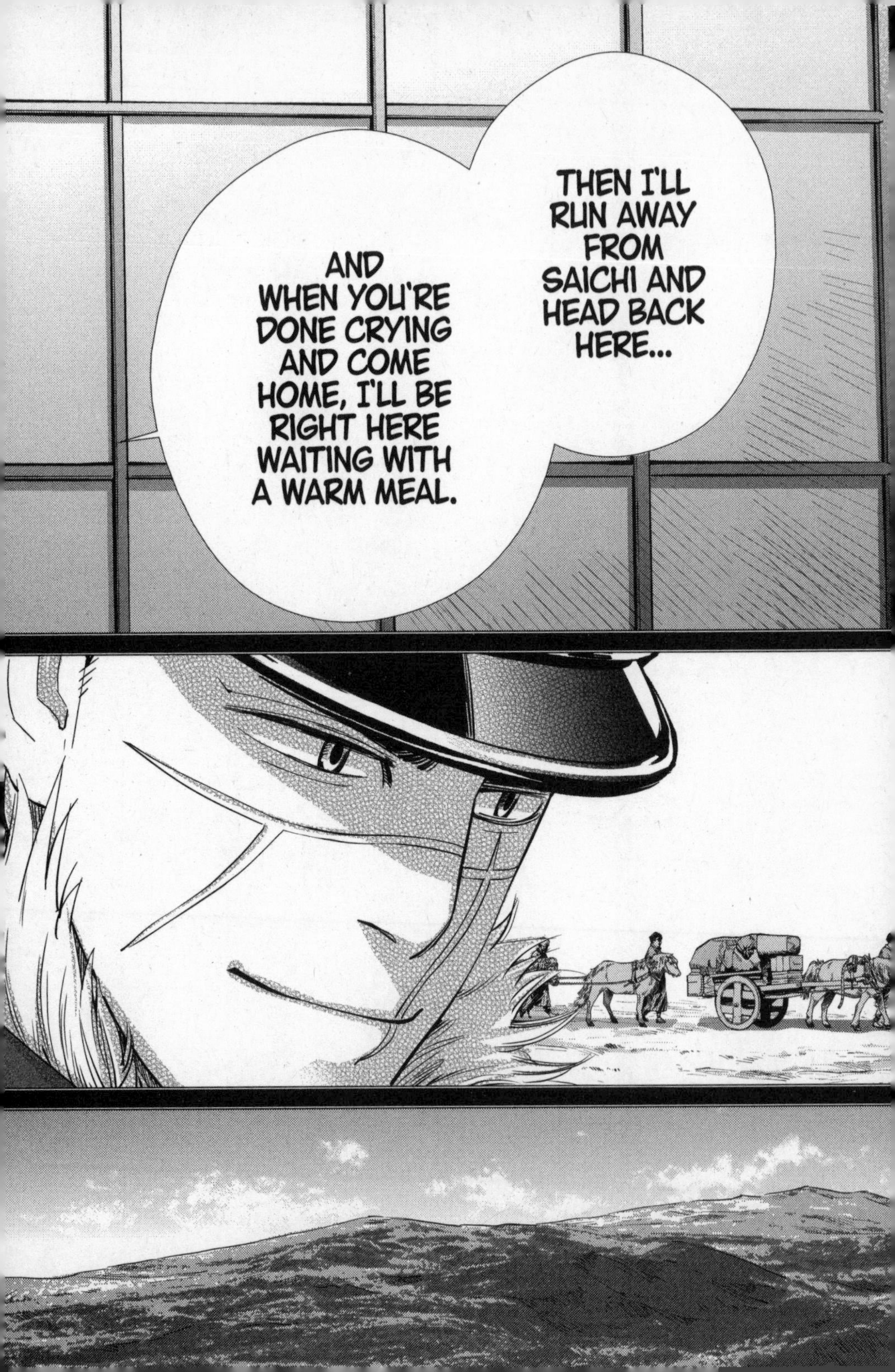
THEN I'LL RUN AWAY FROM SAICHI AND HEAD BACK HERE...
AND WHEN YOU'RE DONE CRYING AND COME HOME, I'LL BE RIGHT HERE WAITING WITH A WARM MEAL.

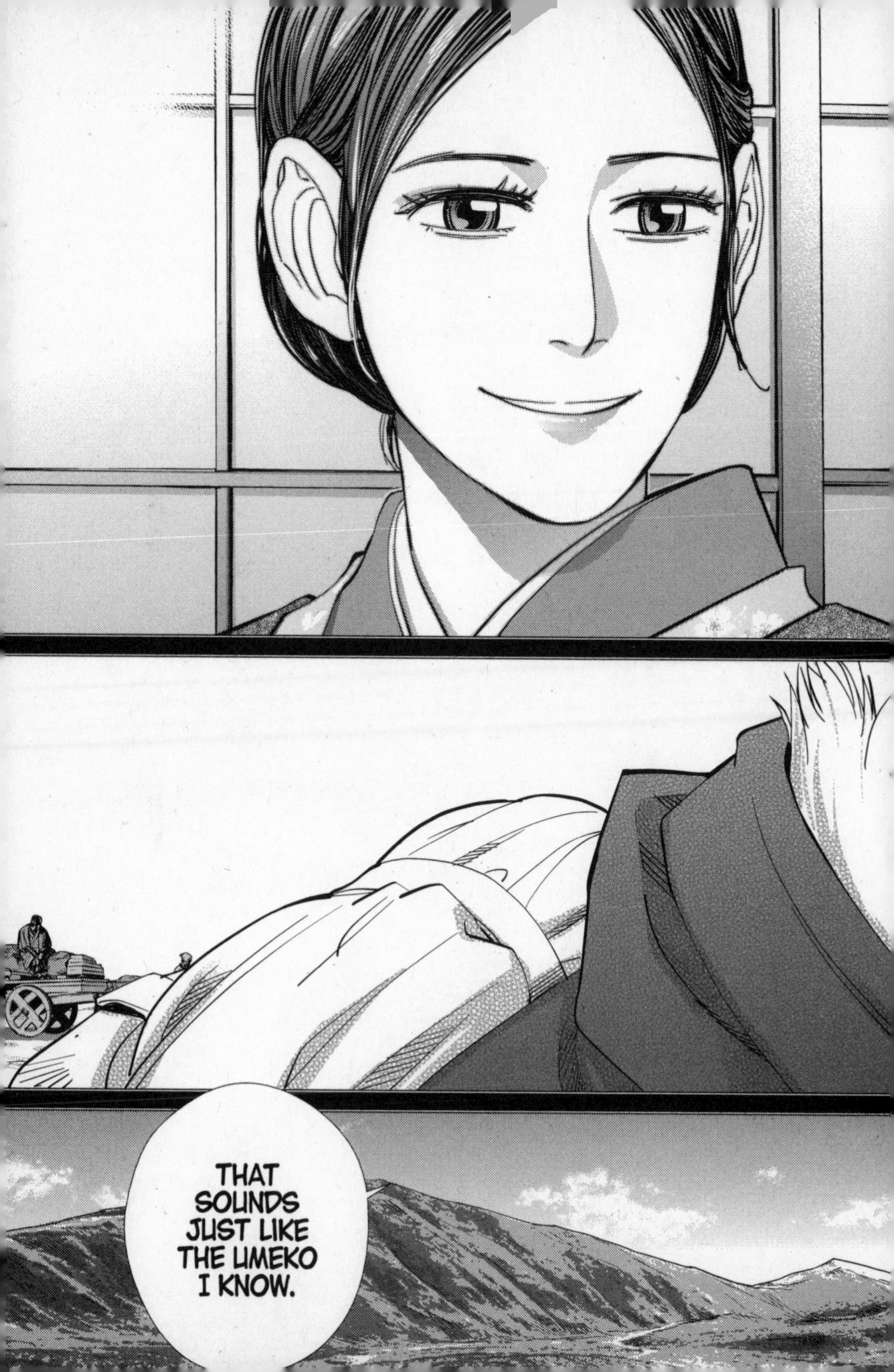
THAT SOUNDS JUST LIKE THE UMEKO I KNOW.

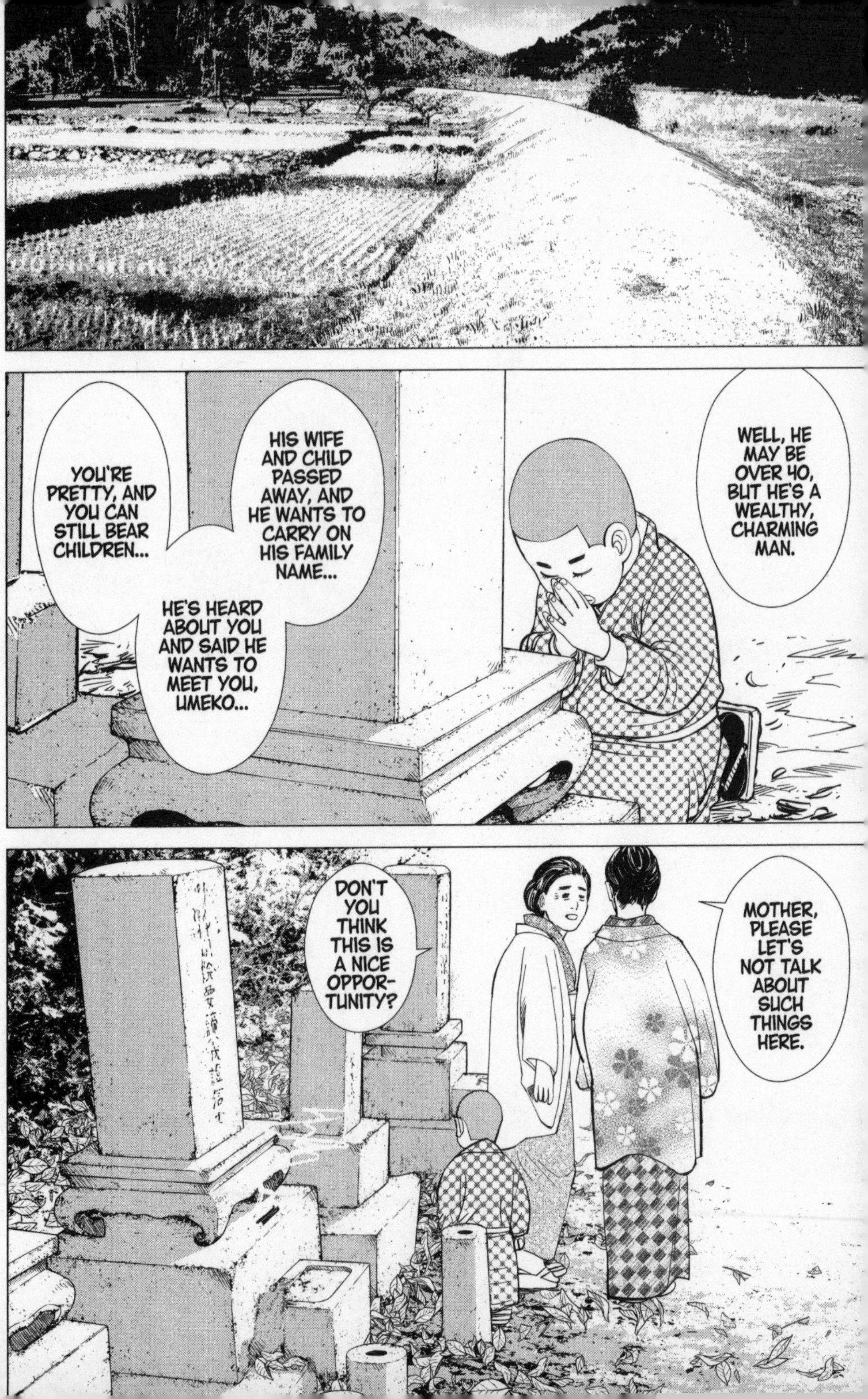
WELL, HE MAY BE OVER 40, BUT HE'S A WEALTHY, CHARMING MAN.
HIS WIFE AND CHILD PASSED AWAY, AND HE WANTS TO CARRY ON HIS FAMILY NAME...
HE'S HEARD ABOUT YOU AND SAID HE WANTS TO MEET YOU, UMEKO...
YOU'RE PRETTY, AND YOU CAN STILL BEAR CHILDREN...
MOTHER, PLEASE LET'S NOT TALK ABOUT SUCH THINGS HERE.
DON'T YOU THINK THIS IS A NICE OPPOR-TUNITY?

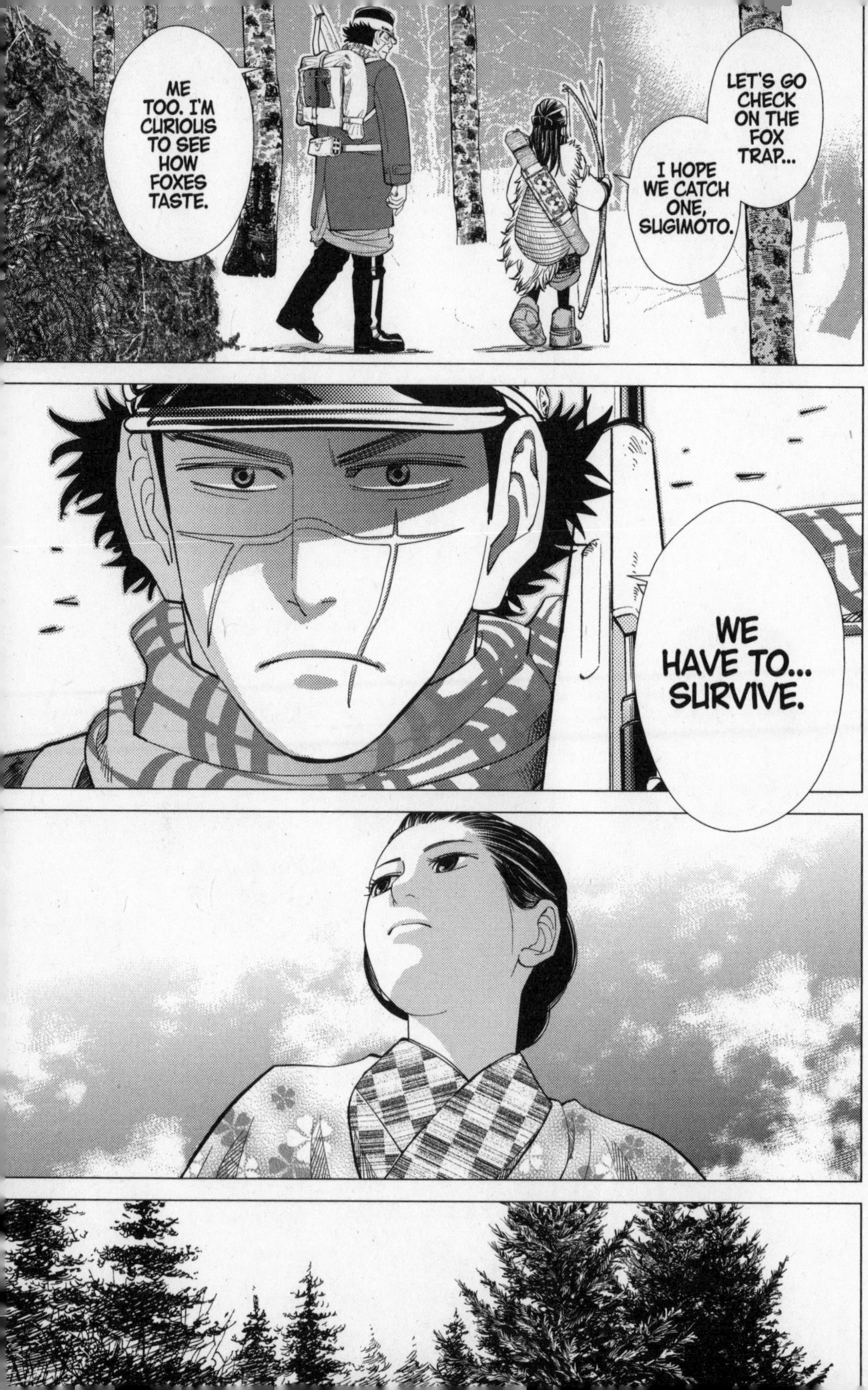
LET'S GO CHECK ON THE FOX TRAP...
I HOPE WE CATCH ONE, SUGIMOTO.
ME TOO. I'M CURIOUS TO SEE HOW FOXES TASTE.
WE HAVE TO... SURVIVE.

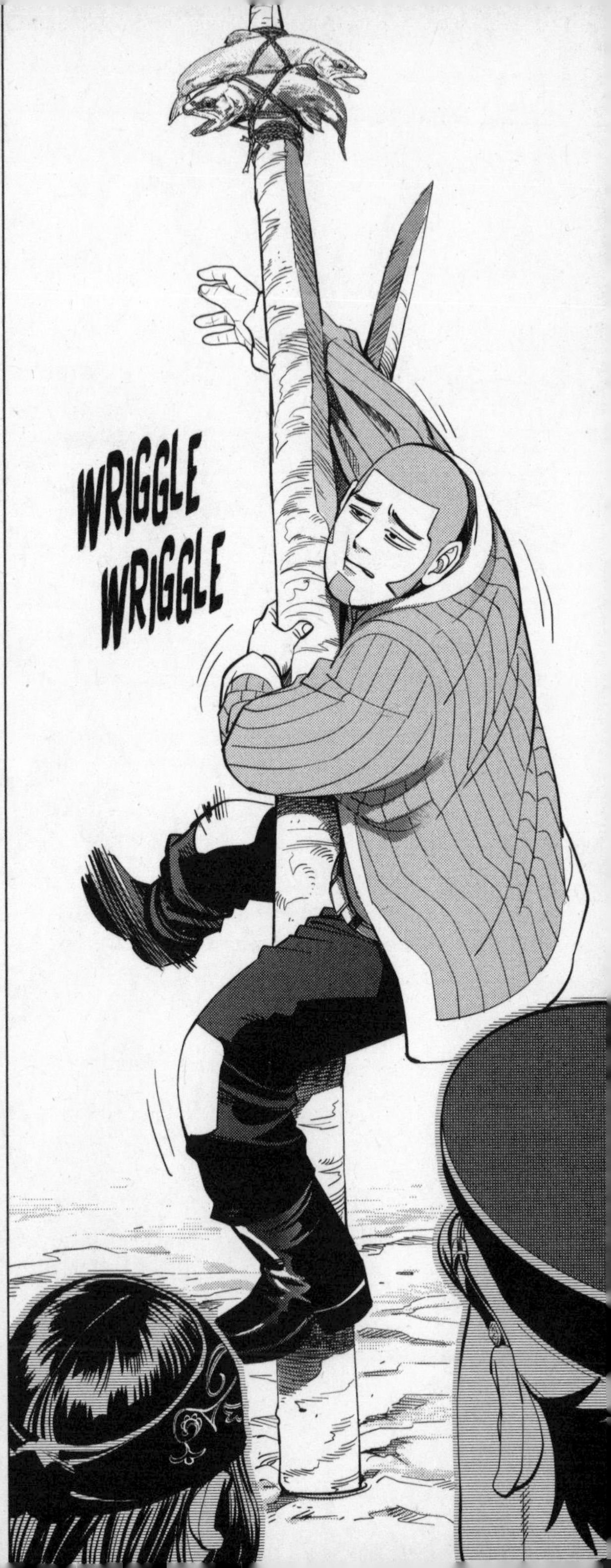
WRIGGLE
WRIGGLE
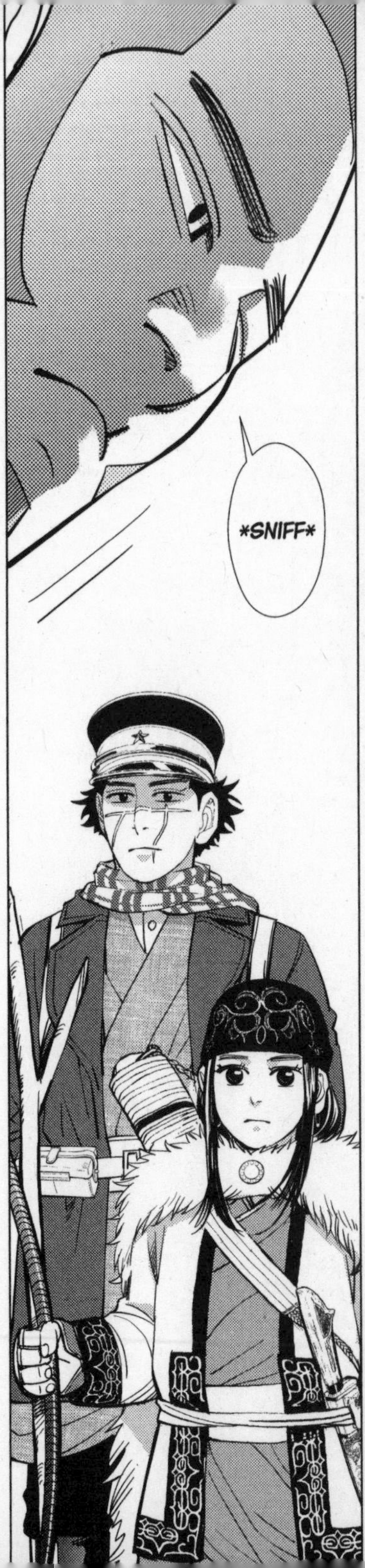
SNIFF

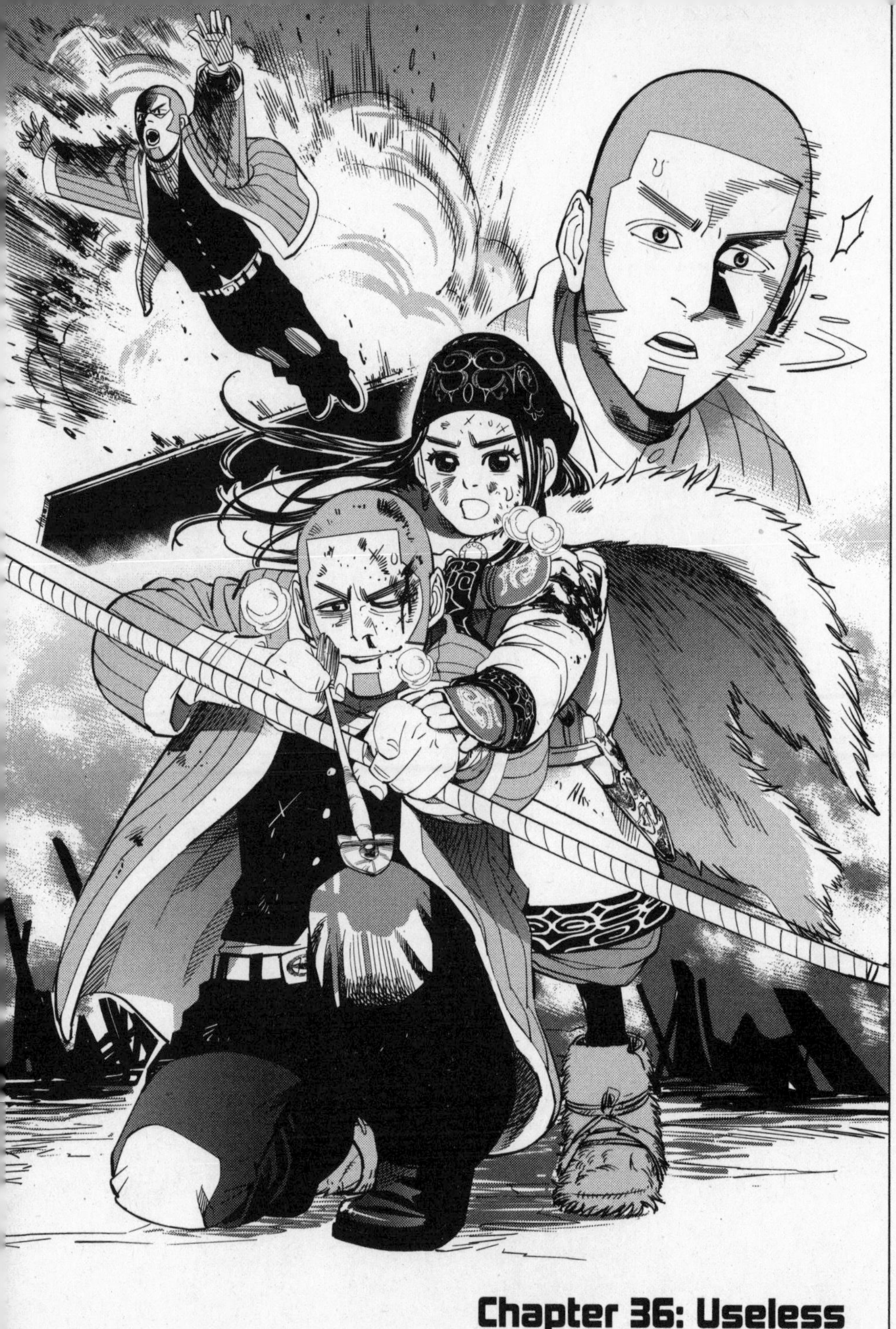

Chapter 36: Useless

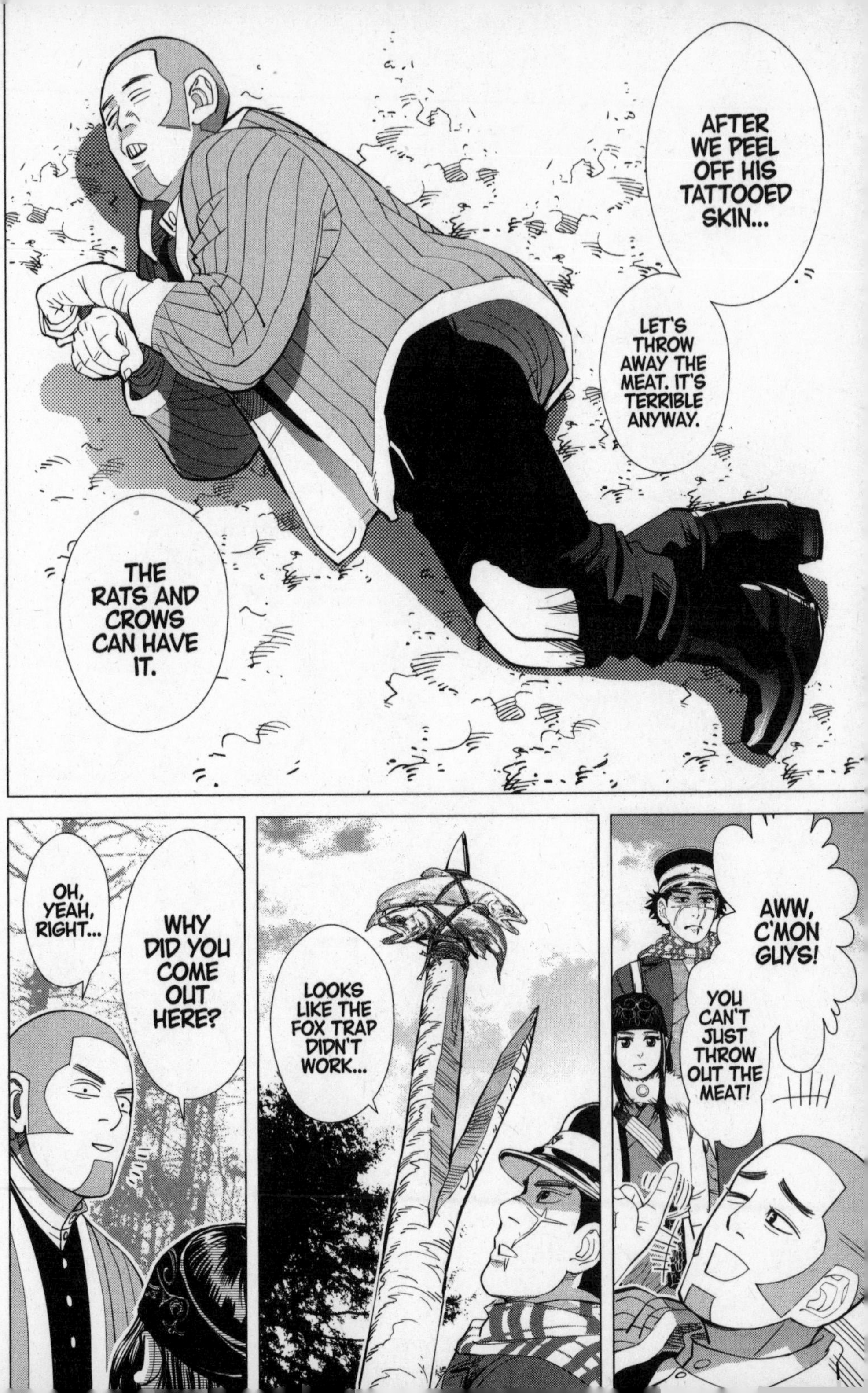
AFTER WE PEEL OFF HIS TATTOOED SKIN...
LET'S THROW AWAY THE MEAT. IT'S TERRIBLE ANYWAY.
THE RATS AND CROWS CAN HAVE IT.
AWW, C'MON GUYS!
YOU CAN'T JUST THROW OUT THE MEAT!
LOOKS LIKE THE FOX TRAP DIDN'T WORK...
WHY DID YOU COME OUT HERE?
OH, YEAH, RIGHT...

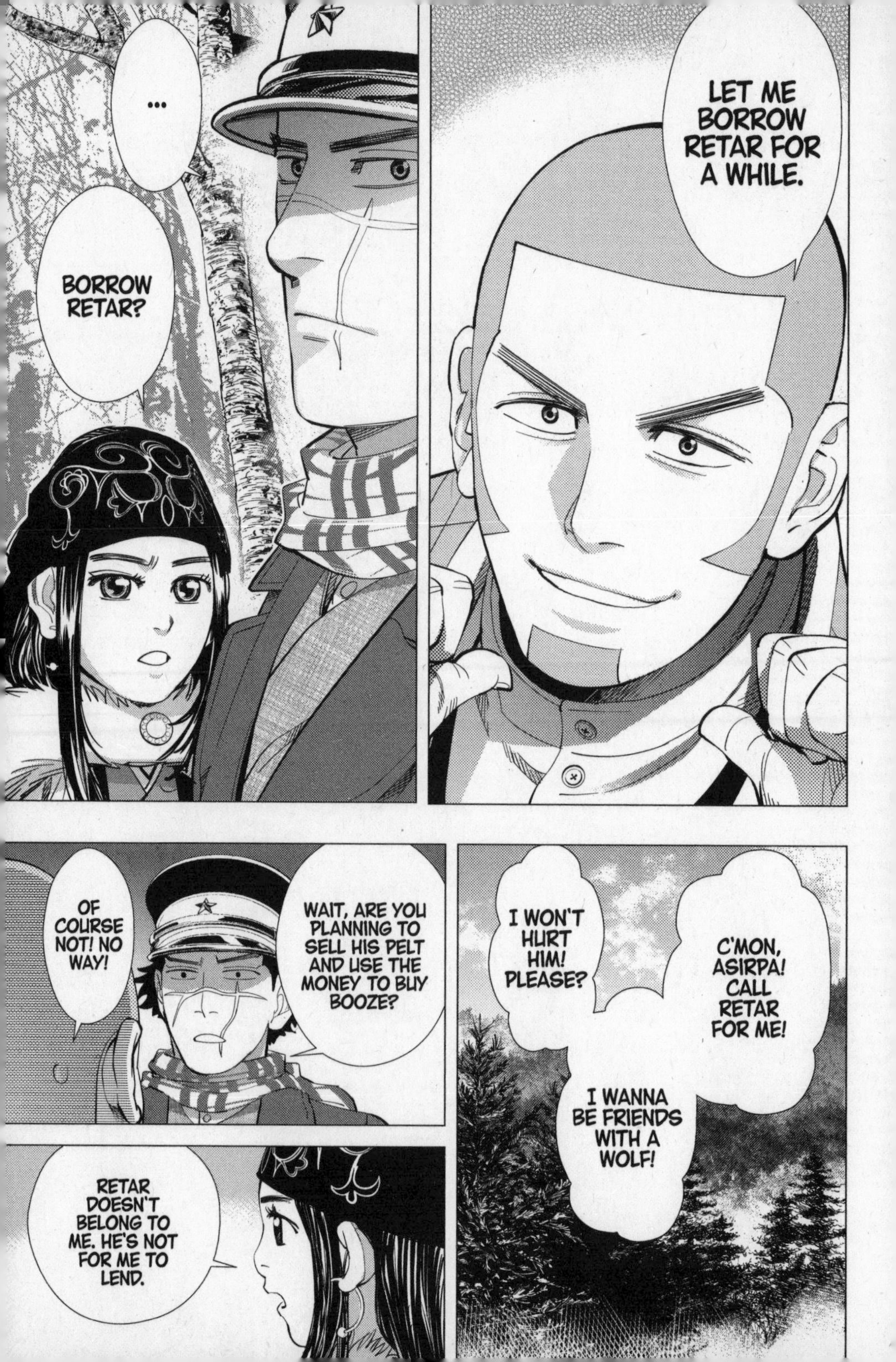
LET ME BORROW RETAR FOR A WHILE.
...
BORROW RETAR?
C'MON, ASIRPA! CALL RETAR FOR ME!
I WON'T HURT HIM! PLEASE?
I WANNA BE FRIENDS WITH A WOLF!
WAIT, ARE YOU PLANNING TO SELL HIS PELT AND USE THE MONEY TO BUY BOOZE?
OF COURSE NOT! NO WAY!
RETAR DOESN'T BELONG TO ME. HE'S NOT FOR ME TO LEND.

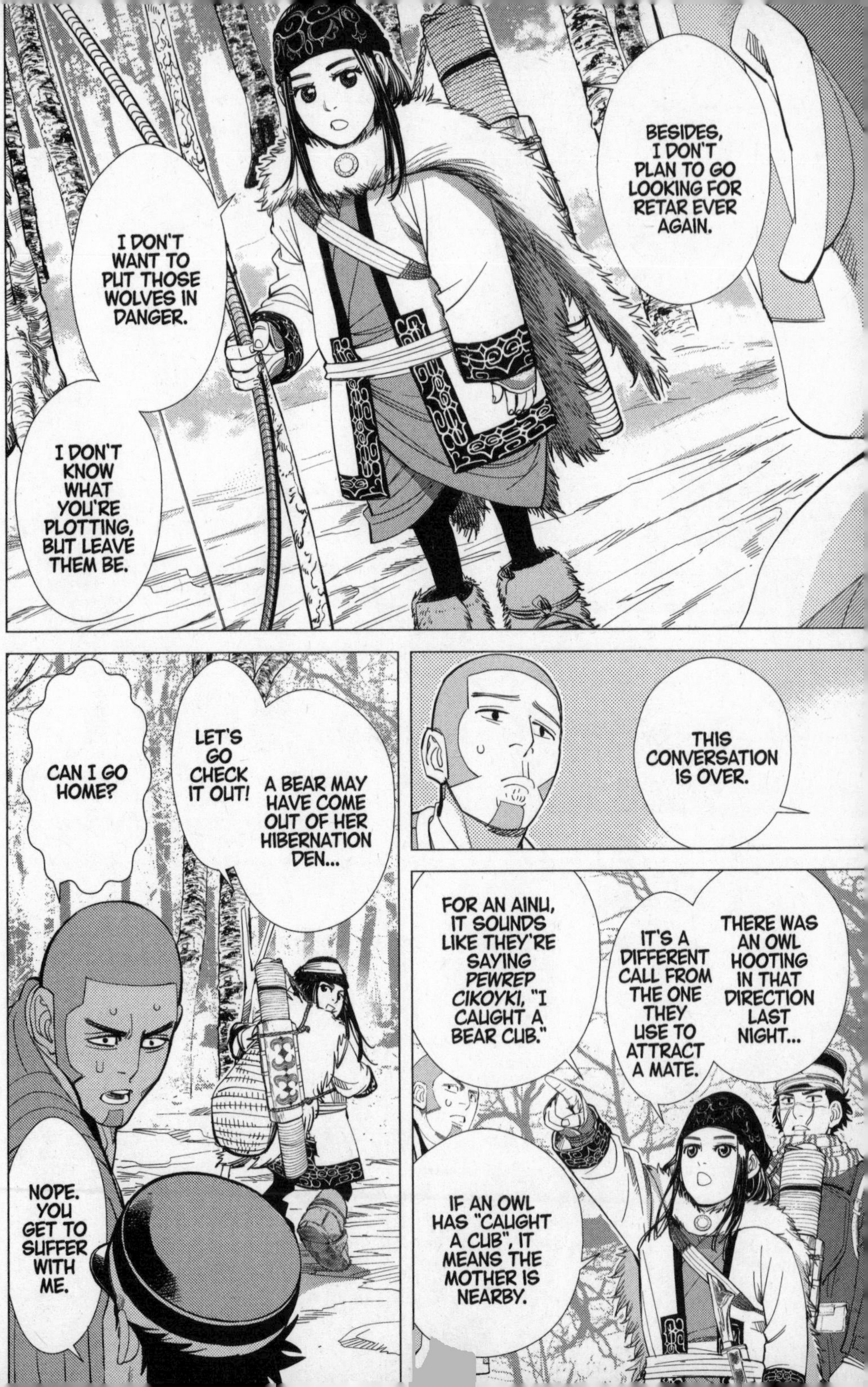
BESIDES, I DON'T PLAN TO GO LOOKING FOR RETAR EVER AGAIN.
I DON'T WANT TO PUT THOSE WOLVES IN DANGER.
I DON'T KNOW WHAT YOU'RE PLOTTING, BUT LEAVE THEM BE.
THIS CONVERSATION IS OVER.
THERE WAS AN OWL HOOTING IN THAT DIRECTION LAST NIGHT...
IT'S A DIFFERENT CALL FROM THE ONE THEY USE TO ATTRACT A MATE.
FOR AN AINU, IT SOUNDS LIKE THEY'RE SAYING PEWREP CIKOYKI, "I CAUGHT A BEAR CUB."
IF AN OWL HAS "CAUGHT A CUB", IT MEANS THE MOTHER IS NEARBY.
LET'S GO CHECK IT OUT!
A BEAR MAY HAVE COME OUT OF HER HIBERNATION DEN...
CAN I GO HOME?
NOPE. YOU GET TO SUFFER WITH ME.

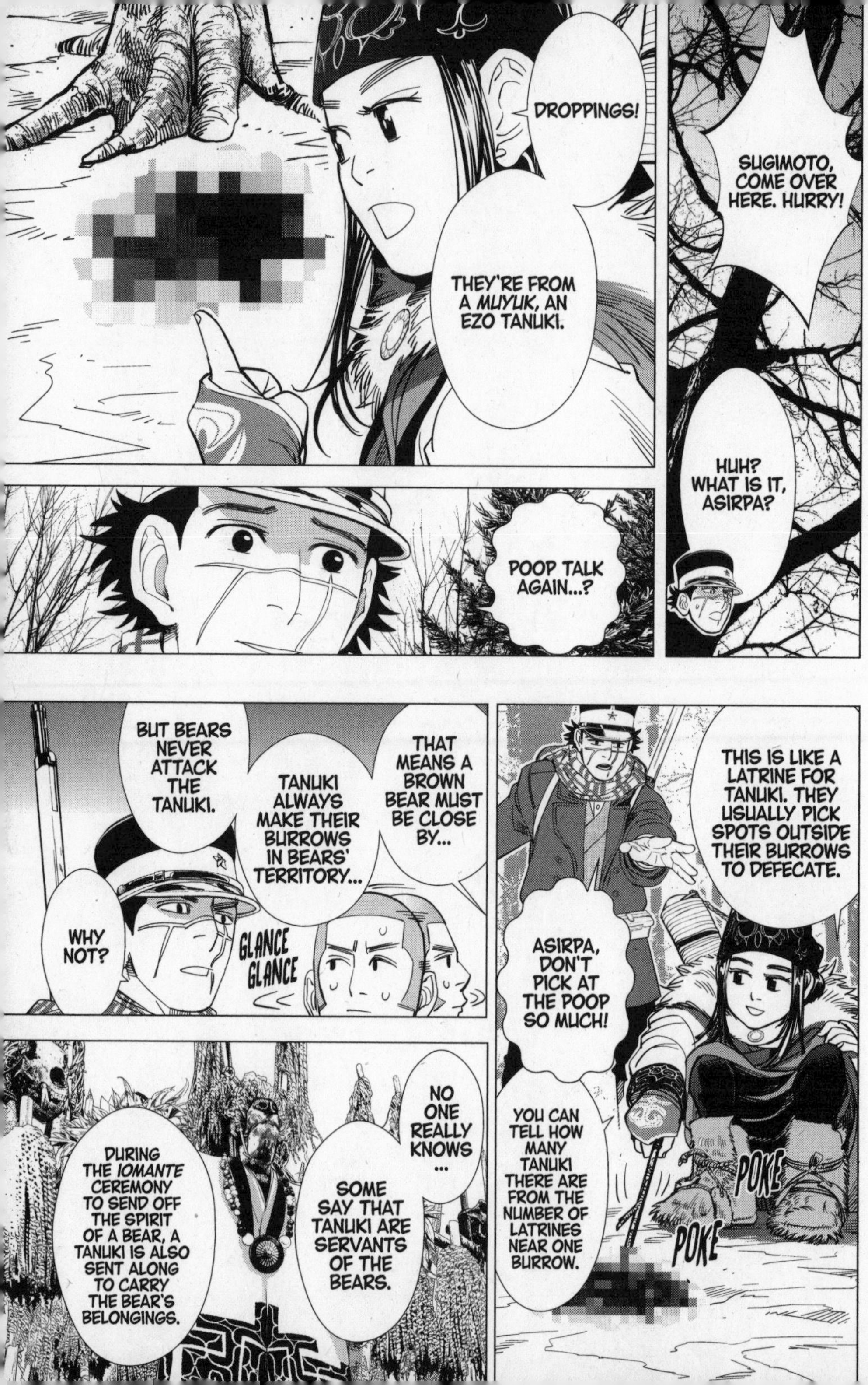
SUGIMOTO, COME OVER HERE. HURRY!
HUH? WHAT IS IT, ASIRPA?
DROPPINGS!
THEY'RE FROM A *MUYUK*, AN EZO TANUKI.
POOP TALK AGAIN...?
THIS IS LIKE A LATRINE FOR TANUKI. THEY USUALLY PICK SPOTS OUTSIDE THEIR BURROWS TO DEFECATE.
ASIRPA, DON'T PICK AT THE POOP SO MUCH!
YOU CAN TELL HOW MANY TANUKI THERE ARE FROM THE NUMBER OF LATRINES NEAR ONE BURROW.
POKE
POKE
THAT MEANS A BROWN BEAR MUST BE CLOSE BY...
TANUKI ALWAYS MAKE THEIR BURROWS IN BEARS' TERRITORY...
BUT BEARS NEVER ATTACK THE TANUKI.
WHY NOT?
GLANCE GLANCE
NO ONE REALLY KNOWS...
SOME SAY THAT TANUKI ARE SERVANTS OF THE BEARS.
DURING THE *IOMANTE* CEREMONY TO SEND OFF THE SPIRIT OF A BEAR, A TANUKI IS ALSO SENT ALONG TO CARRY THE BEAR'S BELONGINGS.

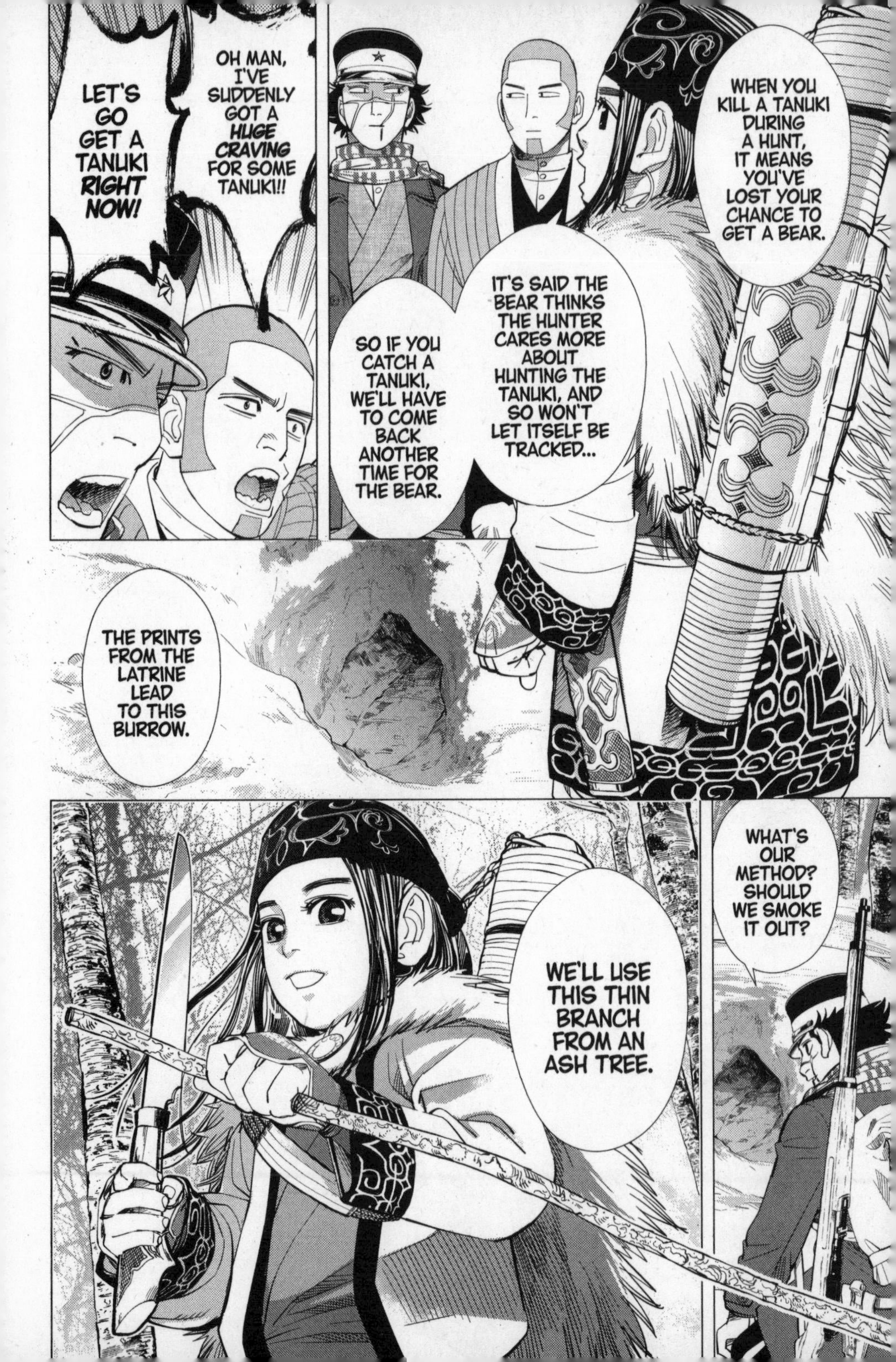
WHEN YOU KILL A TANUKI DURING A HUNT, IT MEANS YOU'VE LOST YOUR CHANCE TO GET A BEAR.
IT'S SAID THE BEAR THINKS THE HUNTER CARES MORE ABOUT HUNTING THE TANUKI, AND SO WON'T LET ITSELF BE TRACKED...
SO IF YOU CATCH A TANUKI, WE'LL HAVE TO COME BACK ANOTHER TIME FOR THE BEAR.
OH MAN, I'VE SUDDENLY GOT A HUGE CRAVING FOR SOME TANUKI!!
LET'S GO GET A TANUKI RIGHT NOW!
THE PRINTS FROM THE LATRINE LEAD TO THIS BURROW.
WHAT'S OUR METHOD? SHOULD WE SMOKE IT OUT?
WE'LL USE THIS THIN BRANCH FROM AN ASH TREE.

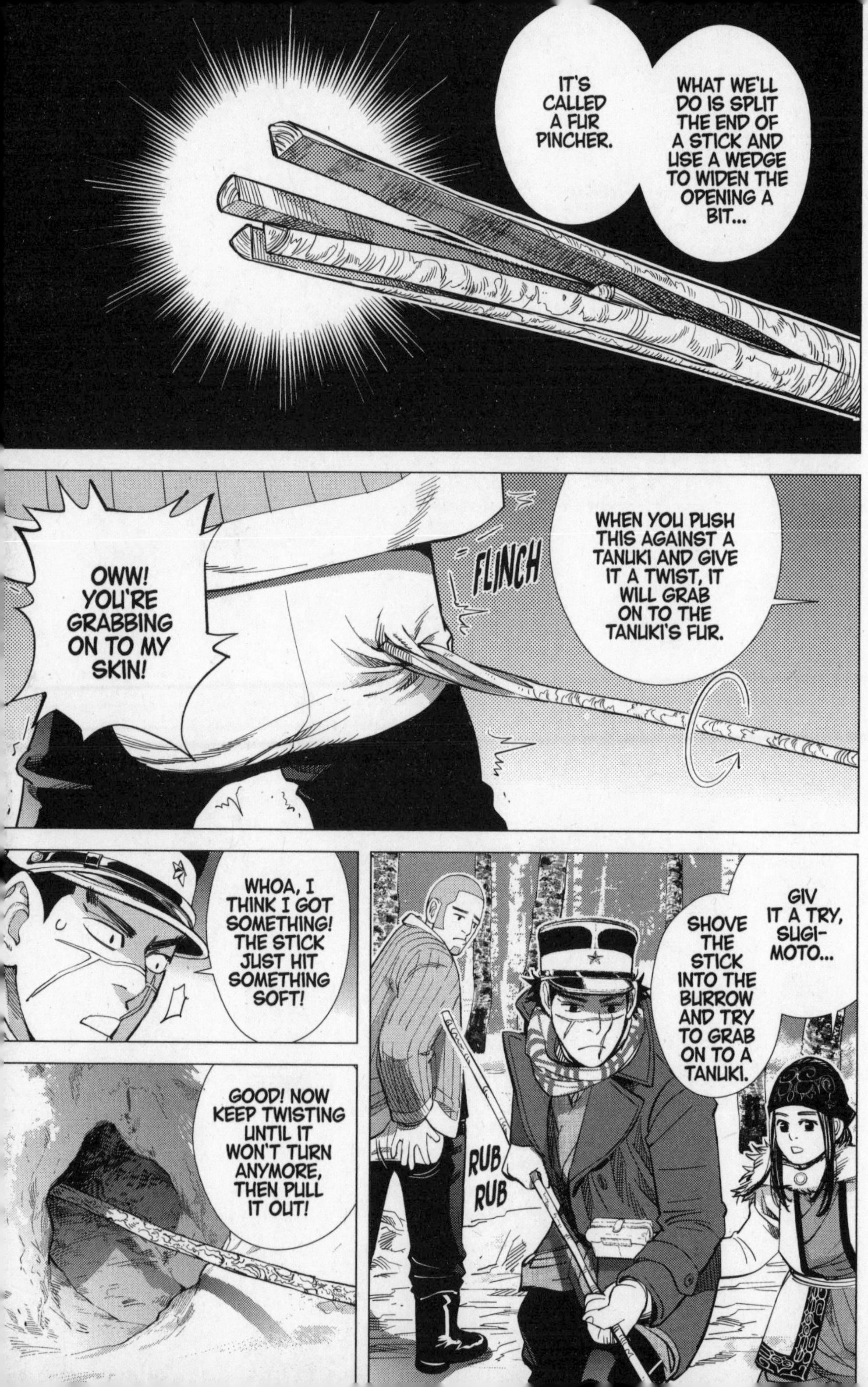

WHAT WE'LL DO IS SPLIT THE END OF A STICK AND USE A WEDGE TO WIDEN THE OPENING A BIT...
IT'S CALLED A FUR PINCHER.
WHEN YOU PUSH THIS AGAINST A TANUKI AND GIVE IT A TWIST, IT WILL GRAB ON TO THE TANUKI'S FUR.
FLINCH
OWW! YOU'RE GRABBING ON TO MY SKIN!
GIV IT A TRY, SUGI-MOTO...
SHOVE THE STICK INTO THE BURROW AND TRY TO GRAB ON TO A TANUKI.
RUB RUB
WHOA, I THINK I GOT SOMETHING! THE STICK JUST HIT SOMETHING SOFT!
GOOD! NOW KEEP TWISTING UNTIL IT WON'T TURN ANYMORE, THEN PULL IT OUT!

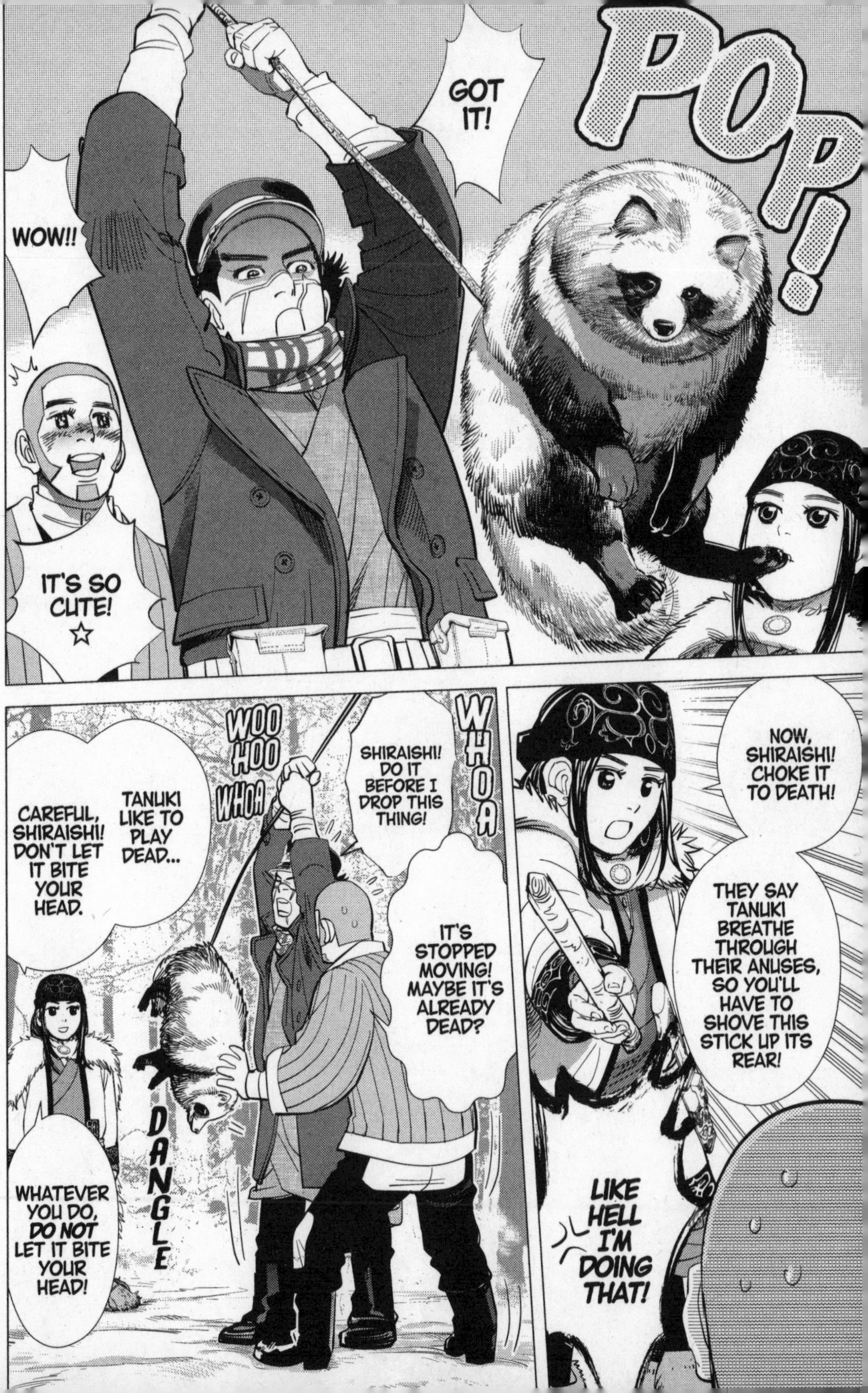
POP!
GOT IT!
WOW!!
IT'S SO CUTE! ☆
NOW, SHIRAISHI! CHOKE IT TO DEATH!
THEY SAY TANUKI BREATHE THROUGH THEIR ANUSES, SO YOU'LL HAVE TO SHOVE THIS STICK UP ITS REAR!
LIKE HELL I'M DOING THAT!
WHOA
SHIRAISHI! DO IT BEFORE I DROP THIS THING!
WOO HOO WHOA
IT'S STOPPED MOVING! MAYBE IT'S ALREADY DEAD?
TANUKI LIKE TO PLAY DEAD...
CAREFUL, SHIRAISHI! DON'T LET IT BITE YOUR HEAD.
DANGLE
WHATEVER YOU DO, DO NOT LET IT BITE YOUR HEAD!

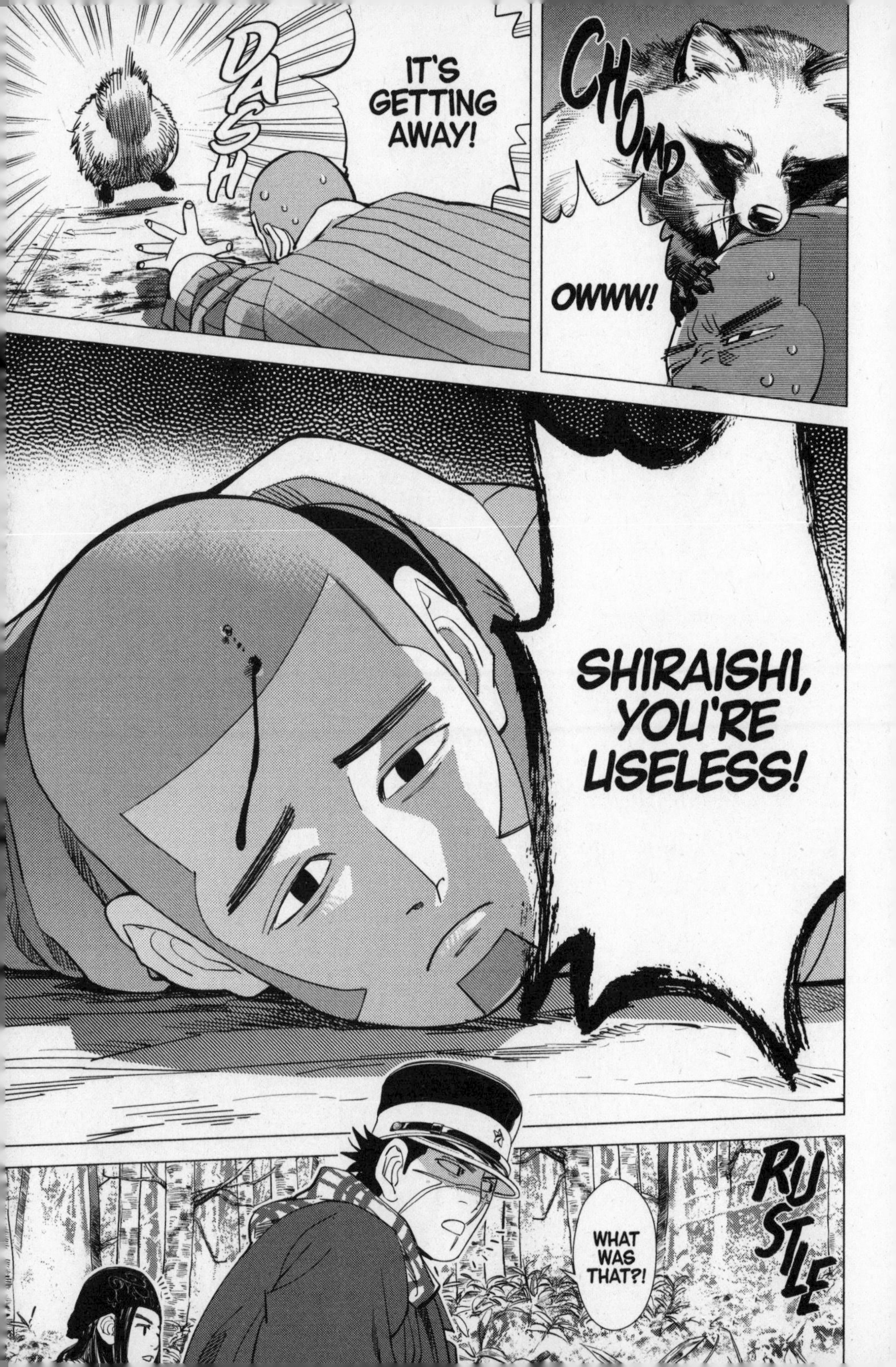
CHOMP
OWWW!
DASH
IT'S GETTING AWAY!
SHIRAISHI, YOU'RE USELESS!
RUSTLE
WHAT WAS THAT?!

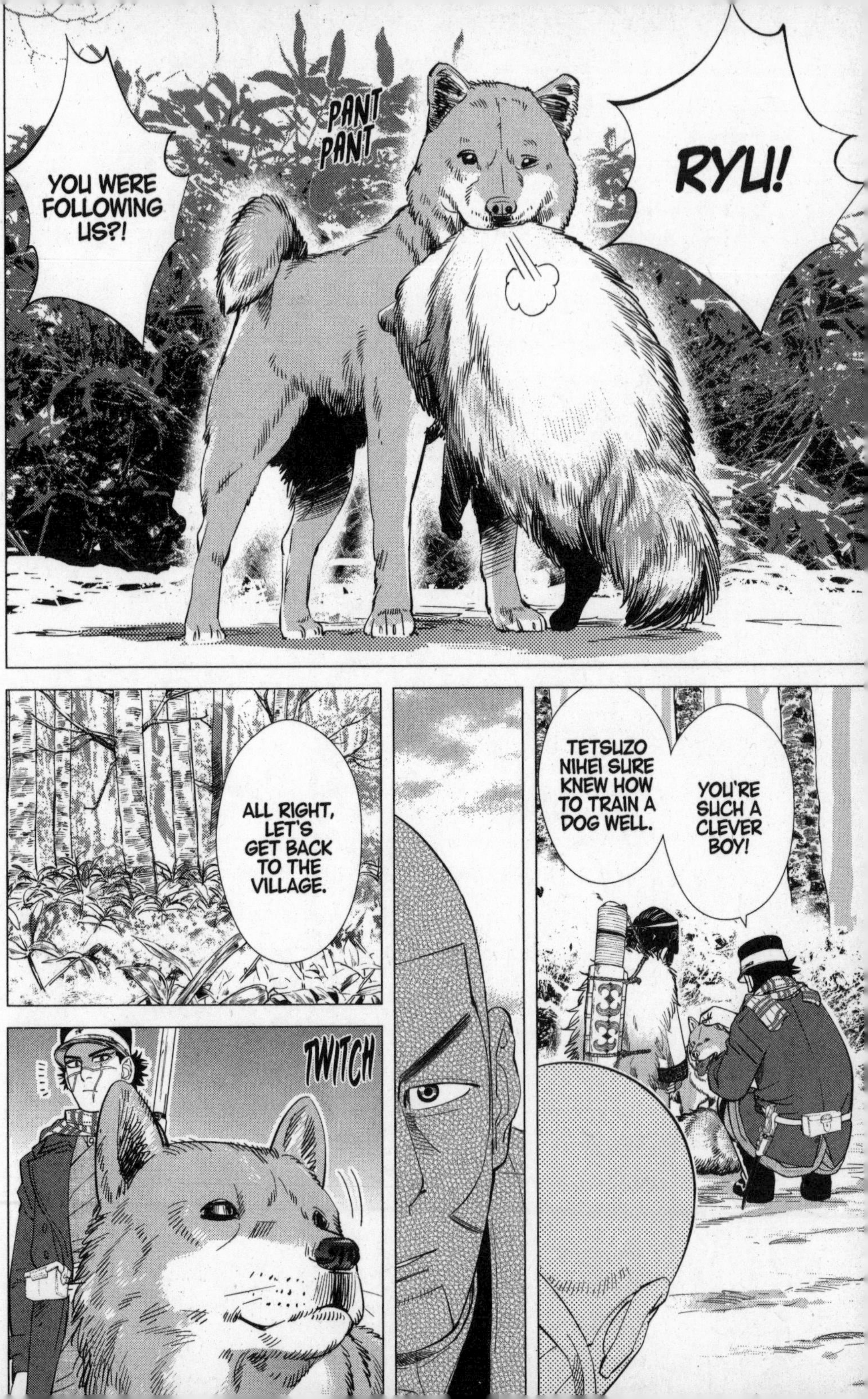
RYU!
PANT PANT
YOU WERE FOLLOWING US?!
TETSUZO NIHEI SURE KNEW HOW TO TRAIN A DOG WELL.
YOU'RE SUCH A CLEVER BOY!
ALL RIGHT, LET'S GET BACK TO THE VILLAGE.
TWITCH
......

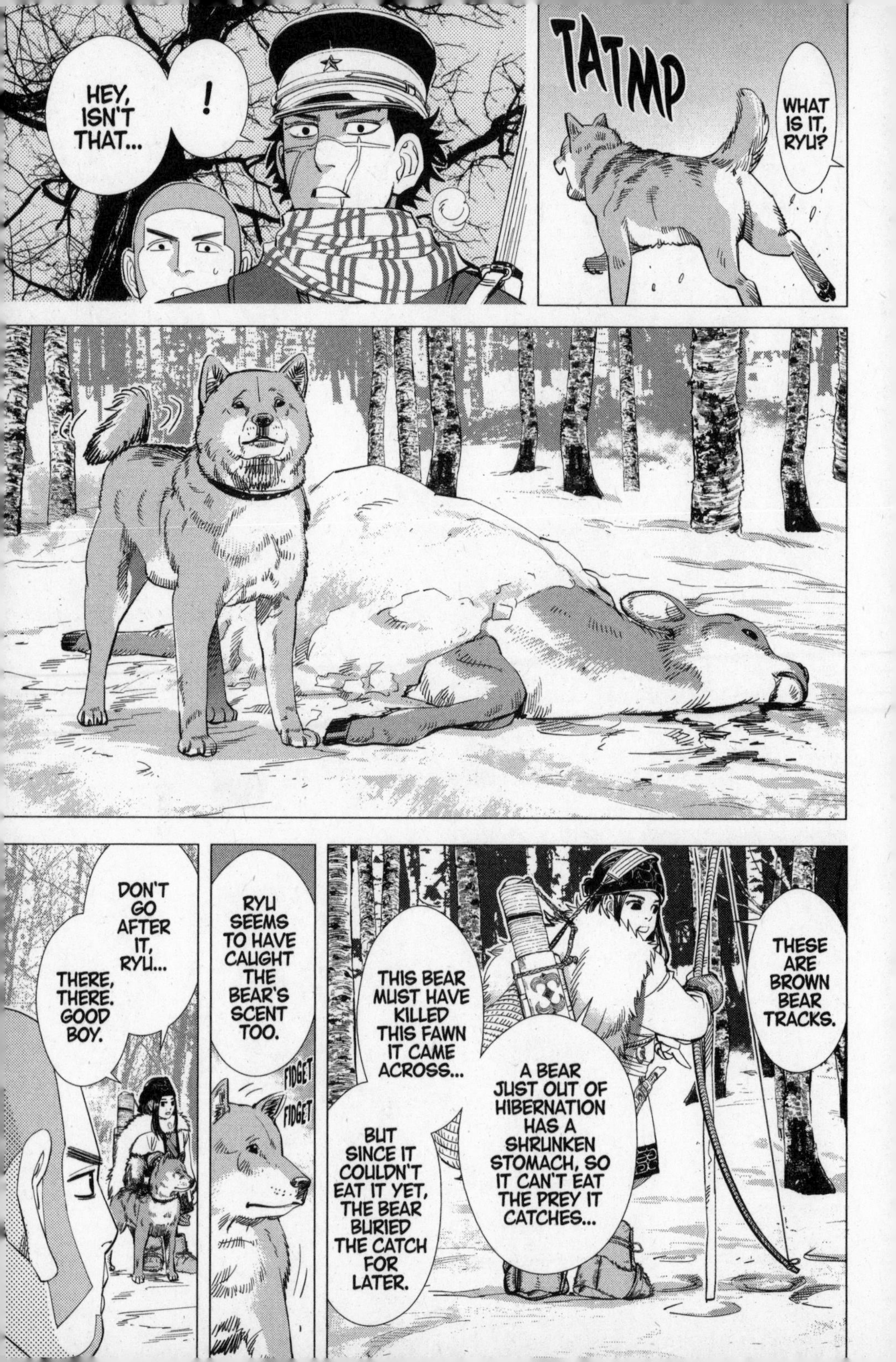
TATMP
WHAT IS IT, RYU?
HEY, ISN'T THAT...
!
THESE ARE BROWN BEAR TRACKS.
THIS BEAR MUST HAVE KILLED THIS FAWN IT CAME ACROSS...
A BEAR JUST OUT OF HIBERNATION HAS A SHRUNKEN STOMACH, SO IT CAN'T EAT THE PREY IT CATCHES...
BUT SINCE IT COULDN'T EAT IT YET, THE BEAR BURIED THE CATCH FOR LATER.
FIDGET
FIDGET
RYU SEEMS TO HAVE CAUGHT THE BEAR'S SCENT TOO.
DON'T GO AFTER IT, RYU...
THERE, THERE. GOOD BOY.

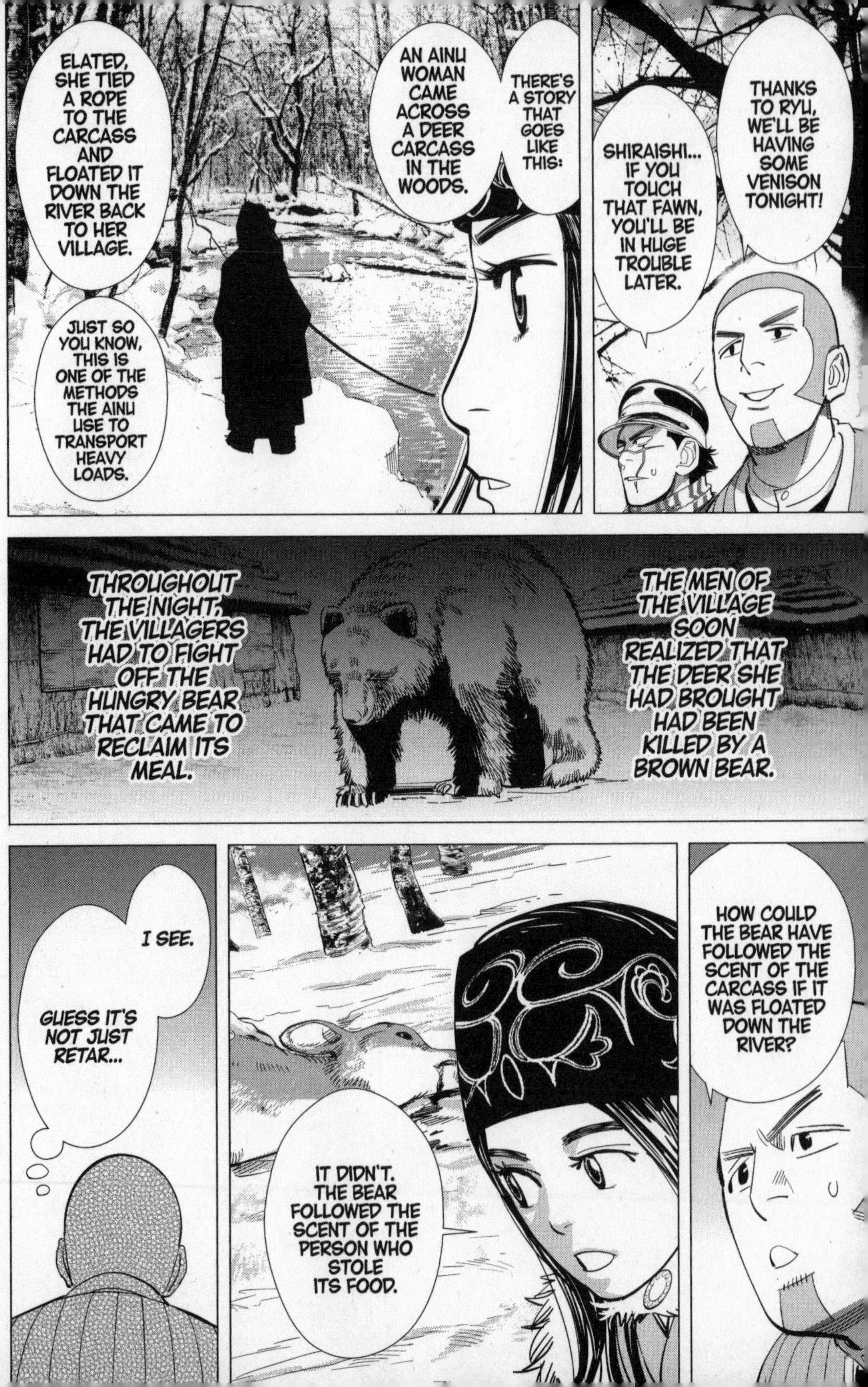
THANKS TO RYU, WE'LL BE HAVING SOME VENISON TONIGHT!
SHIRAISHI... IF YOU TOUCH THAT FAWN, YOU'LL BE IN HUGE TROUBLE LATER.
THERE'S A STORY THAT GOES LIKE THIS:
AN AINU WOMAN CAME ACROSS A DEER CARCASS IN THE WOODS.
ELATED, SHE TIED A ROPE TO THE CARCASS AND FLOATED IT DOWN THE RIVER BACK TO HER VILLAGE.
JUST SO YOU KNOW, THIS IS ONE OF THE METHODS THE AINU USE TO TRANSPORT HEAVY LOADS.
THE MEN OF THE VILLAGE SOON REALIZED THAT THE DEER SHE HAD BROUGHT HAD BEEN KILLED BY A BROWN BEAR.
THROUGHOUT THE NIGHT, THE VILLAGERS HAD TO FIGHT OFF THE HUNGRY BEAR THAT CAME TO RECLAIM ITS MEAL.
HOW COULD THE BEAR HAVE FOLLOWED THE SCENT OF THE CARCASS IF IT WAS FLOATED DOWN THE RIVER?
IT DIDN'T. THE BEAR FOLLOWED THE SCENT OF THE PERSON WHO STOLE ITS FOOD.
I SEE.
GUESS IT'S NOT JUST RETAR...

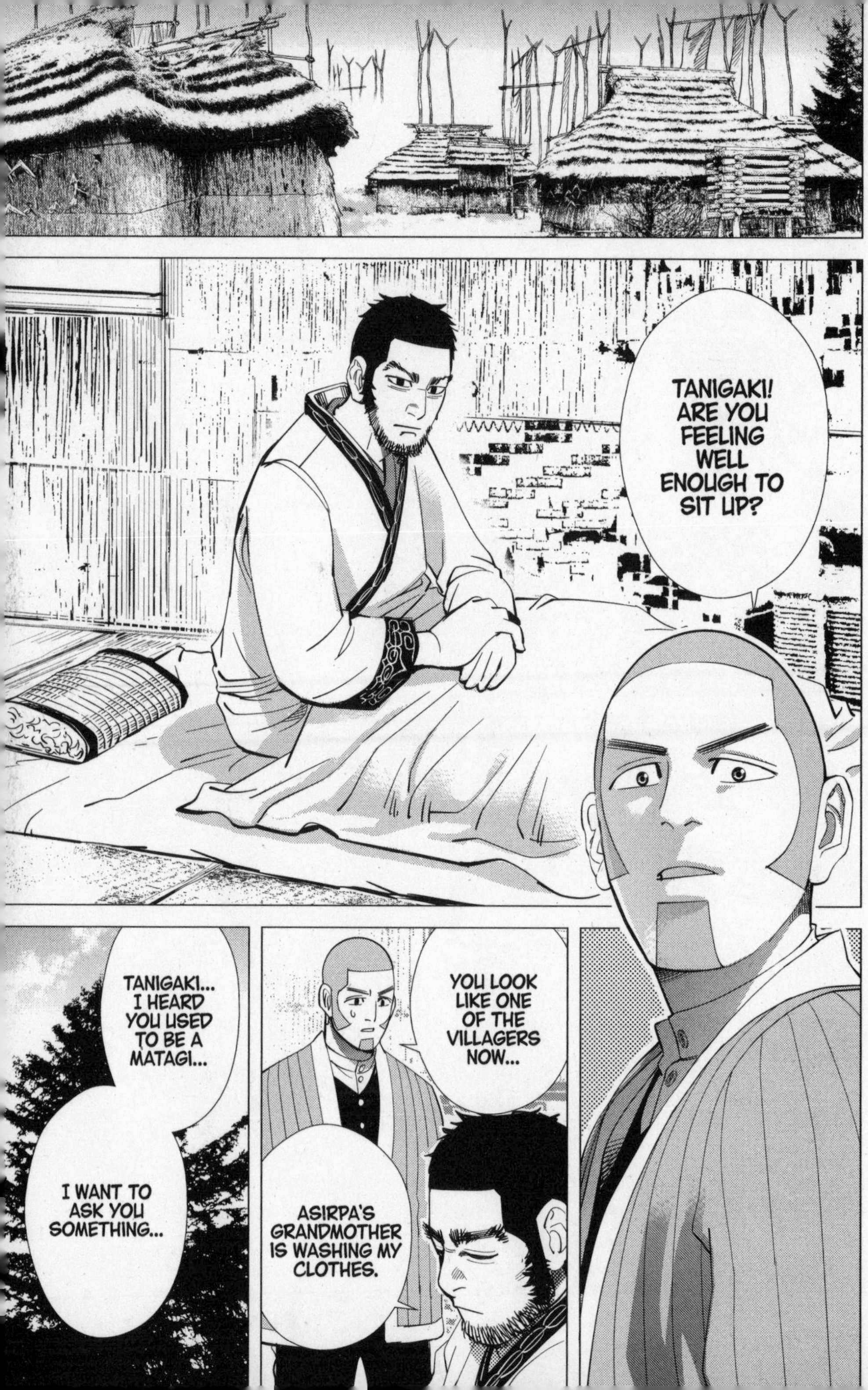
TANIGAKI! ARE YOU FEELING WELL ENOUGH TO SIT UP?
YOU LOOK LIKE ONE OF THE VILLAGERS NOW...
ASIRPA'S GRANDMOTHER IS WASHING MY CLOTHES.
TANIGAKI... I HEARD YOU USED TO BE A MATAGI...
I WANT TO ASK YOU SOMETHING...

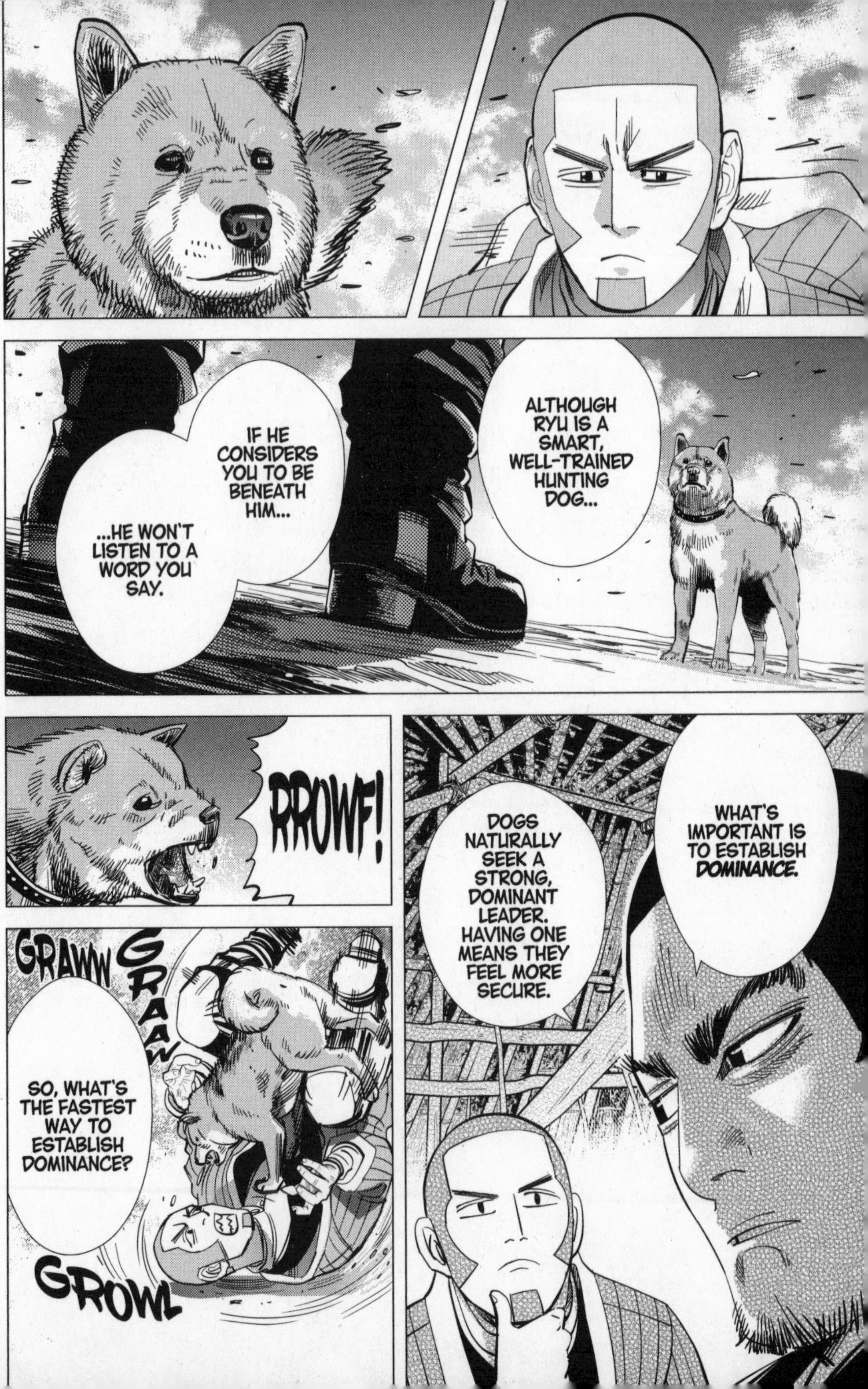
ALTHOUGH RYU IS A SMART, WELL-TRAINED HUNTING DOG...
IF HE CONSIDERS YOU TO BE BENEATH HIM...
...HE WON'T LISTEN TO A WORD YOU SAY.
WHAT'S IMPORTANT IS TO ESTABLISH **DOMINANCE.**
DOGS NATURALLY SEEK A STRONG, DOMINANT LEADER. HAVING ONE MEANS THEY FEEL MORE SECURE.
RRROWF!
GRAWW
GRAAW
SO, WHAT'S THE FASTEST WAY TO ESTABLISH DOMINANCE?
GROWL

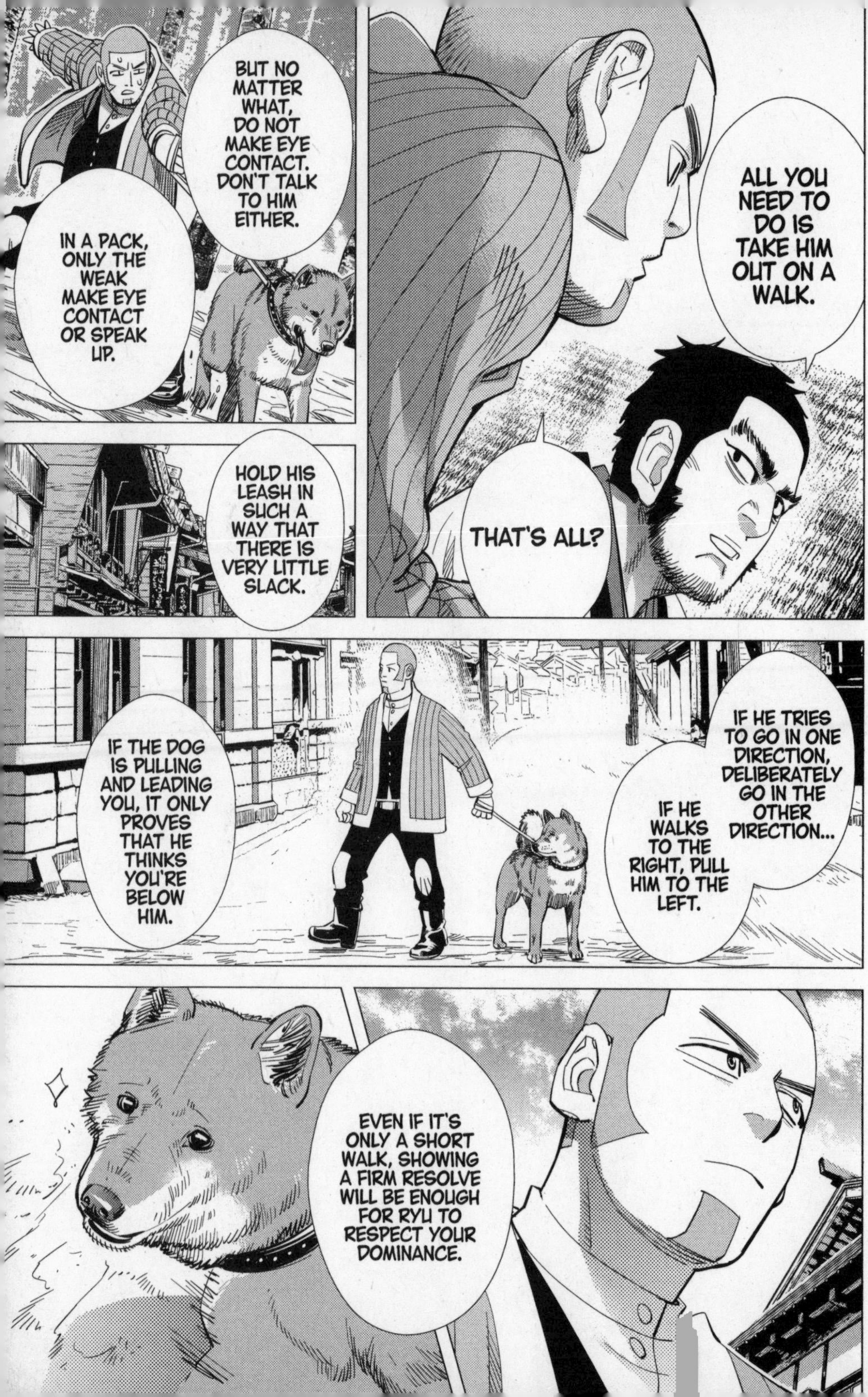
ALL YOU NEED TO DO IS TAKE HIM OUT ON A WALK.
THAT'S ALL?
BUT NO MATTER WHAT, DO NOT MAKE EYE CONTACT. DON'T TALK TO HIM EITHER.
IN A PACK, ONLY THE WEAK MAKE EYE CONTACT OR SPEAK UP.
HOLD HIS LEASH IN SUCH A WAY THAT THERE IS VERY LITTLE SLACK.
IF HE TRIES TO GO IN ONE DIRECTION, DELIBERATELY GO IN THE OTHER DIRECTION...
IF HE WALKS TO THE RIGHT, PULL HIM TO THE LEFT.
IF THE DOG IS PULLING AND LEADING YOU, IT ONLY PROVES THAT HE THINKS YOU'RE BELOW HIM.
EVEN IF IT'S ONLY A SHORT WALK, SHOWING A FIRM RESOLVE WILL BE ENOUGH FOR RYU TO RESPECT YOUR DOMINANCE.

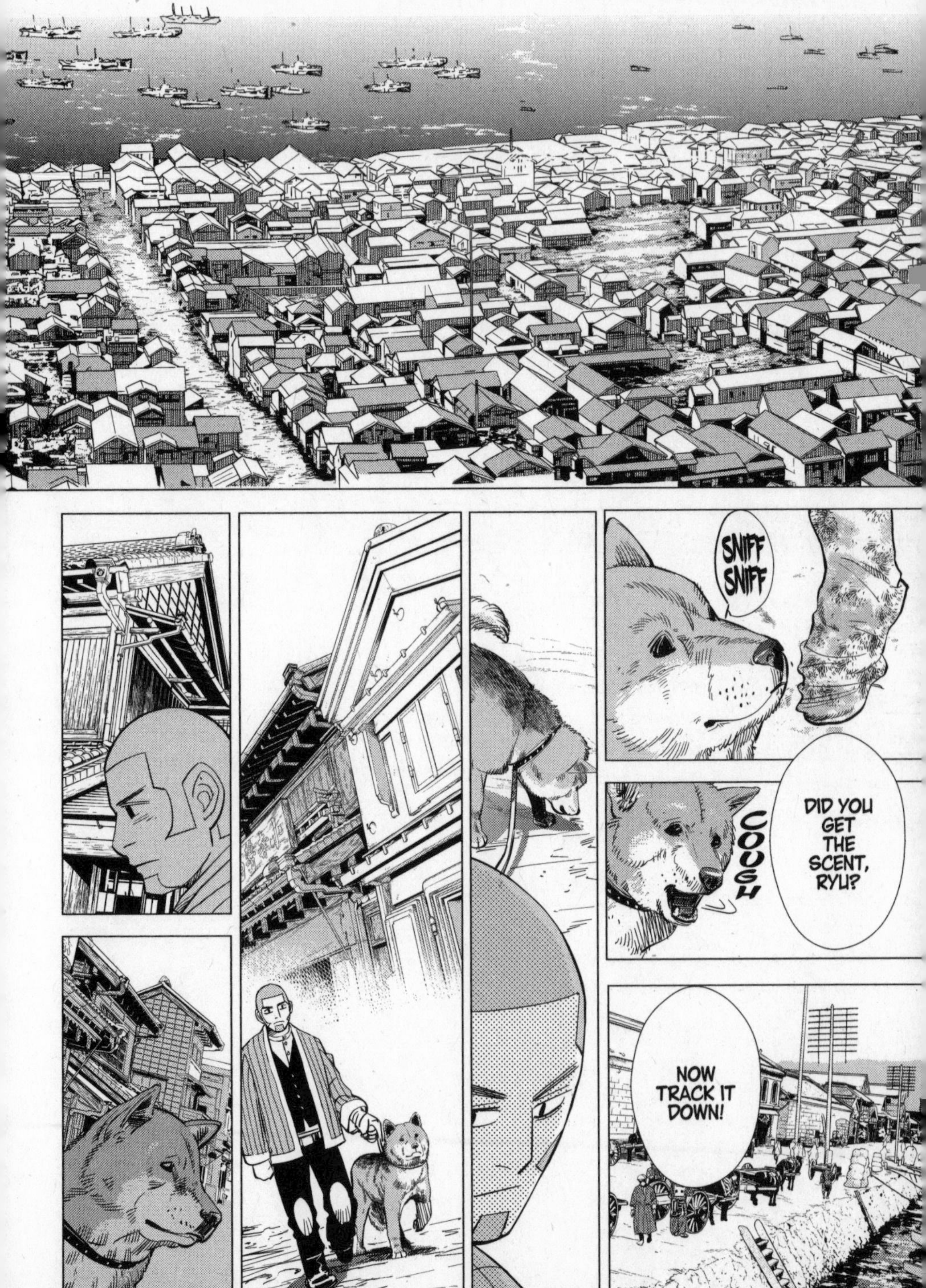
SNIFF SNIFF
DID YOU GET THE SCENT, RYU?
COUGH
NOW TRACK IT DOWN!

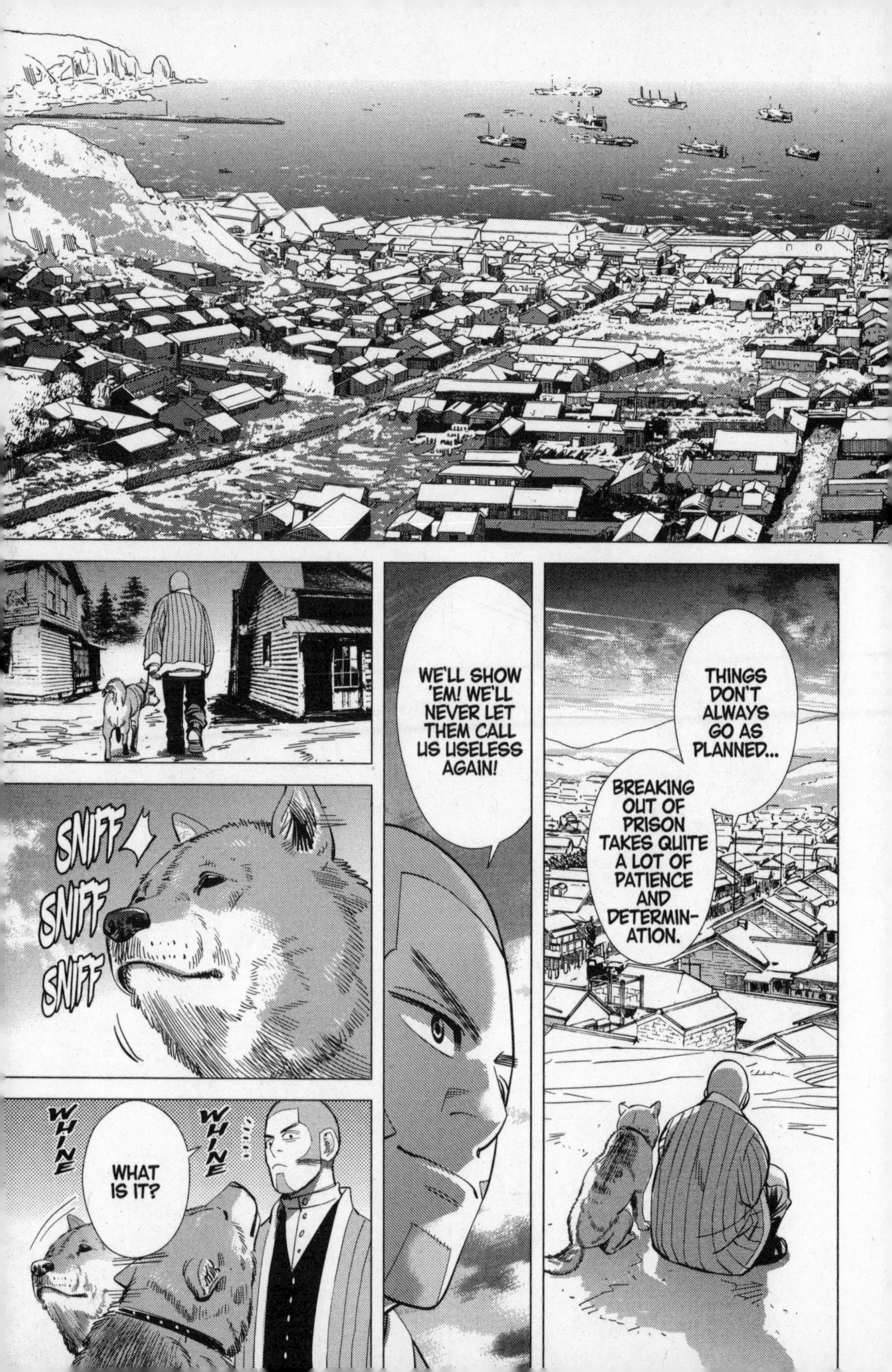
THINGS DON'T ALWAYS GO AS PLANNED...
BREAKING OUT OF PRISON TAKES QUITE A LOT OF PATIENCE AND DETERMIN-ATION.
WE'LL SHOW 'EM! WE'LL NEVER LET THEM CALL US USELESS AGAIN!
SNIFF
SNIFF
SNIFF
WHINE
WHINE
......
WHAT IS IT?

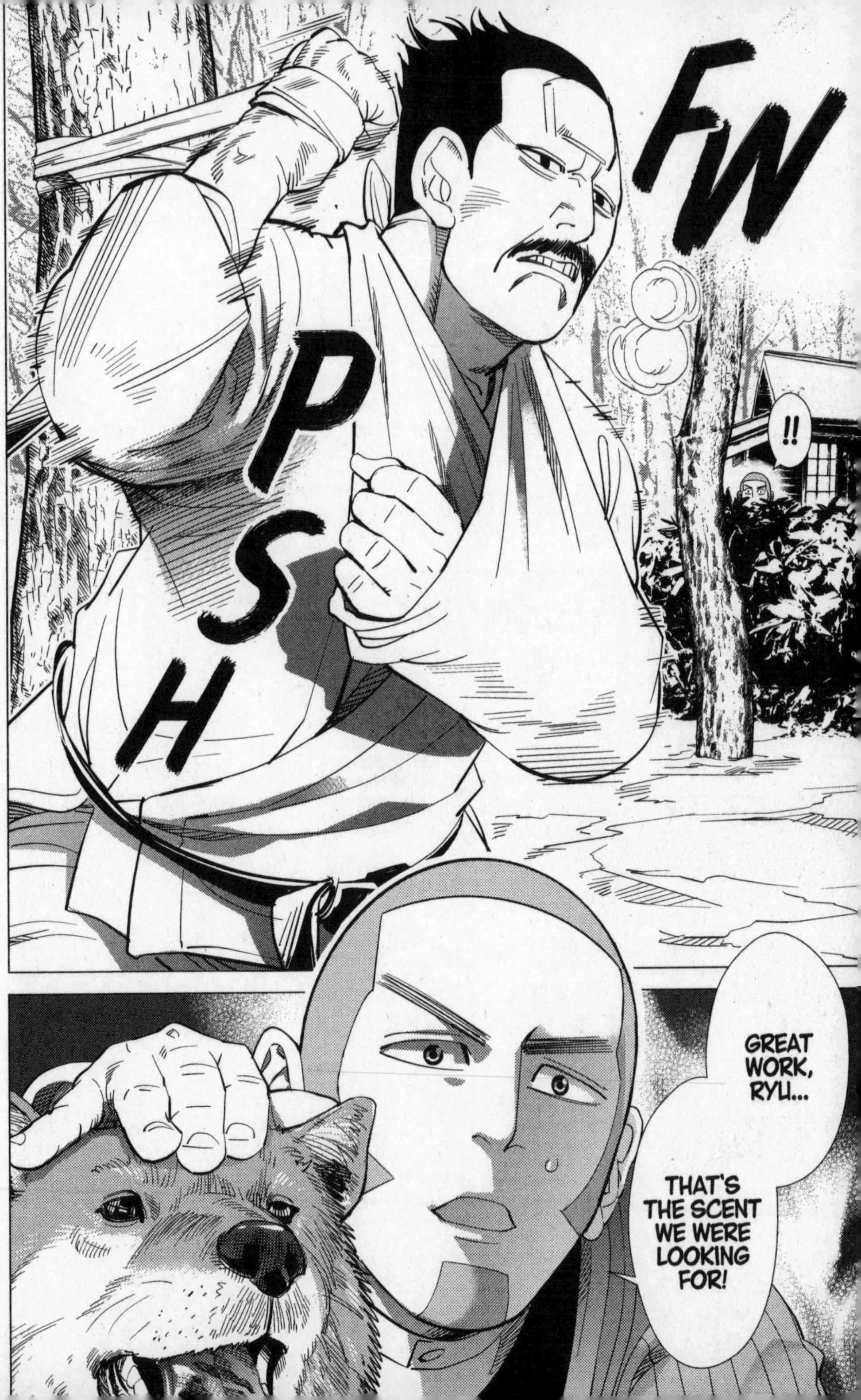
FW
PSH
!!
GREAT WORK, RYU...
THAT'S THE SCENT WE WERE LOOKING FOR!

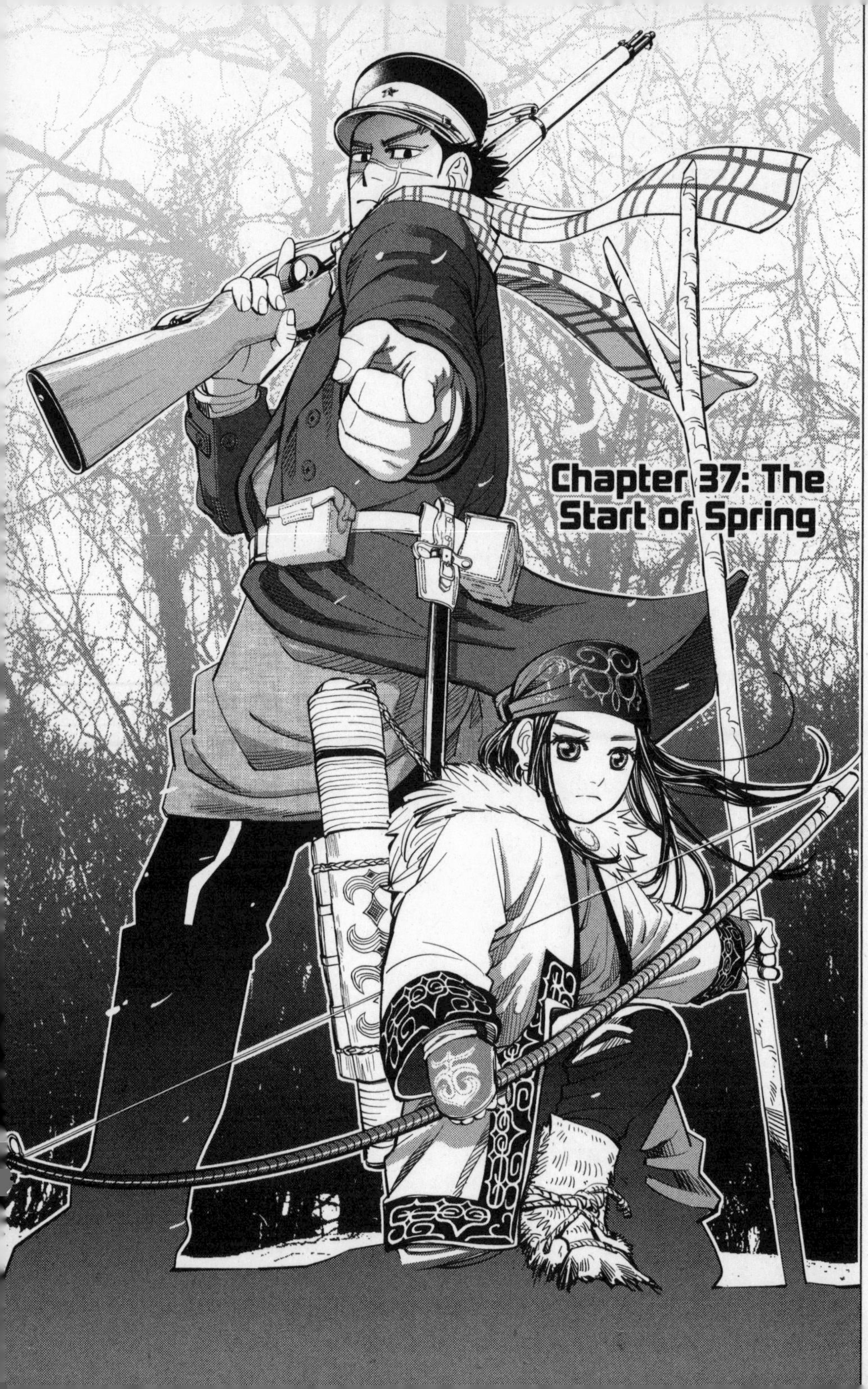
Chapter 37: The Start of Spring

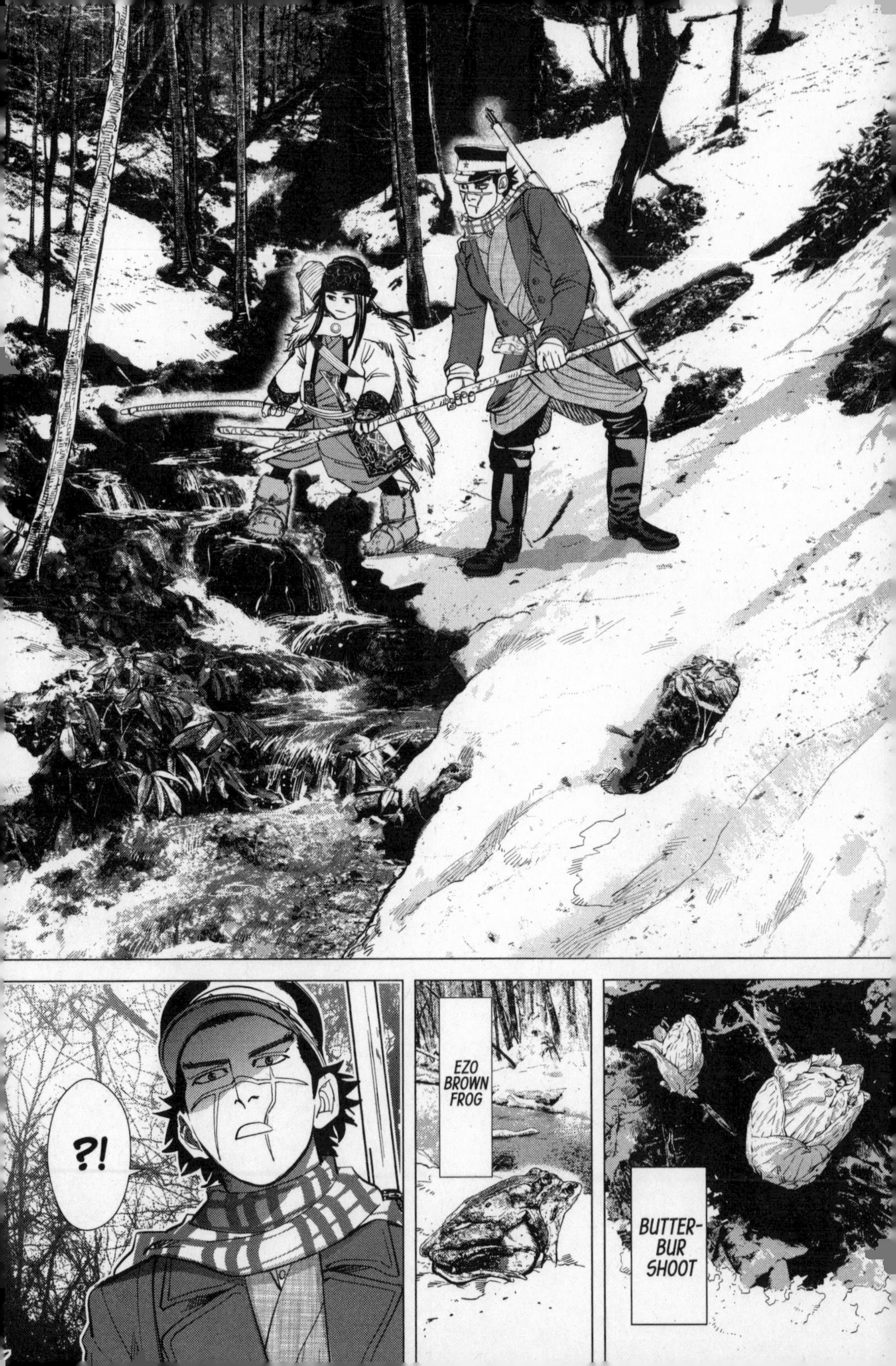
BUTTER-BUR SHOOT
EZO BROWN FROG
?!

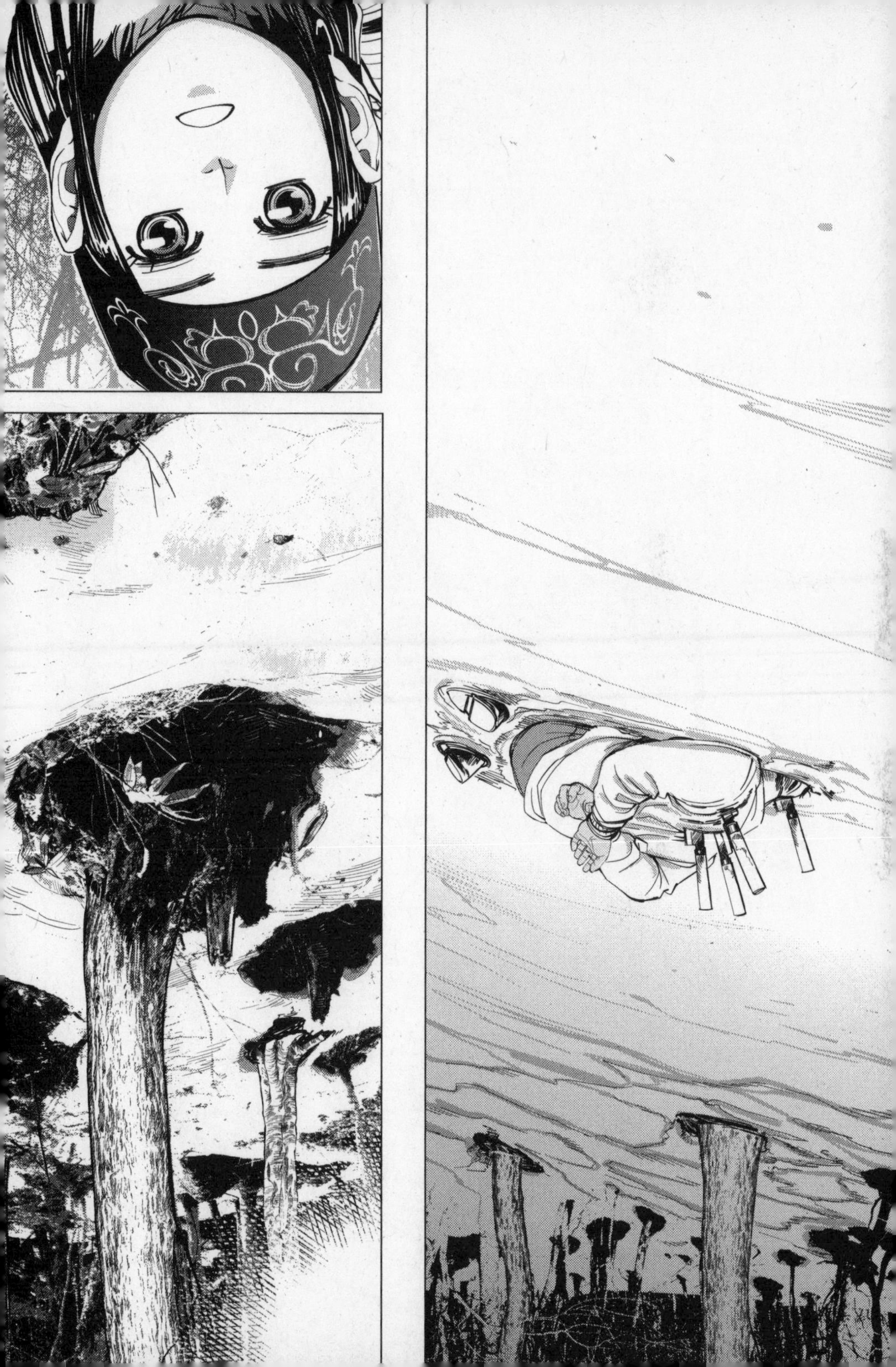

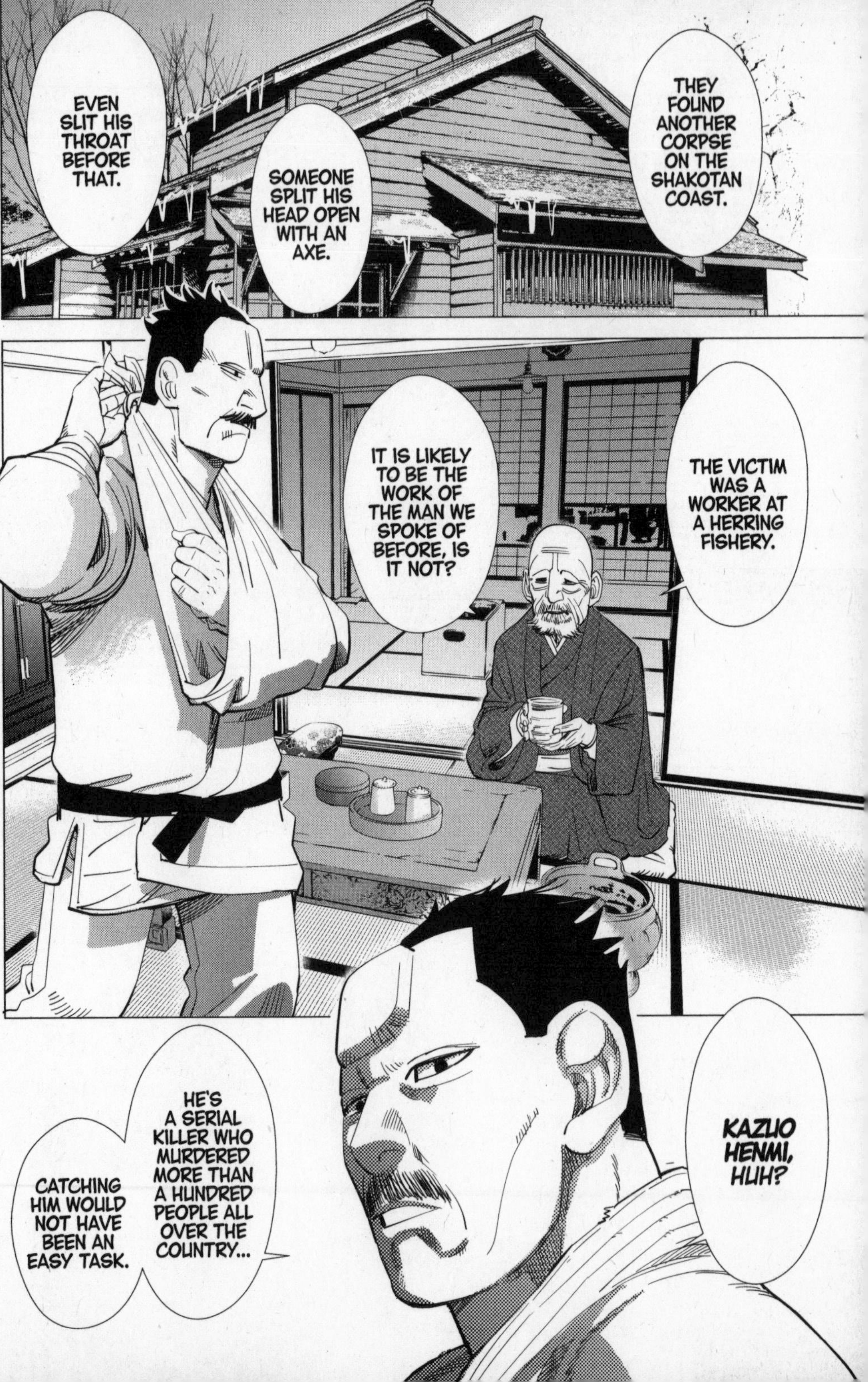
THEY FOUND ANOTHER CORPSE ON THE SHAKOTAN COAST.
SOMEONE SPLIT HIS HEAD OPEN WITH AN AXE.
EVEN SLIT HIS THROAT BEFORE THAT.
THE VICTIM WAS A WORKER AT A HERRING FISHERY.
IT IS LIKELY TO BE THE WORK OF THE MAN WE SPOKE OF BEFORE, IS IT NOT?
KAZUO HENMI, HUH?
HE'S A SERIAL KILLER WHO MURDERED MORE THAN A HUNDRED PEOPLE ALL OVER THE COUNTRY...
CATCHING HIM WOULD NOT HAVE BEEN AN EASY TASK.

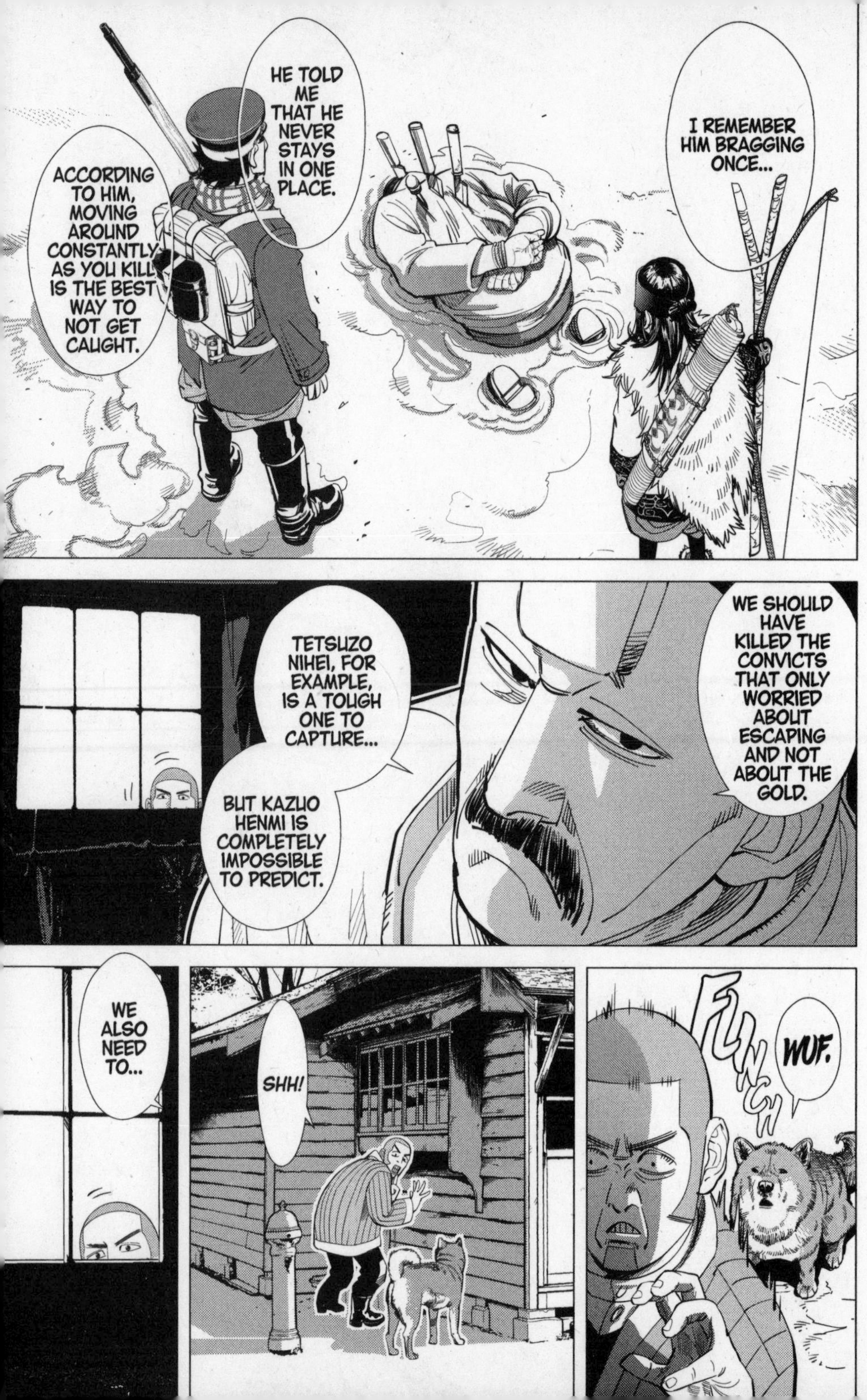
I REMEMBER HIM BRAGGING ONCE...
HE TOLD ME THAT HE NEVER STAYS IN ONE PLACE.
ACCORDING TO HIM, MOVING AROUND CONSTANTLY AS YOU KILL IS THE BEST WAY TO NOT GET CAUGHT.
WE SHOULD HAVE KILLED THE CONVICTS THAT ONLY WORRIED ABOUT ESCAPING AND NOT ABOUT THE GOLD.
TETSUZO NIHEI, FOR EXAMPLE, IS A TOUGH ONE TO CAPTURE...
BUT KAZUO HENMI IS COMPLETELY IMPOSSIBLE TO PREDICT.
FLINCH
WUF.
SHH!
WE ALSO NEED TO...

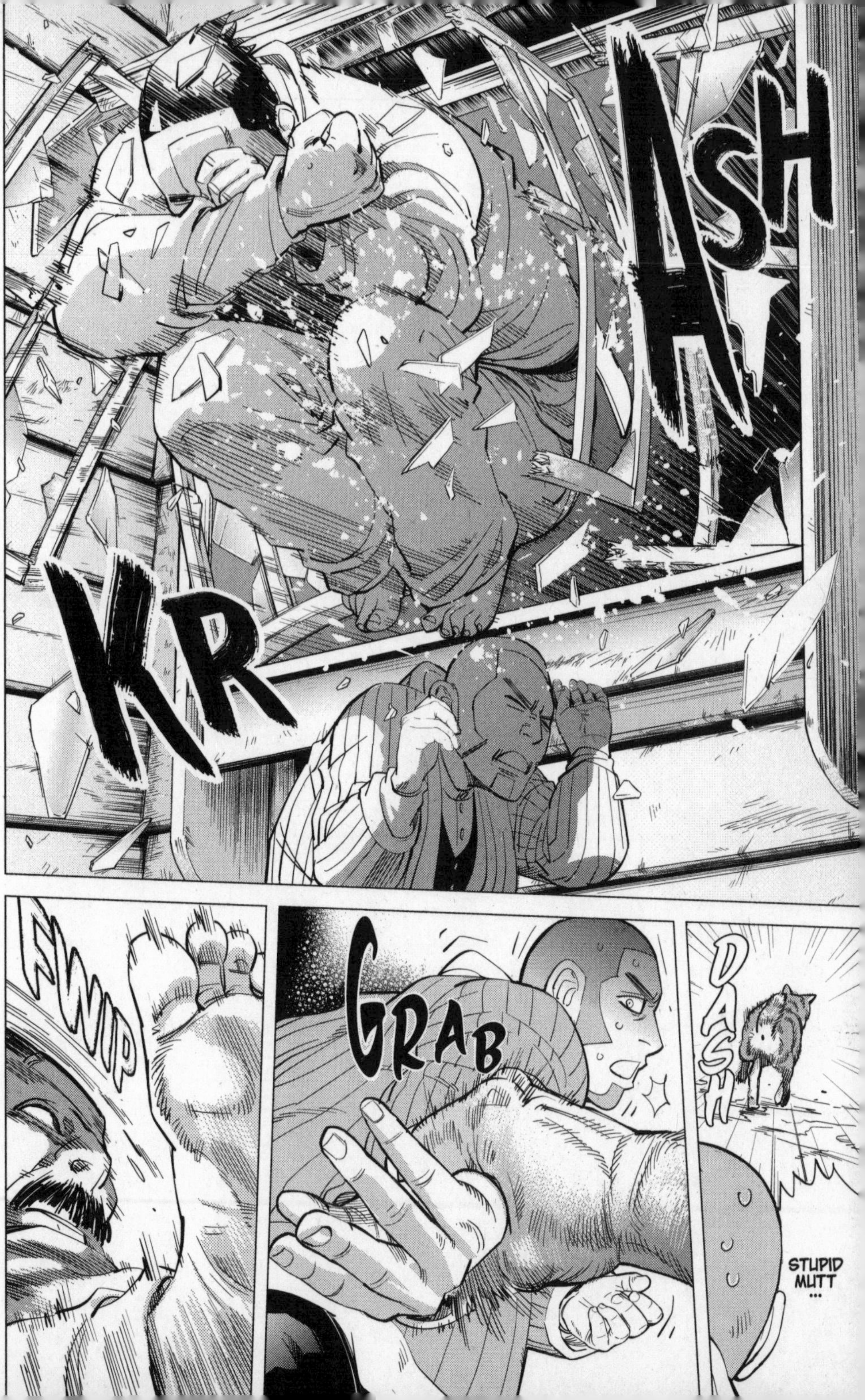
KR
ASH
DASH
STUPID MUTT ...
GRAB
FWIP

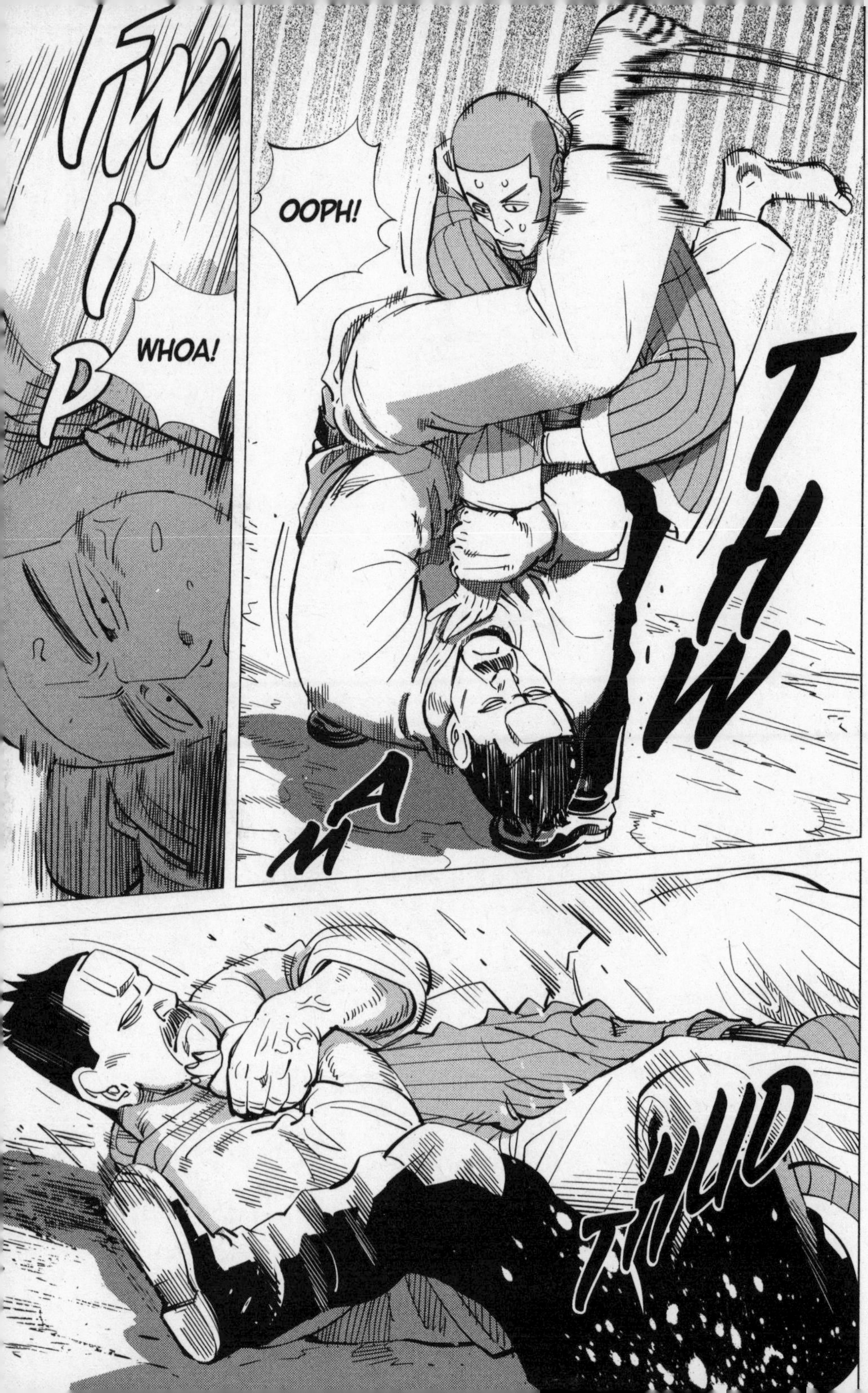
THWAM
OOPH!
FWIP
WHOA!
THUD

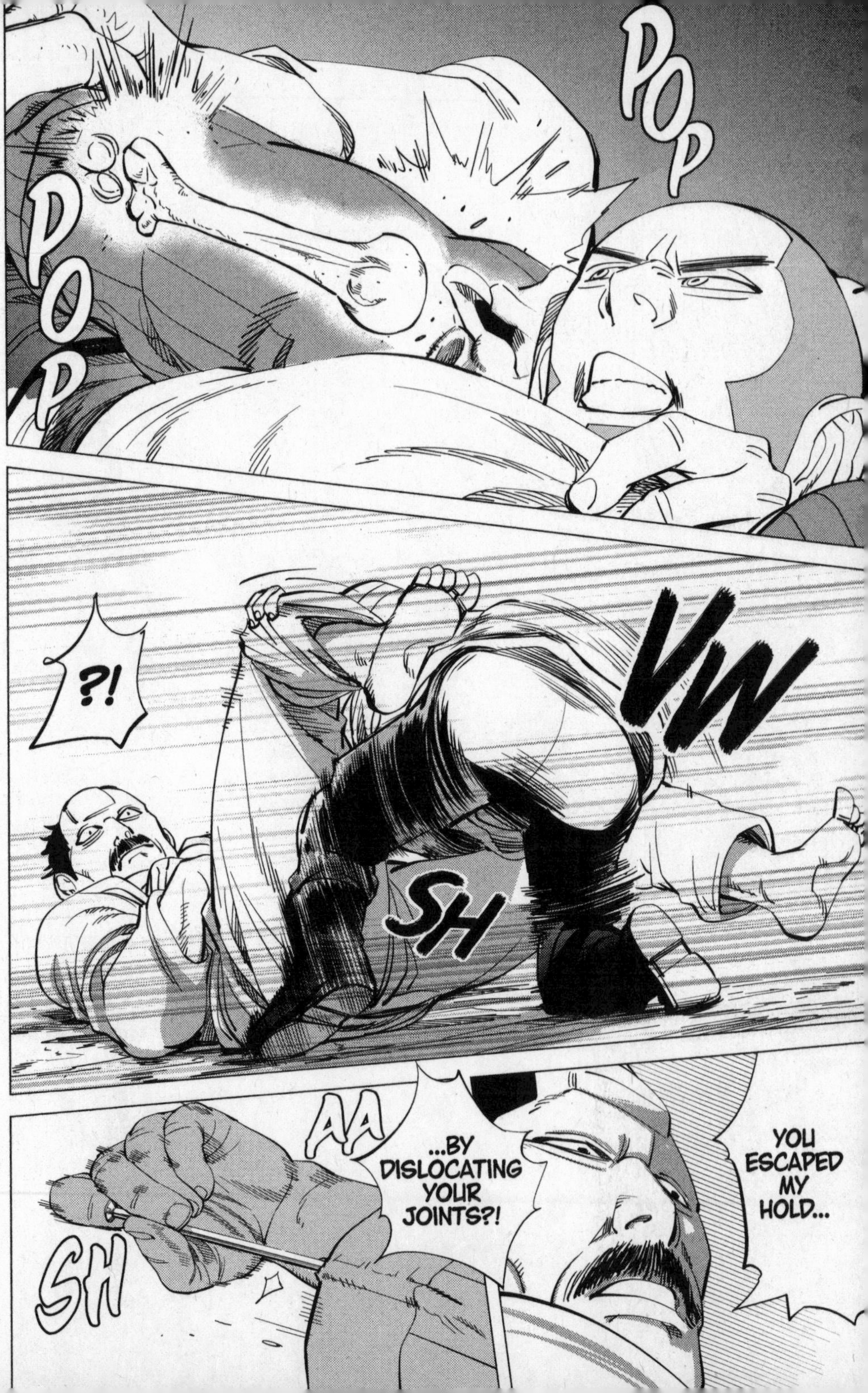
POP
POP
POP
VW
SH
?!
YOU ESCAPED MY HOLD...
...BY DISLOCATING YOUR JOINTS?!
AA
SH

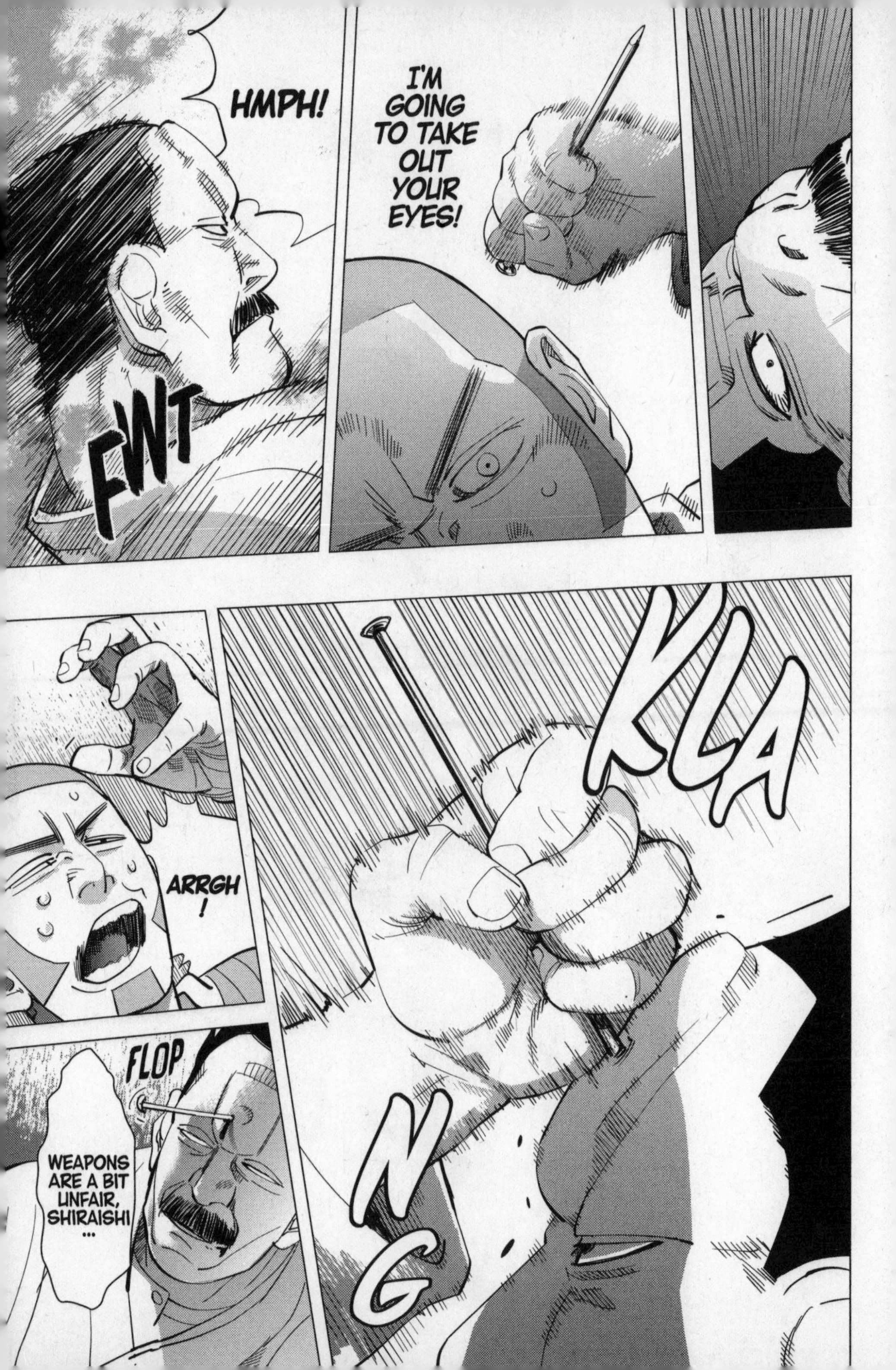
I'M GOING TO TAKE OUT YOUR EYES!
HMPH!
FWT
KLANG
ARRGH!
FLOP
WEAPONS ARE A BIT UNFAIR, SHIRAISHI...

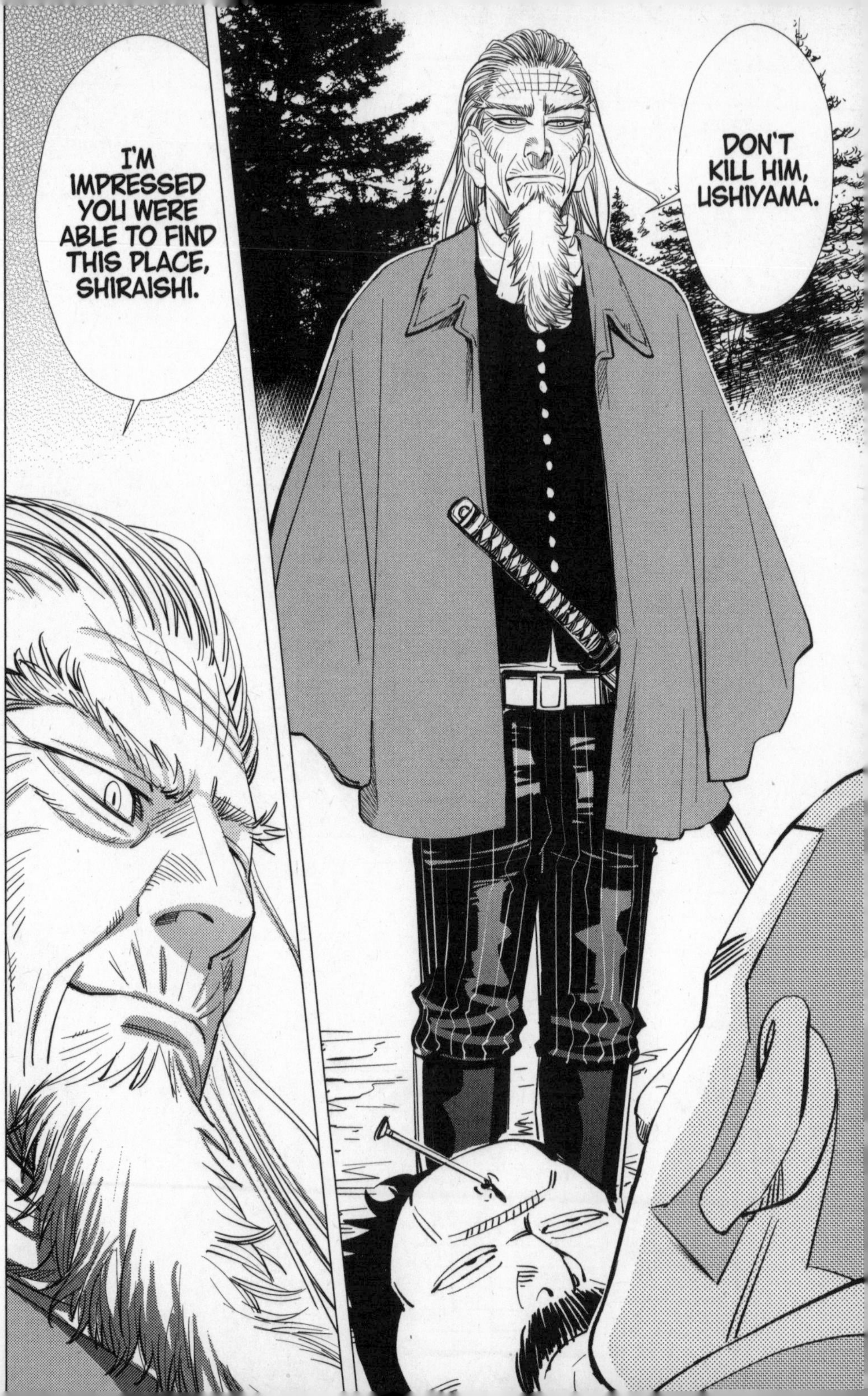
DON'T KILL HIM, USHIYAMA.
I'M IMPRESSED YOU WERE ABLE TO FIND THIS PLACE, SHIRAISHI.

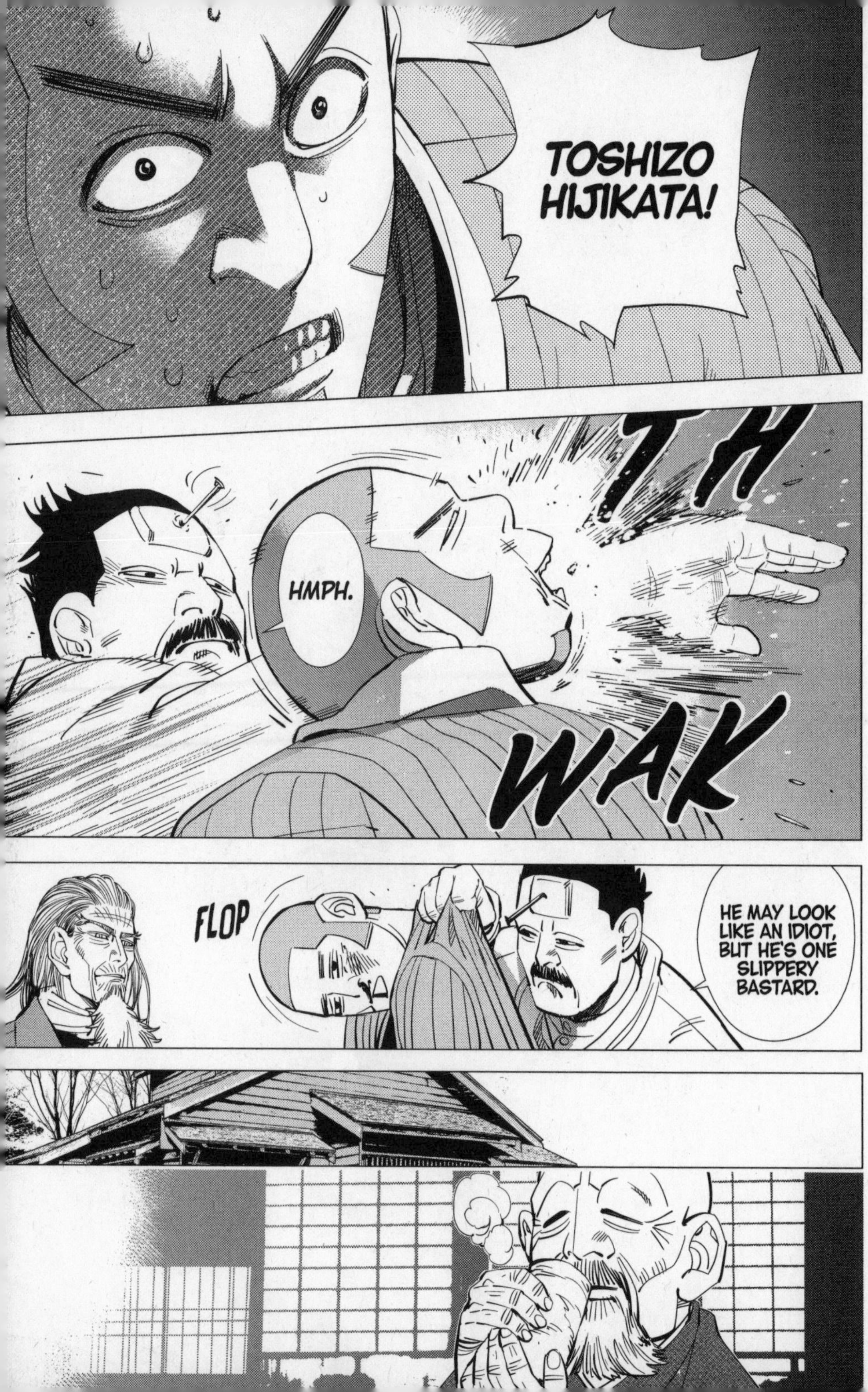
TOSHIZO HIJIKATA!
THWAK
HMPH.
HE MAY LOOK LIKE AN IDIOT, BUT HE'S ONE SLIPPERY BASTARD.
FLOP

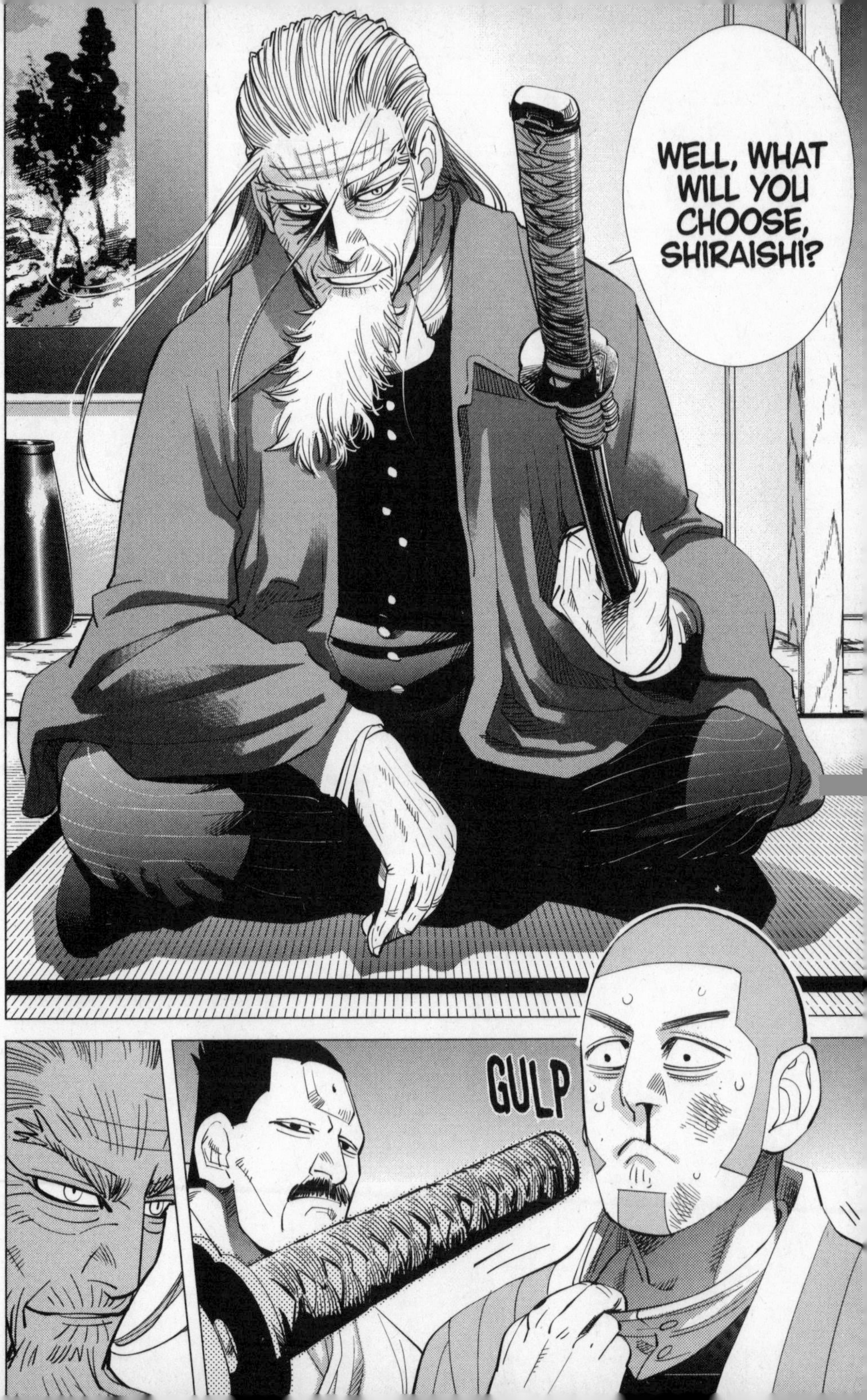
WELL, WHAT WILL YOU CHOOSE, SHIRAISHI?
GULP

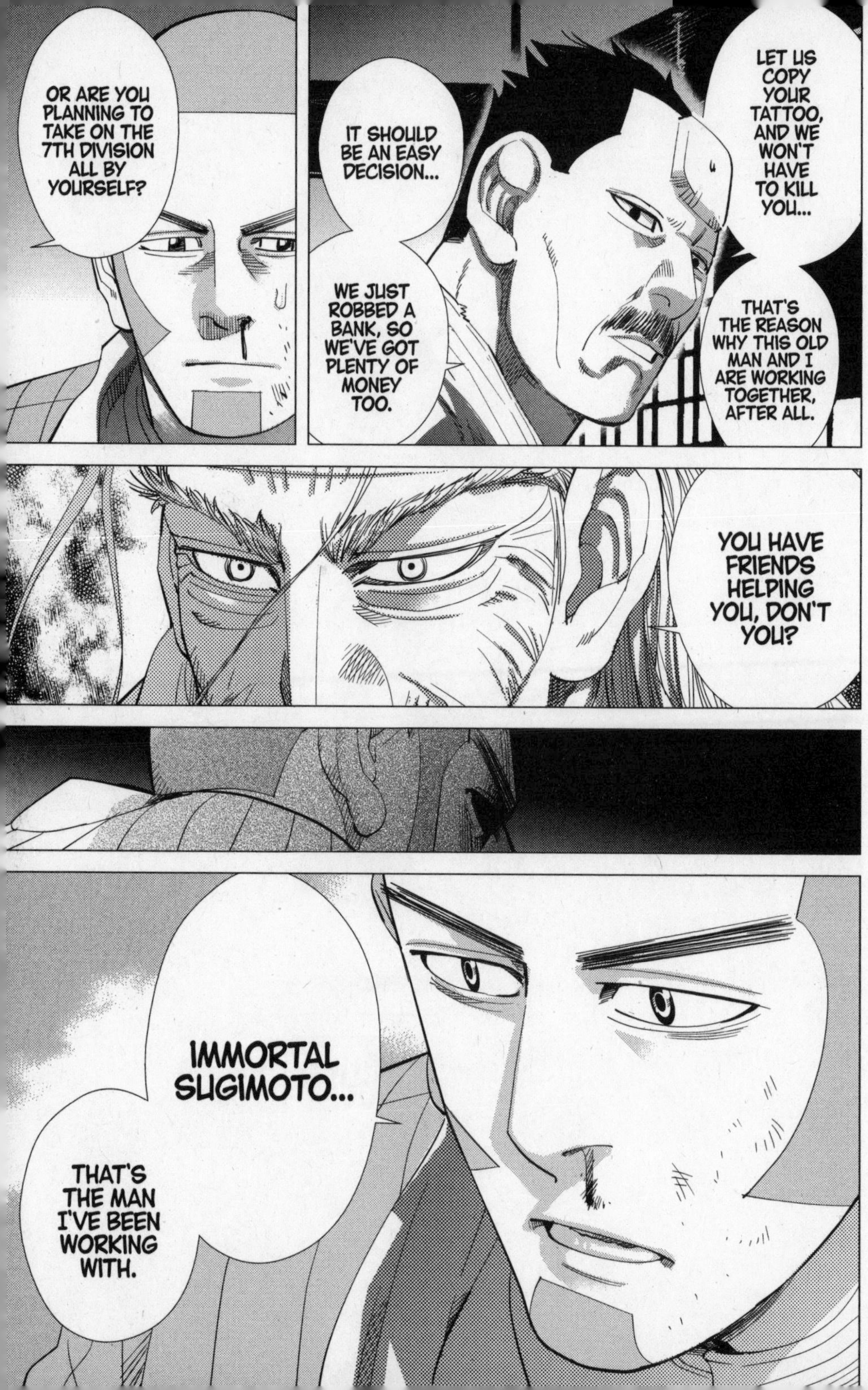
LET US COPY YOUR TATTOO, AND WE WON'T HAVE TO KILL YOU...
THAT'S THE REASON WHY THIS OLD MAN AND I ARE WORKING TOGETHER, AFTER ALL.
IT SHOULD BE AN EASY DECISION...
WE JUST ROBBED A BANK, SO WE'VE GOT PLENTY OF MONEY TOO.
OR ARE YOU PLANNING TO TAKE ON THE 7TH DIVISION ALL BY YOURSELF?
YOU HAVE FRIENDS HELPING YOU, DON'T YOU?
IMMORTAL SUGIMOTO...
THAT'S THE MAN I'VE BEEN WORKING WITH.

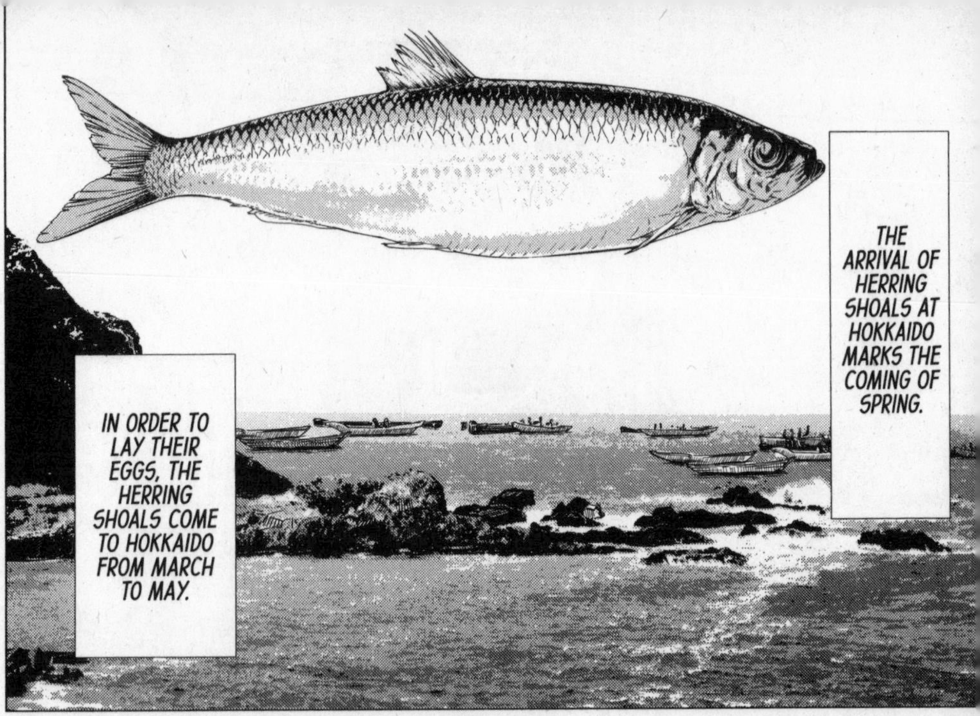
THE ARRIVAL OF HERRING SHOALS AT HOKKAIDO MARKS THE COMING OF SPRING.
IN ORDER TO LAY THEIR EGGS, THE HERRING SHOALS COME TO HOKKAIDO FROM MARCH TO MAY.
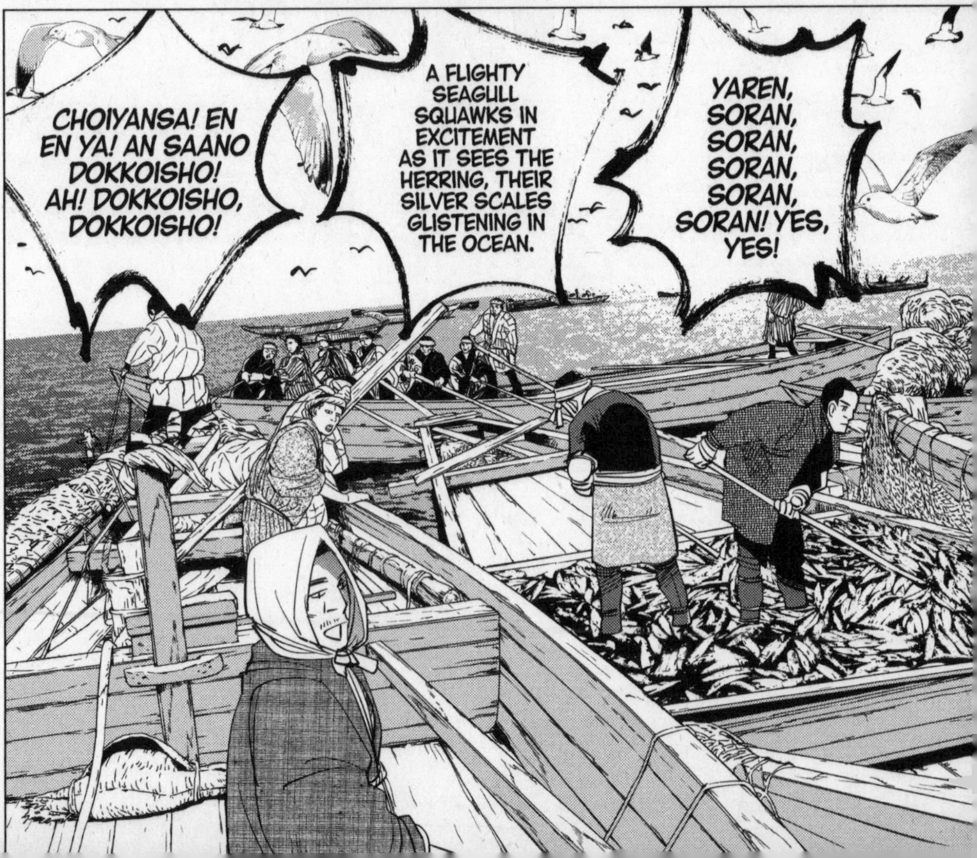
YAREN, SORAN, SORAN, SORAN, SORAN, SORAN! YES, YES!
A FLIGHTY SEAGULL SQUAWKS IN EXCITEMENT AS IT SEES THE HERRING, THEIR SILVER SCALES GLISTENING IN THE OCEAN.
CHOIYANSA! EN EN YA! AN SAANO DOKKOISHO! AH! DOKKOISHO, DOKKOISHO!

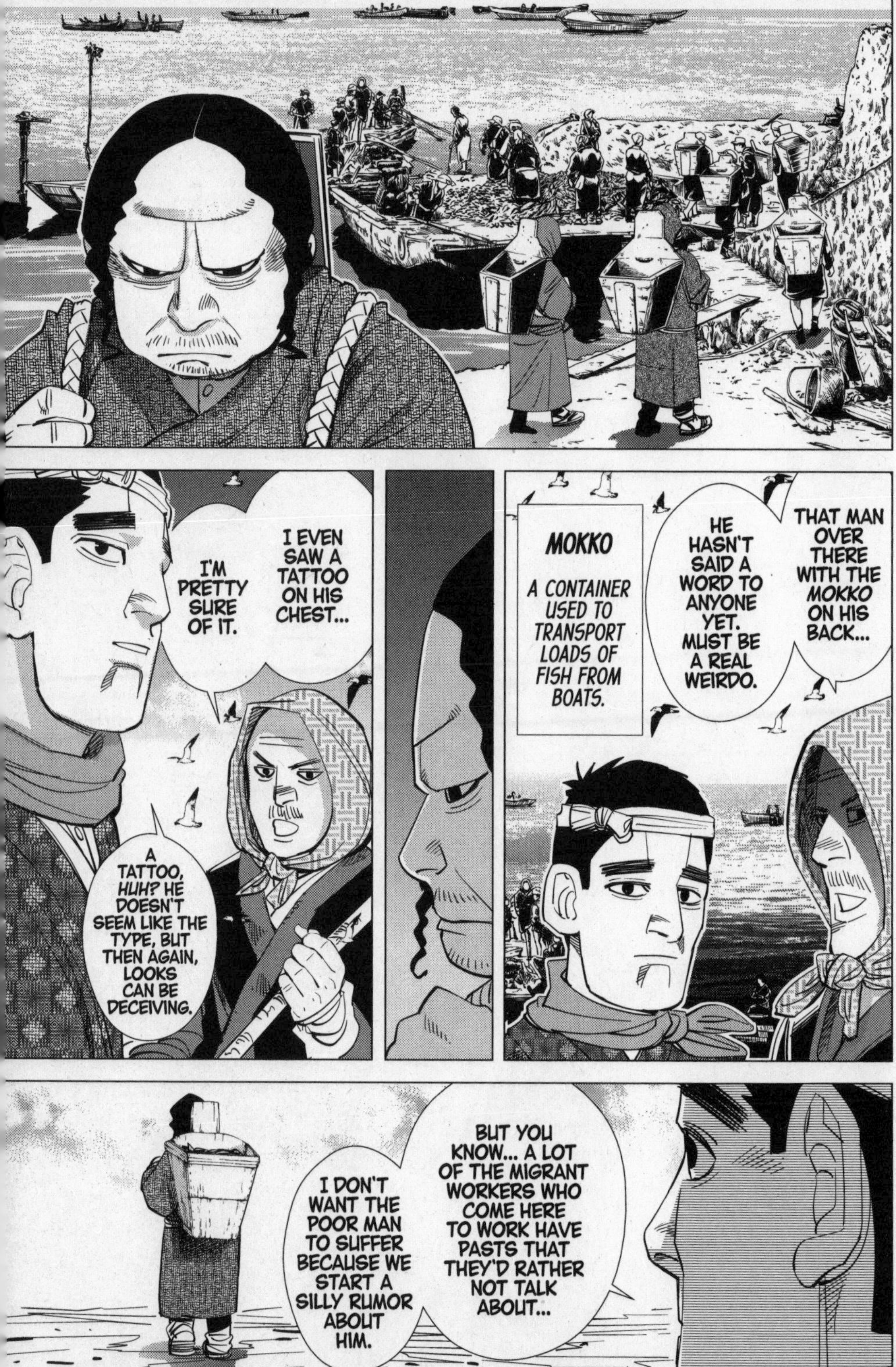
THAT MAN OVER THERE WITH THE MOKKO ON HIS BACK...
HE HASN'T SAID A WORD TO ANYONE YET. MUST BE A REAL WEIRDO.
MOKKO
A CONTAINER USED TO TRANSPORT LOADS OF FISH FROM BOATS.
I EVEN SAW A TATTOO ON HIS CHEST...
I'M PRETTY SURE OF IT.
A TATTOO, HUH? HE DOESN'T SEEM LIKE THE TYPE, BUT THEN AGAIN, LOOKS CAN BE DECEIVING.
BUT YOU KNOW... A LOT OF THE MIGRANT WORKERS WHO COME HERE TO WORK HAVE PASTS THAT THEY'D RATHER NOT TALK ABOUT...
I DON'T WANT THE POOR MAN TO SUFFER BECAUSE WE START A SILLY RUMOR ABOUT HIM.

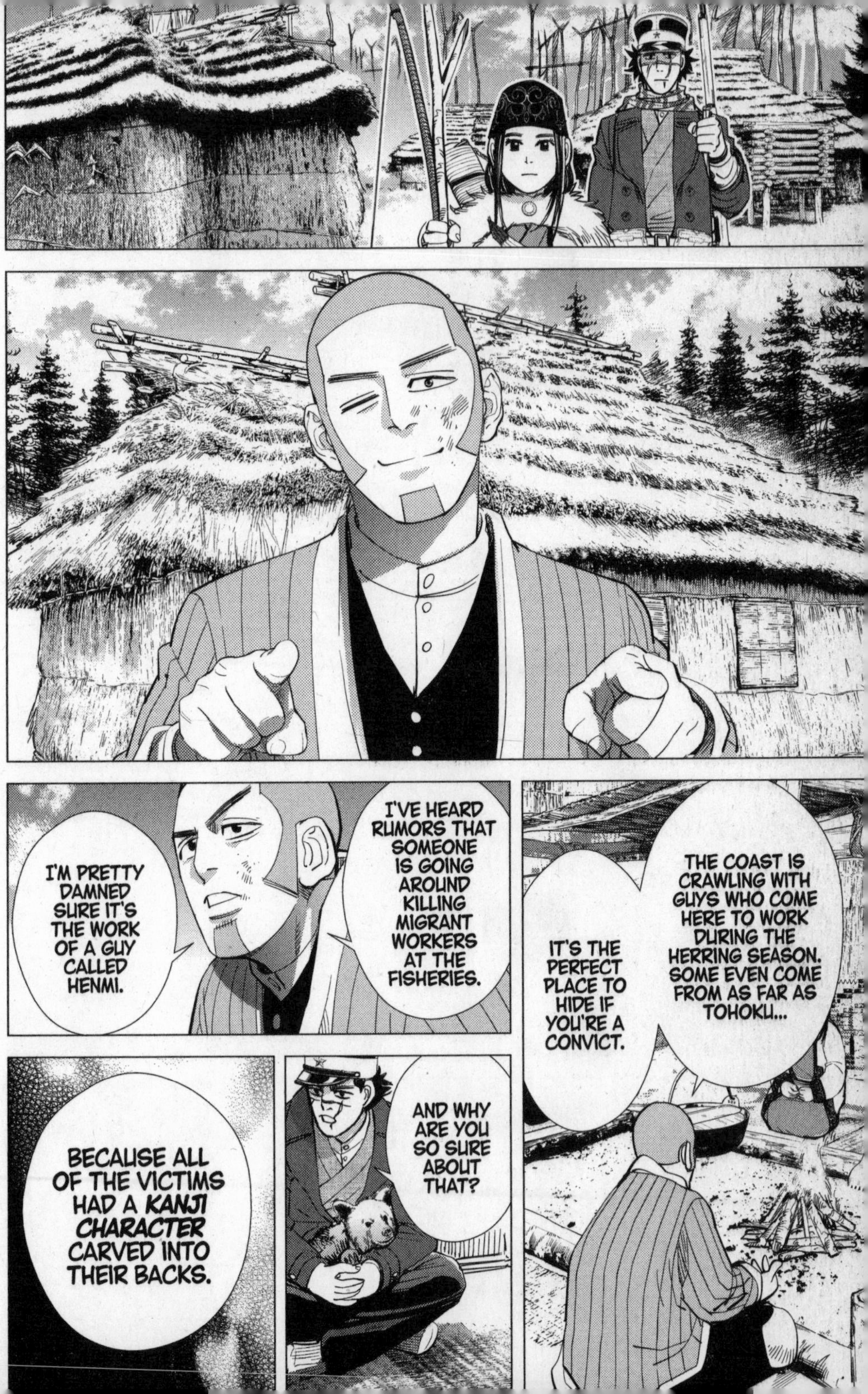
THE COAST IS CRAWLING WITH GUYS WHO COME HERE TO WORK DURING THE HERRING SEASON. SOME EVEN COME FROM AS FAR AS TOHOKU...
IT'S THE PERFECT PLACE TO HIDE IF YOU'RE A CONVICT.
I'VE HEARD RUMORS THAT SOMEONE IS GOING AROUND KILLING MIGRANT WORKERS AT THE FISHERIES.
I'M PRETTY DAMNED SURE IT'S THE WORK OF A GUY CALLED HENMI.
AND WHY ARE YOU SO SURE ABOUT THAT?
BECAUSE ALL OF THE VICTIMS HAD A ***KANJI CHARACTER*** CARVED INTO THEIR BACKS.

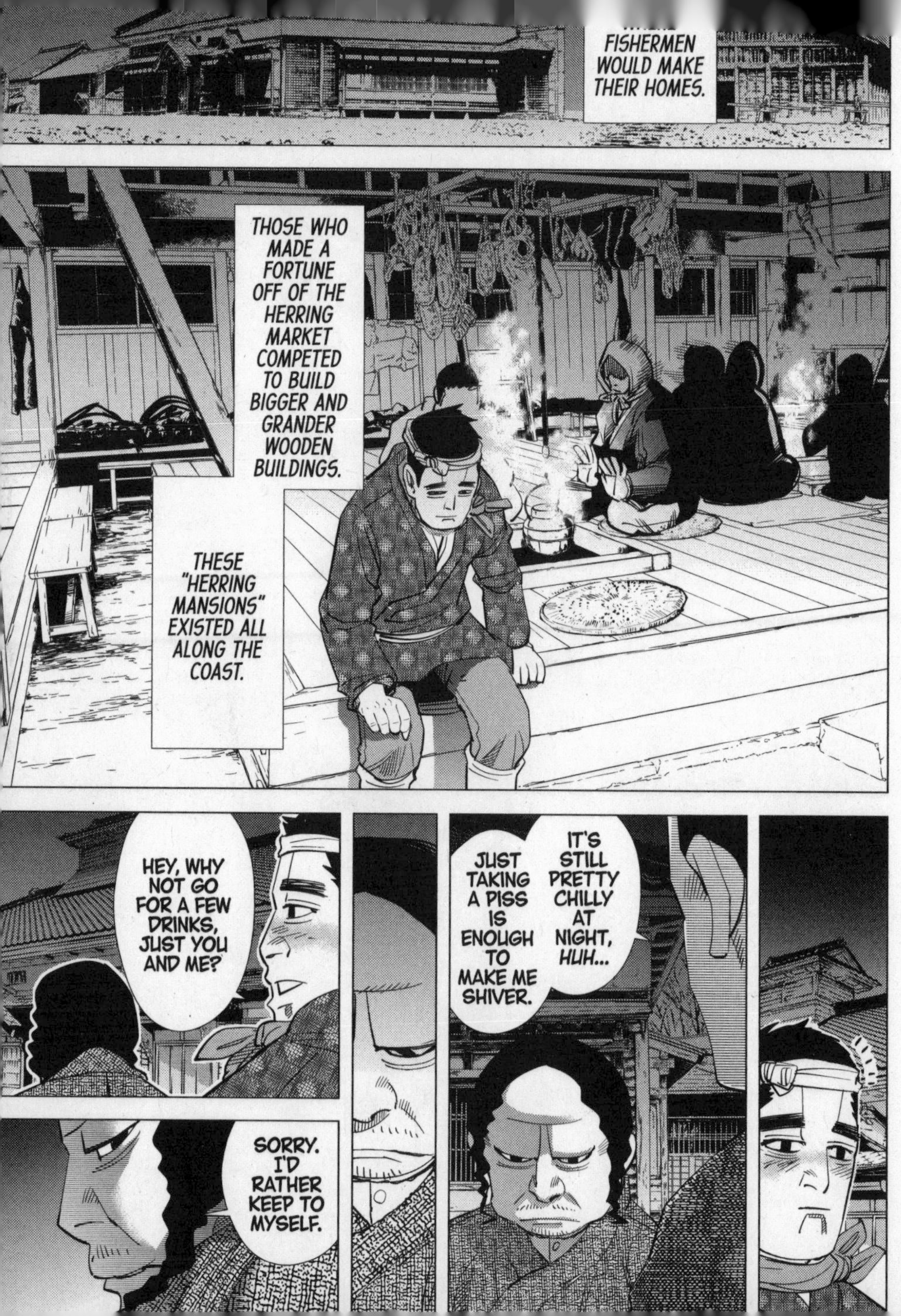
FISHERMEN WOULD MAKE THEIR HOMES.
THOSE WHO MADE A FORTUNE OFF OF THE HERRING MARKET COMPETED TO BUILD BIGGER AND GRANDER WOODEN BUILDINGS.
THESE "HERRING MANSIONS" EXISTED ALL ALONG THE COAST.
IT'S STILL PRETTY CHILLY AT NIGHT, HUH...
JUST TAKING A PISS IS ENOUGH TO MAKE ME SHIVER.
HEY, WHY NOT GO FOR A FEW DRINKS, JUST YOU AND ME?
SORRY. I'D RATHER KEEP TO MYSELF.

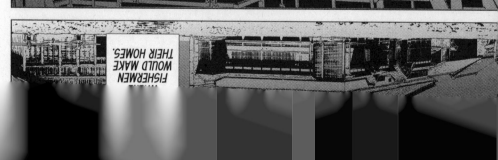

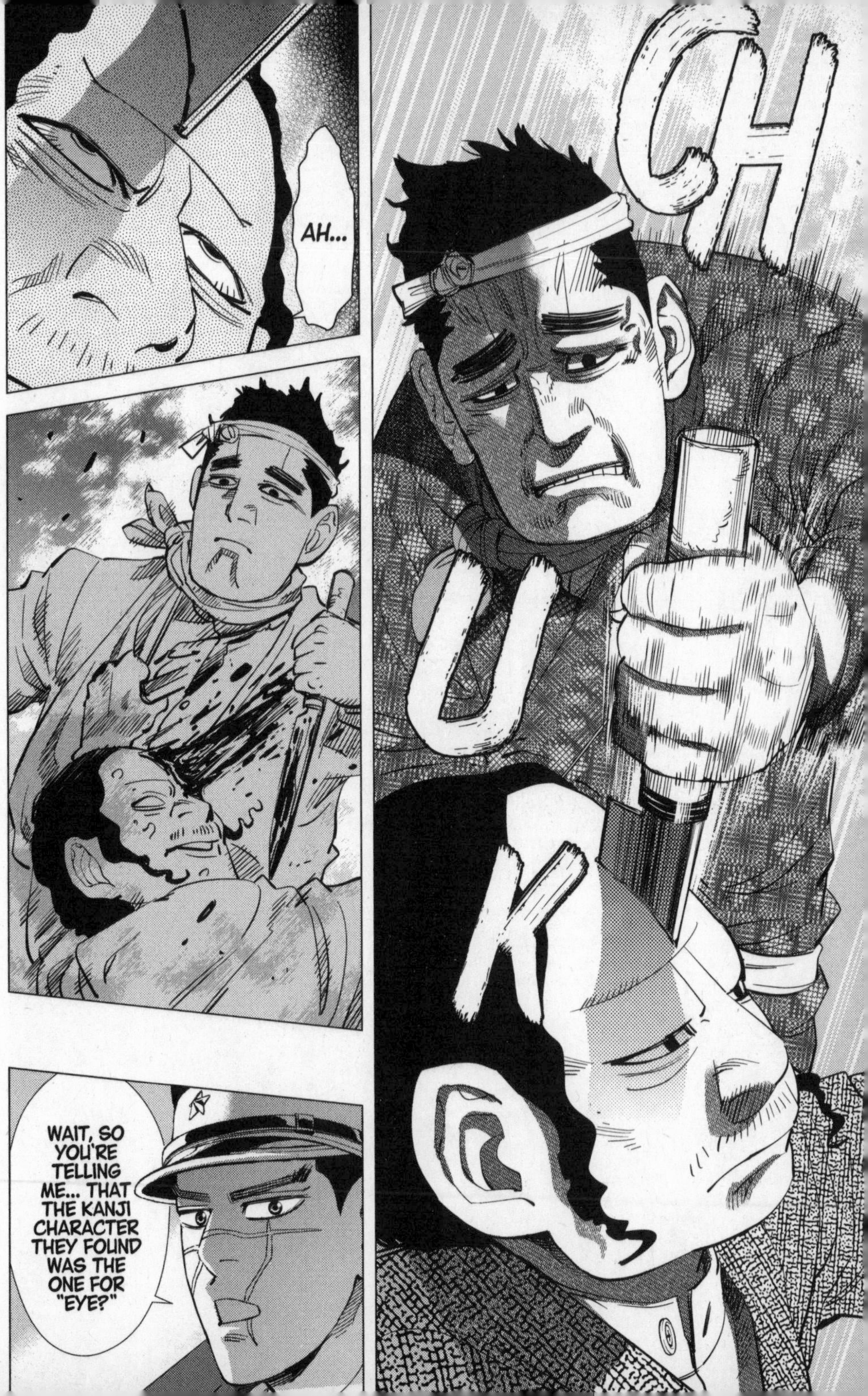
CHUK
AH...
WAIT, SO YOU'RE TELLING ME... THAT THE KANJI CHARACTER THEY FOUND WAS THE ONE FOR "EYE?"

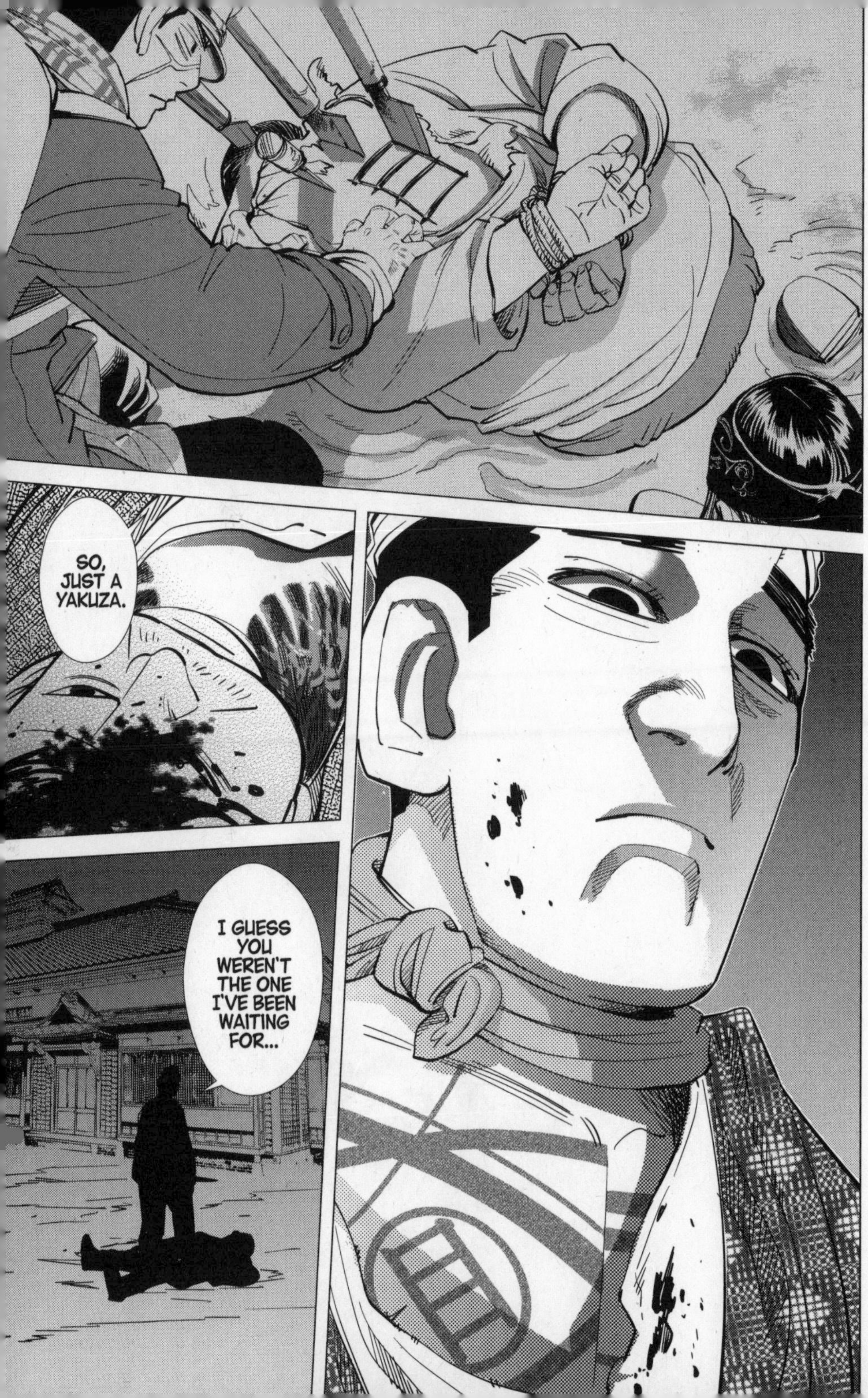
SO, JUST A YAKUZA.
I GUESS YOU WEREN'T THE ONE I'VE BEEN WAITING FOR...

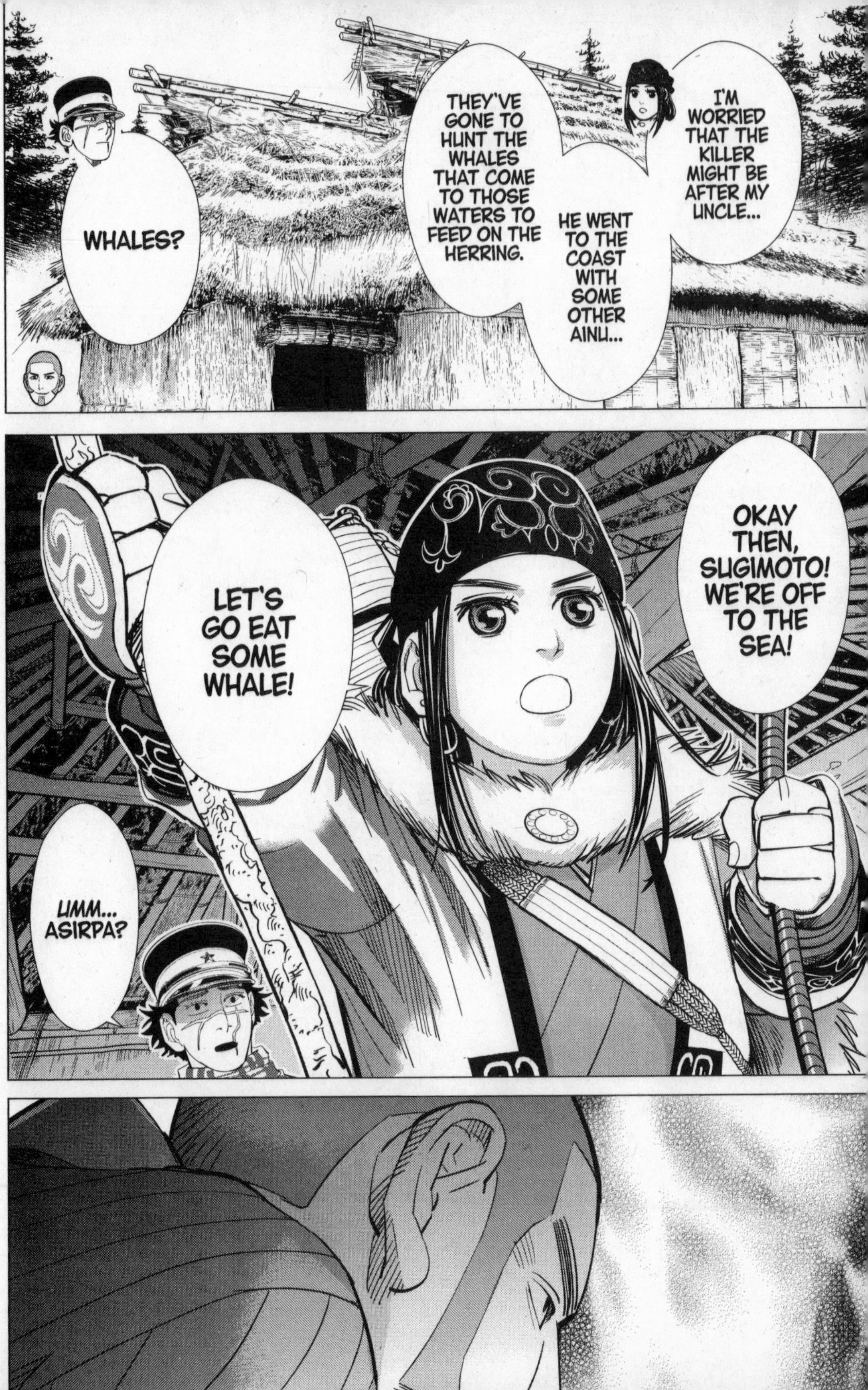
I'M WORRIED THAT THE KILLER MIGHT BE AFTER MY UNCLE...
HE WENT TO THE COAST WITH SOME OTHER AINU...
THEY'VE GONE TO HUNT THE WHALES THAT COME TO THOSE WATERS TO FEED ON THE HERRING.
WHALES?
OKAY THEN, SUGIMOTO! WE'RE OFF TO THE SEA!
LET'S GO EAT SOME WHALE!
UMM... ASIRPA?

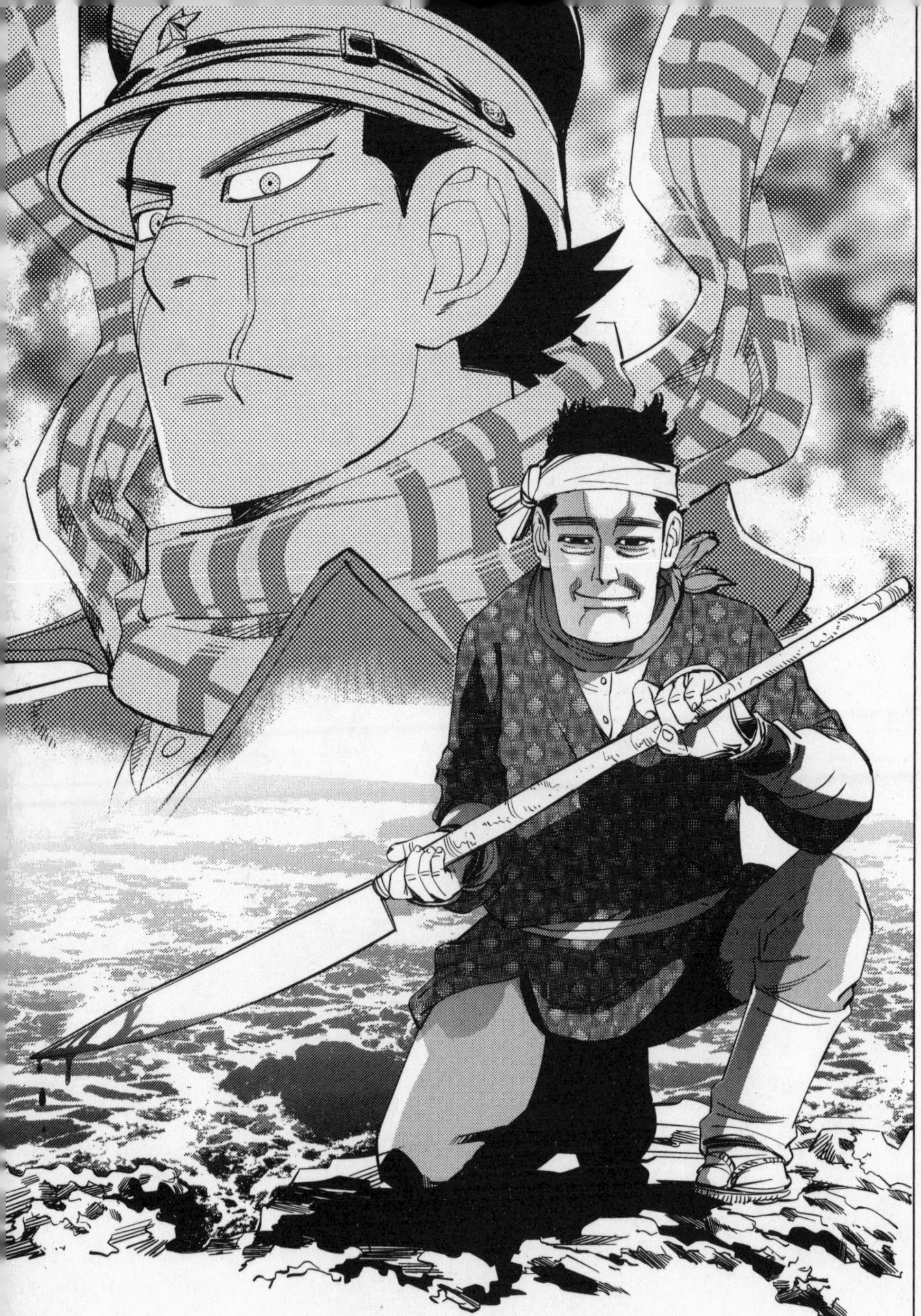

Chapter 38: Humpe

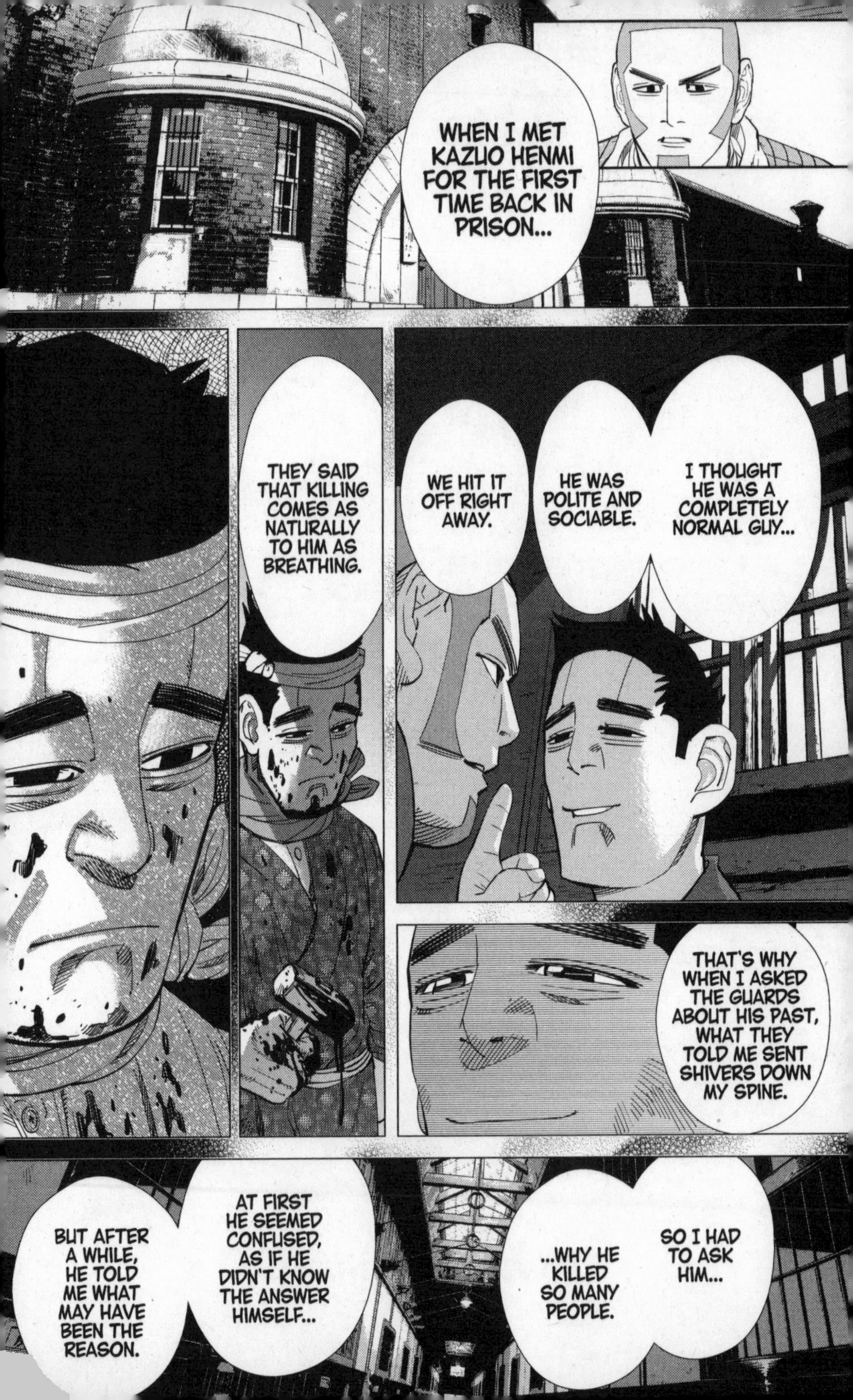
WHEN I MET KAZUO HENMI FOR THE FIRST TIME BACK IN PRISON...
I THOUGHT HE WAS A COMPLETELY NORMAL GUY...
HE WAS POLITE AND SOCIABLE.
WE HIT IT OFF RIGHT AWAY.
THAT'S WHY WHEN I ASKED THE GUARDS ABOUT HIS PAST, WHAT THEY TOLD ME SENT SHIVERS DOWN MY SPINE.
THEY SAID THAT KILLING COMES AS NATURALLY TO HIM AS BREATHING.
SO I HAD TO ASK HIM...
...WHY HE KILLED SO MANY PEOPLE.
AT FIRST HE SEEMED CONFUSED, AS IF HE DIDN'T KNOW THE ANSWER HIMSELF...
BUT AFTER A WHILE, HE TOLD ME WHAT MAY HAVE BEEN THE REASON.

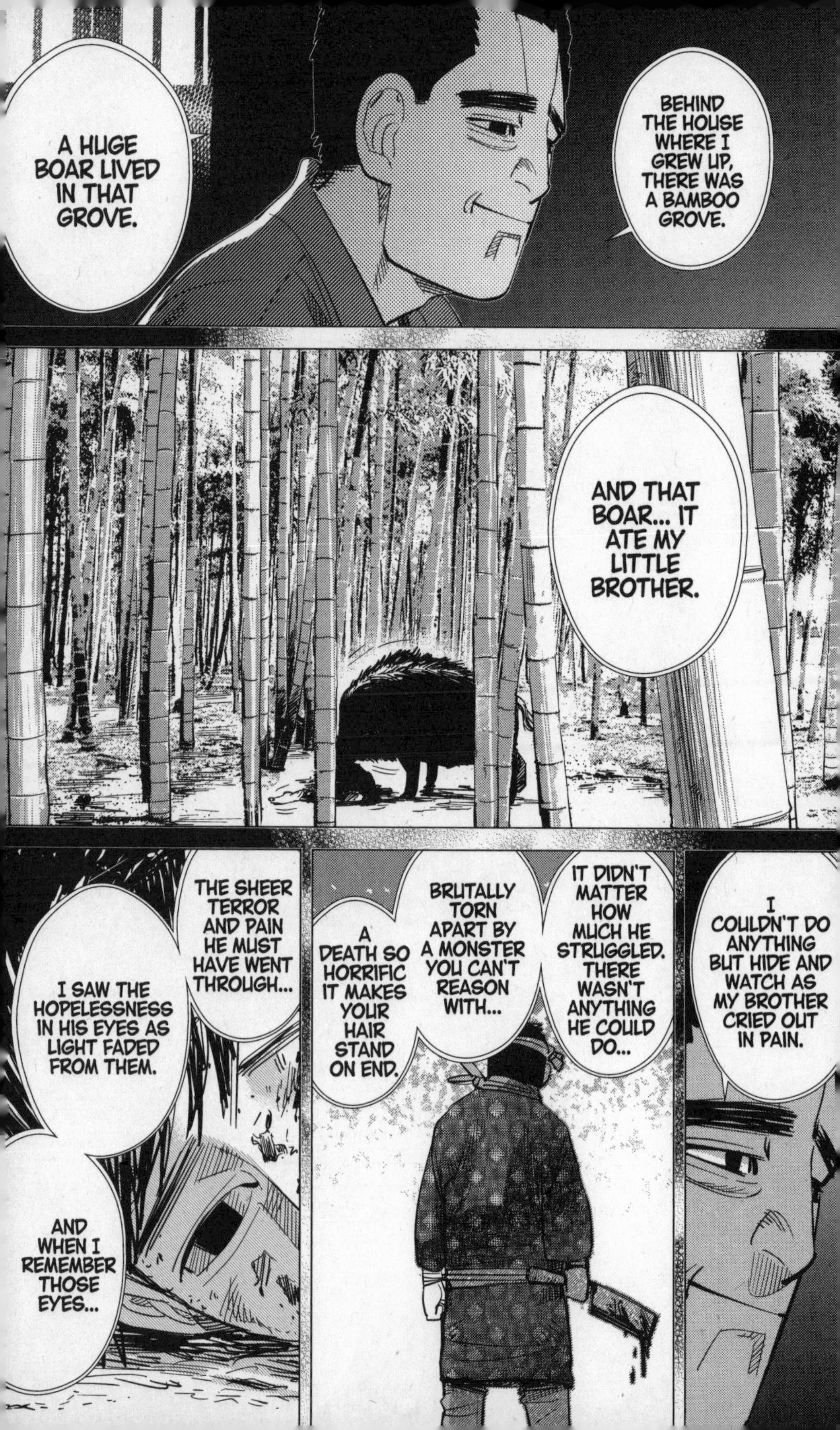
BEHIND THE HOUSE WHERE I GREW UP, THERE WAS A BAMBOO GROVE.
A HUGE BOAR LIVED IN THAT GROVE.
AND THAT BOAR... IT ATE MY LITTLE BROTHER.
I COULDN'T DO ANYTHING BUT HIDE AND WATCH AS MY BROTHER CRIED OUT IN PAIN.
IT DIDN'T MATTER HOW MUCH HE STRUGGLED. THERE WASN'T ANYTHING HE COULD DO...
BRUTALLY TORN APART BY A MONSTER YOU CAN'T REASON WITH...
A DEATH SO HORRIFIC IT MAKES YOUR HAIR STAND ON END.
THE SHEER TERROR AND PAIN HE MUST HAVE WENT THROUGH...
I SAW THE HOPELESSNESS IN HIS EYES AS LIGHT FADED FROM THEM.
AND WHEN I REMEMBER THOSE EYES...

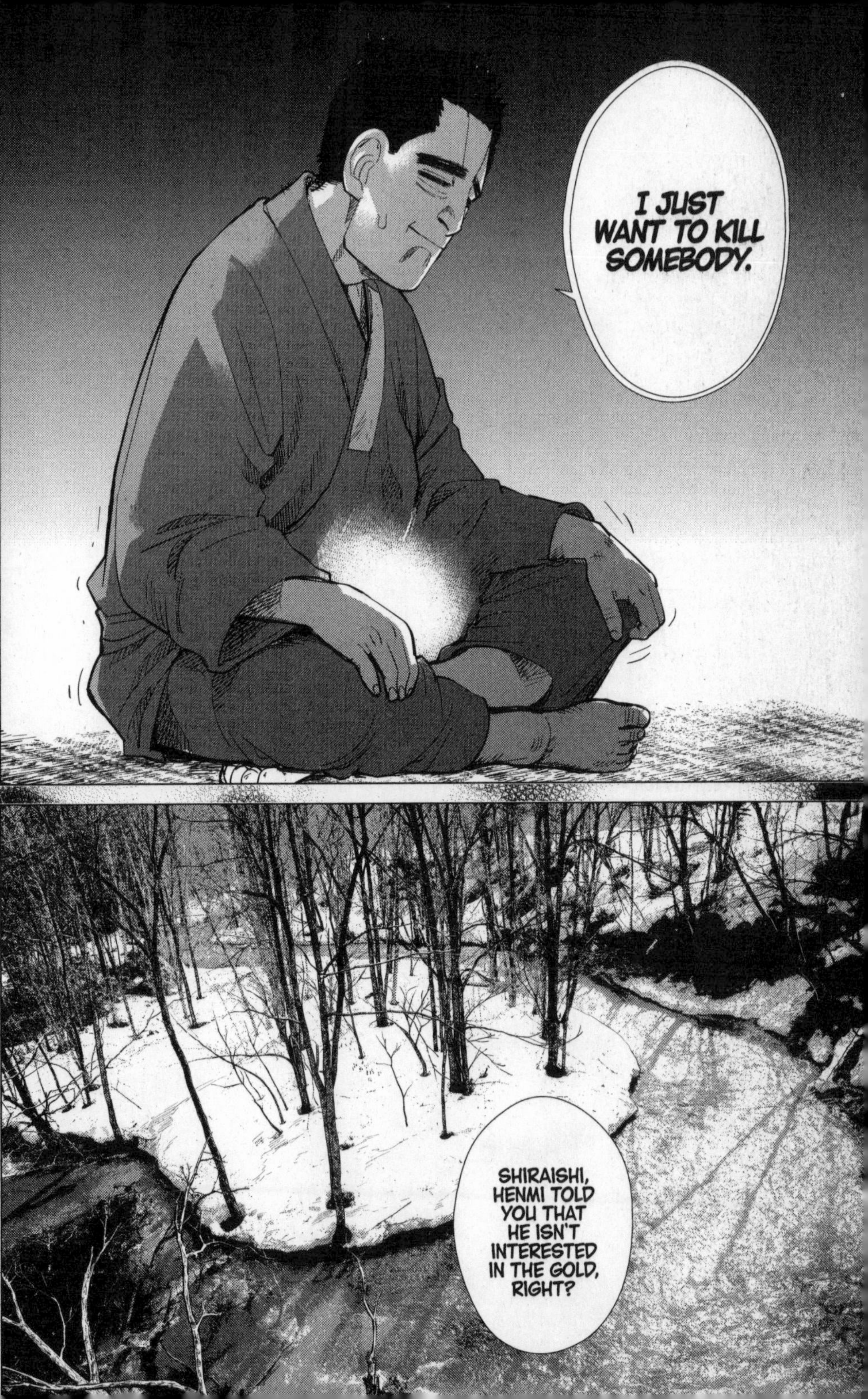
I JUST WANT TO KILL SOMEBODY.
SHIRAISHI, HENMI TOLD YOU THAT HE ISN'T INTERESTED IN THE GOLD, RIGHT?

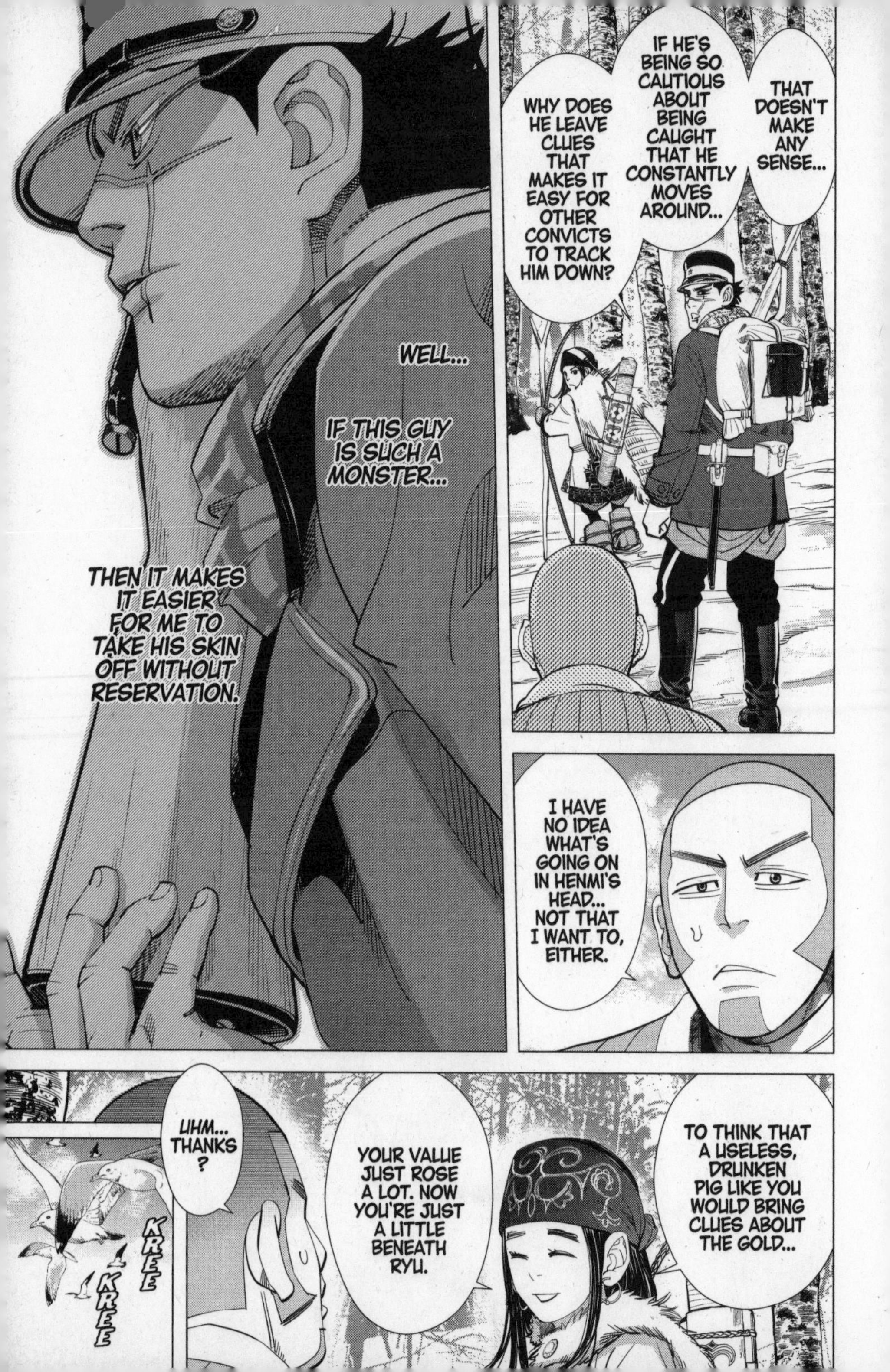
IF HE'S BEING SO CAUTIOUS ABOUT BEING CAUGHT THAT HE CONSTANTLY MOVES AROUND...
WHY DOES HE LEAVE CLUES THAT MAKES IT EASY FOR OTHER CONVICTS TO TRACK HIM DOWN?
THAT DOESN'T MAKE ANY SENSE...
I HAVE NO IDEA WHAT'S GOING ON IN HENMI'S HEAD... NOT THAT I WANT TO, EITHER.
WELL...
IF THIS GUY IS SUCH A MONSTER...
THEN IT MAKES IT EASIER FOR ME TO TAKE HIS SKIN OFF WITHOUT RESERVATION.
TO THINK THAT A USELESS, DRUNKEN PIG LIKE YOU WOULD BRING CLUES ABOUT THE GOLD...
YOUR VALUE JUST ROSE A LOT. NOW YOU'RE JUST A LITTLE BENEATH RYU.
UHM... THANKS ?
KREE
KREE

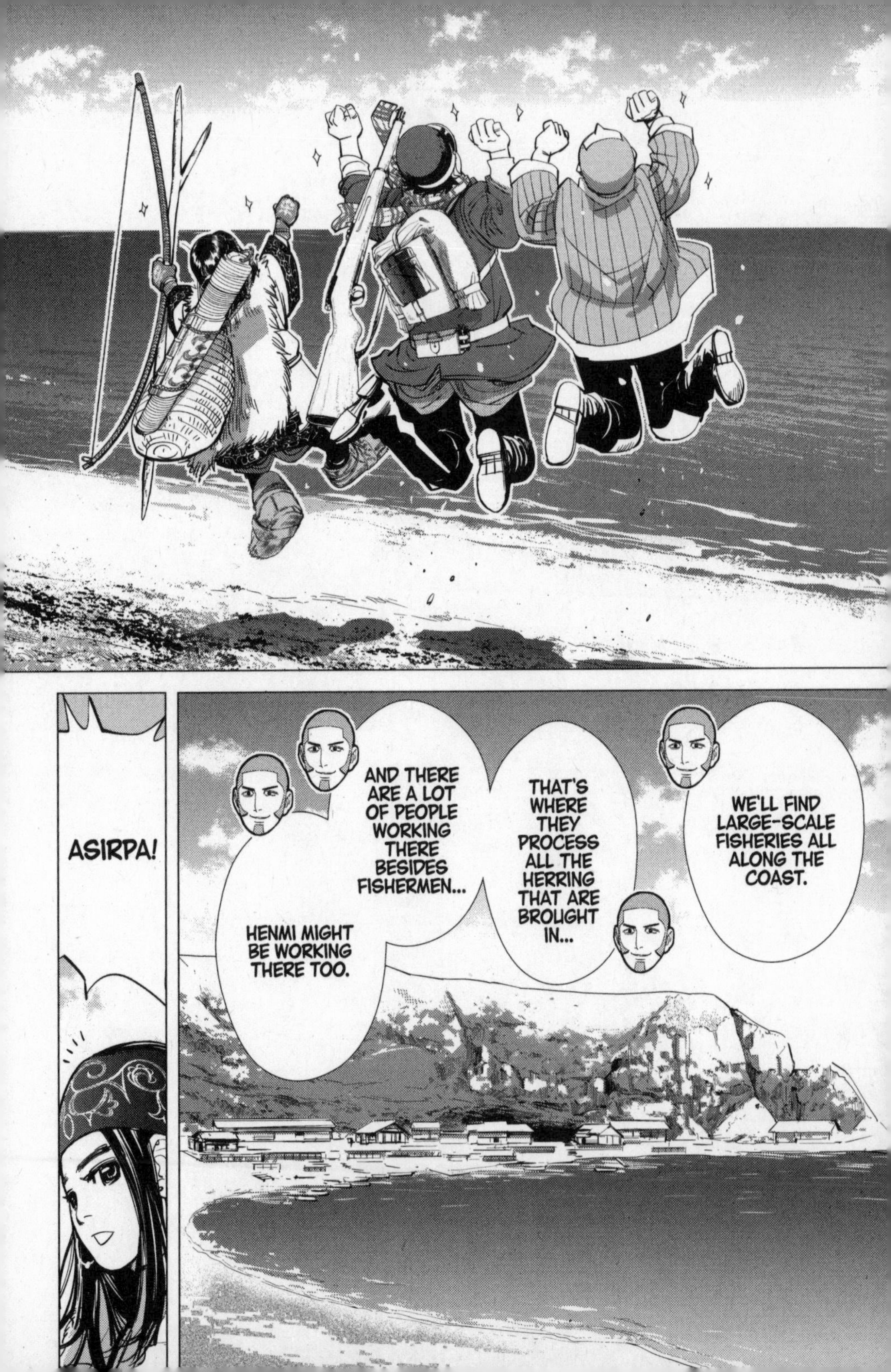
WE'LL FIND LARGE-SCALE FISHERIES ALL ALONG THE COAST.
THAT'S WHERE THEY PROCESS ALL THE HERRING THAT ARE BROUGHT IN...
AND THERE ARE A LOT OF PEOPLE WORKING THERE BESIDES FISHERMEN...
HENMI MIGHT BE WORKING THERE TOO.
ASIRPA!

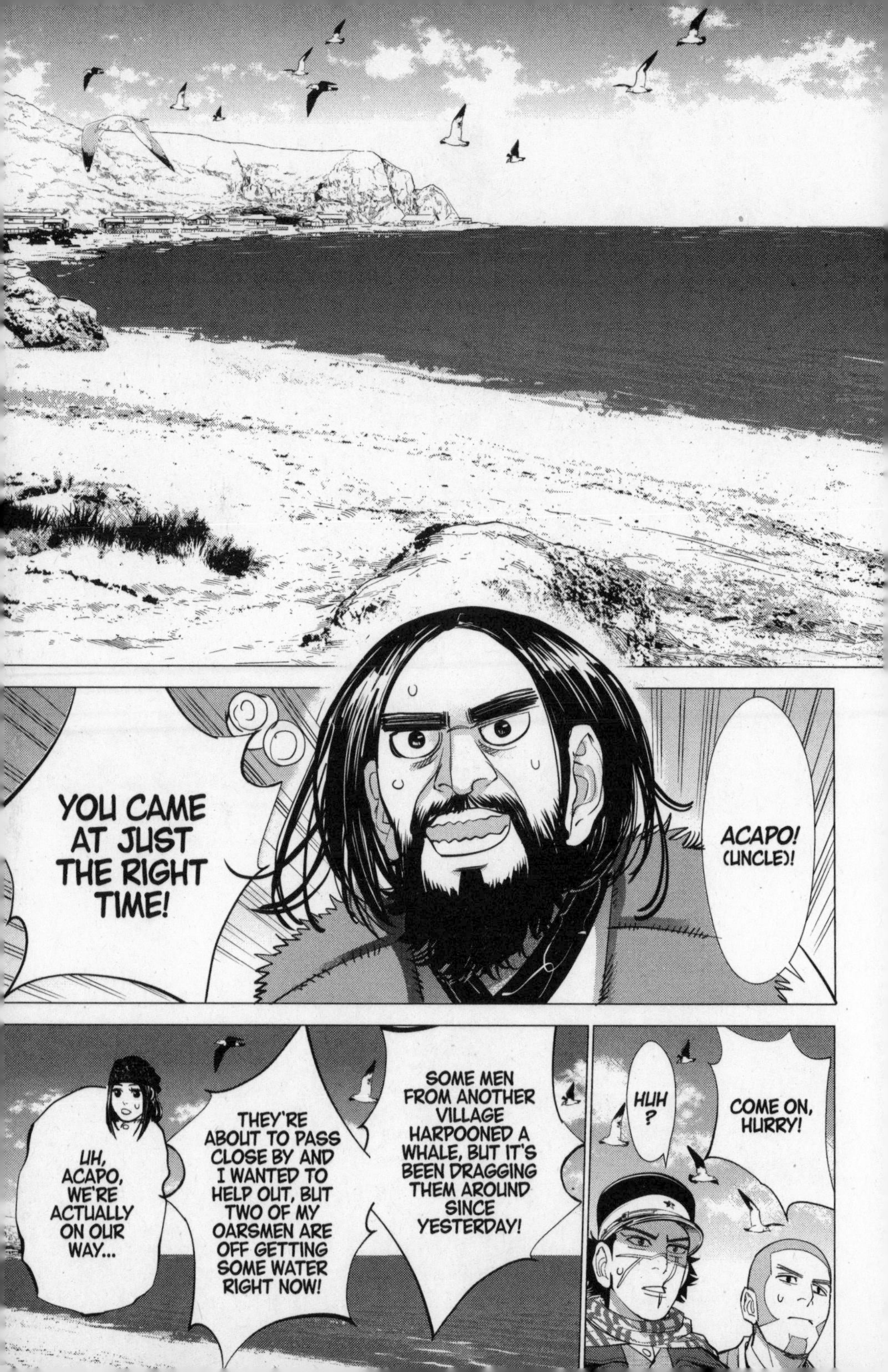
ACAPO! (UNCLE)!
YOU CAME AT JUST THE RIGHT TIME!
COME ON, HURRY!
HUH?
SOME MEN FROM ANOTHER VILLAGE HARPOONED A WHALE, BUT IT'S BEEN DRAGGING THEM AROUND SINCE YESTERDAY!
THEY'RE ABOUT TO PASS CLOSE BY AND I WANTED TO HELP OUT, BUT TWO OF MY OARSMEN ARE OFF GETTING SOME WATER RIGHT NOW!
UH, ACAPO, WE'RE ACTUALLY ON OUR WAY...

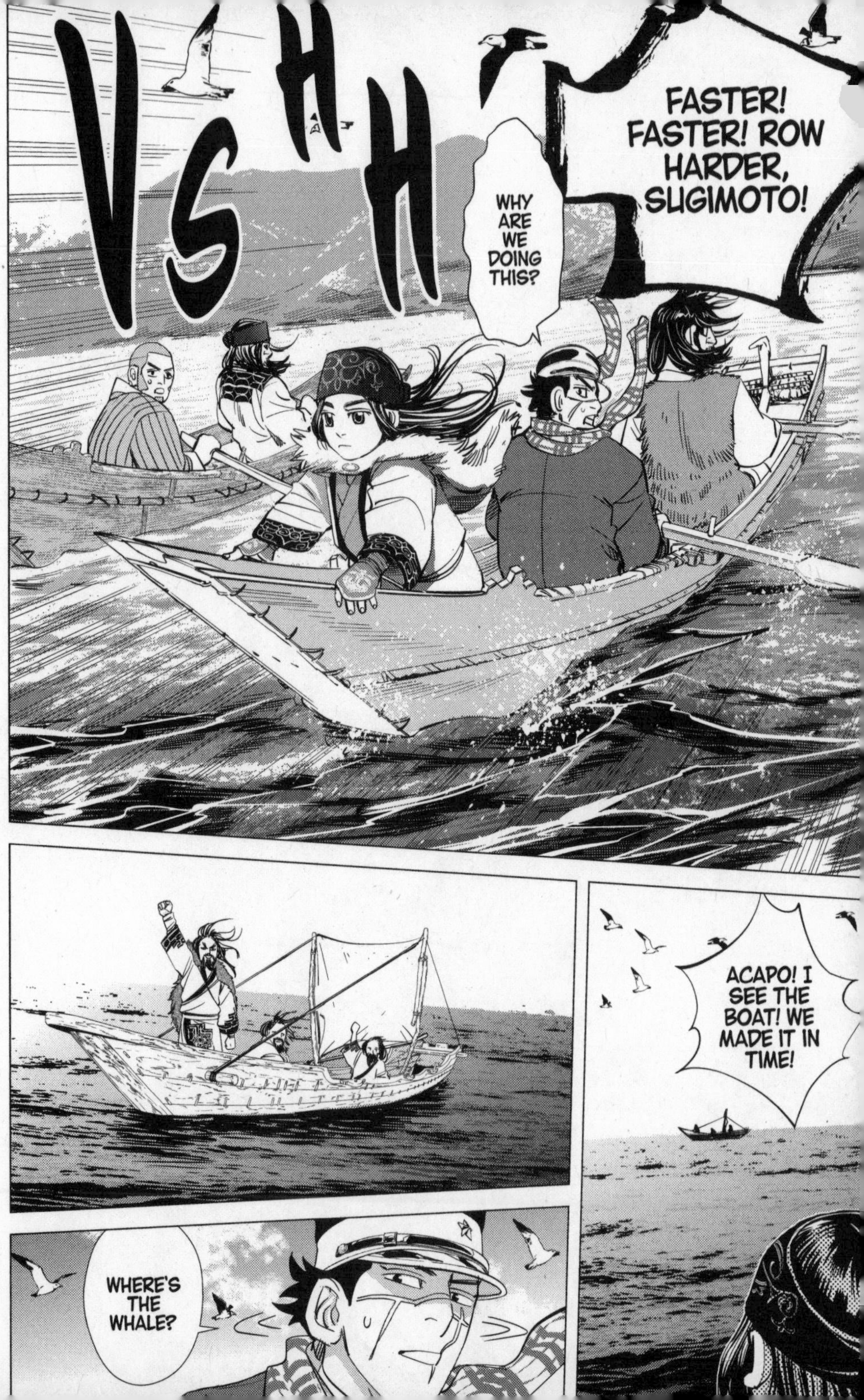
FASTER! FASTER! ROW HARDER, SUGIMOTO!
WHY ARE WE DOING THIS?
VSHH
ACAPO! I SEE THE BOAT! WE MADE IT IN TIME!
WHERE'S THE WHALE?

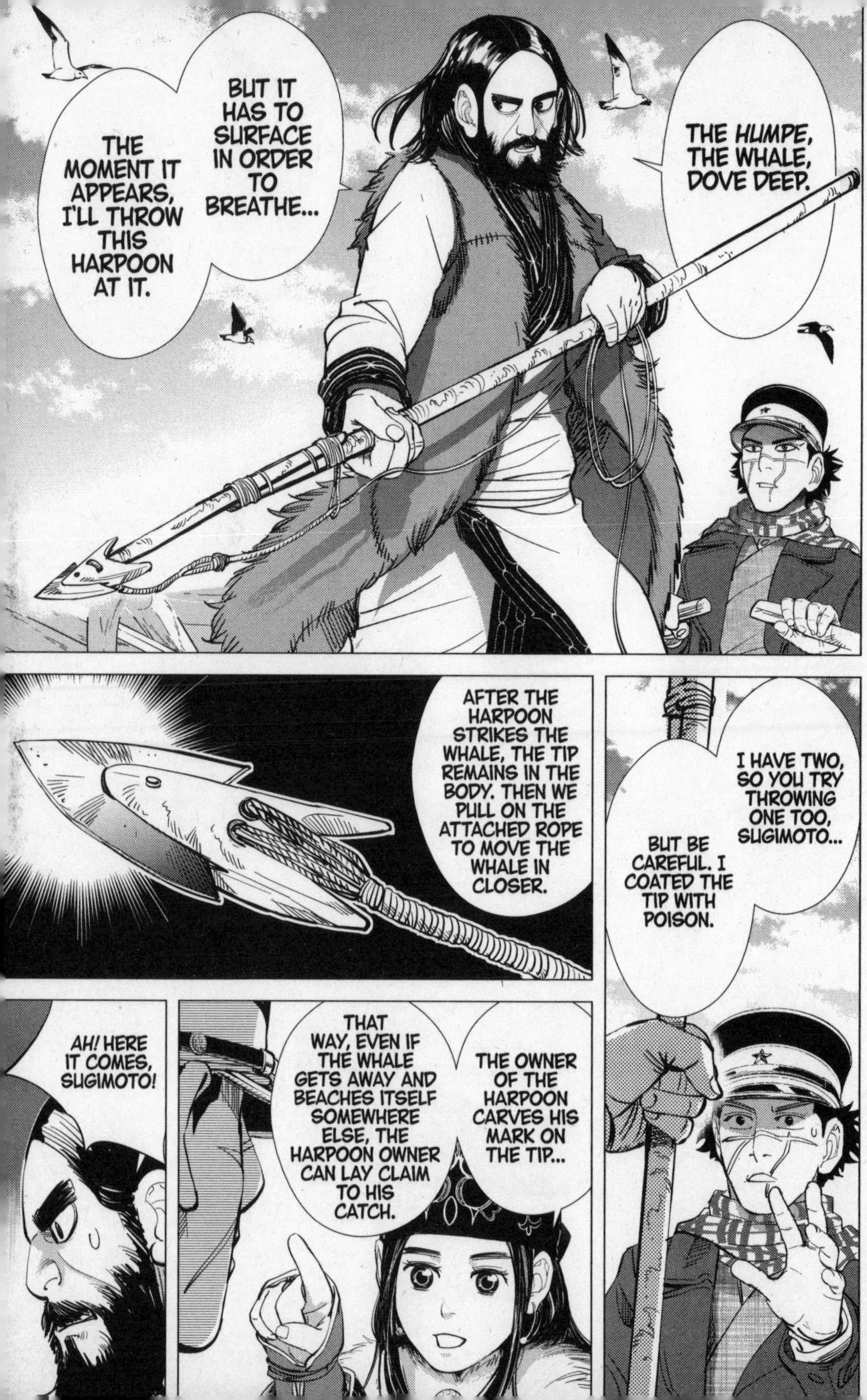
THE HUMPE, THE WHALE, DOVE DEEP.
BUT IT HAS TO SURFACE IN ORDER TO BREATHE...
THE MOMENT IT APPEARS, I'LL THROW THIS HARPOON AT IT.
I HAVE TWO, SO YOU TRY THROWING ONE TOO, SUGIMOTO...
BUT BE CAREFUL. I COATED THE TIP WITH POISON.
AFTER THE HARPOON STRIKES THE WHALE, THE TIP REMAINS IN THE BODY. THEN WE PULL ON THE ATTACHED ROPE TO MOVE THE WHALE IN CLOSER.
THE OWNER OF THE HARPOON CARVES HIS MARK ON THE TIP...
THAT WAY, EVEN IF THE WHALE GETS AWAY AND BEACHES ITSELF SOMEWHERE ELSE, THE HARPOON OWNER CAN LAY CLAIM TO HIS CATCH.
AH! HERE IT COMES, SUGIMOTO!

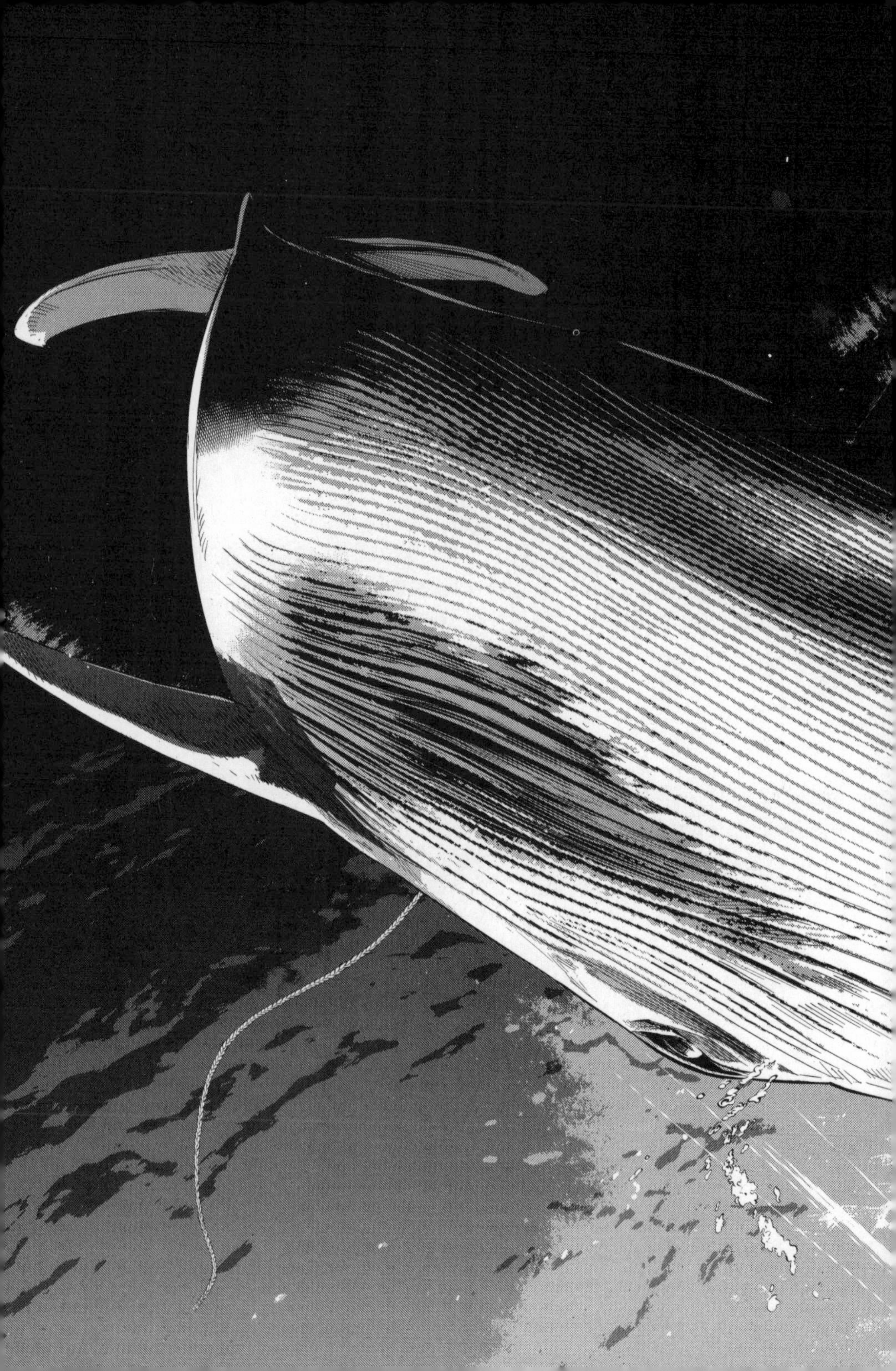

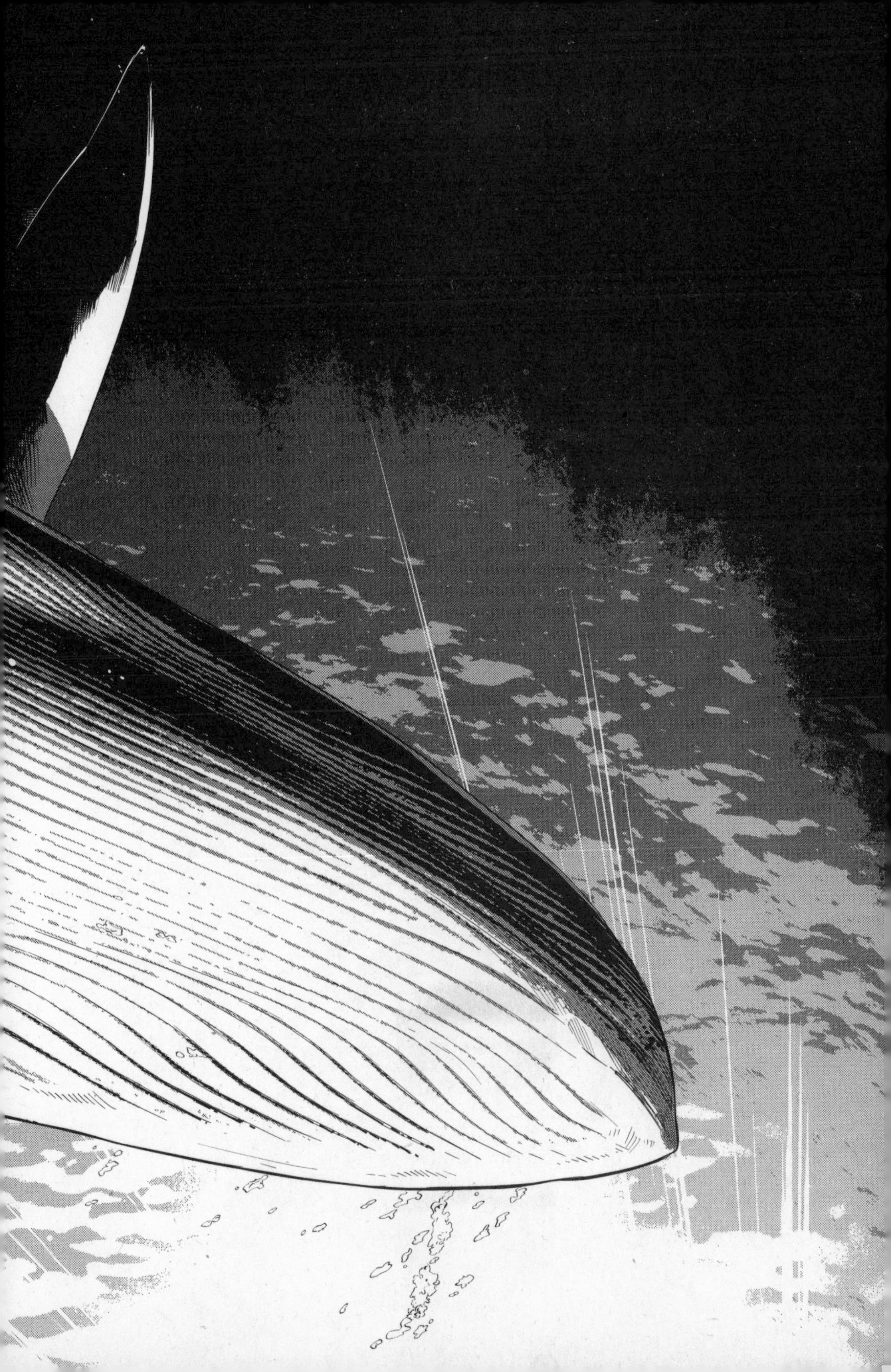

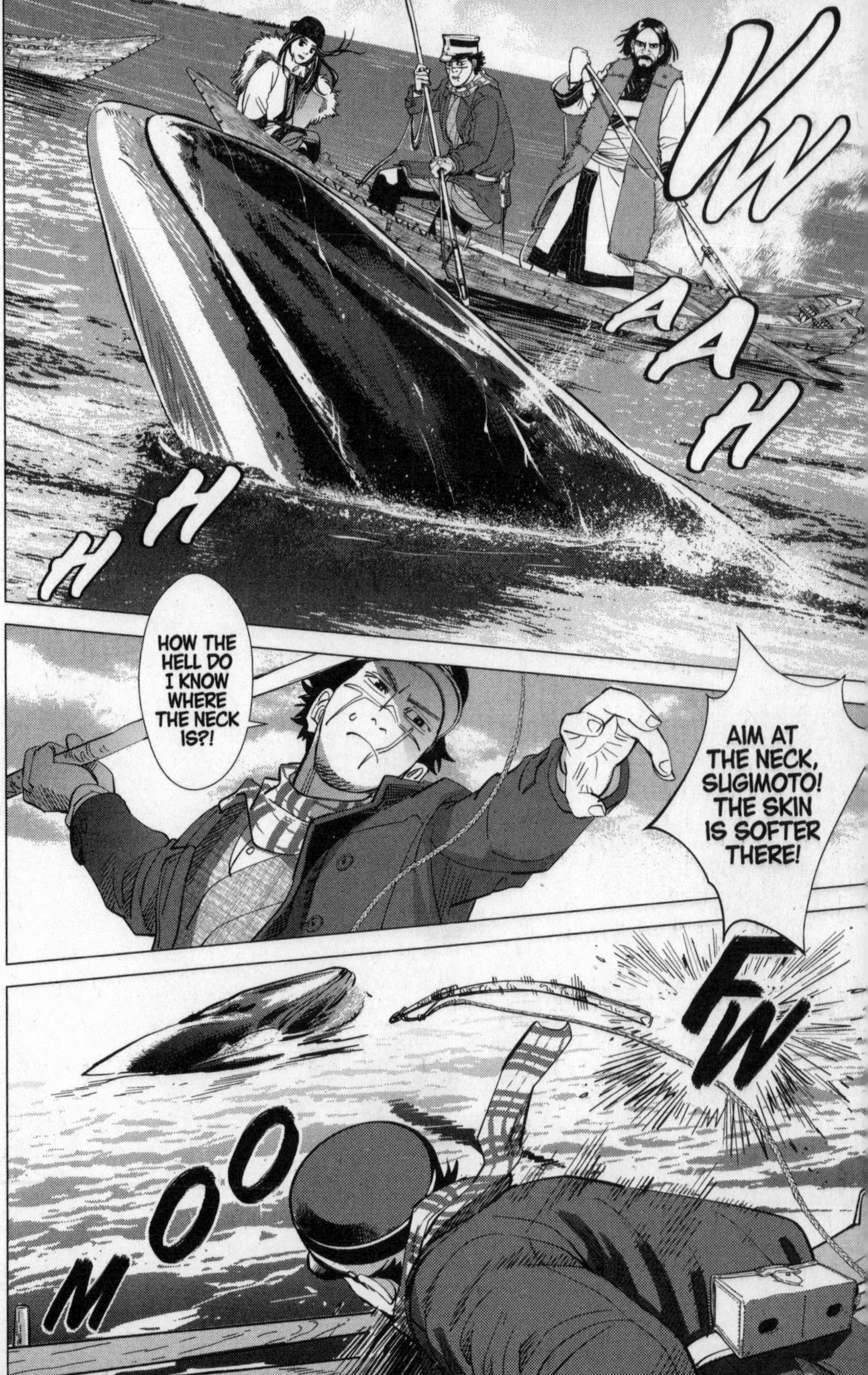
VWAAHHH
AIM AT THE NECK, SUGIMOTO! THE SKIN IS SOFTER THERE!
HOW THE HELL DO I KNOW WHERE THE NECK IS?!
FW
MOOO

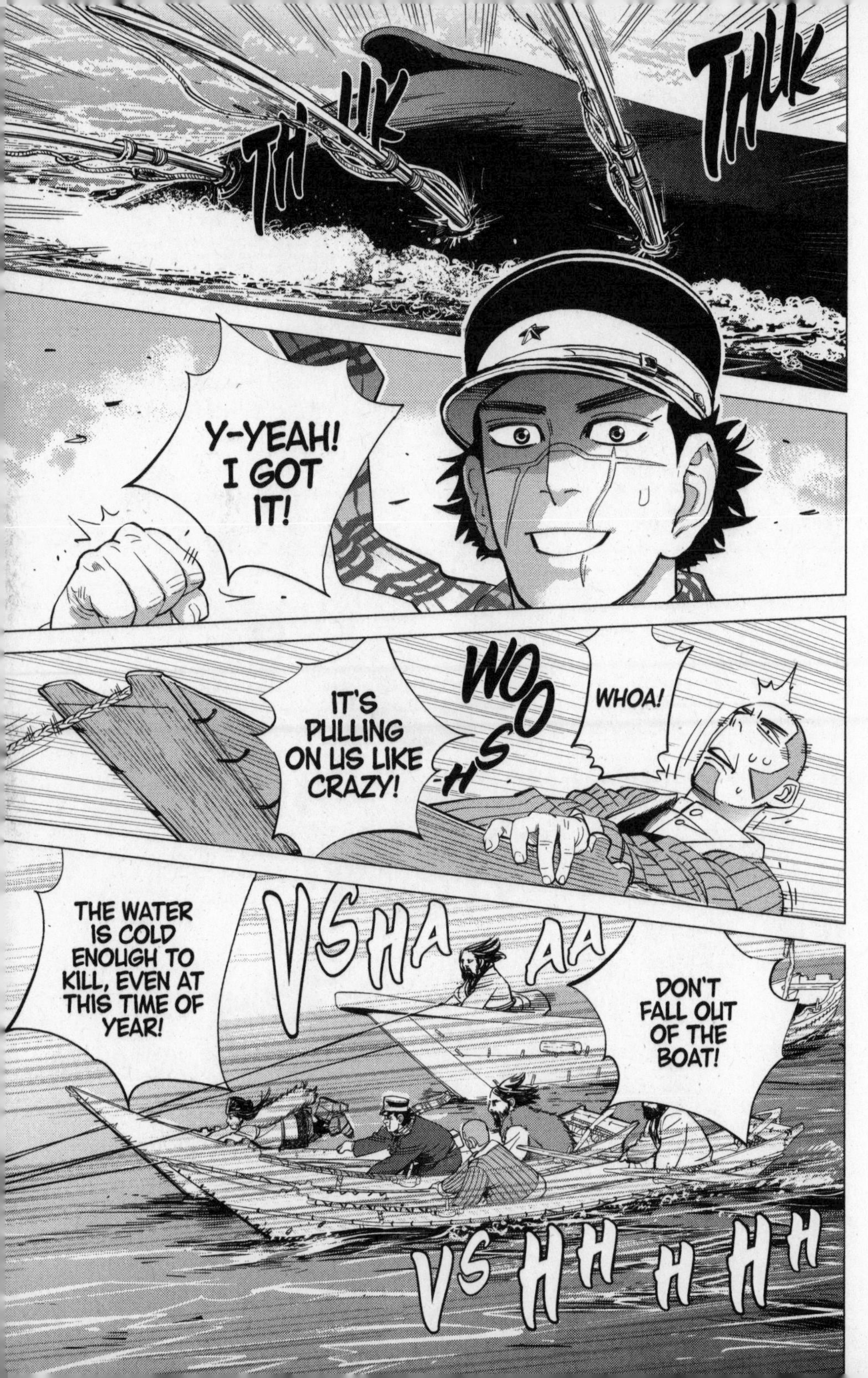
THUK
THUK
Y-YEAH! I GOT IT!
WHOA!
WOOSH
IT'S PULLING ON US LIKE CRAZY!
DON'T FALL OUT OF THE BOAT!
VSHAAA
THE WATER IS COLD ENOUGH TO KILL, EVEN AT THIS TIME OF YEAR!
VSHHHHH

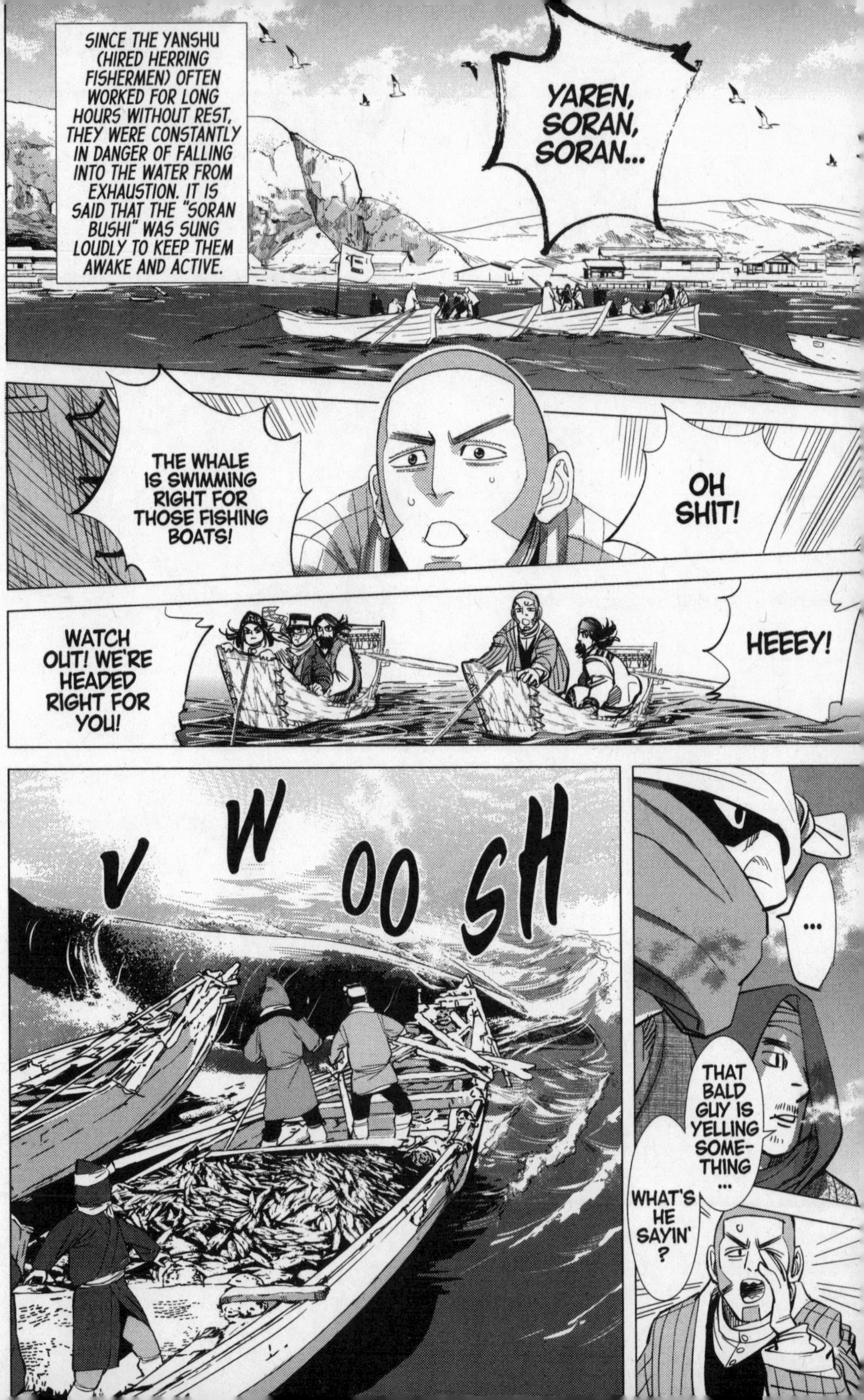
YAREN, SORAN, SORAN...
SINCE THE YANSHU (HIRED HERRING FISHERMEN) OFTEN WORKED FOR LONG HOURS WITHOUT REST, THEY WERE CONSTANTLY IN DANGER OF FALLING INTO THE WATER FROM EXHAUSTION. IT IS SAID THAT THE "SORAN BUSHI" WAS SUNG LOUDLY TO KEEP THEM AWAKE AND ACTIVE.
OH SHIT!
THE WHALE IS SWIMMING RIGHT FOR THOSE FISHING BOATS!
HEEEY!
WATCH OUT! WE'RE HEADED RIGHT FOR YOU!
...
THAT BALD GUY IS YELLING SOME-THING...
WHAT'S HE SAYIN'?
VWOOSH

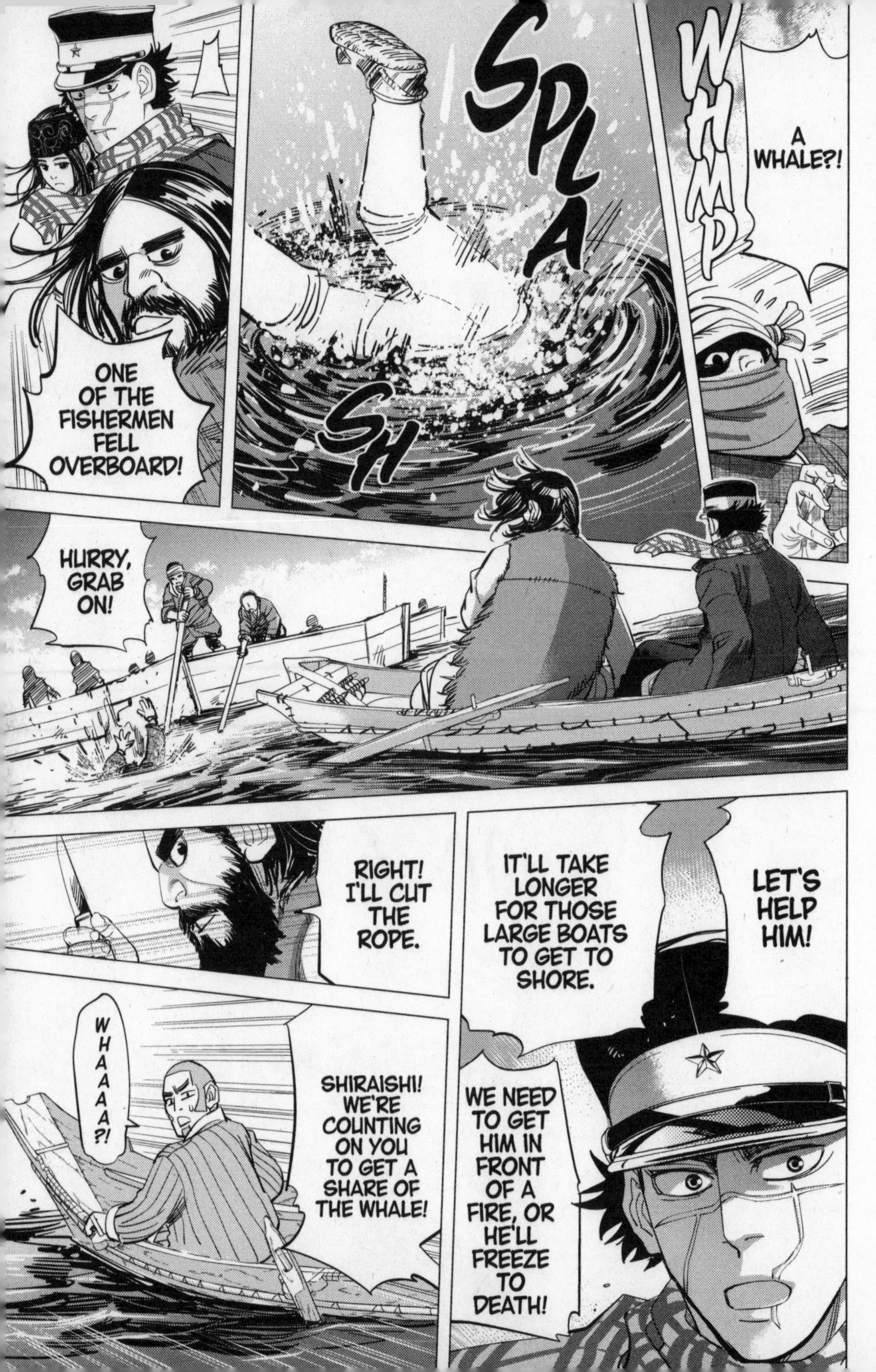
WHMP
A WHALE?!
SPLASH
ONE OF THE FISHERMEN FELL OVERBOARD!
HURRY, GRAB ON!
LET'S HELP HIM!
IT'LL TAKE LONGER FOR THOSE LARGE BOATS TO GET TO SHORE.
RIGHT! I'LL CUT THE ROPE.
WE NEED TO GET HIM IN FRONT OF A FIRE, OR HE'LL FREEZE TO DEATH!
SHIRAISHI! WE'RE COUNTING ON YOU TO GET A SHARE OF THE WHALE!
WHAAAAA?!

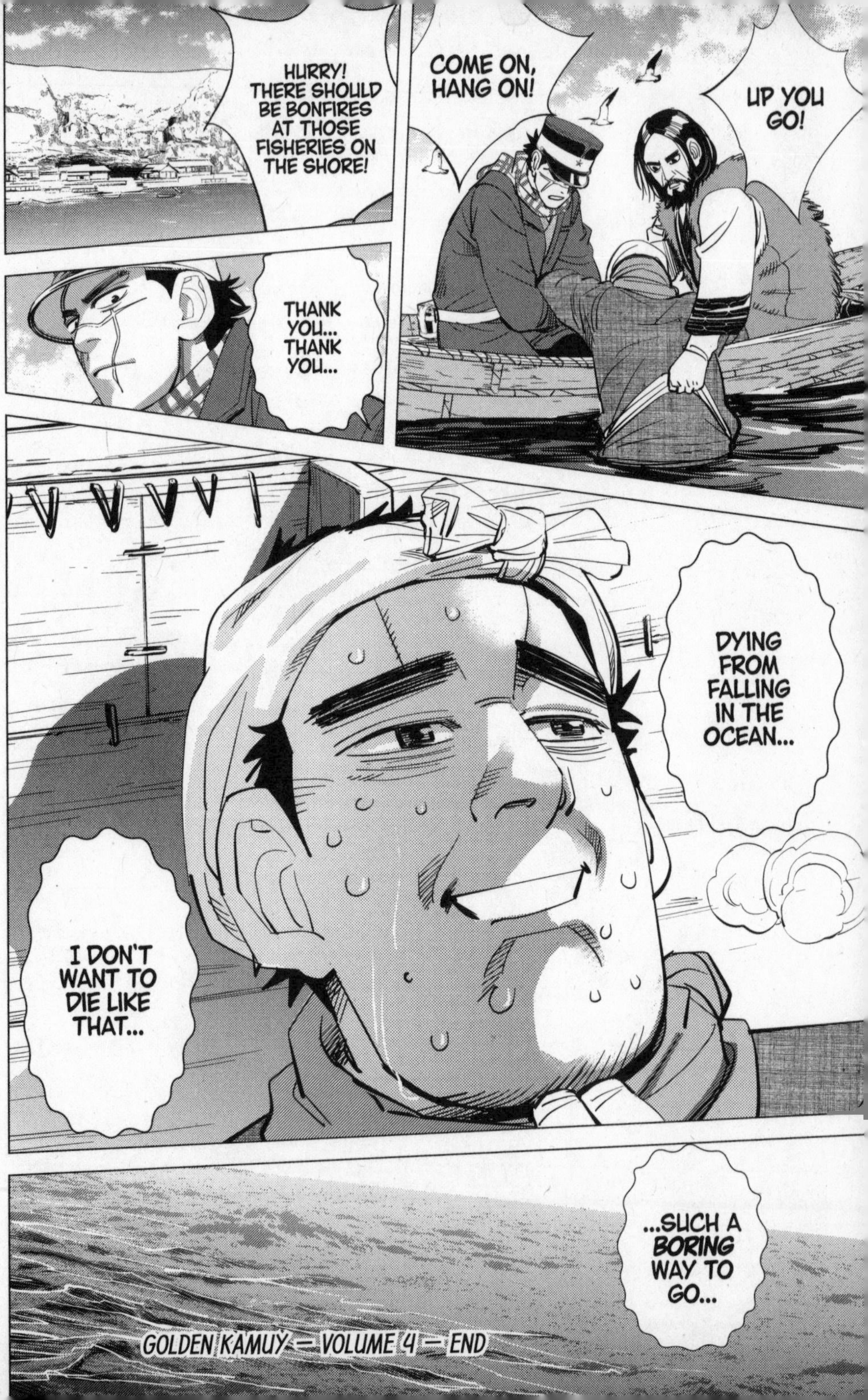
UP YOU GO!
COME ON, HANG ON!
HURRY! THERE SHOULD BE BONFIRES AT THOSE FISHERIES ON THE SHORE!
THANK YOU... THANK YOU...
DYING FROM FALLING IN THE OCEAN...
I DON'T WANT TO DIE LIKE THAT...
...SUCH A BORING WAY TO GO...
GOLDEN KAMUY — VOLUME 4 — END

Ainu Language Supervision • Hiroshi Nakagawa

Cooperation from • Hokkaido Ainu Association
and the Abashiri Prison Museum

Jirota Kitahara • Kazunobu Goto

Photo Credits • Takayuki Monma
Takanori Matsuda

Ainu Culture References

Chiri, Takanaka and Yokoyama, Takao. *Ainugo Eiri Jiten* (Ainu Language Illustrated Dictionary).
Tokyo: Kagyusha, 1994

Kayano, Shigeru. *Ainu no Mingu* (Ainu Folkcrafts). Kawagoe: Suzusawa Book Store, 1978

Kayano, Shigeru. *Kayano Shigeru no Ainugo Jiten* (Kayano Shigeru's Ainu Language Dictionary).
Tokyo: Sanseido, 1996

Musashino Art University - The Research Institute for Culture and Cultural History. *Ainu no Mingu Jissoku Zushu*
(Ainu Folkcrafts – Collection of Drawing and Figures). Biratori: Biratori-cho Council for Promoting Ainu Culture, 2014

Satouchi, Ai. *Ainu-shiki ekoroji-seikatsu: Haruzo Ekashi ni manabu shizen no chie* (Ainu Style Ecological Living:
Haruzo Ekashi Teaches the Wisdom of Nature). Tokyo: Kabushiki gaisha Shogakukan, 2008

Chiri, Yukie. *Ainu Shin'yoshu* (Chiri Yukie's Ainu Epic Tales). Tokyo: Iwanami Shoten, 1978

Namikawa, Kenji. *Ainu Minzoku no Kiseki* (The Path of the Ainu People).
Tokyo: Yamakawa Publishing, 2004

Mook. *Senjuumin Ainu Minzoku* (Bessatsu Taiyo) (The Ainu People (Extra Issue Taiyo).Tokyo: Heibonsha, 2004

Kinoshita, Seizo. *Shiraoikotan Kinoshita Seizo Isaku Shashin Shu* (Shiraoikotan: Kinoshita Seizo's Posthumous
Photography Collection). Hokkaido Shiraoi-gun Shiraoi-cho: Shiraoi Heritage Conservation Foundation, 1988

The Ainu Museum. *Ainu no Ifuku Bunka* (The Culture of Ainu Clothing). Hokkaido Shiraoi-gun Shiraoi-cho:
Shiraoi Ainu Museum, 1991.

Keira, Tomoko and Kaji, Sayaka. *Ainu no Shiki* (Ainu's Four Seasons). Tokyo: Akashi Shoten, 1995

Fukuoka, Itoko and Sato, Kazuko. *Ainu Shokubutsushi* (Ainu Botanical Journal). Chiba Urayasu-Shi: Sofukan, 1995

Hayakawa, Noboru. *Ainu no Minzoku* (Ainu Folklore). Iwasaki Bijutsusha, 1983

Sunazawa, Kura. *Ku Sukuppu Orushibe* (The Memories of My Generation). Hokkaido, Sapporo-shi:
Miyama Shobo, 1983

Haginaka, Miki et al., *Kikigaki Ainu no Shokuji* (Oral History of Ainu Diet).
Tokyo: Rural Culture Association Japan, 1992

Nakagawa, Hiroshi. *New Express Ainu Go*. Tokyo: Hakusuisha, 2013

Nakagawa, Hiroshi. *Ainugo Chitose Hogen Jiten* (The Ainu-Japanese dictionary). Chiba Urayasu-Shi: Sofukan, 1995

Nakagawa, Hiroshi and Nakamoto, Mutsuko. *Kamuy Yukara de Ainu Go wo Manabu*
Learning Ainu with Kamuy Yukar). Tokyo: Hakusuisha, 2007

Nakagawa, Hiroshi. *Katari au Kotoba no Chikara – Kamuy tachi to Ikiru Sekai*
(The Power of Spoken Words – Living in a World with Kamuy). Tokyo: Iwanami Shoten, 2010

Sarashina, Genzo and Sarashina, Hikari. Kotan Seibutsu Ki <1 Juki / Zassou hen>
(Kotan Wildlife Vol. 1 – Trees and Weeds). Hosei University Publishing, 1992/2007

Sarashina, Genzo and Sarashina, Hikari. *Kotan Seibutsu Ki <2 Yacho / Kaijuu / Gyozoku hen>*
(Kotan Wildlife Vol. 2 – Birds, Sea Creatures, and Fish). Hosei University Publishing, 1992/2007

Sarashina, Genzo and Sarashina, Hikari. *Kotan Seibutsu Ki <3 Yachou / Mizudori / Konchu hen>*
(Kotan Wildlife Vol. 3 – Shorebirds, Seabirds, and Insects). Hosei University Publishing, 1992/2007

Kawakami Yuji. *Sarunkur Ainu Monogatari* (The Tale of Sarunkur Ainu). Kawagoe: Suzusawa Book Store, 2003/2005

Kawakami, Yuji. *Ekashi to Fuchi wo Tazunete* (Visiting Ekashi and Fuchi). Kawagoe: Suzusawa Book Store, 1991

Council for the Conservation of Ainu Culture, Ainu Minzokushi (Ainu People Magazine). Dai-ichi Hoki, 1970

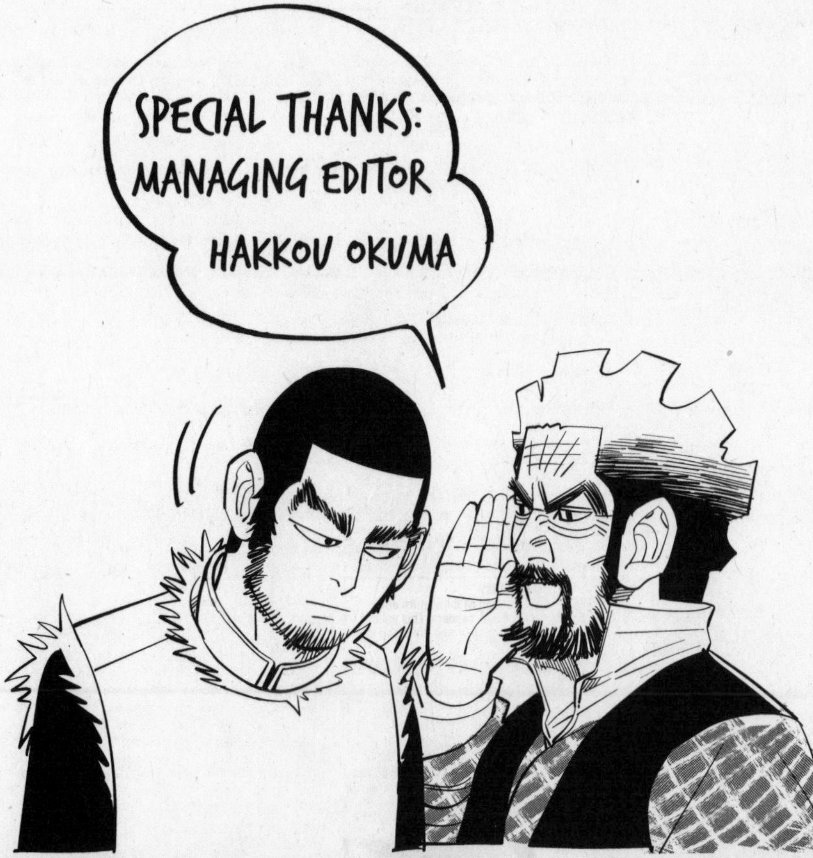
SPECIAL THANKS: MANAGING EDITOR HAKKOU OKUMA

GOLDEN KAMUY

Volume 4
VIZ Signature Edition

Story/Art by Satoru Noda

GOLDEN KAMUY © 2014 by Satoru Noda
All rights reserved.
First published in Japan in 2014 by SHUEISHA Inc., Tokyo.
English translation rights arranged by SHUEISHA Inc.

Translation/Eiji Yasuda
Touch-Up Art & Lettering/Steve Dutro
Design/Izumi Evers
Editor/Mike Montesa

Printed in the U.S.A

Published by VIZ Media, LLC
P.O. Box 77010
San Francisco, CA 94107

10 9 8 7 6 5 4 3 2 1
First printing, March 2018

VIZ
media
www.viz.com

VIZ SIGNATURE

THIS IS THE LAST PAGE.

1
2
3
4
1
2
5
6
7
8
3
4
9
5
142

←Follow the action this way.

GOLDEN KAMUY has been printed in the original Japanese format in order to preserve the orientation of the original artwork.

Please turn it around and begin reading from right to left. Unlike English, Japanese is read right to left, so Japanese comics are read in reverse order from the way English comics are typically read. Have fun with it!

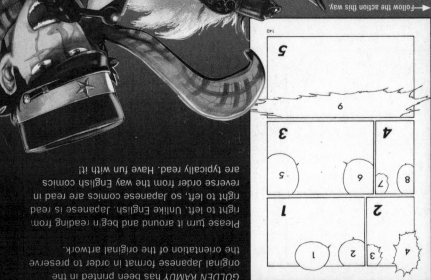

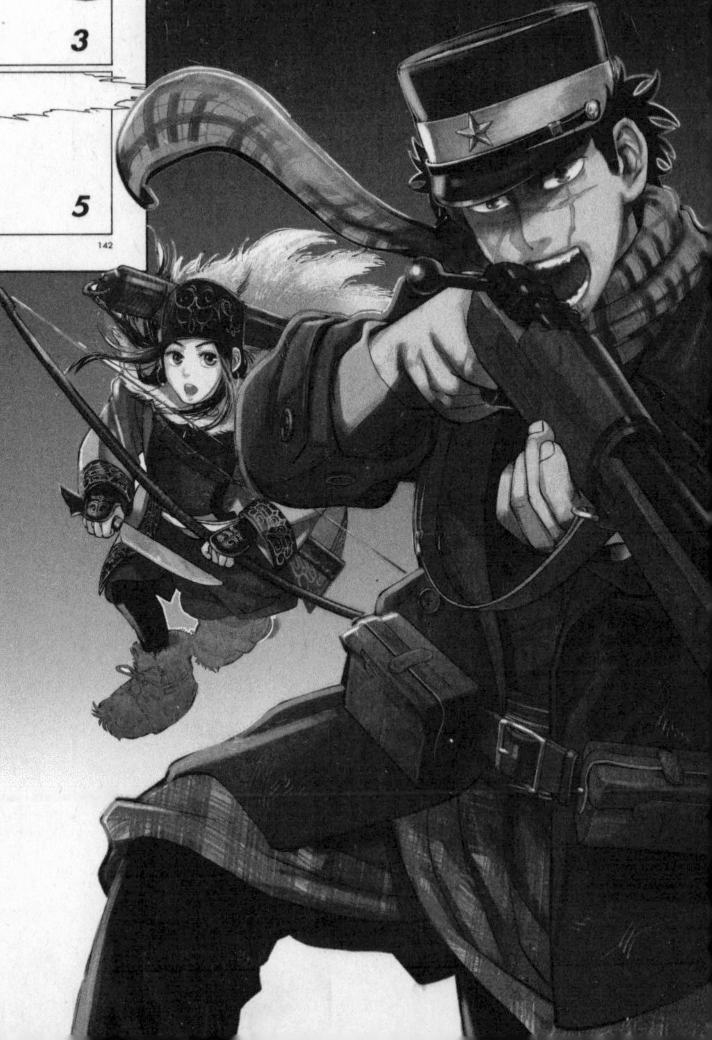

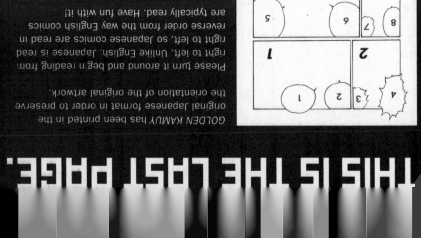